Enterprise Strategy – New Horizon

Enterprise Strategy – New Horizon

By Zhang Xiuyu

NA

NorthAmerican

Business Press

Atlanta – Seattle – South Florida - Toronto

North American Business Press, Inc
Atlanta, Georgia
Seattle, Washington
South Florida
Toronto, Canada

Enterprise Strategy – New Horizon
ISBN: 9780985394912
© 2012 All Rights Reserved.

Along with trade books for various business disciplines, the North American Business Press also publishes a variety of academic-peer reviewed journals.

Library of Congress Control Number: 2012951022

Library of Congress
Cataloging in Publication Division
101 Independence Ave., SE
Washington, DC 20540-4320
Printed in theUnited States of America

First Edition: 9780985394912

ABOUT THE AUTHOR

Mr. Zhang Xiuyu, male, was born in 1942, university diploma, professor, senior management consultant, certified management consultant, former dean of business administration department of Beijing Institute of Economic Management. In 2003, he retired from the university. In 2005, he found Beijing Successful Key Consulting Co., Ltd. He acts as the chairman of the board of directors and the general manager of the company.

Professor Zhang Xiuyu is the special researcher of Peking University, the leading cadre graduate student tutor of Party School of the Central Committee of C.P.C, the guest professor for presidents class, MBA, EMBA of many famous universities, such as Peking University, Tsinghua University, Renmin University of China, China Europe International Business School(CEIBS) etc. He is also member of editorial board of *China Middle and Small Enterprises Financial Service Guideline* (management consulting column) of Ministry of Industry and Information Technology of the People's Republic of China, a member of the tutor group, member of the Middle and Small Enterprises Expert Consultant Committee of Beijing City. He has been the senior management consultant and strategy consultant of many enterprises.

Professor Zhang Xiuyu integrates *Science of Strategy*, *Management Science* with *Success Science*, combines the research with the application of *The Art of War* by Sun Tzu and *Three Kingdoms*. He is the strategy expert, management expert and consulting master with the rich understanding and flexible application, who dynamically integrates the modern enterprise strategy management theory with the Chinese traditional culture. He also is the founders of China success science.

Professor Zhang Xiuyu engages in the teaching, scientific research, training and consulting work on enterprise strategy management and operation management for long time. He has published 11 works such as *Enterprise Strategy Management*, *Strategy Management*, *Management Science Principle*, *Total Competition Management*, *Welcome Challenge-How the Enterprise Practice the Internal Power*, *How to be Successful*, *China Human Resources Development and Research*, *Human Resources Management*, *Labor Quota Formulation and Management*, *Labor Remuneration Science*, and *China First Resource – Human Resources Development Utilization Theory and Practices* etc.

He has undertaken more than 10 province or ministries level research subjects and has published about 100 theses.

Professor Zhang Xiuyu is the author of the text book *Enterprise Strategic Management* published by Peking University Press. The first version has been printed in 2002 and the second version has been printed in 2005. It has been printed for 16 times in about 80 thousand volumes. It is the most printing times of text book *Enterprise Strategic Management* in China until now. The new modified third version is published and distributed on January, 2011. He also is the author of the first success science book in China – *How to be Successful*, the founder of China success science.

Professor Zhang Xiuyu engages in the consulting and training such as enterprise development strategy, business modes innovation, organization and human resources management etc. for long time. The consulting result not only has the scientific and innovative features, but also has the practical, simple and operative way. It can meet the actual need of the enterprise with convenient and simple operation.

In 1999, Professor Zhang Xiuyu was awarded in honor the excellent teacher and excellent education worker award of Beijing Institute of Economic Management. In 2003, he retired from the university. In 2005, he found Beijing Successful Key Consulting Co., Ltd. He acts as the chairman of the board of directors and the general manager of the company.

On May 30-31 of 2008, Professor Zhang Xiuyu presents "2008 (the second session) APEC Middle and Small Enterprise Dialogue with World Top 500 Fortune Forum" in Qingdao city, China as the honorable guest.

In August 2008, Professor Zhang Xiuyu is the cover figure of the fourth issue of *China CEO* magazine guided by Economics Research Center of State-owned Assets Supervision and Administration Commission of the State Council. The introduction is the innovative and practicable strategy expert, simple and effective management expert, warm-hearted success science master, the research and application expert of *The Art of War* by Sun Tzu and *Three Kingdoms*.

On December 1, 2008, Professor Zhang Xiuyu was awarded in honor "The Seventh Session China Time Excellent New Feature Award" in Beijing Diaoyutai State Guest House.

On January 15, 2009, Professor Zhang Xiuyu is awarded in honor the Eighth Session China Reform Excellent Feature Award in People's Congress Hall in Beijing.

On February, 20, 2009, *China Information* newspaper makes the comprehensive, deep and vivid report of the achievement of Professor Zhang Xiuyu in the whole edition of the newspaper. The title is *Full of Learning in Many years - China consultant master, the founder of China success science, the chairman of the board of directors and the general manager of Beijing Successful Key Consulting Co., Ltd.*

In 2009, in the time of memory of 60th anniversary of the People's Republic of China, Professor Zhang Xiuyu was awarded in honor the glory title of the Outstanding Feature of the People's Republic of China. And he has been awarded the prize Outstanding Feature Crystal Memorial Column of the People's Republic of China.

On January 8, 2011, Professor Zhang Xiuyu was awarded in honor "China Enterprise Innovation Excellent Feature Award" and "China Excellent Innovation Enterprise Award".

Contact us:
Unit name: Beijing Successful Key Consulting Co., Ltd.
Zip code: 100102
Company website: www.cgzy.com.cn
Information address: Edit the short message "China enterprise consulting information" to 12114
Company address: Room 2212, 603 Building, Wangjingyuan, Furong Street, Chaoyang District, Beijing City
Telephone: +86-10-64747217(o)
Fax: +86-10-64747217(o)
Mobile phone: +13641324263
E-mail: zxy9780@yahoo.com.cn

STRATEGIC MANAGEMENT FROM
A CROSS-CULTURAL PERSPECTIVE

Preamble to Enterprise Strategy: New Horizon

Confucius, the great ancient Chinese thinker, statesman and educator has said that **"Worries will soon come if one gives no thought to a long-term plan."** 1. Chen Danran, a famous scholar in Qing dynasty also has said that **"Since ancient times, people cannot work well for short-term and partial interests without consideration of long-term and whole ones."** 2. We can learn that the long-term and overall situations refer to the strategic issue, which determines the fate of a company.

In addition, Sun Tzu, the great ancient Chinese military strategist has said that **"Plans go first in the operations of war."** 3. **"The art of war is of vital importance to the State. It is a matter of life and death, a road either to safety or to ruin. Hence it is a subject of inquiry which can on no account be neglected. Now the general who wins a battle makes many calculations in his temple where the battle is fought. The general who loses a battle makes but few calculations beforehand. Thus do many calculations lead to victory and few calculations to defeat: how much more no calculation at all! It is by attention to this point that I can foresee who is likely to win or lose. "** 4. It means that plans should be made before the war in order to win, which can affect the results.

Similarly, western management scholars, represented by those of the United States, consider corporate strategy as the top class one of enterprise management science.

I pay special attention to strategy during my long-term teaching, research, training and consulting in China due to its paramount status and significance for enterprises. I have written a book to summary my practices in a theoretical way, that is *Enterprise Strategic Management (Chinese version)* published by Beijing University Press. It sells well after its first printing in since February 2002. And it attracts attentions of large range of readers in China, such as chairman, general manager, president, director of companies, as well as MBA, E-MBA and undergraduate students of institution of higher education. Up to July 2004, it has been printed for 5 times. Then, its 2nd Edition is sent to the press in March 2005, and has been printed 11 times by October 2009. So it becomes the textbook with largest market sales in China, with 16 times of printing and almost 80 thousand volumes. Because of this, I make some modification of the second edition, according to requirements of readers and recommendations of Beijing University Press. Now this third version is published in China since January 2011.

This book - ***Enterprise Strategy: New Horizon*** published in the U.S. is a re-edited adaptation based on the U.S. national conditions and needs of American readers. It can help people to learn more about Chinese corporate strategic management by using vivid cases in China. Readers can find systemic explanation of basic theories and methods in relation to introduction to strategic management, strategic formulation, strategic implementation, strategic evaluation, strategic control, strategic change, and so on. Moreover, a thorough discussion about red ocean strategy and blue ocean strategy is made to give a picture of the frontier strategic management thoughts.

This book combines lots of information, for example, strategic thoughts of Mao Zedong, the modern Chinese military strategist, principles of success, as well as classic military doctrines and military wars from Chinese masterpieces like *The Art of War* and *Three Kingdoms*. As a collection of China and other countries, ancient and modern, theory and practice, it is a strategic management textbook covering multidisciplinary. Main features of this book are as following:

First, it concerns not only modern strategic management theories and success science of America, but also Mao Zedong's strategic thinking and selected content from *The Art of War*, *Thirty-Six Stratagems*, and *Three Kingdoms* of China.

Second, it links modern theories of strategic management to actual problems faced by Chinese companies;

Third, it tells both experience of success and lesson from failure in strategic management of Chinese companies;

Fourth, it resorts to systematic and theoretical explanations as well as typical and vivid cases;

Fifth, it talks about practical management experience of other successful people in addition to that of the author.

I have been engaging in teaching, research, consulting and training of business management and strategic management for more than 20 years. After my retirement in 2003, I found a professional management consulting firm - Beijing Key to Success Consulting Co., Ltd. As the chairman and general manager, I want to contribute all knowledge and experience accumulated in my life to the society, which is also a way to carry out my value. Besides, I also serve as senior management consultant and strategic adviser of large and medium-sized enterprises.

I have formulated many strategic plans during my long-term management practice, especially management consulting experiences. They are not only for large enterprises and groups, but also for small and medium-sized enterprise, even for my own consulting company-Overall strategic plan (2005-2015). Many of the cases in this book are some outcomes of my consults.

I always follow three principles of innovation in my career, which is to inherit the good parts of national culture, to learn advanced things from other countries, and to create special uniqueness of my own. I am long to write a book about corporate strategic management in China, and this book is a great try of my dream.

On June 23, 2007, I suddenly receive a long-distance call from the United States. It is from Dr. Emery and Dr. Tian Guang who invite me to work with them to make a comparative study of American and Chinese corporate strategies. The next day (2007-6-24 6:58 pm), the following e-mail is sent to me by Dr. Tian Guang.

Dear Professor Zhang:

My colleague, Professor Charles Emery, (PhD, President of Erskine College Business School) and I are doing a comparative study of American and Chinese corporate strategies. We mainly refer to your book Strategic Management (second edition, University Press, ISBN 7-301-05488-2) as the source of information for the Chinese part.

We are both very interested in writing a book on strategic management from the perspective of contemporary Chinese enterprises. We would like to invite you as a collaborator if possible. Of course, our cooperation can also be extended to other areas, such as staff and student exchanges between two institutions.

If you agree to cooperate with us, please notify us as soon as possible.

Best wishes!

Robert

Dr. Emery is an American, while Dr. Tian Guang is a Chinese American, who lives in Beijing. Once I have asked Tian Guang why they pick up my book from so many handbooks about corporate strategy when he returned to Beijing. He answers me frankly that they have found none but my book that is really a textbook telling about Chinese corporate strategic management. There are so many schoolbooks that are translated or re-edited from American books. But actually, I understand that I am still on the way as well.

Unexpectedly, in 2008, financial crisis breaks out in the U.S., in addition to a heart attack to Dr. Emery; we are not able to work together. But they inform me their wishes to cooperate with me.

Recently, Dr. Tian Guang takes the initiative to invite me again hearing about the publication of my *Enterprise Strategic Management* (3rd Chinese version). He asks whether I could re-edit the book in English according to practical needs of business executives and college students in the United States. Moreover, he introduces the North American Business Press to publish it. This book cannot come into being without Dr. Emery and Dr. Tian Guang, who choose my book from millions of textbooks and give their full recognition, praise, support and advocacy. Therefore, I sincerely thank them! At the same time, I extend my sincere gratitude to people of North American Business Press.

In short, this book I dedicate to is one that inherits the good parts of national culture, learns advanced things from different countries, and creates special uniqueness of my own. It interprets corporate strategic management in China, due to that, it provides American readers with new Horizon, new science, new art and new method.

As we all know, the United States is the world's largest developed country, while China is the world's largest developing country. I hope my book can build a bridge between these two countries for cultural and academic exchanges of corporate strategic management. Moreover, a win-win result is expected during the intercourse.

Finally, your comments and suggestions are appreciated.
Email: zxy9780@yahoo.com.cn
Zhang Xiuyu

Notes:

1. Confucius and Mencius: *The analects of Confucius and the Mencius.* 1st edition. People's Literature Publishing House, February, 2008. p. 189.
2. Chen Danran: *Enlightening words.* Two volumes of version published in the fourth year of the Republic of China (1915). The quotation is from *Enlightening words II: recommendation of moving the capital and building feoff.*
3. Here it refers to analyze objective conditions of two sides of before the war and to predict and plan the outcome. Sun-Tzu(the original), Kung-sun Daoming ed, *Art of War and Thirty-Six Stratagems* 1st edition, Guangxi Ethnic Publishing House, July 1995, p. 6.
(4)Calculation here is a preparation process before war in ancient times. Usually, generals and commanders will hold a meeting in a temple to analyze gain or loss and make plans of the war. Sun-Tzu(the original), Kung-sun Daoming ed, *Art of War and Thirty-Six Stratagems* 1st edition, Guangxi Ethnic Publishing House, July 1995, p. 6.

CONTENT ABSTRACT

The new text book presented to the readers – *Enterprise Strategy: New Horizon*, is designed for America readers on the enterprise strategy management in updated content in English.

The text book is for the people in different fields such as business, education, academy, publishing etc., who are seeking a comprehensive and deep understanding of China, knowing China and studying Chinese enterprise strategy management. The book applies the popular and simple language, the typical and vivid Chinese cases to illustrate in system the basic theory and basic method of modern enterprise strategy management overview, strategy factors, strategy content, strategy nature, strategy core, strategy thinking, strategy types, strategy format, strategy principle, strategy establishment, strategy implementation, strategy assessment, strategy control and strategy change etc. At the same time, the book also makes deep research on the frontier issue in the enterprise strategy management field – red ocean strategy and blue ocean strategy.

The text book is full of the strategy idea of Chairman Mao Zedong, the successful principles of *Success Science*, and integrates with the typical military theory and military cases of *The Art of War* by Sun Tzu and *Three Kingdoms*. etc. It is one of special enterprise strategy management book closely combining with China and foreign theory, ancient and modern cases, and theory and practices application. The main features of the text book are:

I.   The combination with America modern strategy management science, success science and Chinese elites such as the strategy idea of Chairman Mao Zedong, *The Art of War* by Sun Tzu and *Three Kingdoms* etc.
II.   The combination of the theory knowledge of modern enterprise strategy management and the actual condition of China enterprise.
III. The combination of the successful experience and failure lesson in the enterprise strategy management in China.
IV.   The combination of the theory illustration in comprehensive system and the typical and vivid cases study.
V.   The combination of telling the successful management experience of other business and the practical management experience of the author.

In summary, we present the reader one new Horizon and new science with Chinese-featured enterprise strategy management of inheriting the traditional and excellent culture, learning form the foreign advanced theory, creating self-featured science by the way of adopting good points from others and having a own unique style.

TABLE OF CONTENTS

CHAPTER 1

A General Overview on Enterprise Strategy Management

Abstract

This chapter starts with the fable of "the tortoise and the hare," which indicates the importance of enterprise strategy for a company. Then, it explains the roles of entrepreneurs and tasks for strategists in the company, that is, "The task for strategists is not to find out what the company is now, but to predict what it will become in the future." The so called "what it will become" refers to the appearance of the company after 5 years, 10 years, or an even longer. In order to achieve this task, one has to teach enterprise strategy management, the monarch of business management. Then, it cites classic strategies like Zhuge Liang's Analysis of Three Kingdoms and Deng Xiaoping's Three-Step Strategy. Besides, based on cases of Lenovo and Ford, it describes concepts and main points of strategy, enterprise strategy and enterprise strategic management, as well as procedures, characteristics and levels of enterprise strategic management. After that, it states the significance and methods of enterprise strategic management through taking classic examples in the military and comparing them with real business cases of success and failure. At last, it has appendix of cases and comments of "Lenovo Group."

Learning Objectives

- To clarify tasks of strategists in companies.
- To understand concepts and main points of strategy, enterprise strategy and enterprise strategic management.
- To understand the process, characteristics, and levels of enterprise strategic management.
- To deeply understand the significance of enterprise strategic management for companies.
- To master the main ideas and measures to succeed through strategic management.

Introduction

In the new version of fable "the tortoise and the hare," the hare is not very convinced of the results that the tortoise wins the race for it falls asleep on

1

the half way. So it asks to race again. When the race starts, the tortoise tries its best to crawl forward the required line. But when it reaches the end, it doesn't see the hare. It turns out that the hare learns a lesson from the last race and keeps running without sleep. However, it notices the direction is wrong when it is too tired to run any more. This story tells us that a company cannot succeed without the right strategy, which serves as the direction for it to move forward. Even it has a positive attitude, attention to details, diligence. cannot make it without the right strategy.

Lesson

I. To Understand Strategists' Tasks from an Entrepreneur's Perspective

The world changes a great deal since the industrial revolution, and the social economies develop to a new stage along with three technological revolutions. In this historical process, creative work done by working people and forces of science and technology certainly are very important motivations. However, people seldom think about the following questions, such as how to find out social problems and needs of human beings? How to find out the best solutions to work them out? How to discover potential values of science and technology results and to turn them into productivity effectively? How to design new productive jobs for increasing wealth through innovative activities of people?

Nevertheless, there are a group of outstanding individuals who have been discovering problems and try hard to solve them out. They convert contemporary achievements of science and technology into social productivities. Furthermore, they take use of organization form of business firms to efficiently mobilize workers' labor and intelligence to make economical miracles and to push the societal progress. It has been best demonstrated in the US in the third technological revolution. This group of people who makes outstanding contributions is titled as new heroes of country, new generational heroes after Lincoln and Roosevelt. They in fact are entrepreneurs.

This kind of new heroes also appears in China, especially after China becomes a member of WTO. They are represented by entrepreneurs such as Zhang Ruimin and Liu Chuanzhi in contemporary China. The trend of times creates heroes and the heroes change the way of things is going. China is facing the best situation and opportunities in the world. The era of reform

2

and open is the time to make new generational heroes-entrepreneurs, and everyone who is full of strong wishes should make effort to become one of them.

In an army, there must be a marshal; similarly, in a business firm there must be an entrepreneur. Positions and roles of an entrepreneur in a company are as same as these of a marshal in an army. In army there is a saying that "a soldier who does not want to be a marshal cannot be a good soldier." It can be changed into "an employee who does not want to be an entrepreneur cannot be a good employee." in a company. Both entrepreneurs and marshals are not born, but grow to be through practice. So everyone can become an entrepreneur.

An entrepreneur should serve at least the following five roles:

Firstly, an entrepreneur is a business operator. An entrepreneur must assure the survival of a company. Then, makes plan for its development healthily, stably, and continuously from small to big, weak to strong.

Secondly, an entrepreneur is a creator. It becomes more difficult to run a business today than before. Without protection of government, facing no economic shortage, entrepreneurs have to deal with problems such as more and more rivals in the industry, changes in the market, faster update of science and technology, as well as products, less resources and high demands for environmental protection. In such a situation, an entrepreneur has to become a creator who is skilled in innovating in order to effectively run a company.

Thirdly, an entrepreneur is an organizer. A company has to allocate a variety of resources, such as workshops, warehouse, machine, rural materials, semi-finished products, finished products, managers, front line workers, and so on. Moreover, generally speaking, business firms are located in crowded and limited spaces in urban areas but in countryside, grassland or barren region. All these factors must be scientifically organized to become real productivity, to create products and to generate effectiveness. Therefore an entrepreneur must be an organizer.

Fourthly, an entrepreneur is a director. Regardless of the size of the companies, it is important to have a director. This is true especially for those giants consisting of many different departments and employees. It is just like an orchestra with many players and different

3

instruments. To make all departments and employees think and work together as a whole, someone must stand out as a director. That is what an entrepreneur will do.

Fifthly, an entrepreneur is a strategist. There must be an overall design before an entrepreneur plays the above roles. It will come out as expected only when the overall design is carried out. Otherwise it could only get half the result with double the efforts, or lead to an absolute loss. This overall design is strategy. And an entrepreneur should be the one who make it.

Which one should rank first among these five? As Wang Jinyu, general manager of Beijing Futian Corporation, suggests "leaders' main role in a company in the market economy should first be a strategist. He has to study, predict, and control the future of the company. Only in this way can a business stand firmly and make progress in a fierce competitive market."

What are the tasks for Enterprise strategists? John W. Diz indicates that "The task for strategists is not to find out what the company is now, but to predict what it will become in the future." According to the international convention, the so called "what it will become" refers to appearance of the company after 5 years, 10 years, or an even longer time.

To fulfill this task, entrepreneurs need to learn the skills of eagles. Strategist Frederick Geroke indicates that "A strategist must make the balance between wideness and depth of information he obtained. An eagle has to fly high enough to find a hare from a widen point of view; meanwhile, it has to fly low enough to target and attack it. A strategist acts similarly to maintain balance, which is the task for him or her alone." It means that an entrepreneur should on one hand act like an eagle when it flies high to see far away so that it can identify the subject for the company, such as good opportunities, good projects, good products, good services, good resources, and good markets; on the other, act like the eagle when it flies low to target and attack the subject, which will continuously create beneficial result for the company. This is the major task for an entrepreneur, a task that no one else can do instead.

Of course entrepreneurs are human beings, who cannot fly like an eagle. However, there indeed is a science and art that will enable entrepreneurs stand higher and see farther, so that they can see what their companies will be in the future. That is enterprise strategic management, which is entitled as this science and art is respectfully titled as monarch of business management in the western world, which is termed enterprise strategy.

II. To Learn Strategy from Three Classical Cases: Zhuge Liang's Analysis of Three Kingdoms, Mao Zedong's On Protracted War, and Deng Xiaoping's Three-Step Strategy

(I) Military connotation of strategy

Strategy, the art of war in ancient time, is a vocabulary in military. The definition of strategy in dictionary reads "It is a noun for military use and refers to plan and command for a whole war. It is determined according to military, political, economic, and geographical factors of both sides, considering overall situation of the war in every aspects. Besides, it specifies the mobilization and use of military forces."

Initially strategy is mainly used in military. In English, strategy comes from Greek word stratagia, which is also a word related to military. In *Concise British Encyclopedia,* strategy is defined as a science and art to reach the goals of the war by military means in war. Many famous militarists have incisively elaborated strategy. For example, the famous Germany military strategist general Fen Calasweizi once says that "Strategy is the use of battle for realizing goals of the war. Strategy must specify a goal for the entire military actions that is in consistence with the purpose of the war." Another famous Germany military strategist Moltke, Helmuth von also says once that "Strategy is a detailed practical plan of a commander for using the tools in hand in order to reach his pre-designed goals."

Except for military, strategy is more and more used in other areas such as politics, economies, science and technology, culture and education.

(II) Three classical strategic cases

Case one: Zhuge Liang plans three kingdoms in Long Zhong

In "Zhuge Liang Plans For The Three Kingdoms; Sun Quan Attacks Xiakou To Take Revenges," Chapter 38 of the classical Chinese novel *The Three Kingdoms*, the author describes historical plot in details about Liu Bei, Guan Yu, and Zhang Fei visiting Zhuge Liang three times and inviting him to come out from the mountains to help them restore the state. Zhuge Liang is an excellent politician, thinker and strategist in the period of the Three

5

Kingdoms. After he learns Liu Bei's ambitions to promote righteousness in the kingdom as well as considers Liu Bei visiting him three times, Zhuge Liang decides to serve in the Shu Kingdom as the chief military advisor. He presents his strategy to Liu Bei in his small thatched cottage - the historically famous "Long Zhong Dialogue." Based on his analysis of the real situations faced by Cao Cao, Sun Quan, and Liu Bei, Zhuge Liang proposes his strategy to Liu Bei.

Zhuge Liang tells Liu Bei that "Cao Cao is not as powerful as Yuan Shao, but he overcomes Yuan Shao by seizing the favorable moment and using his soldiers properly. Now he is all-powerful; he rules an immense army and, through his control of the court, the various feudal lords as well. You cannot think of opposing him. "

"Then the Suns have held their territory in the South Land for three generations. Their position in that old state of Wu may not appear too secure, but they have popularity to appeal to. You can gain support but win no success there."

Zhuge Liang then tells Liu Bei "As you are a scion of the Family, well known throughout the land as trustworthy and righteous, a whole hearted hero, who greatly desires to win the support of the wise, if you get possession of Yiazhou and Jingzhou, if on the west you are in harmony with the Rong Tribes, on the south win over the ancient states of Yi and Viet, make an alliance with Sun Quan of Wu, and maintain good government, you can await confidently the day when Heaven shall offer you the desired opportunity. Then you may depute a worthy leader to go to the northeast while you take command of an expedition to the northwest, and will you not find the warmest welcome prepared for you by the people? Once done the completion of the task will be easy. The Hans will be restored. And these are my counsels in all these operations if you will only undertake them."

"You, General, will be the lord of Human and complete the trinity. Jingzhou is to be taken first as a home, the Western Land of Rivers next for the foundation of domination. When you are firmly established, you can lay your plans for the attainment of the whole empire."

Case two: Protracted War

Comrade Mao Zedong makes a famous speech "On Protracted War" in Yanan Anti-Japanese War Consortium from May 26 to June 3, 1938. The content of

6

this speech is very abundant and profound. As a response to the criticism against both the pessimistic and over-optimistic view towards the anti-Japanese war at that time, Mao concludes the anti-Japanese war would be a protracted war and China could finally win this war. The main points of the protracted war strategy are as follows:

1. Critiques of the idea that China will be conquered by the Japanese. The "conquered nation" viewpoint believes that Japan is too strong and China is too weak, China would lose the war.
2. Critiques of the idea that China would win the war very quickly. This viewpoint believes that Japan is not that strong and China would be able to defeat them very quickly.
3. Proposes "protracted war" strategy, this strategy believes that the anti-Japanese war would be a protracted war and China could finally win this war.

The protracted war strategy is based on four basic facts between the conflict of China and Japan: a) Japan is strong and China is weak at the time, b) Japan is in retrogress while China is in progress, c) Japan is a small country but China is a large country, d) Japan gets few helps but China gets many helps.

He indicates that the anti-Japanese war would go through three main processes including strategic defense, strategic balance and strategic counter attack.

Apparently, protracted war is the strategy that comrade Mao Zedong designs for anti-Japanese war.

Case three: Three-Step strategy

Development strategy is the core of Deng Xiaoping's strategic thought. With regard to the strategic steps for development, he links long-term goals with arrangements for each step of development and sets a realistic "three steps" development strategy.

First step is that, from 1981 to 1990, we should double our gross national product and basically solve the problem of food and clothing. So far we have already realized the first objective.

Second step is that, by the end of this century, our goal is to have our GNP reach $1 trillion, with a per capita income of $800 to $1,000. In other words, the strategic goal is to reach a level of comparative prosperity.

7

Third step is that within the ensuing 50 years, China shall strive to approach the level of developed countries and basically realize the strategic goal of modernization.

(III) The Concept and main points of strategy

Strategy is the positioning of the organization's tasks as well as the plans and policy decisions that refer to the organization's overall, long term, and leading principal goals. It contains the following main points:

1. Strategy first refers to plan and policy decision;
2. The main subject of plan is "organization," here the organization refers to a substance that is composed of people who share the clearly defined common goals and systematic structure. This substance could be a nation, an army, a business firm, an institution, a school, or an association.
3. The contents of strategy are the positioning of the organization's tasks as well as the plans and policy decisions that refer to the organization's overall, long term, and leading principal goals.

4. Strategy generally has three specific properties, namely the overall vision, the long term objective, and the leading principal goals.

5. The concept and main points stated here are in accordance with the three cases presented above. Therefore plan and policy decision can be considered strategy no matter in which area as long as it meets the aforementioned criteria.

III. To Learn Enterprise Strategic Management from the Rapid Development of Lenovo Group

(I) Lenovo Group's magic tool for winning

Lenovo Group is established on November 1, 1984. It starts from 200 thousand RMB Yuan, a small cottage and 11 people. After 15 years of arduous struggle, it has total assets of 7.8 billion, net assets of 5.5 billion, and 12 000 employees. Its business size increases from 3 million RMB Yuan in 1985 to 2.7 billion in 2000. By 2000, its total sales revenue reaches 10.35 billion, and tax of 2.6 billion, which is 1.3 times of the original investment. It also gives returns of 160 million to shareholders, Chinese

Academy of Sciences and institution of Computing, which is 800 times of the original investment. In 1994, the group is listed on the Hong Kong Stock Exchange. Now its market value is worth 90 billion, and the company ranks among the top ten companies with the highest market value in the Hong Kong stock market. Moreover, the company's brand "Lenovo" ranks the fourth in the list of "500 most valuable Chinese brands" in 2004 with its brand value of 60.165 billion RMB Yuan and in 2009 it raises to the second with brand value of 68.2 billion. It is China's first large-scale information industry group, and one of the 120 pilot enterprise groups. What's more, it achieves many by being the first national electronic group, the first national high-tech enterprises, and the first national computer industry. Details can be found in the case of this chapter.

Lenovo' practice, performance and experience is called "Lenovo phenomenon" or "Lenovo miracle." at home and abroad. Well what does Lenovo mainly rely on to achieve its rapid development?

Is that capital? No, because Lenovo has only 200 thousand RMB Yuan as total venture capital.

Is that technology? No. Because Lenovo starts with neither its own technology patents, intellectual property rights, nor its own products.

Then, what is it indeed? There are many reasons for its development; however, the following main reasons are very important:

A good mechanism and a good leader is the first key reason from an objective perspective. That is the personnel, financial and operational autonomy as well as strong support of leaders represented by Zeng Maochao.

A good strategy formulated by the leaders group headed by original president Liu Chuanzhi is another core from a subjective view. They make many right strategies, for instance, comprehensive development strategy of combining trade, industry and technology; lone-term development of entering the world market; and strategy to fully develop of technology, network and e-commerce in the information industry. Just as what Liu Chuanzhi says, "The right and artistic strategy is the magic tool for Lenovo Group's winning."

(II) The concept and main points of enterprise strategic management

Enterprise strategy is the positioning of the enterprise's tasks as well as the plans and policy decisions that refer to the enterprise's overall, long term, and leading principal goals.

The main points of enterprise strategic management are the followings:

1. Enterprise strategy is the plans and policy decisions of an enterprise.
2. Its subject is the enterprise.
3. Its purpose is to seek sustainable and stable development as well as to adapt to changes in the futures.
4. Its contents are the positioning of the organization's tasks as well as the plans and policy decisions that refer to the organization's overall, long term, and leading principal goals.
5. Enterprise strategy also has three specific properties, namely the property of overall, the property of long term, and the property of leading principal goals.

We can see that development strategy of Lenovo Group is accordance with the concept and main points of a company's Enterprise strategic management. Therefore, plans and policy decisions that match the concept and main points can be called as Enterprise strategy.

IV. To Learn Enterprise Strategic Management from the Legend Development of Futian Automobile Co. Ltd.

(I) The legend development of Futian Cooperation's

The success of Beiqi Futian Automobile Co. Ltd. (hereafter as Beiqi Futian) is a rare flower in the reform and open era in Beijing's industry filed. The development process it experienced is full of legend. It can be used to best illustrate the implication of strategic management.

Beiqi Futian starts initially as a company to make and sell vehicles for peasants' usage. It starts to produce and sell the first generation of vehicles for peasants in 1989 with an annual output of 1000 vehicles and one million RMB Yuan profits. In 1992, its general manager Wang Jinyu realizes that the economic reform and continuous development of the economy in China is increasing, the consumption levels in the countryside consistently increases as well. After examining the company's strategy, people of Beiqi Futian decide to form a joint venture with automobile manufactures. It aims to achieve Futian Company's surpassing conventional development by taking advantage of the automobile industry's technology and other advanced factors that are accumulated through the state investment in last 50 years. On January 18, 1994, Zhucheng Vehicle Manufacture and Beiqi Motorcycle Company cross regionally establish Futian Cooperation, by allocating its state-owned assets.

Its 2310 series vehicles produced using 1022 small truck body for peasants are very successful in the market. It starts a revolution in agricultural vehicles industry by creatively using automobile technology. In 1995, the company's sales increase to 10,000 and its rank in the industry is promoted to the ninth. Shortly after a comprehensive market and industry research, they realize that the stated owned enterprises (SOEs) would hardly survive under the market economy conditions if they do not reform the current business model. The best solution is to thoroughly reform to establish modern enterprise system. Accordingly they make a proposal to establish a company that has multiple ownerships. Their proposal is supported by the leaders of Beijing city at all levels. On August 28, 1996, "hundred legal men" launch the establishment of Beiqi Futian Automobile Co., Ltd., it makes the company's ratio of assets to debt lowered to less than 70% and the financial situation becomes much better. The newly established cooperation spends 50 million Yuan to technologically renovate Beijing Huairou Vehicle Plant, whose productivity is increased to 10,000 in the same year. The sales of the new company are 26030, which is the highest in agricultural vehicle industry history.

The strategy that Futian Cooperation adopts can be illustrated this way: the first step is to acquire assets across regions by market forces. The second step is using the capital market to combine the operations of both production and capital by selling shares in the stock market to raise the working capital. On June 2, 1998 "Futian Ltd." accepts IPO in Shanghai Stock market, acquiring 323 million Yuan, thus opening a channel for the company in capital operation, which makes it possible for combining both production operation and capital operation so that they are able to obtain capital resources for long run business operations. Meanwhile, due to the stock market, the ownership of the cooperation becomes even more multiplied and the legal men system is more perfect which builds a solid foundation for the cooperation to further reform the business model and product portfolio. The third step is to adjust the strategy to create new competitive advantage. After IPO, Futian Cooperation has formed its operational center and strategic management center in Beijing.

Firstly, it moves construction material and construction machinery business to Beijing from Shangdong to form the cooperation's business operation center depending on two larger markets of Beijing and Tianjin.

Secondly, it moves all agricultural vehicle production business to Shangdong Zhucheng to maintain the competitive advantage by using local resources, market, and lower cost advantage.

Thirdly, it establishes an agricultural equipment and machinery center in Shandong Weifang, which produces and sells harvesters, large and middle sized tractors and other agricultural equipment to the domestic market; in preparation for entering into the international market.

Fourthly, it establishes Changsha Vehicle Manufacture in Changsha to produce and sell low and mid end vehicles according to the principle of close market and suitable scales.

Fifthly, it jointly invested 334.9 million Yuan to establish Futian Motor Cooperation with 48 legal men business firms, such as Xindongfang Cooperation, Wuxi Weifu Cooperation, and Beinei Groups etc.

After 10 years of experience with trails and hardships, the general manager Wang Jinyu says "Under market economy conditions the principal administrators of business firms should be strategists first, they need to continuously study, predict, and uphold the future of the firms. Only in this way can they assure the firms stability and develop fierce market competition. The strategic management of Futian Cooperation has experienced a process from zero to some, from superficial to depth, from short term to long term, from crossing the river by touching stones to slow perfection, step by step forming a current strategic management system, and takes the firm to the core level of strategic management." Wang Jinyu believes that "A business firm must clearly set up its own long term goals. Without long term goals, firms definitely have no future. Strategy is the symbol of the firm's cohesive force; it is the firm's motivation and synergy. If a firm has not specified long term goal, it will lose its cohesive force, its motivation, and its synergy. Only when a firm establishes its own strategic management can it use the attainable goals to demand itself and not get lost in the ongoing environmental changes."

(II) The concept and main points of the enterprise strategic management

Strategic business management is the general term that refers to all these activities related with enterprise strategy: plan, implementation, evaluation, adjustment, and change, it is a comprehensive and complex process, is a synthesized, multi-functional and difficult science and art.

The main points of Enterprise strategic management are as follows:

It is a "comprehensive administrative activity," in other words, enterprise strategic management includes not only include devising the strategy, but also the activities of implementing, evaluating, adjusting, and changing the strategy.

It is an "endless management process." In other words, enterprise strategic management is not a one-time administrative work but is an endless management process, it may have a starting point but does not have an end point. As long as the firm exists, it needs to implement strategic management.

It is a "decision making science and art," in other words, enterprise strategic management is a science of decision making, as well as an art of decision making. It is a "science" because it reflects the objective law and systematic knowledge of enterprise strategic management; it is an "art" because its value is in its implementation and practice. As long as implementing it into practice, there will certainly be variation in styles, models, and effects; this is various forms of art. Moreover, there are two special points for this "decision making science and art": one is its synthesis and another is its multiple functions. Therefore to learn and to apply the science and art of Enterprise strategic management one must spend time and energy on it.

V. Enterprise Strategic Management Process, Features, and Management Levels

(I) Enterprise strategic management process

There are four mutually and closely connected stages in enterprise strategic management, namely strategic analysis stage, strategic selection stage, strategic implementation stage, and strategic control stage (see Figure 1-1).

Figure 1.1 Enterprise Strategic Management Process

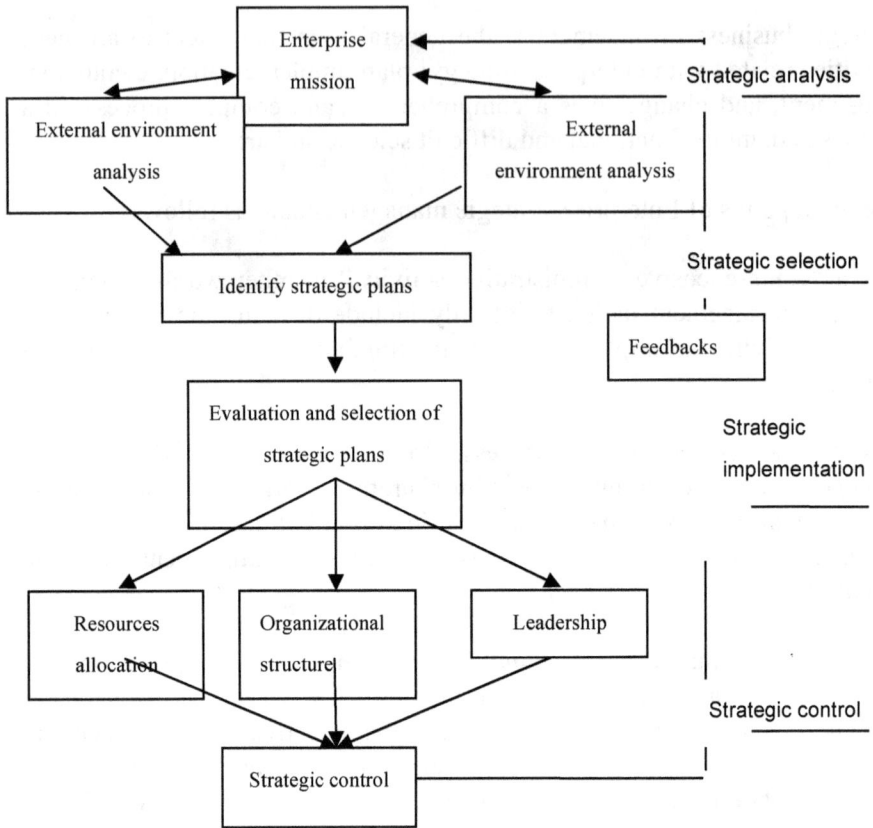

Source: Editing group of required MBA core courses, *Business strategy,"* 2001 edition, China International Radio Press, September, p. 22.

1. Strategic analysis stage

In this stage the principle work for enterprise strategy personnel are the followings:

(1) Specify the enterprise mission, includes describing business goals, business philosophy, business objectives, an evaluation of enterprise stakeholders and their expectations to the enterprise. The specification of cooperate mission statement cannot be separated from the analyses of

14

external and internal environments;

(2) Evaluate internal conditions of the enterprise, it is especially needed to analyze the advantages and disadvantages of the enterprise;

(3) Analyze external environments of the business, it is especially needed to evaluate the opportunities and challenges that the firm is facing.

2. Strategic selection stage

In this stage the main work for enterprise strategy personnel are the followings:

(1) Make several strategic plans for selecting according to the external environment and internal capacity, as well as the enterprise operational mission;

(2) Analyze and evaluate all possible strategies;

(3) Select one best strategy that is executable;

(4) Make policies and plans for implementing the strategy.

3. Strategy implementing stage

In this stage the main work for enterprise strategy personnel are as follows:

(1) Allocate resources to different departments/divisions in the firm;

(2) Design the organization structure that in accordance with the strategy, this structure should guarantee the strategic tasks, responsibilities, and the decision making powers are rationally allocated within the firm.

(3) Assure the cooperate culture matches the strategy;

(4) Play the leadership role;

(5) Resolve various problems and conflicts.

4. Strategic control stage

In this stage the main work for enterprise strategy personnel are the followings:

(1) Make the standard for effectiveness;

(2) Measure the real effectiveness;

(3) Evaluate the real effectiveness;

(4) Make correction mechanism and contingent plan.

From the above statement we know that enterprise strategic management is a very complicated and difficult administrative work.

(II) Features of enterprise strategy

Although people have difference opinions about connotation of enterprise strategy, they have no that much difference on its features.

To summarize, the enterprise strategy has the following features:

1. Totality

Symbolically speaking, enterprise strategy is the firm's development blueprint, which determines all the activities of business management. Enterprise strategy is the guiding principle of plan and design that specifies the business future and goals. It provides a universal, total, and authoritative direction for overall business operations and managements. In short, so called totality is to specify the general goal according to the overall business situation.

To make the enterprise strategy with the feature of totality, firms should make the efforts in the following fields:

(1) Must keep consistency with the world economic and technologic development trend, in other words, must have a "global view."
(2) Must keep consistency with the national development trend (such as national long term development plan, as well as industrial, technological, resources, and environmental policies).
(3) Must keep consistency with the industrial development trend.
(4) Must keep consistency with the firm's real situation and development trend.

2. Principle

The direction of development, strategic goal, and basic policies specified by the enterprise strategy are all principle and generalized guide lines for business operations. In practice we must further develop and break them down to realize them. This does not mean enterprise strategy is empty slogans without renal contents; to the contrary, every single generalized principle is full of meaningful contents.

3. Competition

Enterprise strategy is just like military strategy, which aims at beating enemy down and winning the war. So competition is the most inner feature of enterprise strategy. It has specified competitors and goals for competition, which is to gain competitive advantages in the competition, to conquer the rivals and to develop one's business so that the firm will stand in an unconquerable position. As such, it is full of "the smell of gunpowder" and by no means is a plan in "peaceful" status.

4. Long term

What enterprise strategy plans are the overall development issues of the firm in a long term. Therefore it must handle the relations well today, yesterday, and tomorrow. To properly handle the relations among these three, we must understand what is going on today, make a reference about yesterday, and plan for tomorrow. The enterprise strategy needs to foothold today but to pay more attention about the future, whose main point is looking for the long term development and long term interests. According to the international conventions, long term generally refers to more than five years, and for some large companies, long term even involves several dozen years.

5. Risk

Risk refers to the enterprise strategy that plans for the future of the firms. It may not always be realized, and therefore it will bring risks to firms. The leaders of enterprises must be well aware of this and have prepared the contingent plans for it.

Why there are risks of enterprise strategy? The main sources of risks are from long term business operations. As strategy has long term elements, in other words, it aims to plan the future, resulting in two types of situations: one is that many factors are not predictable, such as natural disasters, wars, causing risks easily. The other is that although some factors are predictable, there are gaps between the predictions and reality, which are hard to be controlled, such as scientific and technology development. Therefore they also bear uncertainty thus bring risks.

Why we still need to make enterprise strategies since there are risks? In fact it is for taking advantage of the opportunities. Clearly, good opportunities can disappear shortly, opportunities and risks go hand in hand, in other words, profitability and risk are directly correlated. Accordingly, to have profitability, especially to have big profitability we must dare to take the risks. Moreover, the nature of strategic decision is to challenge the future risks, if sacred by the risks the strategic decision can hardly be made. Just as the CEO of Heir Group Mr. Zhang Ruiming well put it "The risks for decision making are always there, but we cannot give up making decisions because of risks. If you do not wish the fire catch you, do not want to get trouble for yourself, then you make decisions by voting. In this way you personally will not run into risks for sure but the risk for business will be maximized to the end! Because when everyone can clearly see it as a good thing I will see the opportunity is gone. Therefore, although sometimes the risk is great when facing an opportunity, the benefit will also be great after success. When everyone believes it is a good decision with one hundred percent confidence the result of the decision will be certainly failure." However, taking risk does not mean we can take risks at will but need to be well prepared for the risk. Then what is the best channel to prepare for the risk? To be creative is the best way for handling risk.

6. Creativity

Creativity refers to making enterprise strategy not by copying or following the enterprise strategy models of other firms, but by making a unique strategy that suits real situations of the business according to their own business environments and conditions, strategic decision makers must be daring to create and good at creating. Then, what type of strategy is the best strategy? Professor Porter clearly indicates: "For a given business, its best strategy will be the one that is unique and reflects the firm's real situations. (1)

(III) Enterprise strategy levels

Generally speaking, for a typical middle to large scale firm, enterprise strategy can be divided into three levels, namely corporate strategy, strategic business unit strategy, and functional strategy (see the Figure 1-2).

Figure 1-2 Strategy Levels

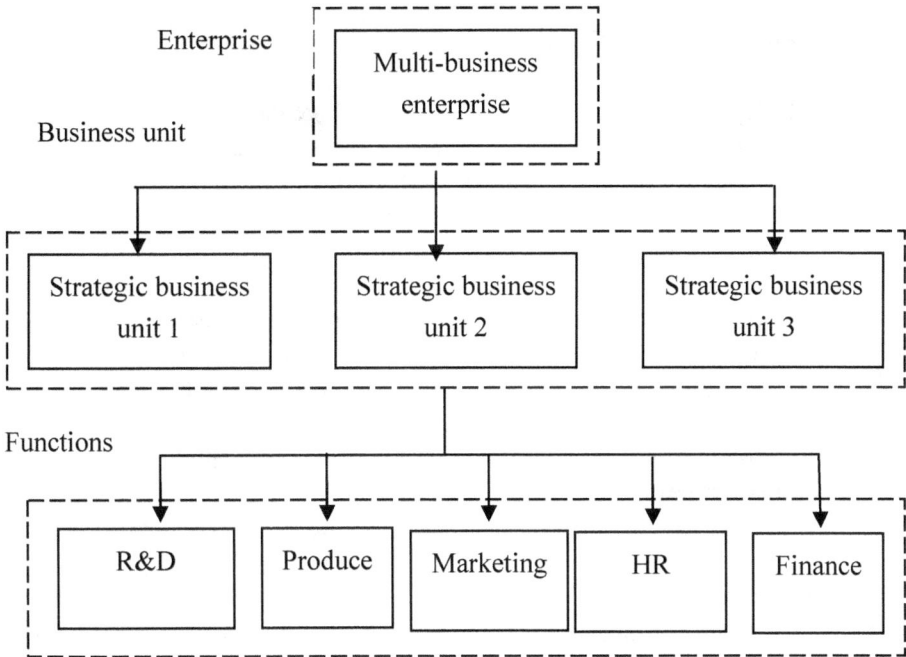

1. Reason for strategy levels

The goals of a business are multi-levels, they include general goal for the corporate, goals for internal levels, and goals for various projects. These multi-level goals form the completed system of goals. Enterprise strategy not only need to illustrate the general goals for the business and the means to reach these goals, but also need to illustrate the goals and the means to reach these goals for every level, every business and every aspect. Therefore, in a business firm usually the head office will make the general corporate strategy; strategic business units make the strategies for themselves, and departments make functional strategies.

2. Enterprise strategy levels

Different types of business have different needs strategy levels, some small and middle sized business firms may not need to make their strategies into

19

three levels because they do not have internally independent business units. The three levels discussed here are mainly based on the large and middle sized business firms' strategy models.

(1) Enterprise overall strategy

Overall strategy, or corporate strategy, is the general strategy for the business, it is the highest business guidelines for the highest administrative level to run and control the business. The general strategy's target is the overall business. In large and middle sized business firms, especially in the firms that have multiple businesses, the overall strategy is the highest strategy of the enterprise strategy. It must specify the areas in where the firm has competitive advantage compared with business rivals based on the corporate goal, and effectively allocate the resources for business operations so that every aspects of the business can support each other and to be coordinated internally. The content of general strategy include all factors, including corporate business development direction, coordination of all the business units, effective use of business assets, as well as the establishment of overall view of business values and the corporate cultural environment.

The overall strategy mainly answers the question like "in which business areas that the firm should conduct the business activities?" In other words, to respond to "what kind of business combination do we need to have."

From the perspective of strategic management, the overall strategy contains the following three main points:

Firstly, to determine the corporate mission. It is about in which areas the firm should conduct the business activities, to serve what type of consumers, and to develop in what areas;

Secondly, to determine development plans for the strategic business units and strategic business;

Thirdly, to determine the strategic goals for major strategic business units.

The features of overall strategy are:

Firstly, from the nature of its formation, the overall strategy is for the overall development of the firm. It refers to whole and long term strategic business activities;

20

Secondly, from the personnel's perspective, making and implementing general strategy mainly involves the administrators at the highest level;

Thirdly, from the degree of its impact on the development of the enterprise, the overall strategy is closely linked with the organizational structure. When a business firm's organizational structure is simple with a single business goal, the overall strategy is the strategy for this single business, or operational strategy. However, the overall enterprise strategy will become complex, such as become multiple enterprise strategies when the firm's organizational structure becomes complex to fit in the environmental changes, as well as businesses and goals become multifold. Nevertheless, because the strategy is made according to business environmental changes, it has counteractions to the organizational structure and thus demands the organizational structure to be changed at a certain period of time. For example, when the firm is prepared to use a part of internal resources to make a joint venture, the firm's organizational structure is requested to be changed.

(2) Business unit strategy

Business unit strategy refers to strategy of strategic business unit, business department, or sub-company. Under the guidance of general strategy, it plans for operation of a strategic business unit as a sub-strategy and serves for the need of overall strategic goal. In large business firms, especially the company groups, usually several business units or part of these units are put together to increase the effectiveness of coordination, as well as to enhance and control the implementation of strategy. Every strategic business unit will have its own products and segment markets. Internally, if every business department has it is unique products and markets; it can be treated as an independent business unit.

The main focus of business unit strategy is to improve the strategic business unit's competition in its field or segment market. It answers to the question such as "how shall we compete in every business field?" It involves in problems of how to compete in its business fields, which role should it play in its business fields, as well as how to effectively allocate resources.

The business unit strategy mainly pinpoints to the continuously changed external environment so as to ensure that the business unit can effectively compete in its own business fields. To assure competitive advantage, every business unit must effectively control the resources to be allocated and used.

Meanwhile, the business unit strategy should coordinate all functional strategies and make them become into a united one.

The business unit strategy stresses on how to achieve the enterprise mission, analysis of opportunities and challenges for enterprise to development, analysis of internal condition, the enterprise overall goals and demands, determination of the focus of business unit strategy, strategic stages, as well as main strategic measures.

Business unit strategy differs from the overall strategy in the following areas:

First, the overall strategy is about long term overall strategic plan for the whole enterprise, it will generate a great impact for the whole enterprise development in long term. However, the business unit strategy just takes care of partial strategy of the enterprise that related with internal business departments or subdivisions, whose influences are limited in particular products and market of individual business departments or subdivisions. And it only influences the achievement of the overall strategy at certain degree.

Second, highest managers participate in the formation and implementation of overall strategy while managers of the business departments or subdivisions take part in that of the business unit strategy.

(3) Functional department strategy

The functional department strategy, also called the functional level strategy, is the strategy designed for the specific business functional department to support the implementation of overall strategy and business unit strategy. It answers the question such as "how to support the overall strategy and business unit strategy". It is short term strategy for the functional departments within a business firm. It will help the managers of functional departments to better understand their responsibilities in facilitating the implementation of overall enterprise strategy. Accordingly it will effectively make use of functions of R&D, marketing, production, finance, and human resources to assure the realization of the strategic goals of the enterprise.

Generally, the functional department strategy includes marketing strategy, human resource strategy, financing strategy, production strategy, R$D strategy, public relation strategy, and so on. From the strategic management's perspective, the main points of functional department strategy include: how to realize the overall goal of the business; determine the functional objectives and the details, such as the production scales and productivity, main product and brand objectives, quality objectives, technology advance objectives, marketing objectives; determine functional department strategic principles, strategic stages and major strategic means; risk and the capacity of contingency analysis in the process of implementing strategy.

The major differences between functional department and enterprise overall strategies are:

First, time period. The functional department strategy is used to determine and coordinate short term business activities, whose time period is short, usually is about one year. The main reasons for short time period of functional department strategy can be explained in two ways, one is that the managers of functional department are able to focus on present tasks that need to be done according to the general strategy, another one is that the managers of functional department can better understand their departmental business conditions to promptly adapt to the conditional changes and make necessary adjustments.

Second, specification. The functional department strategy, compared with the enterprise overall strategy is more specific in contents. Overall strategy points out directions of the enterprise in general terms, while the functional department strategy gives specific directions to the managers who are responsible for annual business objectives, and tells them how to reach the annual objectives. Meanwhile the functional department strategy will help to improve the functional department managers' capacity to fulfill the strategy. There are three reasons why specification can make the functional strategy to be successful: the first reason is that the specification increases the real meaningful contents of the strategy and clarifies the tasks that must be fulfilled by the internal functional departments, thus enriched and perfected the strategy; the second reason is that specified functional department strategy provides information to the senior administrators of a business about how individual functional department prepared to implement general strategy, as such the confidence of senior business administrators to implement and control the general strategy will be increased; the third reason is that the specified functional department strategy can be used to illustrate the strategic relationships and potential conflicts among all the functional departments in a business firm, it will benefit the coordination of individual functional departments.

Third, authority and participation. The senior administrators in a business firm are responsible for determining the long term business goals and making overall enterprise strategy. The managers of functional departments, empowered by the head office, are responsible for making the annual business objectives and the department strategy. The managers of functional departments, by participating in the process of making department strategy, will make them more consciously do the works to implement functional department strategy, increase their responsibilities to fulfill the strategy so as to successfully realize their departments' annual business objectives.

In short, to determine and implement overall strategy, business unit strategy, and functional department strategy is, in fact, an outcome of comprehensive discussion and cooperation among managers at all levels. These three levels of strategy make the strategic system of a business firm.

VI. Significance of Strategy Obtained From Classic Examples in the Military.

(I) Why Liu Bei can have his kingdom among the three?

During the Three Kingdoms period, there are three political forces, which are leaded by Cao Cao, Sun Quan and Liu Bei. Among them, Cao Cao has the strongest power, followed by Sun Quan, and Liu Bei is the weakest. However, Liu Bei is able to form his own kingdom as good as the other two parts. The reason lies in his three visit of Zhuge Liang for asking him as military advisor and Zhuge Liang's brilliant "LongZhong dialogue," which makes a key strategy of the recovery of the central plains for Liu Bei. It is the implementation of this strategy that allows Liu Bei to gradually set up his own kingdom among the three from a weaker start. There is no doubt that Liu Bei says he is like the fish that get water when he gains the support of Zhuge Liang.

(II) Why can't Cao Cao become emperor when he is alive?

Everyone wants to be treated as emperor from ancient times. Cao Cao, the strongest in the Three Kingdoms period, dreams to be an emperor. However, he doesn't make it until he is dead. The reason is that he hasn't defeat Sun Quan and Liu Bei for uniting the whole country. While the other two parts resist the attacks of Cao Cao and form a competition of three parts. It attributes to strategy made by Zhuge Liang and Lu Su, military advisors of these two parts to a great extent. It tells the idea of getting together to fight against Cao Cao. Therefore, a wise strategy is equal to millions of soldiers.

(III) Advices Sun Bin gives to Tian Ji

Sun Bin, a military strategist in ancient China, serves as counselor of Tian Ji after he is rescued from Wei State, and later as a military advisor of King of Qi. He, with general Tian Ji, takes charge of the military forces of Qi. During that period of time, he makes a lot of wise strategic plans for Tian Ji. Among them, two classic ones are widely spread.

First one is "Horse race of Tian Ji and King of Qi." Both sides (Tian Ji and King of Qi) have horses of similar strength (upper, middle and lower grade horses) . In this case, So Sun Bin suggests changing the deployment of troops to break the balance of power situation. It is an important way to create the relative competitive advantage of every race and finally achieve victory. Finally Tian Ji wins the race by winning 2 rounds among 3.

The second is "besiege Wei to rescue Zhao." This is a strategy to relieve the besieged by besieging the base of the besiegers. Sun Bin suggests attacking capital of Wei State instead of its main army who are attacking Zhao. Therefore, it results in winning without fighting the soldiers.

Sun Tzu says in *Art of War* that "Thus the highest form of generalship is to balk the enemy's plans; the next best is to prevent the junction of the enemy's forces; the next in order is to attack the enemy's army in the field; and the worst policy of all is to besiege walled cities. The rule is, not to besiege walled cities if it can possibly be avoided. " He also says "Hence to fight and conquer in all your battles is not supreme excellence; supreme excellence consists in breaking the enemy's resistance without fighting." (2)

(IV) A military event that Mao Zedong is most proud of

After the Chinese Revolution, Montgomery, commander of allied army in the World War II tells Mao Zedong that the "Three Battles" (Liaoxi-Shenyang Campaign, Beiping-Tianjin Campaign, Huaihai Campaign) he command is comparable to any great battle in the world. However, Mao Zedong shakes his head after hearing it. He tells Montgomery that what he is most proud of is "Crossing Chishui River for Four Times" other than these three battles. He explains that People's

Liberation Army wins the three battle as a stronger against weaker, so it cannot be counted as a clever winning. While Central Red Army then wins as a weaker versus stronger this is a really capable victory. (3)

VII. Discuss the Significance of Enterprise Strategic Management: the Real Business Cases of Success and Failure

I. Strategic Success Cases

Case One: How does Haier Group go out to the world market?

Originally, Heir is a small plant that produces electronic calabashes with less than 100 employees and 147 million Yuan deficit, and now Haier Group's total assets is over 10 billion Yuan. In 2003, its annual revenue from whole world market is over 80 billion Yuan, with a growth of 9 billion Yuan compared with the year of 2002, and with an average growth of 70%, which is 22988 times of those 17 years ago. In 2004, Heir is selected as one of the "100 most influential brands in the world," the brand equity increases to 61.237 billion Yuan, and continuously ranks the most valuable brand in China. Heir Group's CEO Mr. Zhang Ruimin ranks 19th among 25 outstanding non-American business leaders who are selected by the USA *Fortune* magazine in August, 2003. He is the only entrepreneur from China. How does Heir succeed?" Heir CEO Zhang Ruimin believes it because Heir implements three great strategies in various stages:

The first stage (1984 to 1991) is to implement brand strategy. It takes seven years to make good refrigerators and create Heir brand.

The second stage (1992 to 1998) is to implement multiplied strategy. It changes color of products from white to black and then to rice yellow.

The third stage (1998 to now) is to implement the internationalization strategy. The goal is to build a large transnational cooperation, to create a world brand Heir, and to become one of the world 500 best business firms.

Case two: How does Hongta Group make the miracle?

Yuxi Tobacco Manufacture, the predecessor of Hongta Group, is a small least known tobacco plant. However, in 2004 Hongta's brand equity is 52.968 billion Yuan, making it the sixth brand in China. How does Hongta Group make the miracle? After research and investigation, the experts unanimously agree that three major strategic decisions make 70% of the contribution to it.

First, it is the first to import first class equipment from all over the world.

Second, it establishes an operational system that combines manufacturing, marketing, purchasing, production and sales together.

Third, it directly produces tobacco leaves, which introduces the first process of producing Yunnan cigarettes system into the field?

II.Strategic loss cases

Case one: Why are 40 billion investments wasted?

In the middle of 1990s, Beijing, Tianjing, Shangdong, Guangdong, and Hunan launches five ethylene projects. Among them, each project is invested 8000 million Yuan, costing 40 billion RMB Yuan in total. However after these five projects are completed, none of them is profitable, and shortly they all go into bankruptcy and look for companies to take over. Thus the 40 billion Yuan investment is like a stone dropped in water. The main causation is that they make wrong investment decisions in two areas:

One, they make the investment decision that is against the law of scale economy. According to the law of scale economy, for ethylene project, only when the scale of production reaches 300 thousand tons annually is it possible to be profitable. When all these five projects are all designed with a production scale of 150 thousand tons annually, how can they be expected to make profits?

Two, they make the investment decisions that repeat previous projects. China Government has already set up several ethylene projects that produce 300 thousand ton annually. For example, in Beijing, it builds a 300 thousand tons project in Yanshan Petroleum Corporation, whose scale is to increase to 450 thousand tons later. Then, why bother building Dong Fang Hong Chemical Factory beside Yanshan Petroleum? Isn't it a duplication of similar projects?

Case two: Why does Juren Group go into bankruptcy?

Zhuhai Juren Group is originally developed as a software company, who is ambitious to be "the Blue Giant of China." However it starts to invest in biological project to produce brain gold when it is far away from becoming "juren," and to invest in real estate business before brain gold becomes successful, dreaming ambitiously to build the highest building in China, "Juren Mansion." Due to its massive business scale, the group collapses while "Juren Mansion" is under construction and shortly goes to bankruptcy. Clearly, the enterprise strategic loss is the reason that helps explain why Juren Group collapsed. More specifically, its investment strategy is wrong, so its business extension strategy blindly multiply its businesses.

Case three: Why is Sichuan Great Wall Special Steel Factory merged by others immediately after going public?

Sichuan Great Wall Special Steel Factory raises 500 million Yuan from the stock market in earlier 1997 after it is reformed into a limited public-share-holder corporation. Without the newly raised 500 million RMB Yuan, the firm can manage to survival; but after going public, the firm suffers loss and soon gets into bankruptcy in less than one year. Finally it is acquired by another company. The problem resides in the use of the newly raised capital. There are two opinions on how to use it. One is to renovate equipment, adopt newly operational process, revive the accumulated assets for intentional expansion so that the firm would have new vitalities; another is to build a new plant, introduce new equipment for intentional expansion.

The second one was chosen by the company decision makers. Soon after that, every day the firm would lose three million RMB Yuan, which is accumulated to 497 million before the end of 1997. As a result, the provincial government of Sichuan has to announce its bankruptcy. In the end not only the establishment a new factory failed, but also the myth that "the company will be better once it gets the stocks sold to the public" ended.

For cases like this factory, Yuan Baohua, a famous business manager in China indicates that "If the leaders direct the business resorting the way of planned economy, their companies will find it difficult to win in the market economy even if they get listed in the stock market and raised a certain amount of capital."

To get public in the stock market does not mean the firms become success. It is easy to make mistakes when operating in the market economy with old thoughts of the planned economy. It matters not only the positions of the leaders, but also the future of the company, livelihood of its employees and the investment of stockholders.

Just "words" means no change in practice. Leaders have to continuously learn market economy knowledge and to improve their own psychological diathesis. Only in this way can they make the strategic decisions in accordance with the market economy laws.

Similar contrast of cases can be found in many industries in China.

In the IT industry, Lenovo succeeds while Juren fails;

In the appliance industry, Haier succeeds while Huanyu fails;

In the communications industry, Huawei succeeds while IDALL fails;

In the meat industry, Shuanghui succeeds while Chundu fails;

In the real estate industry, Vanke succeeds while Jintian fails;

In the beverage industry, Wahaha succeeds while Jianlibao fails;

In the joint sales industry, Gome succeeds while Asia fails;

In the family companies, "Four Brothers of Liu "(Liu Yonghao, Liu Yongxing, etc.) succeeds while "Four Brothers of Tang"(Tang Wanli, Tang Wanxing, etc.) fail;

And so on.

In the same industry and the same macro-situation, why some enterprises succeed while others fail? Obviously, the reason lies not outside of enterprises but inside. There may be more than one internal reason, but the most important one is surely the wrong strategic decisions made by managers.

III.Significances of enterprise strategic management

From the above two types of cases we can get a specific conclusion that the reason for the successful businesses is that the decision makers of those businesses are able to make and implement scientific and correct development strategies; while the reason for failed businesses is that their decision makers make wrong strategies. The expert of Lander Company in USA says clearly that "Among every 1000 large bankrupted corporations in the world, 85% of them are due to careless decision-makings by their leaders." Clearly, the enterprise strategic management is not only necessary and important, but also imminent. To summarize, the significances of enterprise strategic management are:

1. Strategic management is the inevitable trend of practice and theory development of enterprises in advanced countries.

2. Strategic management is the necessary demand to the business of developing socialist market economy.

3. Strategic management is very imminent for business firms in our country to join the international competition.

4. Strategic management is a development indicator for development direction of an enterprise.

5. Strategic management is an unlimited resource of employees' motivation.

6. To well take charge of strategic management is the first task for entrepreneurs.

Then, from the perspective of enterprise itself, how can a firm take use of strategic management and realize strategic success?

(1) Must enhance the responsibility sense for strategic decision
(2) Must increase the sensibility of implementing strategic management
(3) Must fully use "extra brain" ----think tank
(4) Must learn well about enterprise strategic management, a science and an art

Case Study

Lenovo Group (4)

Established on November 1, 1984, Lenovo Group is invested by Institute of Computer, the Chinese Academy of Sciences with 200 thousand RMB Yuan as well as 11 scientific and technical personnel. Today, it has grown into a large enterprise group gets diversified development in the information industry. Lenovo' practice, performance and experience is called "Lenovo phenomenon" or "Lenovo miracle." at home and abroad. It has been chosen by Harvard Business School as a teaching case for MBA course "Competition and Strategy." Liu Chuanzhi, chairman of the board is invited to launch a speech at Harvard Business School in the United States on April 12 2002. Meaning of "Lenovo phenomenon" is quite rich; this case is just a brief introduction to its development strategy and tactics.

Creation background

Institute of Computer Technology, CAS is large-scale research institute engaging in application study of integrated computer technology. It has totally more than 1,500 people, including 863 scientific and technical personnel, 196 senior research staff (including engineers), and 437 intermediate researchers. In addition, there are more than 600 research managers and craftsmen proficient in a variety of processing technologies. For more than 30 years after its establishment, it has developed two tube computers, two transistor computers, a large integrated circuits computer and an integrated circuit vector computer. Many heads of states in the world have visited the computers developed by the institute. These computers also contribute to the development of "two bombs" (atomic and hydrogen bombs). However, very regrettably, none of these computers could be transferred to commercial goods. So people who visit the institute often wonder why all these computers can only act as cocks that cannot lay eggs?

In fact, this is not just a joke. It points out the crucial weakness of the Chinese Academy of Sciences directly. That is the old research system. In the old research system, scientific research result refers to conduct of scientific experiments, development of samples and prototypes and report of the paper. Seldom of them are aimed to apply to national economy development. Therefore, numerous research results can only be shelved, becoming the so-called "cock" that cannot lay eggs.

In response to these shortcomings, the Party and the State Council decides to make changes. A new market-oriented operating system is planned to set up, which combines technology and economy together to adapt to highly competition of commodity production. It will promote the transformation of scientific research to products effectively and that of science and technology to productivity rapidly. In this historical background, hundreds of high-tech companies emerge in Beijing's Zhongguancun. It strongly shock institute of computer, CAS. Then, the institute decides to implement two systems in one unit and chooses an "enlightened mother in law" - Maochao as director.

On November 1, 1984, the predecessor company of Lenovo Group, CAS Computer Technology Institute Company is officially founded. Two systems in one unit come into effect. Director Zeng Maochao, its "enlightened mother in law" puts up with the idea to "attack with two fists." Before the establishment of the company, Zeng Maochao has met with the general manager and vice president of the company, Wang Shuhe, Liu Chuanzhi and Zhang Zuxiang. He admits that there are no more investments than 200 thousand RMB Yuan, but the institute hands over three rights. The first is decentralization of personnel, financial and operational autonomy rights. The second is right to resort to thousands of scientific and technical personnel in the institute. And the third is the right to use name of "Institute of Computer Technology." He further explains the purpose of establishing the company is to combine the company with the institute in order to change scientific and technological achievements into products and commodities rapidly. The company is a bridge for the economic construction.

Under the leadership and care of Zeng Maochao, two systems in one unit come into effect and the predecessor company of Lenovo Group, CAS Computer Technology Institute Company is officially founded on November 1, 1984.

Small business in the basket

When the company is founded, there is almost nothing besides 200 thousand RMB Yuan investment, 20 square meters house, and 11 people. The house where all 11 people stay is changed from the original janitor's cottage. No other department as well as signs, even no product for them to sell. Because the 11 people have stayed in the laboratory for decades, they never run business and don't know how to do. As managers, researchers and senior engineers, they feel ashamed to shout for selling. Although they sell small items, such as electronic watches, roller blades and so on, they never shout for business rather than stand away from their stalls before the canteen and storage shed. It happens that they are almost born in the year of hare, so people say the company will live as short as rabbit's tail. Thus the general manager has to decide to withdraw all goods.

However, they are lack of capital. Then they think of the terminology of political economy - capital accumulation. So they take advantage of themselves to accumulate capital. Some of them repair and maintain machines, some of them give lectures, some of them help others overcome technical problems, and some of them serve as sales agents of companies like IBM. Soon, Wang Shuhe and Liu Chuanzhi hear that there are imported "Apple" machines to be tested in the institute and gain the task. They do their bests to work day and night. They ignore every accident and disease they encounter and overcome all difficulties in their lives. Because they feel they find themselves back, not in the mirror or photos, but in reality.

Months later, they actually earn 700 thousand RMB Yuan and 60 thousand U.S. Dollars. They feel happy for their first major victories of capital accumulation. Primitive accumulation is usually to extract people crazy, while these scholars are crazy to extract themselves. With 700 thousand RMB Yuan, they have the necessary funds to develop competitive products. Later, Liu compares the hard work in this early start period as "small business in the basket."

Alone and roving "boat"

Since its establishment Lenovo always adheres to its sole aim "to contribute to the national economy with our research results."

At that time, China has imported hundreds of thousands of PC microcomputer. But due to words barriers and limited staff excel in computer science; a large number of them are left unused or used only as a typewriter. They make no economic and social benefits. This serious phenomenon is cause by the problem of Chinese localization. Localization is a problem of international concern. Leaders of Lenovo keen to see the relationship of Chinese localization of computer and construction career of China. They also understand that with localized computer, they can win customers, and further contribute to social economy. Then Ni Guangnan, general engineer as a trump card of the company, is assigned to work that out with 5 to 6 people. They strive to work for several sleepless days and nights squeezing in a small house. Finally in November 1985, "Lenovo Han-card" is formally identified by the Chinese Academy of Sciences. Identification considers this system "is the most powerful Chinese character system." Scholars of other countries believe "the Chinese character information processing technology of Chinese Academy of Sciences ranks first in the world," and it is "a great contribution to Chinese character development."

Lenovo Group starts by developing Lenovo Han card and gets famous due to it. After continuous improvement, it has 8 software versions and 6 models of associative character systems, which are widely used in six major areas. Then, it develops many high-tech products making significant social and economic benefits in a succession, including FAX communication systems, CAD super-character system, GK40 programmable industrial controllers, Lenovo PC 286, and so on.

Lenovo has its own product development process. Before research and development, it will collect information from market at home and abroad. Then it decides to do the project after calling developers, managers, and chief engineers to hold a joint demonstration meeting. Later it will sign a contract with decision-making department. During the process, it will put adequate resources in to the research and development in an efficient way. It will produce designed trial samples and test various properties comprehensively in order to check quality of products. The trial samples later will be send to trade fairs at home and abroad for trial use and marketing, then they will be improved according to demands of users. After all development process, it will conduct mass production, advertise products, popular technology and train staff to develop new market. Also it will support after sales service and adjust the products according to views of users before starting to develop new projects.

In order to transfer products into productivity, the company applies science and technology to other process including production, processing, market development, and after sell service in addition to product research and development. Each time a new product is introduced to the market, science and technology will accompany in the whole process of product consumption till users feel satisfied. Therefore, the company holds a large nationwide technical exchanges exhibition twice in a year. Its training center train more than 5 thousand social computer workers for free. It also sets 36 service outlets in the country. At the same time, it establishes a set of comprehensive transformation system within the enterprise, that is, an industrial structure consists of a virtuous circle of development, production, marketing, information, and services. To adapt to this industrial structure, the company builds several departments. For example, it establishes business department to make a dozen of branch companies form a products distribution network in the country. It sets up engineering department to manage two production bases and a pilot plant respectively in Hong Kong, Shenzhen and Beijing. It has a training center and two research and development centers separately in Hong Kong and Beijing. In addition, it has a user's association with more than 500 units as members and 36 service stations. This way, a large set of tight market feedback and social service system is formed. In this system, sensitive feedback, efficient product development, strict quality control, rapid capital flows and timely maintenance services, constitute a thriving technology products market. It leads to the technological and economic high-speed operation, and enable technology companies with strong vitality and competitiveness. It firmly links the broken connections between science, technology and economy. This is what Lenovo do in specific practices.

After 5 years of struggle, Lenovo has developed 156 utility computer technology products, of which 27 has obvious economic benefits. The turnover of own made products and secondary developed products accounts for above 80% of the total. In 1988, *Economic Information Daily* lists Institute of Computer Science as the top among computer enterprises with computer science and technology development benefits. High-tech products manufactured by the company are widely used in various industries throughout the country, and some are also exported to international markets. Meanwhile, the company's assets, personnel, turnover, profits and taxes, etc. are growing rapidly. However, Liu Chuanzhi, president of the company thinks "Our Company is still an alone and roving boat, which may not bear the impact of storms." He clearly states "we will strive to establish a first-class export-oriented computer industry in a few years in order to make more contribution to the economy of China." In order to achieve this strategic goal, since 1988, the company formulates and implements an overseas development strategy to explore ways to enter overseas markets.

To go into overseas markets

Creating export-oriented high-tech industry is Lenovo's goal. In order to achieve this strategic goal, since 1988, the company formulates and implements an overseas development strategy. This strategy includes a "trilogy" and "three development strategies."

(I) Trilogy

First step is to establish a trading company in overseas so as to enter the international circulation.

Purpose is to understand the overseas market conditions, explore commercial laws and accumulate capitals. More important is to find a breakthrough in development of export-oriented products. In April 1988, Lenovo Computer Co. Ltd. is set up in Hong Kong with investment of 900 thousand Hong Kong dollars, which is recovered within three months. Its first annual turnover is up to 120 million Hong Kong dollars.

The second step to establish a multinational company with research and development center, production base, and international distribution network.

This is the focus of the entire export-oriented business, and also is the key step. On November 14, 1989, Beijing Lenovo Computer Group Corporation is formally established. It stands as an important symbol of the accomplishment of this step.

The third step is to go public in the overseas stock market in order to realize scale economy and rank among computer industries of the developed countries.

After about six years of struggle, this trilogy is completed in 1993.

(II) Three development strategies

Lenovo forms a unique of overseas development strategy in development of overseas business. That is the three development strategies.

1. "The blind carries the lame on back" strategy - Industry Development Strategy

It means to take use of complementary advantages of each other. Lenovo Hong Kong is a joint venture company of three investors. They all have their own advantages. Of them, Hong Kong Daoyuan Company is familiar with local and European markets, it has a long experience in overseas trade; another Chinese technology transfer company can provide a reliable and solid legal guarantee for the loan sources; and Beijing Lenovo has the advantage of technology and personnel strength, which is unparalleled in Hong Kong. Not only in company combination, but also in the industrial structure at home and abroad, complementary principle is used. Hong Kong is an international trade center suitable for engaging in development and trade with sensitive information, unblocked channels; but due for its expensive land and labor, the production base is needed to be built in the mainland. Meanwhile, with high trend of immigration, Hong Kong is lack of high-tech talent. On this basis, the company decides to send a group of highly skilled personnel to establish a research and development center and build production bases mainly in the mainland. The company chose its headquarter as a base to enter overseas market and overseas company is responsible for unified command and deployment of personnel, money. These two sides cooperate with each other and build an enterprise team with competitive and strong anti-risk abilities.

2."Tian Ji's horse race" strategy - research and development strategy

In Warring States Period, there is a person names Tian Ji who has a horse racing with King of Qi State, resulting in three losses. Later, under the guidance of Sun Bin, his strategic advisor, he use his best horse against the king's middle grade one, his middle grade against the worst one and wins the race by just one time loss. Companies in China always try to catch up with strong fast horse depending on their slow horses, getting nothing but failure. However, Lenovo changes the practice by identifying the market demand, selecting the right breakthrough, concentrating a superior force, and achieving success in one area. At that time, 286 computer has a very broad market in Europe and America, and its suppliers are companies mainly from China Taiwan and Korea. In the international market, technically speaking, 286 is just a middle level technology. So Lenovo decides to compete with them using the best products. Lenovo inputs adequate funds and first-class technical talent leaded by chief engineer Ni Guangnan. They carefully analyze all types of 286 in the international market and design their product according to advanced ideas. Due to the use of international, most integrated and the latest components, products are superior to these from Korea, China Taiwan and Hong Kong in performance. Therefore, Lenovo finally squeezes into the international market. Although

286 is not the world's most advanced computer technology, it has a broad market, which allows Lenovo to earn a lot of foreign exchange.

3."Fen liquor and Erguotou liquor" strategy - Product Management Strategy

Leaders of the company seldom see Chinese products in their several visits to European and American computer fairs. They understand that the product must with high quality and low price in order to have a position in the international market. With its technical and personnel strength, cheap domestic labor and low production costs, Lenovo can make it. Lenovo 286 has the quality equal to "Fen liquor," famous, expensive and high quality liquor in China, but it is sold at a price of "Erguotou liquor," famous, cheap liquor in China. Thus Lenovo finds an opportunity for its products and succeeds in entering the international market. People of Lenovo firmly believe they will get a room to stand.

After several years of practice in the overseas market, they clearly understand the difficulties to run overseas business. It exceeds the imagination of domestic scientific and technical personnel that the sudden replacement of overseas products, demanding product requirements of overseas customers, intense degree of price competition, and brutal strife between enterprises. Battle of the computer market overseas is a contest of technology, intellectual and determination. Lenovo almost inputs half of its possession to develop 286 PC. Ni Guangnan, the chief engineer, almost never takes a rest for more than six months. There are also some problems in the production in Hong Kong. This step is really very hard to take. Decision-makers of the company, represented by Liu Chuanzhi, clearly notice that the overseas market is like a vast ocean, where at any time a storm may form. In this sea, in order to reach the beach steadily, their enterprise can never stay as an alone and roving boat, it has to become a "Big Ship." Thus, it is imperative to construct technology enterprise management mode and main corporate culture of "Big Ship structure."

"Big Ship structure"

Lenovo's decision-makers realize that it is not possible to make it without an organized team with strong fighting strength to enter overseas markets. In this context, they propose a "Big Ship structure" management model. Originally, "Big Ship model" is a set of internal management structure and methods for meeting the needs of enterprise survival and development.

Later, it has been extended to use in the corporate development strategy, overseas strategy, and in the company's thought patterns. It has become the dominant ideology and a unique main corporate culture.

"Big Ship model"

The main features of this model are "centralized command and division of labor." Specifically it includes the following five points:

1. Centralized command and coordination

Company takes development, production, operation systems as the main focus. It will set up a decision-making system and a service system for them. Staff will be under centralized command and funds will be unified managed. There will be only one supply channel and one financial sector. According to the market laws of competition, inside the enterprise, management by results and mandatory work style will be implemented to unify thinking and orders. It is close to the quasi-military management.

2. Implement of economic contract system in each "cabin"

In 1988, the company is divided into professional units by the nature of the work. For example, there are professional units Han card, computer, network, minicomputers, CAD industrial, software, data and so on in the business department. All units serve as cabins of the ship, with clear mandates and flow line production. It helps to improve the quality and efficiency of distribution according to work, also, it is conducive to mobilize the enthusiasm of workers and show the status of corporate owners.

3. Gradually institutionalized management

Since 1998, the company begins to improve and perfect various enterprise management systems. For example, the financial system, "interface" system, staff training system, cadre appointment system, warehouse management system, and do on. Pains to standardize corporate governance aim to make preparation for the establishment of large-scale export-oriented industries. Implementation of system management links every "cabin" to cooperate. It forces each unit to not only improve the efficiency of their work, but also consider the overall objectives and interests. Institutional management not only provides the company with a powerful dynamic mechanism, but also establishes a corporate self-discipline mechanism to ensure the normal operation of high-speed enterprise.

4. Collective leadership of the company with General Manager's Office under the Board

General Manager's Office has four members, two in Hong Kong, and two in the mainland. The company is under united command at home and abroad. The company attaches great importance to the unity of leaders and their exemplary role. In order to maintain the collective leadership, they abide by several principles: (1) regular exchange of ideas to make common understanding and unified speeches; (2) transparent discussion of issues with different views on the table; (3) fearless treatment of contradictory points with clear attitude, and sincerity; (4) responsibility to maintain unity, abide laws, work hard and undertake tasks. Because members of leadership have common ideals and common ideological basis, in addition to their harmony cooperation under guidance of above principles, the general manager becomes the strong core of the company, who has a strong appeal to employees and can ensure the correctness of business decisions.

5. Combination of ideological and political work as well as strict organizational discipline

General Manager's office is open for every staff so that general manger can timely communicate with the staff and exchange feelings. The company attaches great importance to change of people's thoughts, as well as unity of thinking and understanding. It conducts ideological and political work in every process including scientific research, production, operation, management and so on, even business in overseas market. The company is concerned about the ideological and personal growth as well as interests of various types of workers equally, actively offers various benefits, and resolves various practical difficulties and problems. Besides, the companies consciously develop a cadre group to play the role of Party organizations. The company is committed to training young people. It not only devotes effort to help, guide and encourage them, but also restricts them with strict disciplines in order to promote the rapid and healthy growth of their abilities and integrities as new technology enterprises talent.

Lenovo has strict discipline (known as "law of heaven"), including: no part-time job, no kickbacks, no "red envelopes," not private gains from works and so on. For employees who make outstanding contributions, the company will give rewards as incentives to, which may be increasing bonus, promoting post or positional title, study or work abroad, and so on. For those who make mistakes or violate "law of heaven," the company will punish them in forms of criticism, withholding bonuses, handing over to Human Resource Department or even dismiss. Under the right guidance and restriction of the company, staff of Lenovo at all ages is united and vibrant.

Through practice, they fully understand the superiority of "Big Ship model." it is reflected by the overall benefits of "1 +1> 2," once the enterprise is formed a strong a powerful unit as a whole. Because of the "Big Ship structure," Lenovo has a good influence and reputation in the community, wins the trust of customers, and gains the support of various State departments. "Big Ship structure" enables people of the company with the ability to develop a series of high-quality leading products. Thus an integrated industry of technology, industry, trade, information and services are formed. Then Lenovo has the ability to extensively develop new markets. It is helpful to enhance the competitiveness and anti-risk ability of enterprises and is conducive to cultivation of management talents of technology enterprise. Only enterprises with the big ship structure model can enter the international market. In addition, "big ship structure" is good for the company to achieve the aim "to contribute to the national economy with our research results." Therefore, Lenovo people believe that "big ship structure" not only is the experience of their business success, but also is ideal for enterprise management.

"Big ship culture"

"Big ship culture" is the experience sublimation of Lenovo in the reform and opening up historical conditions and in the process of creating new technology company. Generally it includes six aspects:

1. Indoctrinate new values

First one is the idea that contribution but toil counts. Evaluation of scientific and technical personnel is not based on their qualifications, experience and research results, but resorts to economic benefits that they earn. Second is to promote "researchers behind the counter," which requires them to improve products according to the market demands in order to make benefits. Third is to require developers to strengthen the sense of market, users, time and efficiency. In addition, the company makes comprehensive evaluation of employees and appoints post in accordance with ability, excluding personal grievances.

2. Foster the common career ideal

"Found the computer industry and enter the world market" is the common ideal of Lenovo Group. Common ideal and grand goal are sources of its cohesion.

3. Foundry of company's overall sense

Lenovo Group considers global awareness, cooperation, consciousness, etc. as its guiding philosophies. It strongly opposes any activities that threaten the unit. The company advocates transparent relationships, emphasizes on internal cohesion, and stimulates centripetal force. Lenovo requires staff to try their best to strive for the common goals as a science and technology enterprises team.

4. Shape the social image of high-tech enterprises

Lenovo Group takes product quality, company reputation and after sales service as three pillars of its survival. Therefore, it invests 2 / 3 of its staff and considerable amount of money to guarantee product quality and social services. Moreover, it puts up with many slogans like "the user is our queen," "reputation is precious than gold," "the whole process of quality control" and ensures their seriously and resolutely implementation.

5. Promote the entrepreneurial spirit of the company

There is a famous slogan in Lenovo Group, saying, turn "5% of the hope into 100% of the reality." Lenovo sets goals and plans cautiously and carries out them trying its best. It encourages staff to march forward cutting off retreat.

6. Develop a sense of home and proud of the group and promote close and harmonious relations within the company.

It guides staff to closely combine their future and its development together through common ideals and values. It makes staff feel sense of ownership and belonging. Besides, it encourages and attracts long-term or even lifelong employee business services.

Lenovo's decision-makers think that a new career needs new ideas, new methods, new culture and new talents.

The prominent features of "big ship culture" are the overall awareness. Lenovo Group not only takes itself as a whole, but also considers the Group and its subsidiaries, business and society, market and customers, technology and economy, China and other countries as an organic one. That allows Lenovo to make comprehensive benefits relaying on coordinated development.

The essence of "big ship culture" is creation. It means the creation of first-class products, first-class industry, and a new technology enterprise with scientific world view, wisdom, ability and fighting spirit.

The task of "big ship culture" is to build a team, one that can fight hard battles for scientific and technological enterprises.
Three elements of management

After more than ten years of efforts, Lenovo Group gets rid of small workshop-style business model and sets up a coordinating business model of large group. It is cooperative management that can help a high-tech enterprise in China to be competitive in future international competition. The essence theoretical basis of business management of Lenovo Group is "bucket effect," which means to continue to find the shortest piece and try to make it longer.

Team, leadership and strategy are the three elements of management. They are organically linked and are continuously changing.

Team here means to first, the organizational structure at different times in order to making the most efficient operation; second, the corporate culture that can strengthen cohesion to the maximum; third, management model that guides and restrict staff; fourth, incentives that can maximize the creativity of young intellectuals of modern China.

Most important of these three is leadership. Lenovo has trained senior managers aiming at solving problems, including how to remain united, how to improve leadership and how to lead. They believe no strategy can be achieved without united and spiritual leadership.

Property Rights Reform

Lenovo encounters property rights problems several years after its establishment. Liu Chuanzhi notices that there is no clear policy about state-owned enterprise though there are many discussions in academic and public fields. Thus he thinks Lenovo can succeed as long as it seizes the right opportunity in this complex situation. Then, he decides to wait and prepare for that rather than asks for property rights directly and immediately.

Since 1989, he starts to take steps slowly. Within the company, he increases salaries and bonuses of the staff step by step. In the Chinese Academy of Sciences, he continues to persuade the trend of reform. Finally, Lenovo is approved 35% of the dividend rights in 1984.

However, the dividend rights are not equal to equity. He doesn't rush, for knowing property rights of public owned enterprises are sensitive issues. Although the Beijing Municipal Industry and Commerce Bureau in 1998 reveals those more than two thousand high-tech enterprises in Zhongguancun is in the trip for the issue of property rights, Liu Chuanzhi doesn't move to do anything. He proposes to turn dividend rights in the last 5 years into equity till the State Council approves the construction of the Zhongguancun Science Park in June 1999.

Under the support of the Chinese Academy of Sciences, Liu Chuanzhi continues to walk steadily on the way of dividend rights transition for 10 years. The transition of dividend rights into equity doesn't means to the end of the journey. Liu Chuanzhi is still waiting for opportunity for Lenovo to take off.

Today, the dividend rights have been successfully turned into equity, which lays a solid foundation of property rights for the Lenovo's long-term sustainable development. Liu Chuanzhi holds share worth more than 9 million RMB Yuan as an individual. He is also named Outstanding Entrepreneur of Zhongguancun, and hands over his post perfectly. Besides, his name is impressively engraved on the wall of entrepreneurial culture in the Zhongguancun Science Park. Therefore, the media praise that he is one of the "representatives who get both fame and fortune." People in the industry also think his retreat is the perfect one.

Outstanding performance

Established on November 1, 1984, Lenovo Group is invested by Institute of Computer, the Chinese Academy of Sciences with 200 thousand RMB Yuan as well as 11 scientific and technical personnel. Today, it has grown into a large enterprise group gets diversified development in the information industry, with net assets of 5.5 billion RMB Yuan and more than 12 thousand employees. In fiscal year 2002, its turnover is up to 20.2 billion Hong Kong dollars. In 1994, it is listed in Hong Kong (stock code 992), and becomes one of constituent stocks of the Hong Kong Hang Seng Index. In 2002, Lenovo's market share is 27.3%, ranking first in domestic market for 7 consecutive years since 1996. By March 2003, sales of Lenovo have been the first in the Asia Pacific market (excluding Japan) for 12 consecutive quarters in a row. In the second quarter of 2002, sales of Lenovo's Desktop PC enter the top five in the global market for the first time of which that of consuming companies ranks the third. In face of information and network technology challenges, in April 2000, Lenovo Group has conducted a large-scale strategic restructuring, forming two subsidiaries: Lenovo Computer Inc. and Lenovo Digital China Ltd., which prints a new picture of network age and new pattern of economy.

Lenovo establishes separately a modern production base in Beijing, Shanghai and Huiyang, Guangdong to produce desktop computers, servers, laptops, printers, handheld computers, motherboards and so on. Their production capacities reach 5 million units (PC). In addition, it has a large mobile phone production base in Xiamen.

In the past ten years, Lenovo Group is consistently adhering to the philosophy of "let users get better." It has always been committed to provide Chinese users with the best and the latest technology products and to promote the development of China's information industry. In future, as an IT technology and service provider, Lenovo will be comprehensive customer-oriented and will provide targeted information products and services to four categories of customers, including families, individuals, SMEs, and major industries.

In today's increasingly technology competition, Lenovo continues to increase R & D investment in technology and R & D system. Currently, a research and development system has been set up leading by Lenovo Institute. Beside, many products have been developed independently. For example, Lenovo Deepcomp 1800 computer developed on August 27, 2002.

Its operations reach up to 1.027 trillion times per second, which is identified by a group of experts, including 6 academicians. In 2003, Lenovo is approved as main grid node of 863 national network plans and develops "Deepcomp 6800" supercomputer whose operations rate is more than 4 trillion times per second. "Deepcomp 6800" is announced as a national major project of national 863 plans. It is also rank 14 in terms of speed in the list of national supercomputer top 500 which is published on November 16, 2003. It is the best position Chinese supercomputers have ever obtained. In December 2002, the first Lenovo Technology Innovation Conference (Lenovo World) is held in Beijing. On which Lenovo officially launches the "associated applications strategy," and takes it as the company's technology vision and layout of the development in the new century. On July 31, 2003, Lenovo Technology Tour 2003 (Lenovo Tech Show) start successfully in the "Pearl of the Orient," Shanghai. The tour experiences more than thirty major cities nationwide, showing Lenovo's spirits of technology and innovation to the whole country.

In 2002 fiscal year (April 1, 2002 to March 31, 2003), Lenovo Group applies for a total of 572 national patents, which account for 50% of invention patents. It is the enterprise with most national enterprise technological innovation and intellectual property rights granted by the State Intellectual Property Office. It also forms a core technology system with independent intellectual property rights. Due to its advanced sense and excellent performance of quality management, in September 2002, Lenovo wins the "National Quality Management Award," as the only one IT enterprise among six winners. Lenovo steps ahead in terms of quality management compared with other Chinese companies.

In September 2002, Lenovo Group ranks the sixth among top 100 companies in China published by *Fortune* magazine. In January 2003, Lenovo also wins all the first prizes in the selection of the eleventh (Best-Managed Companies) held by *Asian currency* magazine, including "Best Managed Company," "Best Investor Relations," and "Best Financial Management." In 2004, as "the most valuable brand," "Lenovo" ranks the fourth with brand value of 60.165 billion RMB Yuan.

Go out in the future to develop in the international market

On March 26, 2004, Lenovo Group is the first Chinese company who signs a cooperation agreement with the International Olympic Committee, becoming a global partner of IOC. Lenovo Group will be the sole provider of computer equipment and financial and technical support in 2005-2008 for Olympic Committee and Olympic delegations of 2006 Torino Olympic Winter Games, 2008 Beijing Olympic Games and Olympic Games in more than 200 countries and regions in the world.

In April 2003, Lenovo Group officially announces to use new symbol, replacing the original English logo with "Lenovo" and register it in the world. In China, Lenovo will keep using "English + Chinese" sign, while in overseas only English alone.

In the new century, Lenovo sums up its mission into four parts. For customers, to provide information technology, tools and services to enable people to live and work more simple, efficient and colorful. For its staff: to create more space for their development, value improvement and life quality enhancement. For shareholders: to earn long-term interests. For the society: to make contributions to social progress. Lenovo's entrepreneurs and the young people all hold the idea of making Lenovo a long-term, large scale high-tech enterprise, and ultimately a world-class high-tech industry group.

After studies successful experience of large technology companies in Japan and Korea, Liu Chuanzhi clearly states that the formulation of a right strategic goal is the key to success of Lenovo. It requires the understanding of development laws of the information industry and the consistence with practical situations of the company. Therefore, a right and ingenious strategy is the magic tool for Lenovo."

He also clearly points out "The so-called to break a strategy down into specific tactical steps to achieve strategic objectives can be interpreted into specific stages to achieve goals. First is to put up with long-term goals; second is to carry out in several steps; third is to determine the most recent goal; fourth is to choose the way to achieve it; and fifth is to consider whether adjustment is needed."

According to above requirements, Lenovo sets the recent, medium-term and long-term development goals:

Long-term goal is to enter the list of top 500 largest companies in the world published by the U.S. *FORTUNE* magazine as a high-tech enterprise before 2010.

Medium-term goal is to make turnover of 10 billion U.S. Dollars and to gradually approach the range of top 500 selections by 2005.

Most recent goal is to complete make turnover of 1 billion U.S. Dollars with profits of 100 million U.S. Dollars and to enter top 60 in the world computer industry by 2000.

Lenovo Group conducts an ad-hoc study on the development of the world computer industry and Chinese high-tech enterprises.

Based on the above analysis, Lenovo Group learns a lesson in making its most recent goal. It takes domestic market as main business field and sales as breakthrough point. It also pays more attention to technological elements in the following four aspects.

1. Domestic computer market
2. Domestic systems integration
3. Sales agents
4. PC-board for the international market

These four aspects are important sources of achieving Lenovo's $ 3 billion of income in 2000. In addition, there are also two steps Lenovo takes to ensure the success of its strategy.

The first one is new industrial projects. It sets up factories and sales channels with joint venture partners overseas of CD-ROM, hard disk with changeable disk groups, large screen displays, and so on.

The second is the establishment of a Lenovo Huiyang Science and Technology Park in Guangdong. It is expected to expand to two square kilometers in size around 2000.

These two steps are called "food in the pot" in a joking way, and form the market advantage of Lenovo Group in 2000 accompanying with "food in the bowl," which are businesses of computers, systems integration, agent distribution, and board manufacturing. Lenovo has already reached is the most recent goal by entering top 10 in the world computer industry.

As for the medium-term goal, that is, sales reach 10 billion U.S. dollars, both Liu Chuanzhi and Yang Yuanqing think it is too far to achieve. For that, Lenovo puts too much in diversity which many resources needs but get few, especially leadership.

Liu Chuanzhi states "Recently we make a new three-year plan to ensure Lenovo can do the right things by reducing business and adjusting team. It means Lenovo will turn back to the PC business.

After the strategic adjustment, in mid-November 2004, Lenovo Group announces its interim performance in the 2004/05 fiscal year in Hong Kong. Its overall turnover is 11.533 billion Hong Kong dollars, equal to that of last year and its net profit increase 16.2%. PC sales growth in the second quarter reaches 14.6%, surpassing the market average. Growth of Laptops, cell phones and other key business is a bright spot, increasing respectively 43% and 105% in sales comparing with same period last year. Market share of its PC business rises to 27%, leaving behind the second with a gap of 13.1% in the Asia Pacific market. Liu Chuanzhi is very happy about these achievements and he says that the change of Lenovo has begun to yield significant results in terms of its performance in September. He also believes there will be a considerable progress of what investors concern in the future, including market share and profit.

Go out to emerge like a "snake" can swallow "elephant"

Diversification and internationalization are two options of an enterprise to develop. Through 3 years of practice, Lenovo abandons the former and chooses the latter.

Liu Chuanzhi often says that "Lenovo cannot perform well if it refuses to go out. It is difficult to increase revenue and profit just in domestic market, which will disappoint investors as well as us." (5)
He stresses it again on the 8th annual CEO conference of Lenovo in 2004 that "PC business has to go abroad even it will encounter many difficulties." (6)

On December 8, 2004, Liu Chuanzhi, chairman of Lenovo Group announces a major agreement of Lenovo Group's 12.5 billion U.S. Dollars acquisition of IBM's personal computer division. It includes all the businesses of IBM's global desktop computer and laptops. Lenovo owns the qualification to build a PC manufacture company with more than 10 billion U.S. dollars annual income in the world. It ranks the third among the PC manufactures. Therefore, Lenovo enters the world market besides that in China and Asia. (7)

Hearing that, the audience breaks out of a long applause and cheers.

If count sales of the two sides in 2003 together, then PC shipments of Lenovo will be up to 1.19 million units with sales up to 12 billion U.S. Dollars. The deal makes Lenovo's current PC business grow 4 times than before in scale. Lenovo's business, as well as business of "Think" of IBM in China can bring 160 countries worldwide distribution and sales network.

Liu Chuanzhi says that "As one of the company's founders, I am very excited to see that Lenovo will make a breakthrough step in international development. In the past 20 years, Lenovo has become the first of the PC business in China. But we always adhere to the unwavering goal of becoming an international enterprise. It changes logo in 2003, becomes a global partner of the International Olympic Committee in 2004, and makes strategic alliance with IBM today. I see that Lenovo is becoming a truly world-class enterprise." (8)

Lenovo's current president and CEO Yang Yuanqing says that "The development of the Internet brings opportunities and challenges for the PC industry. Only company with world-class scale, leading technology, highly efficient operations is able to win the victory in the future. Through the acquisition of IBM's global PC business and formation of the strategic alliance with IBM, Lenovo will be able to integrate their strengths, and acquire global brand recognition, global customers and extensive distribution network. It can also get a richer product mix, higher operational efficiency and leading technology, which makes Lenovo can use the powerful global brand IBM to help build its brand on the international market. "

Chen Jinhua, chairman of China Enterprise Confederation and China Entrepreneurs Association, comments the deal of Lenovo's acquisition of IBM's personal computer business division. He says that "It leaves an impression in the history of the development of Chinese companies from whatever point of view. The cross-border asset restructuring of Chinese enterprises is extraordinary. So is Lenovo's transition from a regional brand to an international brand. It makes Lenovo directly enter the top 500 in the world from ranking 37 in the list of top 500 Chinese enterprises published by China Enterprise Confederation. We can see that it is just the first step of its internationalization, which is also an exceptional challenge for

Lenovo's integration of capability, international business management, and development potential." (9)

Chen Jinhua stresses that "Lenovo's practice of forming strategic alliance with the IBM proves the trend of international development of Chinese enterprises. There must be positions for Chinese advanced enterprises among the world leading companies. It is a trend that can never be stopped." (10)

Liu Chuanzhi writes in the end of *Succeed in 2000* that "There is saying that 21st century is the Chinese century, and the economy will be dominated by high-tech industries in the future. Without doubts, information industry is an important component of Chinese economy. Today, Chinese information product market is turning from lab of advanced technologies and flea market of outdated products into a real economic competitive market. Chinese national high-tech enterprises have the ability to grow into a world-class high-tech industry group taking advantage of their comparative advantages, and the national industrial policy, as well as macroeconomic regulation and control."

Turn losses to gains by attacking with two fists

On February 5, 2009, Lenovo releases the performance report of fiscal year 08/09, with the annual net loss of 226 million U.S. Dollars. It is the biggest loss since its establishment, and also the first full-year loss in the past 10 years. At the same time, Liu Chuanzhi returns to the position of chairman to solve the difficulty. It shocks everyone in the industry. When replies to the media, Liu Chuanzhi says that "as the founder of Lenovo, I treat Lenovo as my own life. In this case, I should stand out to work for it. That the reason why I return. I can't withdraw when it is in trouble. I will never retreat until things go back to normal again. I am already 65 years old, but I believe it will realize in 2 years, or 3 years at most."

For the reason to the loss, Liu Chuanzhi admits that these difficulties are expected. The most direct factor is the international financial crisis. Lenovo computers in abroad are mainly sold to large corporate customers. Along with the arrival of the international financial crisis, many companies cut costs, reduce procurement of computers, and thus Lenovo's turnover has been greatly affected. Of course, there also exist many problems in the management of Lenovo.

For problems in the management, Liu Chuanzhi clearly makes new strategies for Lenovo. That is to focus on consumption and emerging markets. He says that "Lenovo's long-term and present strategies are clear, namely to maintain market shares in Europe and the United States. Products for these markets are commercial products for large customers. While in emerging markets like China, India, Russia, and Brazil and so on, we will strive for further development. Goods for consumption will gain greater development. "

After one year of struggle, Lenovo is gradually recovering from the loss in the early 2009. Recently, Lenovo Group announces earnings of the third quarter in 2009 / 2010 fiscal year (by December 31, 2009), it shows Lenovo's consolidated sales growth increases 33% over the previous year, reaching 4.8 billion with net income of $ 79.52 million U.S. Dollars. It makes profits in two consecutive quarters from the restructuring. It realizes the promise of turning losses into gains ahead and it is also exciting news for the global PC industry.

So, what makes the Lenovo to make profits again in the short term? How does Lenovo go through the crisis depend on strategic adjustments?

In early 2009, facing the enormous loss, Lenovo makes a strategic adjustment and begins to implement the strategy known as the "two fist" internally. It means that one "fist" is used to maintain core businesses in the Chinese market and overseas market; the other is used to explore new markets and consumer businesses, as well as to fine new channel partners. It gets more than 2300 new business partners only in the mature market.

It is reported that Lenovo's worldwide PC shipments rise 42% than last year, well above the industry average of 17%. Its share records in the global PC market for the third consecutive quarter, reaching 9%. Yang Yuanqing, CEO of Lenovo says that "This is mainly due to market share increase in most regions in the world, especially in China and emerging markets. Meanwhile, the growth in global demand situation also indicates the growth of the IT industry."

From the report, market share of Lenovo in the third quarter in China increase by 2.8%, reaching a record high of 33.5%, which is the biggest increase in a single quarter for 9 years. It accounts for 47% of the total global sales of the entire group, which is particularly crucial to enhance Lenovo's performance. In emerging markets, Lenovo's third-quarter consolidated sales reach 857 million U.S. dollars, accounting for 18% of worldwide sales of the entire group. Benefit from rising demand for business PCs in North American regions, total sales in mature markets of Lenovo in the third quarter increase by 16% over last year, succeeding in improving its profitability in mature markets.

At the same time, Lenovo believes that the past way of getting market share is not proper anymore, more importantly now is innovation. Lenovo has to accumulate strength and to increase investment in technological innovation. The introduction of innovative products based on CES of Lenovo is a good start, which marking the Lenovo will fully enter the fast-growing mobile Internet market.

In addition, Lenovo will continue to introduce other innovative products and continue to enrich the product portfolio to meet needs of different types and different prices. Lenovo firmly believe that it can gain sustained growth as long as it continues to focus on the implementation of these strategic priorities.

Run the mobile Internet business

On November 27, 2009, Lenovo Group (0992.HK) announces to buy back all the rights and interests of the Lenovo Mobile Communication Technology Co., Ltd. (hereinafter use "Lenovo Mobile" for short) it has sold 2 years ago with 2 thousand million U.S. Dollars. It is the next strategic direction following the new strategies since Liu Chuanzhi returns to the Chairman of the Board and Yang Yuanqing returns to CEO position. That is mobile Internet business. Currently, Lenovo mobile ranks within the top three in Chinese mobile phone market as the top domestic mobile phone brand. In first half of 2009, it earns more than 40 million RMB Yuan pre-tax profits.

Liu Chuanzhi, chairman of the Board says that "Two years ago, we have no choice but to sell mobile phone business. At that time, Lenovo mobile losses 20 to 70 million RMB Yuan, which affects the performance of the whole company and will further has bad influence on its main business. Now although Lenovo pays more 100 million than before, it acquires a profitable business, which is also the strategic direction of Lenovo in future. Thus it is worth doing." He stresses "There will be huge development space for the PC industry along with the development of 3G and the popularity of mobile Internet in the world. In addition, Chinese government is

53

encouraging the standards making of three networks, which will bring Lenovo new opportunities.

Yang Yuanqing also says that "in the next several quarters, we will continue to expand the PC business, focusing on grasping the growth opportunities in the mobile Internet. It means that we will pay special attention to products like mobile Internet hardware devices, tablet PCs, and Music Phone. It will become a major way to overcome our challenges and get market returns from our innovations.

Review

Lenovo' practice, performance and experience is called "Lenovo phenomenon" or "Lenovo miracle." at home and abroad. Well what does Lenovo mainly rely on to achieve its rapid development?

Is that capital? No, because Lenovo has only 200 thousand RMB Yuan as total venture capital.

Is that technology? No. Because Lenovo starts with neither its own technology patents, intellectual property rights, nor its own products.

Then, what is it indeed? There are many reasons for its development; however, the following main reasons are very important:

A good mechanism and a good leader is the first key reason from an objective perspective. That is the personnel, financial and operational autonomy as well as strong support of leaders represented by Zeng Maochao.

A good strategy formulated by the leaders group headed by original president Liu Chuanzhi is another core from a subjective view. They makes many right strategies, for instance, comprehensive development strategy of combine trade, industry and technology; lone-term development of entering the world market; and strategy to fully develop of technology, network and e-commerce in the information industry, especially the international strategy to merge PC business unit of IBM.

Just as what Liu Chuanzhi says, "A right and artistic strategy is the magic tool for Lenovo Group's winning." He warns Chinese entrepreneurs according to the experience of Lenovo that, "Formulation and implementation of strategy is the key to enhance the international competitiveness of Chinese enterprises. It is a severe test for China's enterprises to make correct strategies."

Questions

1. What is strategy? What are its main points?
2. What is enterprise strategy? What are its main points?
3. What is strategic management? What are its main points and significance?
4. What are the characteristics of enterprise strategy? What are stages of enterprise strategic
5. management?
6. What are levels of enterprise strategy? What is the relationship between each level?
7. What are the roles of entrepreneurs? Which is the primary role? What are main tasks of enterprise strategists?
8. According to your own experience, what is the significance of strategic management for a company?
9. According to your own experience, how to conduct and improve strategic management?

Notes

(1) (U.S.) Michael Porter, Competitive Strategy, Introduction, Huaxia Publishing House, 1997, p.33.
(2) Sun Tzu, "Attack by Stratagem," Art of War.
(3) In time of the "Three Battles," the People's Liberation Army has transferred from weak to strong, while the KMT from strong to weak, whose army has been wiped out from 8 million soldiers to less than 2 million. At the time of "Crossing Chishui River for Four Times," the KMT takes use of dominated military advantage. Chiang Kai-shek personally directs the 400 thousand soldiers to besiege the Central Red Army, who has only 20 thousand, of which there are many sick and injured soldiers as well as the elderly, women and children.
(4) This case study is written by the author based on the publications, lectures and other materials of Lenovo Group. It is first published in Principles of Management, a book the author participates in editing, Higher Education Press, 1999, p. 171-184 pages. Then again, in 1999, it is put into Asia Pacific Management Cases (first series) by the Management Development Centre of Hong Kong, which is published in the Asia Pacific

region. This time it is modified according to the latest materials of Lenovo.

(5) Ding Feiyang: "Prepare to pay costs for internationalization," China Business, August 16, 2004.

(6) Ding Fei Yang, "Behind the Silence: Arrangement of Lenovo and IBM on PC business," China Business, November 2004.

(7) Liu Hongwei, "Lenovo swallows global PC business of the 'Big Blue'," Chinese Companies, December 9, 2004.

(8) Liu Hongwei, "Lenovo swallows global PC business of the 'Big Blue'," Chinese Companies, December 9, 2004.

(9) Liang Xin, "Trend that can never be stopped," Chinese Companies, December 13, 2004.

(10) Liang Xin, "Trend that can never be stopped," Chinese Companies, December 13, 2004.

BIBLIOGRAPHY

Mao Zedong, *Elected Works of Mao Zedong,* four volumes, People's Publishing House, Beijing, 1966.

Deng Xiaoping, *Elected Works of Deng Xiaoping,* three volumes, People's Publishing House, Beijing, January, 1989.

Art of War commentary group of War Theory Research Department of Academy of Military Sciences, CPLA, *New Commentary of Art of War*, 1st edition, Zhonghua Book Company, January 1977.

Sun-Tzu (the original), Kung-sun Daoming ed, *Art of War and Thirty-Six Stratagems* , 1st edition, Guangxi Ethnic Publishing House, July 1995.

Editorial board of *Art of War and Strategy for Business and Politics*, *Art of War and Strategy for Business and Politics*, 1st edition, Blue Sky Press, May 1997.

Luo Guanzhong, *Romance of the Three Kingdoms*, 1st edition, Changjiang Literature Press, January, 1981.

Guo Jixing, Li Shijun, *Romance of the Three Kingdoms and Business Strategic Management*, 1st edition, Guangxi People's Publishing House, June, 1988.

Yao Youwei, *Strategies in the Three Kingdoms and Tips for Commercial War*, 1st edition, Donghua University Press, August, 2006.

﹝U.S.﹞ Peter Drucker, *The Effective Executive,* 1st edition, Qing-Wen Printing Co.Ltd., March, 1978.

﹝U.S.﹞Peter Drucker, *The Practice of Management*, 1st edition, China Machine Press, January, 2006.

﹝ U.S. ﹞ Peter Drucker, *Management: Tasks, Responsibilities, Practice*,1st edition, China Social Sciences Press, June 1987.

﹝U.S.﹞ Michael Porter, *Competitive Strategy*, 1st edition, Huaxia Publishing House, January 1997.

﹝U.S.﹞ Michael Porter, *Competitive Advantage*, 1st edition, Huaxia Publishing House, January 1997.

﹝U.S.﹞ Michael Porter & Gary Hamel, The Future of Strategy Management, 1st Edition, Sichuan People's Publishing House, April 2000.

〔U.S.〕Jack Trout, *Trout on Strategy*, 1st edition, China Financial and Economic Publishing House, October 2004.

〔U.S.〕Arthur A. Thompson Jr. & A. J. Strickland, *Crafting and executing strategy: the quest for competitive advantage concepts and cases*, 10th ed, Duan Shenghua, Wang Zhihui trans., Xu Erming revision, Peking University Press, 2004.

〔U.S.〕Fred. R. David, *Strategic Management*, Like Ning trans., 1st edition, Economic Science Press, June 1998.

〔CAN.〕Henry Mintzberg, *Strategy Safari*, 2nd edition, Machinery Industry Press, June 2006.

〔British〕Gerry Johnson & Kevan Scholes, *Exploring Corporate Strategy*, 1st Edition, Jin Zhanming & Gu Xiumei tran, Huaxia Publishing House, April 1998.

〔Japanese〕KenichiOhmae, *Strategic Minds of Entrepreneurs*, 1st Edition, SDX Joint Publishing Company,　January, 1986.

〔U.S.〕Stephen P.Robbins, *Management*, 4th Edition,China Renmin University Press, 1998.

Wang Chao ed, *Transnational Strategy: International Business Management*, 1st edition, China International Business and Economics Press, January, 1999.

Sheng Ding ed, *Harvard Business School MBA*, 1st edition revision, The Economic Daily Press, May, 1997.

Ouyang Yun ed, Latest Cases Study of *Harvard Business School*, 1st edition revision, The Economic Daily Press, May, 1998.

Editing group of required MBA core courses, *Business Strategy*, 1st edition, China International Radio Press, September 1997.

Editing group of required MBA core courses, *Business Strategy*, 1st edition revision, China International Radio Press, 2000.

Liu Jisheng ed, *Company Operation Strategy*, 1st edition, Tsinghua University Press, April 1995.

Xu Erming ed, *Company Strategy Management*, 1st edition, China Economic Publishing House, May 1998.

Si Yan ed, *Win by Strategy—Key to Business Success*, 1st edition, China Citic Press, July, 1994.

Chiang Yuntong ed, *Company Operation Strategic Management*, 1st edition, Company Management Press, April 1996.

〔U.S.〕 Napoleon Hill, Everyone Can Be Successful, 2nd edition, Hubei People's Publishing House in February 2001.

Zhang Xiuyu, *How to be successful*, 1st edition, Enterprise Management Press, January 2005.

Sun Qingguang, *Run to Success*, 1st edition, Enterprise Management Publishing House,   January, 1997.

CHAPTER 2
Enterprise Strategy: Nature and Scope

Abstract

The first chapter introduces the primary functions of enterprise strategy which include six components: business scope, strategic goal setting, strategic action, resource allocation, competitive advantage, and coordination. It then explains the concept of enterprise strategy by addressing key questions such as: What line of business should we be in? How long do we pursue a strategy before changing course? How do we get there? Next, it elaborates on the nature of business strategy and concludes with cases and comments in "Strategic Decision-making of Beiren Group."

Learning Objectives

- To understand the components of enterprise strategy.
- To understand the implication of enterprise strategy.
- To implement an effective enterprise strategy.

Introduction

What are the components, implications and makeup of enterprise strategy? This chapter will attempt to understand and respond to these questions as this understanding is the foundation of enterprise strategic management.

Lesson

Components of Enterprise Strategy

From a narrow perspective m enterprise strategy consists of six factors which include business scope, strategic goal setting, strategic action, resource allocation, competitive advantage, and the coordination of these functions.

Business scope

Business scope defines the environment in which a firm operates. It mirrors the degree of the firm's interaction with its external environment, as well as the demand for interaction of its business plan with the environment. A firm should determine its business scope according to the industry it engages in, its products and its market.

Business goal

Strategic goal setting is attained by reaching a target market of customers in the firm has decided to serve. Two methods are used to measure the business outcome level: one is to use quantitative measures such as total sales revenue or profits in Yuan. Another is to use relative measures such as market position within ones industry or the firm's relative market share. Relative market share is considered more important because it measures business strength.

Strategic action

Strategic action refers to specific steps the firm plans to take in realizing its strategic goal. For example, one business planned to increase its sales from RMB Yuan 100 million to 200 million: it may add production lines or introduce more advanced equipment. Strategic action takes a longer term perspective and should not be confused with the day to day operations or tasks needed to reach these strategic goals.

Resource allocation

Firms allocate resources that are in alignment with its long term goals and objectives as this use of resources directly influences the achievement of the firm's goals. When a firm is forced to change direction because of changes in the external environment, it should make the necessary adjustments to its use of company resources.

Competitive advantage

Competitive advantage means the competitive position a business reaches through decision making processes as it pertains to resources allocation and business scope.Competitive advantage is unique to each firm and differs from its rivals in the market. Competitive advantage can come from the position of a business in terms of product and markets; it can also come from the correctly using of company resources.

Coordinative Function

Coordinative function reflects efficiencies effectiveness gained through the decisions making on resources allocation models and business scopes. Generally speaking, a firm's coordinative function can be divided into four classes:

1. Investment coordinative function. This function comes from internal and joint uses of the firm's equipment, raw materials in stock, R & D investment, as well as special tools and skills by all individual internal business units.

2. Operational coordinative function. This function is gained from fully using the current human resources and equipment, as well as advantages gained through shared experience.

3. Marketing coordinative function. This function is generated from a firm's common shared marketing channels, sales agents, promotions and products brands.

4. Management coordinative function. This function comes from experience accumulation and scale merit in the development of management. For example managers can apply their managerial experiences to manage new business, thus reduce the management cost.

To study the constitutive factors of Enterprise Strategy is very significant. On one hand it can help the business better understand influences these factors have on its overall effectiveness and efficiency; on the other it can enable managers to realize that these six factors exist in various strategic levels, and have various relative significances in each level.

Implications of Enterprise Strategy

To understand the implications of enterprise strategy one needs to answer three questions: What line of business should we be in? How long do we pursue a strategy before changing course? How do we get there?
These questions intend to identify the direction in which the company can compete most effectively. For example, the firm decides which industry it should compete and what products and services it will supply.

What does the company want to do? That depends on the subjective requirements of management. Generally these are influenced by company values, interests' hobbies, expertise and so on.

What can the company do?

It depends on current circumstances, industry structure, and the overall business environment in a particular society. These environmental factors can include science, technology, materials, equipment, and machinery and so on. If any material, which is needed for a product is not provided, then a company cannot produce that. For example, a firm could never manufacture the light bulb if Edison had not invented it, or if there are no support technologies, materials, equipment, and machinery currently available.

What does the company do better than its competitors?

What a company thinks it does better than its competitors is often subjective. But as it is often said, you cannot make something out of nothing. Subjective in this context refers to real firm resources as perceived by management that will be needed to offer its product or service.

What should the company do?

What the company should do is decided in part by what its competitors are doing. Sun Tzu has said if you know the enemy and know yourself, you need not fear the result of a hundred battles. If you know yourself but not the enemy, for every victory gained you will also suffer a defeat. If you know neither the enemy nor yourself, you will succumb in every battle.

In determining what to do, the company assesses the current market situation and industry trends and competition. If there are many strong rivals or some who control most of the market, then the company should consider choosing another industry to compete.

In short, strategy describes what you want to do, what you can do, what you are able to do and what is worth doing. A business that feels comfortable with the answers to these questions understands the fundamentals of business strategy. The most typical deficiency of corporate strategy in China can be illustrated in two forms: one is that a firm has not properly assessed the subjective and objective market conditions, and the company has underestimated market demand.

64

How far should a company go before changing course?

The company needs goals. A goal should include the following five points:

1. Brand goal: to be the "leader" or "follower" in the industry.
2. Regional objective: to develop domestic or global market.
3. Life target: to be short lived or sustainable over time.
4. Economic objective: these include operating income, taxes, profits and salaries.
5. Social responsibility: these would include things like promoting harmony, save energy and protecting the environment.

How is this done?

Peter Drucker believes 90% of strategic management problems are similar among all firms and only 10% are unique to individual firms. These next twelve questions serve as a guide to understanding common strategic plans in industry.

1. What kind of industry structure is desired?
2. How to cultivate corporate culture by focusing on the company's mission and vision and values.
3. What company systems need to be established?
4. What organizational structure needs to be set?
5. What leadership teams need to be formed?
6. How to select and train employees?
7. How to improve technology and product innovation?
8. How to improve quality and marketing management?
9. How to improve financial management?
10. How to improve capital management?
11. How to prevent risks?
12. How to build a corporate brand?

Nature of Enterprise Strategy

Although there are three implications of enterprise strategy, there is only one nature of it, which is "how to do right things". "How to do right things" and "how to do things right" seem too alike, however, there are differences in nature, which can be seen in Table 2-1.

Table 2-1 "How to do right things" ≠ "how to do things right"

	How to do right things	How to do things right
Function	Plan	Implement
Scope	Overall	Part
Time	Future	Present
Level	Senior Level	Middle and Lower levels
Objective	Effectiveness	Efficiency
Strategy/Tactics	Strategy	Tactics

Clearly, "how to do right things" is a study of strategy, while "how to do things right" is a research on tactics. Then which should be the focus of major business leaders? Peter Drucker famous American management master indicates that the most important work for the managers is to do the right things (improve effectiveness) but not to do things right (improve efficiency). The world famous American strategic management expert Michael Porter points out that although leaders in many firms are tasked with managing for better performance, their roles are wider and more important than that particular task. The general manager is not only responsible for the management of a single function; on the contrary, his core business is that of strategy.

Therefore, business leaders, especially major leaders, must decide on their strategies. If not, they miss the purpose of their duties. They can become recognized in the firm as long as they study and formulate the right strategy, guiding the firm to "do the right thing." Otherwise, they could be the ones that lead the firm to troubles. Therefore, all business leaders must pay attention to strategic decision making.

Case study

Strategic decision-making of Beiren Group

Beiren is the abbreviation of Beiren Group Corporation and Beiren Printing Machinery Co., Ltd. It is originally a small state-owned company built in 1952 whose main products are civil engineering machinery, mining machinery and semi-automatic printing machines at beginning. In 1956, it begins to produce stop cylinder press, sheet-fed press and other mechanical presses. It focuses on the production printing machinery in the late 60s. After fifty years of development, it has become China's largest printing press manufacturer, the only listed company in China's printing industry, and one of the top 500 Chinese industrial companies. Beiren brand offset press is famous at home and abroad. Beiren has become a well-known national brand and an excellent model in China's printing industry.

Its leaders take the development strategy of the company very seriously. Chairman Zhu Wuan often stresses that "It is essential to understand the development strategy of the company at the beginning. Besides market analysis, the success of a company is inseparable from the guidance of strategy. An Enterprise Strategy leads people to achieve their goals. A company without long-term development strategies will be destined to fail. Therefore, it is an important task of the company's leaders to start with the right business development strategy and to guide staff to achieve the strategic goals." Leaders of Beiren set a great example themselves and make several strategic decision-makings:

The first to exit out of the machinery manufacturing industry, and focus on the printing press manufacturing industry

In 1952, under the leadership of the Beijing Municipal People's Government, Beijing People's Machine Factory, the predecessor of Beiren Group is formed from 22 small fragmented ironwork firms. For a long time, the factory produces a variety of goods, including printing machinery like platform printing, hand casting machine and stapler, as well as other machineries such as floating concentrator, tramcar, industrial valves, and construction machinery.

In 1981, Beijing People's Machine Factory is renamed Beijing Printing Machinery Factory. Zhu Tanlin is its first director. Under the guidance of related government departments, he decisively changes the factory's positioning from machinery manufacturing to printing equipment manufacturing. It identifies Beiren's positioning, establishes the firm's later wellbeing, stability and sustainable development direction and lays the basis for its right strategy.

Michael Porter, father of competitive strategy points out that strategy is a kind of beneficial positioning. It involves a variety of operational activities. These activities must be designed according to the market conditions and its own situations, which are unique and difficult to imitate. Jack Trout, the world's master of corporate strategy consulting also believes that positioning is the core of strategy. Strategy is what makes the company and its products unique. In the 1980s, machinery manufacturing industry is very popular in China. Facing the current industry competitors and the potential rivals, leaders of Beiren, led by Zhu Tanlin, are wise enough to assess the situation and make the right decision. It's an excellent example of business strategic decision-making.

To produce offset printing press instead of letterpress printing machine decisively

In 1981, Beiren is facing a critical shortage of letterpress printing machines. It has just won the national silver medal. Customers have to pay in advance before the delivery. At this time, Zhu Tanlin notices the trend that offset printing press will surpass letterpress printing machine. It is based on his study of development of the industry at home and abroad, in particular the latest technologies and products.

At this time, people are not quite aware of this major strategic turning point in the industry. There are large numbers of people who feel uncertain of the trend. In spite of this, Zhu Tanlin decides to immediately give up the production of letterpress printing machines and begin to manufacture offset printing presses. In 1982, Beiren develops the first folio duplicate offset press in China. Afterwards, it manufactures different varieties. New products are welcomed in China's technological transformation of the printing industry, and sell very well. It meets the market needs, makes long-term profits for Beiren and lays foundation for its leading position in China.

In the 1980s, it is rare to find case studies from leading firms like Beiren. They have made a good strategic move and change their product line from letterpress printing machines to offset printing presses. It is at least 3-5 years ahead of its competitors in the industry, in which many have gone bankrupt for missing their strategic opportunities.

To seize the opportunity to pre-empt the implementation of joint-stock

In 1993, Zhu Wuan, vice general manager recommends Zhu Tanlin to take the company public. It is really a fresh idea at a time when people still believe stock and stock markets are bad things as described in the novel *Midnight*. The company does not know how to value its assets or how to hire accountants and lawyers, or understand the process of going public. The Beijing government selects only one company in Beijing that can go public. Beiren seizes the opportunity by actively preparing and applying for a stock offering and are surprised many other companies reject this opportunity.

In 1993, Zhu Wuan begins the process of restructuring. He starts to study the rules for listed companies, as well as related Chinese policies and laws. He organizes assessments, designs the organizational structure and drafts relevant documents on his own. Finally, Beiren's application of going public gains the approval of government and Hong Kong stock exchange. Beiren then issues H share in Hong Kong, raising 200 million HKD. In 1994, it issues a share in the Shanghai stock market, raising RMB Yuan 250 million. This infuses Beiren with large amounts of capital. Beiren also becomes the first and only limited company in both Hong Kong and the Shanghai stock market in Chinese printer industry. It is also the first one in Beijing with modern company systems as well as capital. That lays a specified and long-term basis for its development. In this process, Zhu Wuan's pragmatic innovation and forward-thinking spirit, courage and ability to rise to the challenge, and ideas are clearly visible to everyone.

To focus on core businesses and resist the temptation of a mixture of investments

Beiren gets its first funding for development through financing in 1993 and 1994. It makes use of tools such as additional shares allotment. For instance, the company issues more A shares in January 2003, raising a large amount of funds. At that time, many companies blindly invest in real estate, security and diversified operations as a way to expand their business. Beiren never puts its capitals into those other areas, but reinvests in its core business. At that time, public opinion and some so-called experts doubt its choice and criticize it by saying that Beiren doesn't know how to operate capital and make use of it. It stands firm and lays a solid industrial foundation for the company's growth and hence keeps the leading position in the printer equipment industry.

To devise the tenth five-year development strategy.

In 2000, Zhu Wuan serves as party secretary and chairman of the company. He makes it clear that he advocates bringing these products to the market. After careful consideration and brainstorming, leaders of Beiren make the tenth five-year development strategy in accordance with Beiren's product line. It announces that Beiren will produce sheet paper and roll paper offset production as its main business, explores development in upstream and downstream printing press products and industry, coordinates products production and capital operation, and creates a world famous brand to solidify its leading position.

Beiren's efforts prove successful. Sales income in 2004 is 2.54 times greater than in 2000, increasing up to 153.64% with at an average annual growth rate of 27.68%. Total profit in 2004 is 2.02 times greater than in 2000. Beiren conducts its expansion and restructuring efforts at a low cost and merges 4 companies relying on its technological, market, brand and management advantages. It extends the industrial chain, realizes the industrial upgrading, refines the primary business and optimizes the allocation of resources.

To promote the development of company, seizing relocation opportunity

To move into Beijing's Economic and Technological Development Zone (BDA) is the company's most important strategic decision in the firm's history. It is also the biggest ever strategic move. This issue is particularly important considering the present market conditions. That is, is it just a simple change in location or a historic opportunity for taking drastic measures to adjust and transform, and improve the company's strategic position?

The strategy has pays off. Income in 2004 is 2.54 times greater than 2000; an increase of 153.64% with an average annual growth rate of 27.68%. Total profit in 2004 is 2.02 times what it was in 2000. Beiren executes its expansion and restructuring at a low cost and merges 4 companies using its technological, market, brand and management expertise. It extends the supply chain, refines the primary business and optimizes the allocation of resources.

Zhu Wuan, chairman of the Board clearly states that relocation can provide excellent opportunities for company development. Beiren can re-integrate, adjust organizational structure and production facilities, construct a more modern facility and eliminate unproductive assets. Therefore, allocation and adjustment of resources provide synergies.

After careful consideration he sets forth a plan to modernize the facilities that will keep the facility running efficiently for the next 30 years. It is a significant decision because many firms have failed because the leader

70

made the wrong decision. Mistakes in investment or process strategy can bankrupt a company.

At the same time, he proposes a "16 words" general relocation policy, namely, "continue to manufacture products, maintain existing market shares, input available personal capital, and build a united team." He takes a hands on approach in delegating much of the work, and encourages managers to collaborate with each other personally, He leads by example to promote the smooth distribution of work, pays close attention to building positive culture among mid-level managers, strives to adjust the layout of process, accelerates technological transformation, reduce costs improve product quality and manufacturing standards.

The company adopts technology transformation by setting up 6 production lines of drum and shaft rollers. It also conducts organizational restructuring, which clarifies the duties of managers of both the company and its branches. Quality and efficiency are improved after downsizing. So, the company achieves the success of both distribution and development. Moreover, the design of the new plant applies the principles of "five fines:" fine production, fine measurement, fine assembly, fine control and fine management. The workshop building takes the form of joint workshops. A multi-functional large-scale integrated production system is utilized resulting in the shortening of the distance between storehouses and the processing plant. The new plant covers an area of 160,000 square meters, with a construction area of 100,000 square meters. Thus we see the emergence of a new transformed Beiren Group.

Sources: "A wonderful success in China's Pinter industry: Why Beiren can continue to succeed", a research paper of Beijing Successful Key Consulting Co., Ltd. December, 2005.

Review

The experience of Beiren, along with that of many other companies proves that the success of a company is primarily determined by strategy than by details. This is because a company cannot succeed without the right strategy. Without the correct strategy the firm will go farther and farther away from success.
Jack Trout, the well-known expert in strategic consulting has said "What

I've learned over and over again is that success isn't about having the right people, the right attitude, the right tools, the right role models, or the right organization. They all help, but they don't put you over the top. It's all about having the right strategy."

Therefore, the development and success of a business is first affected by the presence or absence of a scientific, accurate and clearly formulated strategy. With the right strategy, the entire team can move in the right direction and create superior business results. Otherwise, even with a focus on high quality and with enthusiastic team members, companies may not achieve their goals. Just like an army may fail due to the wrong strategy, a company may meet its demise due to poor strategic planning.

Beiren Group sets an excellent example among state-owned or state holding companies by achieving success based on their decision-making and strategic management.

Questions

1. What are the components of enterprise strategy?
2. What is the connotation of enterprise strategy?
3. What is the nature of enterprise sstrategy?

Notes

(1) (U.S.) Michael Porter & Gary Hamel, *The Future of Strategy Management*, Sichuan People's Publishing House, April 2000, p. 30.
(2) (U.S.) Jack Trout, *Trout on Strategy*, 1st edition, China Financial and Economic Publishing House, October 2004, p.1.

BIBLIOGRAPHY

〔U.S.〕 Michael Porter, *Competitive Strategy*, 1st edition, Huaxia Publishing House, January 1997.

〔U.S.〕 Michael Porter, *Competitive Advantage*, 1st edition, Huaxia Publishing House, January 1997

.

〔U.S.〕 Jack Trout, *Trout on Strategy*, 1st edition, China Financial and Economic Publishing House, October 2004.

〔U.S.〕 Arthur A. Thompson Jr. & A. J. Strickland, *Crafting and executing strategy: the quest for competitive advantage concepts and cases*, 10th ed, Duan Shenghua, Wang Zhihui trans., Xu Erming revision, Peking University Press, 2004.

〔U.S.〕 Fred. R. David, *Strategic Management*, Li Kening trans., 1st edition, Economic Science Press, June 1998.

Sheng Ding ed, *Harvard Business School MBA*, 1st edition revision, The Economic Daily Press, May, 1997.

Editing group of required MBA core courses, *Business Strategy*, 1st edition revision, China International Radio Press, 2000.

Liu Jisheng ed, *Company Operation Strategy*, 1st edition, Tsinghua University Press, April 1995.

Xu Erming ed, *Company Strategy Management*, 1st edition, China Economic Publishing House, May 1998.

Si Yan ed, *Win by Strategy—Key to Business Success*, 1st edition, China Citic Press, July, 1994.

BIBLIOGRAPHY

CHAPTER 3
Positioning is the Core of Strategy

Abstract

At first, this chapter makes an outline of the concept for positioning from success stories like Gillette Company. Then it explains the four principles of positioning: first, the market demand is positioning foundation; second, the own strength is the main basis; third, the weaker competitor is important basis and fourth, the public support is a moral law. This chapter focuses on the commonly used methods of positioning: striving to be first positioning and comparative positioning. Finally, it has an appendix of cases and comments of strategic positioning of Successful Key Consulting Company.

Learning Objectives

- To understand and know the concept of positioning.
- To understand and know the principles of positioning.
- To learn to apply the methods of positioning.

Introduction

Our society has become over-communicated. Generation of numerous media like books, newspapers, and television brings a media explosion, which then brings the information explosion. The spread of information through a communication channel to mind can be compared to one Chinese saying, "thousands of soldiers and tens of thousands of horses come across a single log bridge." In this over-communicated society, can anyone read all the information exposed to him? However, nothing can be done without information. Besides, the so-called luck usually originates from successful information exchange. Therefore, the best way to communicate is to send useful and very simple information, so that it can successfully get into people's minds. In addition, positioning is a strategic means through which companies are able to send information about their brands, products, and services into their targeted prospective customers' mind.

Lesson

I. Understand the concept of positioning from success stories like Gillette Company

Founded in 1901 in the United States, Gillette has focused on producing and marketing razors with a history of more than 100 years; the company currently employs about 30,000 workers, and makes up to 90% of the market share in the United States and more than 70% of the global market share. Being the World First, Gillette has no stronger competitor in the market.

"Nail clipper king" Liang Boqiang, only runs a nail clipper business, but his sales jumped year by year; for example, in 1999, his sales are RMB Yuan 40 million; in 2000, RMB Yuan 70 million; in 2001, RMB Yuan 120 million; in 2003, RMB Yuan 200 million. Besides, the goal of the next four to five years is RMB Yuan 400 million and long-term goal is RMB Yuan 2 billion. Currently, the "St. Allen (Shengyalun in Chinese)" brand's market share of Liang Boqiang increases steadily and has reached 50%. In that way, he is the truly "nail clipper king" not only in China but also in the world.

Similarly, the Ya Du Company only produces air humidifier and purifier, while its domestic market share is up to 80%, the first in domestic market and the third in the world. Why does the first company and the second one of the world humidifier industry don't enter China's market? Because they could do no better than the existing Ya Do.

Successes of Gillette "nail clipper king" and "Ya Du" give the inspiration for us that a correct positioning is the key for company to succeed and the most important factor that matters the success. With a correct positioning, it hits half; otherwise, it loses everything.

Company strategy consulting expert Jack Trout has said that "We have become an over-communicated society. In the communication jungle out there, the only hope to score big is to be selective, to concentrate on narrow targets, to practice segmentation. In a word, it is positioning." (1) "In the land of positioning, a successful strategy is based on finding a way to be different from your sea of competitors." (2)

Professor Michael Porter has pointed out that "Company's managers must take into account the positioning problem, and must understand 'who you are competing?' If you really have a strategy, then the answer is 'there is no competitor' because you are unique in the industry." (3)

Then, what is positioning? Positioning is focusing in a particular field. That is, specific industry, product or service, and it is the core of company strategy.

Positioning starts from brand, which may be a commodity, a service, a company and even a person. However, positioning shall focus on prospective customers instead of the brand itself. In other words, there should be a brand position settled in the minds of prospective customers so as to ensure that the brand can occupy a really valuable position in their minds. The above brands are good examples. The Gillette Company is the "Razor King", Liang Boqiang is the "nail clipper King," and Ya Du Company is "air humidifier and purifier king." Once a brand occupies the position as a king in the minds of prospective customers, the brand (product, service, company) will naturally become the preferred selection by the prospective customers and therefore, will gain more profits than the industry average level.

In short, It's a simple, focused value proposition. In other words, what's the reason to buy from you instead of one of your competitors? (4)

II.   Positioning principles

No matter engaging in what sort of industry, trade, product or service business, the company should always follow the following four principles in determining the strategic positioning.

(I) Market demand is positioning foundation.

Market demand is the first principle of positioning. No matter what kind of industry, trade, product or service a company decides to engage in; it has to be based on market demand; otherwise, the positioning will inevitably lead to failure, like water without a source or a tree without roots.

There are two kinds of market demand, one is actual demand, or immediate tangible demand; the other is the potential demand, or the future demand.

When choosing its strategic positioning, and companies should consider both two kinds of demand, especially should pay more attention to the potential demand in order to ensure that present business will not be eliminated within five years, and will not fall behind within a decade.

(II) Own strength is the main basis

Success master Napoleon Hill has pointed out in "rebuild your life, manage your better" when talking about success principles after the failure and before the success, please find the common sense that often overlooked, that is to run your own strengths. Modern success believes that, as long as using your own strengths in the most critical place, you are more likely to succeed. (5)

We are unaware of our strengths, which is often our mistakes to make. We eventually overestimate or underestimate our abilities. If so, we miss time due to indecision on things we are able to do, while we take a risk due to eagerness to win on things, we are unable to do. All these adverse consequences are because of not realizing what can do and what can't do. In real life, there are a large number of such people. Thus, there is no use of too many complaints, and the key to success is to know ourselves, to identify our strengths and to make advantages of them.

So what are our strengths? Strengths are the strongest abilities. The so-called firmest ability refers to the potential capability to reveal oneself with skill and ease as well as to reflect one's maximum value. Depending on one's strengths in life, one gains high probability to success; comparing one's weaknesses with others, one can only hand over the success to others. In addition, after taking advantage of one's strengths, even facing failure, one will not regret too much because it is to the best of one's ability; instead, one will leave more regret. Of course, there is no life without regrets, but it is indeed a pity not finding one's personal strengths. Therefore, we must find our own strengths, and operate our own strengths well, which is the key to change our life.

This principle of success that Napoleon Hill emphasizes is not only for individuals but also for companies. Any company has its own strengths (advantages) as well as weaknesses (disadvantages). When makes strategic positioning, a company must make the best use of its advantages and bypass the disadvantages to achieve success.

(III)   Weaker competitor is an important basis.

Ancient Chinese military strategist Sun Tzu has said that "If you know the enemy and know yourself, you need not fear the result of a hundred battles. If you know yourself but not the enemy, for every victory gained, you will also suffer a defeat. If you know neither the enemy nor yourself, you will succumb in every battle." (6) The Art of War by Sun Tzu (Offensive Strategy). It means that when knows both enemy and oneself, one will not fail conducting many operations; when knows oneself but the enemy, one may have half possibility to defeat; when knows neither enemy nor oneself, one will lose every battle.

Comrade Mao Zedong, one of the modern Chinese strategists has said in (7) Strategy Problems of China's Revolutionary War that the sentence of ancient Chinese military strategist Sun Tzu 'knows you as well as the enemy, and you can fight a hundred battles with no danger of defeat. ' can be applied in two phrases, including to learn and use; that is, the phrases to understand laws of development in practice and to determine one's actions following these laws to defeat the current enemy; thus, we should not underestimate the importance of this sentence. In addition, he also has said in (8) On Protracted War that the law of Sun Tzu,' know yourself as well as the enemy ' is still scientific truth.

As we all know, whether in war or in combat, the strong one will easily defeat the weaker opponent; to apply in the commercial warfare. Therefore, in strategic positioning, the companies must conduct comprehensive, thorough and detailed investigations of competitors before select what kind of industry, product or service to engage in, to really "know yourself as well as the enemy,'" especially "know the enemy." Besides, the companies must be sure that competitors are weaker before engaging in, which is an important basis for positioning.

(IV)   Public support is the moral law.

Company is a cell of society, where it gets all resources needed for its survival and development. So companies must benefit, serve, return society and strive to gain public support. This requires that companies must make social responsibility to run no business that violates social ethics. Companies should be honest and trustworthy, obey the laws, pay taxes, and create jobs, moreover. It should be energy saving, environmental friendly, and create harmonious for the benefit of future generations. They are the moral laws of positioning.

III. Positioning methods

Michael Porter has said that "One approach in formulating strategy is to look for positions in the market where a company can meet its objectives without threatening its competitors. When competitors' goals are well understood, there may be a place where everyone is relatively happy." (9)

In order to establish a favorable and lasting competitive position, the following two points should be ensured:

1. Company should find a strategy so that it can defend existing competitors and new invaders through clear advantages.

2. The strategy should not include strategic actions that may threaten competitors to achieve their main objectives and therefore, may spark intense war.

Positioning is to give the brand of company access to the minds of customers. The way to the mind is the basic method of positioning. Effective methods commonly used are the followings.

(I) Striving to be first

The shortcut to the mind is striving to be first. To leave an indelible impression in people's minds, what needs first is not information but the brain, a pure brain that is not affected by other brands.

To be successful in the market, we must recognize the importance of being first in people's minds for people all prefer the first in their minds. It is hard to erase names of product and company that occupied positions of the initial person, the first peak or the first one from people's memo, here are some examples: IBM of the computer industry, Microsoft of the software industry, Intel of the CPU industry, HP of the copier industry, Kodak of the photographic industry, Coca of the cola industry, Hertz of car rental industry, GE of the electric industry, and so on. In addition, in China, there is Lenovo of the PC industry, Haier of the household appliances industry, Huawei of the communications industry, Mengniu of the dairy industry, Tong Ren Tang of the pharmaceutical industry, Quan Ju de of the food industry,

Beiren of the printer industry, Tsingtao of the beer industry, Wahaha of the beverage industry, etc.

All these brands have been popular with customers, and are therefore, far ahead in the market. History has shown that the long-term market share occupied by the first brand getting into the minds of people is usually twice of the second brand's and three times of the third brand. Moreover, this proportion will not change easily.

Leader – the company with the largest market share – can equally have the highest profit margins in the market. The profit margins of four major U.S. auto manufacturers in 1978 are good proofs:

- GM owns 49% of the market share and 6.1% of the net profit in the market;

- Ford Motor Company owns 34% of the market share and 4.4% of the net profit in the market;

- Chrysler has 15% of the market share and 1.0% of the net profit in the market;

- American Motors Company has 2% of the market share and 0.4% of the net profit in the market;

- Net profit of General Motors (the first brand) is more than 50% of sales of American Motors (the fourth brands).

This indeed could be called that the rich is getting richer and the poor is getting poorer!

The ultimate goal of positioning action should be to gain a leadership position in the product category. Once owns this leading position, a company can be assured to gain a lot for many years in the future. Well, how should a company do if its brand cannot be the first in customers' minds? For many companies, one way to success is re-positioning the competitors according to what they are doing. A specific approach is to get real and simplified information from excessive materials, and gain flexible access to people's minds according to your own advantages.

(II) Comparative positioning

All final destinations of our information dissemination activities come from human minds. The human mind is like the computer memory, which will select a position for any information to keep it.

In order to deal with the product explosion, people learn to classify products in minds. In order to introduce a brand new class of products, the company must find its own ladder. Besides, the new product should be related with the original; otherwise, there are no footholds for it in people's minds. To get a position for the new products or new brands in people's mind, the company can also refer to the comparative positioning method.

Comparative positioning is a method to compare new products or brands with old ones. By bringing them together, it provides a chance for customers to make positioning of the new one according to the old. There are two simple and practical comparative positioning methods.

1. Old and new comparison

When you have a new product, you shall compare the new product with the old one. It can let prospective customers make a new-product positioning reference to the existing ones
so that the new product can access to the mind of prospective customers. For example:

The first car in the world is called horseless car at that time. That name is convenient for the public to make concept positioning for car according to the existing traffic transportation.

The first plane in the world is called flying machine at that time. That name is convenient for the public to make concept positioning for a plane according to the existing machines.

In addition, names like unleaded gasoline, tubeless tires, sugar-free cookies, air bus, and water car all show how a new concept should make positioning referring to the old one.

2. Rank queuing

In the market, the position status of competitors is as important as yours, and sometimes even more important. When a company is difficult to rank the first, it might sensibly to rank the second, or the third. Besides, it must stand on the shoulders of giants in order to make own positioning by using that of these giants.

An early success story is the famous campaign of American Elvis, which is an example of product positioning referring to the leading ones. The slogan is that since Elvis ranks the second in the car rental industry, why you need us? That's because we will work harder.

Elvis loses 13 years in a row. However, it starts to make profits since it admits its rank. The company earns 1.2 million dollars in the first year, 2.6 million dollars in the second year and 5 million dollars in the third year. Then it is sold to ITT Corporation.

The reason why Elvis can make a fortune is that it doesn't compete with Hertz Corporation directly after recognizing its status of the first brand of United States car rental industry.

To understand why the Elvis's campaign is successful, we may first imagine that there is a product ladder with a label of car rental industry in prospective customers' minds. There exists a brand name on every level of the ladder, where Hertz Corporation is on the highest level, Elvis on the second level and nationwide car rental companies on the third level. Many people misunderstand the experience of Elvis. They believe the company's success is the result of harder work, but actually, it is not. It is successful because it puts up a hook with Hertz, That is, it stands on the shoulders of giants.

Establishment of a contrast status is a typical positioning method. If a company does not come out on top, it is better to occupy the second position, firstly. That is what Elvis and "Burger King" does, as does Mengniu. In addition, the other companies in various industries can also follow.

China's Mengniu is a good model in using rank queuing method to make own positioning referring to that of giants. It proposes to create a second brand of Inner Mongolia dairy industry and makes advertising signs like ten thousand arrows shot at once.

3. Empty positioning

There are hundreds of products in each category of species in the market, which makes it far from adequate to find empty space in the market. Take an ordinary supermarket as an example; it displays a million products or brands, which means a young man needs to resolve or classify these kinds of commodities in mind.

Given there are so many product varieties in each category, how can companies advertising puts their products into the people's minds? The most basic marketing strategy must be the re-positioning of competitors.

Because of few opportunities, the company must create an empty position based on the re-positioning of competitors who have already taken a place in people's minds. In other words, in order to make a new idea or new product get into people's minds; we must first edge out the original relevant idea or product from their minds. There are two methods commonly used:

(1) Open to provoke a dispute

Disputes - even among individuals – are able to build a reputation overnight, so never be afraid of disputes. The key to re-positioning is fundamentally shaking the existing concepts.

Dispute of Columbus and the public about the shape of the earth is a good example.

The public believed that the earth was flat; while Columbus said the earth was round, not flat. In order to convince the public to accept this new view, scientists in the 15th century must first prove that the earth is not flat. Sailors can see the mast across the board first, then the sailing ship and finally, the hull. Thus, a more convincing view they proposed was that if the earth is flat, sailors should see the whole boat at the same time.

Once the old ideas are overthrown, it becomes extremely simple to promote new ideas. In fact, people tend to take the initiative to find a new idea to fill the resulting gaps. Therefore, never be afraid of disputes. When a company has a new product or new brand, it should be brave to challenge old products or brands in order to draw maximize attentions of prospective customers. In this way, it can build a reputation overnight, putting new products or brands into the minds of customers, and help products occupy a level on the product ladder.

(2) To comment products of competitors

In order to make re-positioning strategy be effective, a company must comment on competitor's products so that prospective customers change their minds on theirs instead of yours. In the United States, the re-positioning of Tylenol for Aspirin is a good example.

The advertising slogan of Tylenol is for the sake of millions of people who should not take aspirin!

The ad of "Tylenol," says that if your stomach is often uncomfortable... if you suffer from stomach ulcers... If you have asthma, allergies, or iron-deficiency anemia, you should consult a doctor before taking aspirin.

"Aspirin will irritate the gastric mucosa," the advertisement of "Tylenol'" continues, "may cause asthma or allergic reactions, resulting in recessive slight gastrointestinal bleeding."

"Fortunately, there is Tylenol ... ..." and 60 words have passed before the product of the advertiser is mentioned.

Thus, Tylenol breaks through the dominance of aspirin and gains significantly increasing sales. Nowadays, Tylenol has become the first brand of analgesic drugs. Re-positioning strategic enables it reaches the status today through the confrontation with aspirin which everyone is familiar with before.

Coincidentally, there are also examples in China, for instance, washing machines without detergent developed by Haier, wooden air conditioners developed by Aucma. In order to get new products into the customer's mind as soon as possible and rapidly expand the market, they must first comment on aged products before promoting the superiority of their new products, so that to persuade customers to give up old products and buy new products. It is also a re-positioning of old products or competitors with which people are familiar, and ultimately puts new products in the customers' minds to replace the old ones, expanding sales of new products.

Case study

Strategic Positioning of Successful Key Consulting Company

"Successful Key" is the trademark of Beijing Successful Key Consulting Co., Ltd. and the first brand of China's success consulting industry, which means the key to open the door to success. The company's aim is to provide customers with the best success consulting services to help organizations and individuals to succeed! In its early days, the company has developed an "Overall Strategic Plan" (2005-2015) to identify its strategic positioning, to be the first to enter China's success consulting industry and to strive to create the first brand of China's success consulting. The following is the summary of "Overall Strategic Plan":

I.   Features and opportunities of the Chinese consulting industry

On November 26, 2004, the "Third (2004) China Management Consulting Summit" is held by the CEC and CEDA in Beijing. This indicates that China's management consulting industry has gotten into the spring of development. There are several significant features of this period.

(I) Features

1. Number of consulting companies is increasing every year. According to statistics, there are more than 7,000 in Beijing alone; more than 1,800 in Shenzhen, and tens of thousands in China.

2. Industries that consulting service involved in very uneven. Most companies focus on fields like information, technology, finance, securities, and professional management consulting like marketing, quality, finance, human resources, while few focus on success consulting.

3. Objects of consulting are also unbalanced. First of all, most consulting companies only attach importance to the organization consulting, ignoring individual counseling; secondly, they only pay attention to a few companies top in the industry, thinking little for the vast companies in the middle or even behind states.

4. Levels of consulting are also very uneven. For example, a company generally requires three levels of consulting; that is, information consulting (base layer), management consulting (middle layer), and strategic consulting (highest level). However, except for a small number of superpowers like McKinsey and other large companies such as CITIC consulting, Hua Jia Planning and PKU, the vast majority of present consulting companies do not dare and unwilling to take strategic consulting projects. It is because they do not understand strategy themselves, not to mention practical experience in strategic consulting. In addition, only a very small number of industries leading companies currently require engaging in strategic consulting, while most companies still lack the sense and requirements.

5. Most consulting companies have no scientific, clear positioning. There are many companies, tens of thousands of existing consulting companies claiming to guarantee to cure all diseases and as the medicine took effect, the symptoms lessened. They do not have a clear business direction, dreaming to engage in all without consideration of their own resources and conditions. Many companies actually are dummy corporations that solicit all businesses but do none well.

6. Qualities of most consulting companies are quite low. It is understood that employees of foreign consulting industry are generally with at least bachelor's degree or equivalent, three or more years' experience in independent consulting, and with expert accounting for more than 80% of all. Employees are quite different in the domestic consulting industry. Such as consulting companies in Shenzhen, there exist numbers of knowledgeable and proficient pioneers as well as lots of people as mischievous as quacks, while exist no minimum standards for practitioners. In Shenzhen, it can be seen everywhere that RMB Yuan 30 to 50 thousand is spent to start up a consulting company. Among the opening consulting companies, 30% of them even do not have organization introductions, 30% have no company plans, and more than 40% have no training programs. Meanwhile, with their backward consulting methods, low accuracy and low timeliness, they are difficult to play roles of systemic, accurate and timely judgments and decision-making.

7. The consulting industry is in need of uniform standards. There are currently no national trade organizations; in addition, local trade organizations are also not complete. It is missing uniform standards for admittance into industries and quality monitoring standards, and lack of

communication and cooperation with each other; moreover, it does not attach importance to their quality improvements.

8. Benefits of most consulting companies are poor. Because of the above reasons, although currently consulting companies have tens of thousands capital, benefits of most of them are woeful. According to the latest reports, only 3% consulting companies are profitable in China, 7% are breaking even, and 90% are struggling, which may collapse at any time.

(II) Opportunities

Above analysis shows that, tens of thousands of consulting companies in China now are not that much considering consulting industry of the developed countries and the huge Chinese consulting market. More important, since the competition grew, most of these consulting companies inevitably go bust with low quality and poor efficiency. Coupled with the serious imbalance in the development of consulting industry, it provides us with a good entrepreneurial opportunity.

This opportunity is an undeveloped and huge Chinese success consulting market. People with mental health all want to succeed. Pursuit of success is the instinct, desire and responsibility of human. People have the instinct to succeed by nature, and then gradually generate a desire to succeed and shoulder the responsibility to succeed when doing any work. Therefore, everyone wants to work well and to be successful. Whether you realize it or not, success is a sense of each person, which is bound to spawn a huge potential market, a success consulting market urgent needs to develop in China.

To develop this huge market, three competitive products are needed to develop. One is a successful strategy; another is successful management, and another is superior quality. In the modern economy, technology and management conditions, these three are indispensable and necessary for regardless of organizations or staff to get success. People who can pre-empt them will be able to seize the market.

II. Resources and strengths of company

(I) Resources

1. Dozens of full-time and part-time experts with high quality, experience, ability, sound structure and high-profile;

2. Scientific research results with certain reputation in the country, such as Enterprise Strategic Management published by Peking University Press, How to be successful published by Enterprise Management Publishing House, and Full Competition Management published by Reform Publishing House, etc.;

3. A number of consulting results in significant effects. For example, the development strategies of large groups or companies like Lenovo Group, Digital China, China Banknote Printing and Minting Corporation, China Luoyang Float Glass Group Company and so on;

4. Potential market demand and huge client resources of the business;

5. Necessary and adequate capital;

6. A group of lean efficient leaders and sales team;

7. Own web sites and sales channels;

8. Headquarter in Beijing, which makes is convenient to link with both nationwide and the world.

(II) Strengths

1. Good at teaching and formulating successful strategies for customers. It includes teaching and formulating development strategies not only for organizations like companies, but also for individuals, such as students and staff.

2. First to edit and publish the original China successfully monograph "How to be successful" which closely links the theory and practice. In addition, the company also produces a "How to be successful" teaching courseware, and launches a quality education pilot, achieving remarkable results.

3. Adept in formulating implementation plans with five qualities of science, innovation, practicality, feasibility and simplicity. That is, with above five qualities, successful strategies and variety of implementation plans that we offer to customers are convenient to operate and in line with the actual needs of organizations and individuals.

Strategic positioning and mission of company

(I) Company's strategic positioning

The company's strategic positioning is to be the first to enter China's success consulting industry and to strive to create the primary brand of China's success consulting. This positioning cannot only avoid violating vested "cake" of current competitors in the consulting market, but also create and effectively defend a new "cake" needed by customers, which is the successful strategy, the successful management and the success quality.

Why such a position is determined?

1. China's success consulting market is a piece of "virgin land" which has a huge number of potential customers.

As early as a hundred years ago, America's success experts represented by Andrew Carnegie and Napoleon Hill begin to study and create success science and actively develop U.S. success consulting market. However, in present China, success science is still at the initiation stage, and the success consulting market is an undeveloped "virgin land" which draws no attention. China is a country with a population of 1.3 billion and hundreds of thousands of organizations like institutions, companies and groups. Both organizations and individuals want to be successful, and once this sense is developed; China will become a vast market.

2. China's success consulting market is basically without competitors. The first entry is easy.

The father of competitive strategy Michael Porter has said that company's managers must take into account the positioning problem, and must understand "who you are competing?" If you really make strategy, then the answer is "there is no competitor" because you are unique in the industry. Corporate strategy consulting master Jack Trout also believes that in order to make positioning in customers' minds, the company must make differences. Strategy should be competitor-oriented rather than customer-oriented. To capture a mountain guarded by a strong enemy is tantamount to suicide. So the secret is to create competitive differences to enter the minds, firstly, that is, to be the first different one other than follow the better ones. Obviously, despite there are thousands of competitors in the current Chinese market, they are concentrated in fields such as information, technology, management, finance, securities and so on. If we first enter the success consulting market, it is easy to make the original national success consulting brand.

3. Requirements of companies and other organizations for strategic management and critical consulting will inevitably generate

Strategic management is the inevitable development trend of enterprise management practice and theory in developed countries. Throughout its history, people will find that the key to success of companies is changing in different economic development stages.

- The key in the 50s is production;
- The key in the 60s is operation;
- The key in the 70s is finance;
- The key in the 80s is strategy.

Strategic management theory is a new management science as well as an art rises in the United States in 70s of 20th century. It is known as "imperial science" of enterprise management, which lies at the highest level of enterprise management and consulting and provides most difficult and expensive insulting services. By 1980s, strategic management and strategic consulting have been widely used by companies in developed countries. Such as in 1970, 100% of the U.S. companies have developed a strategy. Today's era belongs to strategic management, strategic innovation and strategic victory. This is also the only way for Chinese companies. So requirements of Chinese companies for strategic management and strategic consulting will inevitably generate.

4. Success sense of hundreds of millions of people will develop into desire of success quality.

All people with mental health want to succeed. This success sense is the potential market urgent to be developed, and this market includes a large number of customers. As long as we persevere to publicize and teach various types of customers of success science, we can raise people's success sense, prompt people to strive to improve success quality, and then encourage and help people succeed.

5. Success consulting industry is a noble career which helps organizations, and individuals succeed. It will necessarily get public support, and thus speed up the formation and development of success consulting market.

(II) Company's mission

To provide customers with best success consulting services and to help organizations and individuals succeed!

The mission consists of three main points:

The company's business is to provide customers with success consulting services, including successful strategies and successful management for organizations, in order to help them.

1. Successfully develop and improve the quality of personnel.
2. Clients of the company are first, companies and other organizations; second, individuals.
3. Contribution of the company is to help organizations and individuals to succeed!

Company philosophy

(I) Core philosophy

Depend on all wisdoms to help people succeed! Strive to make customers, employees, shareholders and society satisfied!

(II) Operation philosophy

We teach fishing as well as give fish. Especially, we will inspire customers' motion to go fishing consciously and actively, and let them learn fishing principles, methods and techniques.

Company objectives

(I) Brand objective: to build the first brand of China's success consulting industry!

(II) Economic objective: to achieve operating income RMB Yuan × hundred millions.

(III) Geographic objective: While featuring its international orientation and wide national representation, the company will gradually establish a network covers major regions and cities nationwide based in Beijing, and conduct international exchanges.

(IV) Life objective: to become the first hundred years-old brand of China's success consulting industry!

(V) Image objective: to be the pioneer and leader of China's success consulting industry.

Main objectives of each strategy phase

(I) Start-up phase (2005-2007)
(II) Consolidation phase (2008-2010)
(III) Development phase (2011-2015)

Target decomposition of the start-up stage (2005-2007)

(I) The first year (2005)
(II) The second year (2006)
(III) The third year (2007)

(I) Company's guidelines

    1. Core guidelines

To rely on good faith, and to win with wisdom!

    2. Customer guidelines

To help both organizations and individuals;
To treat elephants and to prefer monkeys.

    3. Strategic directions

Not for the biggest, but for the best;

Not for form, but for practical;
Not for complex, but for simple;
Not for undeserved reputation, but for a result.

Note: The elephant is a metaphor of large companies and groups, while the monkey is a metaphor for small and middle companies.

(II) Company's belief - all wishes come true!

Our company must be successful!
Our company will succeed!

Source: The case is cited from "Overall strategic plan of Beijing Successful Key Consulting Co., Ltd." (2005-2015);

In order to maintain corporate trade secrets, some contents are instead with "omitted" and specific data with "×."

Review

Beijing Successful Key Consulting Co., Ltd. is a professional consulting company. Established in 2005, it is a pioneer, leader and the first brand of success consulting industry in China.

There exist close ties as well as obvious differences between success consulting and management consulting. Management consulting mainly provides programs of management improvement, including strategies, tactics and methods, but doesn't intervene whether these programs can be implemented and whether they are successful. Success consulting should not only provide programs of management improvement, but also help customers improve the success quality, stimulate program implementation motion, guide and track program implementation in order to help customers succeed.

The positioning method of the company is "striving to be first," which is the best way of positioning. Once a company seizes the leading position in the industry, it can enjoy the fruits of leadership in the next many years.

Positioning experience of Beijing Successful Key Consulting Co., Ltd. provides excellent inspiration for Chinese companies, especially those small and medium companies that blindly follow the trend without own positioning.

Questions

1. What is the core of the strategy?
2. What are the principles of the positioning?
3. What are the methods of the positioning?

Notes

AL Ries, Jack Trout, *Positioning*, 2002 edition, China Financial and Economic Publishing House, P 6.

Jack Trout, *Trout on Strategy*, 1st edition, China Financial and Economic Publishing House, October 2004, P 57.

Zhang Jingbo, *Unique*, 1st edition, China Company Press, June 2004, back cover page.

Jack Trout, *Trout on Strategy*, 2004 edition, China Financial and Economic Publishing House, P 157.

Zhang Xiuyu, *How to be successful*, Enterprise Management Publishing House, 1st edition, January, 2005, P49.

Sun-Tzu(the original), Kung-sun Daoming edit, *Art of War and Thirty-Six Stratagems* 1st edition, Guangxi Ethnic Publishing House, July 1995, P 32.

Mao Zedong, *Strategy Problems of China's Revolutionary War*, *Selected Works of Mao Zedong* (four volumes), People's Publishing House, 1966, P 175.

Mao Zedong, *On Protracted War*, *Selected Works of Mao Zedong* (four volumes), People's Publishing House, 1966, P 480.

Michael Porter, *Competitive Strategy* 1997 edition, Huaxia Press, P 58.

BIBLIOGRAPHY

Mao Zedong, *Selected Works of Mao Zedong,* four volumes, People's Publishing House, Beijing, 1966.

Sun-Tzu(the original), Kung-sun Daoming edit, *Art of War and Thirty-Six Stratagems* 1st edition, Guangxi Ethnic Publishing House, July 1995.

Michael Porter, *Competitive Strategy* 1st edition, Huaxia Press, January 1997.

Al Ries, Jack Trout, *Positioning,* 1st edition, China Financial and Economic Publishing House, February 2002.

Jack Trout, Steve, *The new positioning*, 1st edition, China Financial and Economic Publishing House, October 2002.

Jack Trout, *Trout on Strategy*, 1st edition, China Financial and Economic Publishing House, October 2004.

Al Ries, Jack Trout, *Marketing Warfare*, 1st Edition, China Financial and Economic Publishing House, October 2002.

Al Ries, Jack Trout, *The New Marketing Warfare*, 1st edition, China Financial and Economic Publishing House, October 2002.

Arthur Thompson, Stickrod, *Strategic Management: Concepts and Cases*, 10th edition, Duan Shenghua, Wang Zhihui as translators., Xu Erming revision, Peking University Press, 2004.

Zhang Jingbo , *Unique*, 1st edition, China Company Press, June 2004.

Zhang Xiuyu, *How to be successful*, Enterprise Management Publishing House, 1st edition, January, 2005.

CHAPTER 4

Entrepreneur's Strategic Thinking

Abstract

This chapter, from the height of modern strategic study, describes the rich connotations of entrepreneurial strategic thinking, such as being good at grasping development opportunities, excelling at conducting strategic analysis, adapting at solving strategic contradictories and being skilled in clarifying strategic ways of thinking. Finally, it has an appendix of cases and comments of "Market Oriented Entrepreneur- Entrepreneurial Thinking of Wang Hai."

Learning Objectives

- To make it clear the connotations of entrepreneurial strategic thinking
- To understand the importance to grasp development opportunity
- To deeply understand and master five features of strategic analysis
- To understand and properly resolving eight strategic conflicts
- To master and apply four strategic ways of thinking

Introduction

The world-renowned strategist Frederick Geroke indicates that "A strategist must make the balance between wideness and depth of information he obtained. An eagle has to fly high enough to find a hare from a widen point of view; meanwhile, it has to fly low enough to target and attack it. A strategist acts like that in continuous balancing, which is the task for him or her alone." Entrepreneurs should first be strategists, who should have a strategic head and strategic eye lights, should be good at doing strategic analysis, stand high and see far, keep overall business in mind, devise strategies within a command post, and defeat the opponent by a surprise attack. Entrepreneurial strategic thinking refers to ways of thinking when an entrepreneur makes significant decisions on the company's overall, long term, and leading principal goals. This set of scientific ways of thinking include being good at grasping development opportunity, excelling at conducting strategic analysis, adapting while solving strategic contradictories and being skilled in clarifying strategic ways of thinking.

Lesson

I. Good at Grasping Development Opportunity

Enterprise strategic emphasis is driven by the entrepreneur's sense of opportunities and by the current resources possessed by the company. One important responsibility of entrepreneurs is to monitor environmental changes and identify the opportunities from these changes. Most important is to generate good investment ideas and to be about clear how many resources it possesses.

Once the opportunity is identified entrepreneurs will start to look for the means to use the opportunity. Their entrepreneurial nature determines if they believe that opportunity can be exploited. They usually do not hesitate to take financial risks, professional career risks, and family relationship risk; they even do not hesitate to endure great psychological pressures, to start the new business. When faced with opportunities they do not care about statistics that point out all the issues new businesses must deal with before they are successful: new businesses that employ less than 10 employees survival rate in the first year is just a little higher than 75%; only about 1/3 of new firms will be in business for four or more years, all entrepreneurs strongly believe that they themselves belong to the statistical numbers of success.

An entrepreneur will start to think about the resources he needs only after he identified an opportunity as well as the means to explore the opportunity. The order of the entrepreneur's thinking is this: first to think about the resources needed and then to think how to get these resources. It is a sharp contrast to what the typical bureaucratic administrators would do; determine the opportunities to be explored according to what resources they have. Moreover, entrepreneurs usually are fully of imagination to efficiently use very limited resources, and financial resources for supporting new ventures. Venture investment companies make all these things come true, so long as a new idea is sufficiently promised; it is always possible to find the funds to make it happen.

Finally, when the barrier of resources is moved, the entrepreneur will compose the organizational structure, employees, marketing plan, and other factors to realize the general strategy.

II. Excel at Conducting Strategic Analysis

Entrepreneurs should have a strategic head and strategic vision, and should be good at doing strategic analysis, stand high and see far, keep the overall business in mind, devise strategies within a command post, and defeat the opponent by a surprise attack. Strategic analysis is a category that is paired with tactical analysis.

Compared with tactical analysis, the strategic analysis has the following characteristics:

The first is to highlight the sense of the overall situation. To consider the overall situation is the first distinguished feature for strategy. The so called sense of the overall situation means that when conducting an analysis we need to take care of every aspect of the business, as well as various steps of different kinds in business development and their relationships; put it simply, have sense of the overall business situation. Just like comrade Mao Zedong says in his work "On the Strategic Issues of China Revolutionary War" that "The most important thing for the commander who directs the overall situations is, to put all his attention to taking care of overall situations." "If he gives this up but is busy in doing other less important things, then he definitely will suffer from losses." (1)

The second is to highlight the sense of greater situation. The so called sense of greater situation means that to be able to correctly deal with the relations between parts and whole, consciously obey to the general situation, actions under general situation. Entrepreneurs, when making significant decisions, must firmly up hold the sense of greater/general situations. There is a famous saying in Chinese "One who does not know how to plan for the whole will not be able to plan for parts; one who does not plan for long term will not be able to plan for present." Comrade Deng Xiaoping says that "It is encouraged to take care of the whole situation. Something can be done from a partial perspective but cannot be done from a whole perspective; while something cannot be done from a partial perspective but can be done from a whole perspective. In the end we must take care of the whole situations." (2) Entrepreneurs must obey and follow the laws and policies made by the country when doing business and formulating benefits for their firms, in accordance with the interests of the whole and to unify the benefits for parts and for the whole, if there is a conflict between parts and the whole, the interests for the parts should give up for the interests of whole without any hesitations.

The third is to highlight the political sense. The so called political sense is to correctly deal with the relationship between politics and economies as well as the relationships among all the factors in the whole, to assure the firm steps forward along the correct strategic direction and strategic goals. Economies and politics go together hand in hand although the principle jobs for entrepreneurs are for economies; economies are the basis while politics are concentrated reflection of economies and politics also are counteractions to economies. In socialism economic construction, all significant economic issues are full of political meanings. Meanwhile, the economic development also needs strong politics to guarantee success. Only when one is able to well deal with various interests and their relationships from high political perspectives, from the perspectives of political power, government decree, law, and policies, can we realize the economic goals that have been determined. Therefore, to up hold the whole situation from a highly political perspective, always keep a clear-political-minded head; it is absolutely necessary for entrepreneurs.

The fourth is to highlight the global sense. The so called global sense refers to when to analyze and determine serious business issues; one should have the world's eye sights, to be good at using global information and resources, to find the right position for the business, to grasp the development opportunity, to enter into the world market, and to push the business development. To set up a global sense is the historical request for entrepreneurs in our time. In contemporary time, the business development in China cannot be separated from the world. Especially under the situations of economic globalization, the multi-polarization of the world, and our country to become a formal member of WTO, entrepreneurs should even more aware of the global sense, to have a comprehensive eye to view the world, to have the ability to catch the development opportunity in the whole world, and accordingly to make a spot for their own businesses on the stage of the world economic competition.

The fifth is to highlight the sense of a significant point. The so called sense of significant point means that when analyzing and dealing with complex problems, one is able to focus his attention on the issues that determine the whole situations, to break through the main point and push forward the whole business. An entrepreneur should be first a strategist. For the strategic leaders the most important thing is to focus his attention on the whole situation. However, to take care of whole situation does not mean there is no order for light or heavy, pressing or otherwise, it requests strategic leaders "focus his own main attention on the issues or actions that are most important and most determinate to the whole situation under his direction (Mao Zedong)." (3) The so called "determinate issues or actions" refer to the important connection or key step that related to the whole situation's success or fail. Such as the major strategic goal, pivotal connection that impacts the whole situation, "bottle neck" or "breakthrough point" that influence the development in whole, the opportunity and turning point for strategic changes. These important connections usually perform in parts, but they all determine the whole situation. One move gets success the whole will win while one move fails the whole will lose. To put the strategic direction focuses on these key issues means one grasped the main contradiction that influences the whole situation. Once the main conflicting problem is solved all other problems are easily solved.

The above five points are characteristics that tactical analysis does not possess. For entrepreneurs only when they are firmly certain of these five points, can they enhance these five senses; then they can be able to make good strategic analyses, make good strategic decisions, and firmly control the driving power in their own hands.

III.   Adapt to Solve Strategic Contradictories

Contradictions exist throughout the process of strategic management. An entrepreneur should mainly handle these basic contradictions that are related with strategic decision making. In summary, these contradictions can be listed as the following:

(I) Contradictions between organization and environment

Organizations, consisting of people, are a systematically structured group with specific goals. From the nature of the organization it can be divided into two classes, one is economic organization, such as business firms; another is non-economic organizations, such as government, arms, schools, hospitals, and so on. What we are going to discuss here mainly refers to business firms.

No organization can survive in a vacuum, to subsist and to develop an organization usually must rely on its external environment. Environment refers to external structures or forces that have potential influences on the business organization's success. For business firms, environment includes indirect environment and direct environment.

Indirect environment includes macro environment and the environment between macro and micro; this includes global, national, and regional economic factors, political factors, social background, and technological factors.

Direct environment refers to these environments that are directly related with realizing the organization's goals, it is the industrial environment for the business, and it is consisted of those key customers or factors that can generate either positive or negative influences on the success of the organization. Direct environment differs for individual firms and is changing along with the conditional changes. It includes suppliers, customers, competitors, government institutions, and public pressure groups. Generally, the administrators focus their energy on the specific environment for the organization.

The restrictions and influences that environment has to the organizations are in two parts: on one hand it provides a development opportunity for the organizations; on the other hand it creates threats or pitfalls to organization. The first job for administrators is to identify and grasp the opportunity, to avoid the threats, and to find the correct direction and road for organizations.

The essence of contradictions between organizations and environments is to answer where the opportunity for the organization is and where the threat to the organization is. The fundamental purpose for administrators is to study the contradictions between the organization and the environment and to identify the opportunity and avoid the threats from the environment. The so called "opportunity for the organization" refers to the joint part of opportunity from the environment and the resources that organization possessed. Of these two factors, the opportunity from environment is the basis and premise, and the resources organization possesses are the condition, both are necessary for success and neither could be ignored.

(II) Contradictions between resources and goals

There are not only one but several more opportunities for an organization. In other words, the direction for the business operation is not only one choice but several possible choices, such as the choice from industries, from businesses, from products, and from services. However, this does not mean that a firm can blandly run multiple businesses without choices. Because there is a constraints on condition for a firm to do what kind of business and to expect what kind of outcome, which is the resources a firm possesses, it includes resources currently possessed and the resources that can be obtained through certain efforts. If the organization blindly determines the business direction and business objectives without considering the conditions of current resources and obtainable resources, such as manpower, capital, equipment, technology, material, management, and market, it is highly possible to become a loser. Therefore the essence of contradictions between goals and resources is to correctly determine the organization's mission and objectives, to answer the following questions: What business should we be in? What goals should our firm reach? Whether a firm can properly handle the contradictions between resources and goal, correctly determine the mission and objectives, is the critical point for an organization to decide whether to grow and flourish or not.

Peter Drucker puts it well: "No firms can do all things. Even if it has the sufficient capital, it will never have enough manpower. It must separate light from heavy, separate pressing from others. The worst is to do just a little of everything. This will surely accomplish nothing. Choice, even if not the best, is better than not choice at all." (4)

William Cohen also says that "In whatever the situations, the resources a firm possesses will not be good enough for using various opportunities or avoiding threats it faces. Therefore strategy is an issue of allocation of resources. A successful strategy is to allocate the resources to the opportunity that is most decisive." (5)

This should be the guiding principle for organization to handle the contradictions between resources and goals.

(III) Contradictions between new and old businesses

An organization, especially business kind of economic organization, cannot produce one product, provide one service, and conduct one type of business for ever. Because of various reasons, such as the product renovation and upgrade, the service renovation and upgrade, science and technology advances, diversified demanding, the society requests the need of a business firm to get rid of the products, services, and businesses that it has an intimate knowledge of them, and forces the firm to develop new products, new services, and new businesses; otherwise the life of the business will be finished along with its old products, old services, and old businesses. Therefore, the essence of the contradictions between old and new businesses is how to correctly reform the business mission and objectives; this is the key point for keeping the firm vital and in continuously development.

Again, as Peter Drucker puts it "Managers must consistently do management. But a good manager must be an entrepreneur. They must transport resources from the fields with lower profits or diminishing profits to the fields with higher profits or increasing profits. They must get rid of the past, give up what they already know and what already existed, and create the future." (6)

"Entrepreneurial spirit is a given in administrative tasks. Entrepreneur spirit is to create business for the future, to fulfill this task they must be creative." (7)

(IV) Contradictions between subsistence and development

An organization, especially a business organization, must first maintain substance and at the same time to seek for development. If it cannot maintain substance there is naturally no way for development. However, if they do not seek for development, the basis for substance will become weaker and weaker, and finally go downhill. Therefore, substance and development becomes a contradiction internally in an organization, especially a business organization from very beginning to the end. The essence of this contradiction is how to handle the conflict between consumption and accumulative savings. This is a serious difficulty that administrators face.

Consumption and saving is a very complicated contradiction that is difficult to deal with; it not only involves benefit relationships among different interest groups, but also touches upon the relationship between short term benefits and long term benefits for those interest groups. For instances, the shareholders want more dividends, creditors want more interests, employees want higher wages and bonuses, a better benefit package, and consumers want excellent quality and reasonable prices, as well as excellent service. Externally, the governments want to collect taxes and fees, the community want the substantial, and various parts of the society to be sponsored. Therefore, how to handle properly conflicts among those interest groups, and how to properly handle the conflicts between short term benefits and long term benefits for those interest groups, essentially is how to handle the relationships of ratios between consumption and savings; this is a contradiction that every business must properly handle in its strategic management process. Only when properly handled can a firm be able to be safely sustain itself and continue to develop.

(V) The Contradiction between specialization and multiplization

A business firm should be specialization or multiplization; they are two kinds of strategic selections for a business in its development direction. To select specialization or to select multiplization, except for considering pros and cons of these two strategies and their application scope, the most important is to study the specified environment that the firm is in and the conditions that the firm possesses. There is no universal formula to be used, every case is unique and must be analyzed and handled accordingly.

A large number of practices demonstrate that to implement a specialization strategy can be successful, but it also can lead to failure; it is the same that to implement multiplization strategy can also be successful, but could fall in to pitfall as well. In short, no matter specialization or multiplization, they are double edged swords: use it properly and it can conquer the rival and to be a success; use it improperly it can hurt itself and make fail. We often say "a fall into the pit, a win in your wit," but sometimes "a win into the pit, a fall in your wit," it seems like a conflict but in fact unified, a lively real body that is opposed and unitary. Therefore, to be specialization or to be multiplization becomes a common basic contradiction in the strategic management process. Whether a firm can properly handle this contradiction, and make a good decision on the business development direction, is the key button that determines if a firm can healthily developed or not.

(VI) Contradiction between importing and exporting

In the past twenty or more years since its "reform and open" China has been implementing "importing strategy," such as absorbing foreign capitals, introducing foreign technology and foreign experts, three come and one fill, pressing foreign raw materials, and building joint ventures.

The success implementation of "importing strategy" has provided solid basic foundations for the implementation of "exporting strategy," which is an inevitable selection for China reform and open development at the current stage.

In today's world, transnational companies run wild, "firms without nationalities" spreading everywhere. With the advantage of high technology and proficient operational skills, they take knowledge economies as a basis, an information network as a main body, rely on transnational companies, push the global economic wave and rise one after another, and constitute the new great global economic structure.

Facing the threats and opportunities by the globalization of the economy, what shall China do? The general secretary Jiang Zeming says "go outside!"

However, as where to go the individual firms must have a correct selection, never blindly go outside without selection, be especially cautious when expanding to developed countries. We should first select the developing countries for expanding out, such as the developing countries in Africa, Middle East, and South America. The comparative regional advantage is the correct principle for making the selection of "expanding our strategy."

With the waves of economic globalization, "exporting strategy" becomes a key step for China in the new century; it is also a new contradiction for the business firms in the process of strategic management. Therefore, individual firms must high attention to this, carefully study, up hold the fine opportunity, and properly handle it.

(VII) Contradiction between competition and cooperation

Under market economic conditions, the individual business firms are competitors, as well as cooperators. Therefore, the relationship among firms should be competitive but also cooperative, although the emphasis point is not the same in different situations and different periods. Sometimes emphasize competition, sometimes emphasize cooperation, both are necessary.

Experience demonstrates that normally competition is in the first position. This is because without competition there will be no pressure, without pressure there will be no driven force, without driven force, there will be no vitality, without vitality it is very hard for business to develop. This kind of situation usually takes place in the initial and development periods of an industry, especially in the development period. In this period the market structure is not matured, the number of competitors is the largest, the differences of business scale and strength is not too big, no one wants to give in, therefore in this period the competition is fierce, firms compete for every penny and it is impossible to cooperate. After fierce competition, great waves rush away sands, superiors win and inferiors leave, and the number of business slowly becomes smaller and smaller, capital tends to concentrate, the whole industry tends to be mature, and then finally arrives at the decline stage. At this time, the market structure is basically stable; the firms become fewer and fewer, but scale and strength of each firm become larger and stronger, it is very difficult to beat down each other. In this situation, the strategic selection among firms usually will switch from competition oriented to corporation oriented, at this time if over one competes again, especially in a price war, the outcome could be that neither side will gain. All could even perish together.

Apparently, firms need competition as well as corporation; they must be good at combining these two. Competition is an art, corporation is also an art, when combined these two organically will be an art at a higher level. Accordingly, when firms should emphasize competition, when firms should emphasize corporation, and how to combine the two organically, becomes a prominent contradictory that must be studied in the enterprise strategic management process, especially when making competitive strategy. Only when correctly and properly handled well will this contradiction beat the competition.

(VIII) Contradictions between launching new businesses and protecting environments

Businesses need to be started, economies need to be developed, environments also need to be protected, and this is a global contradiction. If we do not start businesses, do not develop economies, the society will not be developed, nor will we reach the higher degree of richness and civilization. However, starting new businesses, developing economies, must be under the presupposition of environmental protection. It is a dangerous if humans destroy the environment when starting a new business and developing economies against that endanger the environment.

Currently, in our country the business firms are lacking an environmental protection sense; many firms stay with the sense of environment protection for just putting pollution under control, some firms do not even consider controlling pollution. Compared with developed countries, they have moved from ending pollution control, preventing pollution from production process;

these two stages lead to the third stage, starting from product design to recycle the waste and reuse it.

To implement an ecological industrial business development strategy, is the essential way to protect the environment. The so called "ecological industrial businesses," refers to a firm following the requests by a general ecological plan, applying principles of ecological economics to design and construct technological processes for manufactures, so that the technology adopted produces no or less waste materials, makes best use of various natural resources and materials, formulates the firm to become a modern firm that has lower investment, lower energy consumption, and lower pollution but higher output.

From the above discussion, we can know that environmental protection is a huge systems project; it does not only restrict the firm's matter of live or die and sustainable development, but also relates to creating a good living environment for our next generations. Therefore, firms must think highly about this global issue in strategic management process. This is a significant promise for the business to healthily, stably, and consistently develop.

IV.   Skilled in Clarifying Strategic Way of Thinking

Qingdao Hair Group CEO Zhang Ruimin says well, "There is no way out without clear way of thinking, when there is a clear way of thinking there will be a way out." As an entrepreneur, we should clarify the guiding way of thinking to direct various works quickly under complicated situations. Specifically in enterprise strategic management, there are four major ways of thinking to be mastered.

(I) Have a foothold on strategic triangle

There are three main roles that must be considered when conceiving a business strategy, namely corporation, customers, and competitors; we term them as "strategic triangle."

From the logics of strategic triangle perspective, the strategist's task is to decide how to gain advantage over the competitors on key factors for success; meanwhile, strategist must have a good measurement if the strategy can make the business strength meet with a specified market force. To maintain the firm's goal in coordination with the market needs is necessary for establishing a continuously stable good relationship; otherwise the firm's long term vitality could be in danger.

However, this coordination is always relative. If the competitors can provide an even better solution, then the firm will continuously exist in a position of disadvantage. If the way a firm interacts with its consumers is similar with that of a competitor's, then the consumers will not be able to identify the differences. It will possibly lead to a price war. Although the price war will benefit the consumers in a short period, the firm and its competitors on both sides will suffer loss. A successful strategy must assure a better and stronger coordination compared with competitors between the firm's strength and consumers' need.

From the perspective of three key roles, the so called strategy is this kind of way of doing business, through this way while the firm using its business strength to better satisfy the customers' need, and at the same time to make the best effort to differentiate itself from competitors (see Figure 4-1).

Figure 4-1 Strategic Triangle

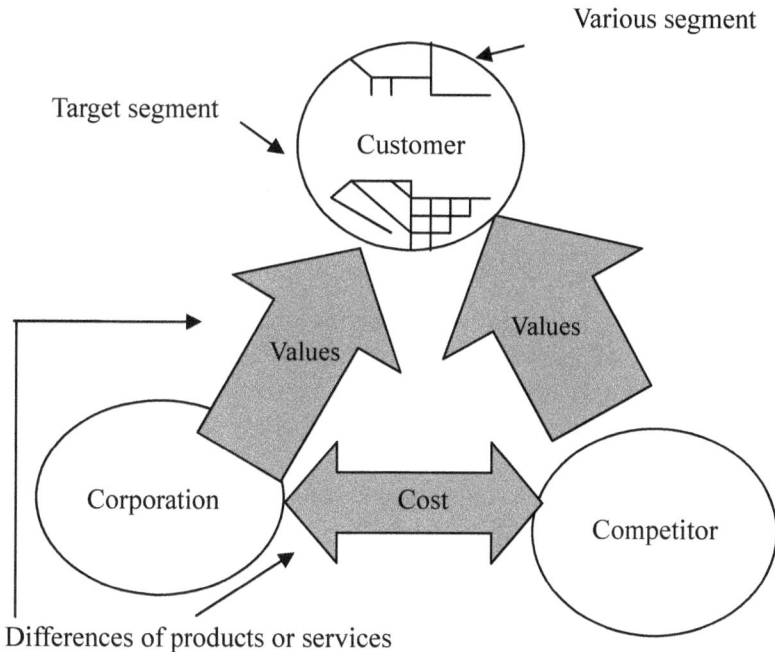

(II) Focus on continuous development

There are three types of business development tendencies: one is "broad-leaved epiphyll flouring for one time," another is "rich no more than three generations," and the third one is continuously developing, which would be businesses with centennial glorious brand name. Apparently continuously developing is the best type.

The core issue for business strategy is to search for businesses subsisting and continuously developing for the future. To do this it is required that entrepreneurs must have a strategic way of thinking as well as foresight and judicious judgment; they must be able to see things earlier and further.

The reason that leaders are leaders is that the decisions they made may not be accepted by the majority today but for acceptance and admiring by people tomorrow. Therefore to make good strategic decisions and to direct the business continuously developing, the leaders must have a leading strategic sense and strategic eye.

Zhang Mintai, the president and CEO of Sichuan Suotuo Corporations, says it well "Successful entrepreneurs should use two thirds of the energy to think about tomorrow." This sentence should be motto to all entrepreneurs.

(III) Search for competitive advantages

To search for competitive advantages is the starting point and the stopping point. The main idea of competitive strategy lies in a favorable and enduring advantageous position established by all forces that determines the industry competition.

There are two central issues for competitive strategic selection: one is the industry's attractiveness which is determined by the industry's long term profitability and its influential factors; another one is the factors that determine the competition's positions among firms within an industry.

Competitive strategy not only reacts to environment, but also molds environment according to business profits.

In the end, competitive advantage comes from the values firms create for their consumers which are beyond their cost. Lowering costs and differentiating are basic formats for firms to search for competitive advantages.

(IV) Timely conduct reform

Business strategy is the legal document at the highest level. Once determined, its seriousness and authority must be maintained, to keep stability. By no means should the strategy contradict itself, by making an order in the morning and changing it in the evening.

However, as the environment changes, the firm also changes. When reaching the firm's goal, or when its goal has not been reached but some uncontrollable event occurs, such as a natural disaster, war, or when the market environment changes, firms should make timely adjustments and reform their strategy. In this area, Hair Group, Double Star Group, and Wahaha Group have provided us good examples.

In short, to "have a foothold on strategic triangle" is the basic point for strategic management; to "focus on continuous development" is the purpose for strategic management; to "search for competitive advantages" is the means for strategic conquer; and to "timely conduct reform" is the key for strategic conquer.

As long the principle business leaders keep a clear understanding about these four ways of thinking, and firmly, elastically, and properly uphold and apply these four ways of thinking, they can certainly and steadily steer the big ship of the business to their destination.

Case Study

Market Oriented Entrepreneur

The entrepreneurial thinking of Wang Hai

There must be an outstanding entrepreneur in an outstanding enterprise. Wang Hai is the one in Double Star Group, and is also the core. No one can deny the fact that there would not be Double Star without Wang Hai. The people of Double Star Group followed his leadership in thirty years of reform to overcome the difficulties and achieve today's glory.

Then what are the reasons of Wang Hai's continuous success? Napoleon

Hill, the world-famous guru of success once said that the power of thinking is the greatest strength; it can build a great kingdom, and it can also ruin one. All concepts, plans, purposes and desires come from thoughts. Thought is the master of all energies; it can solve all the problems. Without learning to think in a correct way, you can absolutely make no outstanding achievement.

Therefore, the main reason for his success is his thinking, especially his entrepreneurial thinking. This article tries to describe, summarize, explain and sublime his entrepreneurial thinking by studying his practice and experience in the 30 years of reform. That shall become a common spiritual wealth of Chinese entrepreneurs, and then more entrepreneurs like Wang Hai and more companies like Double Star will appear.

"I position myself as a professional entrepreneur"
    - A clear positioning and ambitious goals

The experience of many successful entrepreneurs at home and abroad has proved that you must have "a clear positioning and ambitious goals" before you become a successful entrepreneur. It is a prerequisite to the success of entrepreneurs, and Wang Hai is an example.

September 9, 2008 was the 87th anniversary of Double Star's birthday, the 30th anniversary of China's reform and opening up, and the 30th anniversary of Double Star's reform. During the 30 years of China's reform and opening up, labor-intensive industries with low thresholds were the first and the largest influence in the market-oriented competition. The footwear industry, which Double Star originally engaged in, is a typical one. Under the lead of Wang Hai, the former nearly bankrupt shoe factory developed into a large comprehensive enterprise group engaging in eight industries, of which there are five pillar industries including shoes, tires, clothing, machinery, thermoelectric and other industries of printing, embroidery and tertiary. Its products are exported to more than 100 countries and regions in the world; its staff increased from more than 2 thousand to 60 thousand; its fixed assets raised from less than 10 million RMB Yuan to 5.5 billion; its annual sales revenue gave rise to 10 billion from 30 million; its exports add to 1500 million US Dollar from 30 million; and its profits and taxes paid amount to more than 3 billion RMB Yuan.

Wang Hai has been criticized for many reasons many times during the 30 years of reform of Double Star. Almost every step he decided to take and every idea he came up with caused negative comments.

However, achievements of the reform prove the rightness of Wang Hai's new ideas, new concepts, new decisions, and new strategies. They all meet the market's needs in the new era. Thus, Wang Hai is praised for that as outstanding entrepreneur.

Wang Hai treats himself as a professional entrepreneur. Moreover, he publicly declares in many conferences that he will step into markets other than offices. So he refuses the recommendation of deputy mayor who is in charge of industry. He identifies the market target of Double Star is to "Solidify in Shang Dong, develop in China, flourish Asia and roar in the world." It is these well-defined positions and ambitious goals that motivate Wang Hai to strive to pursue success of the company.

Success guru Napoleon Hill has said that "You have to know what you want to pursue in your life and be determined to get it. Focus on your goals and you will succeed. To think and plan your goals, and completely ignore other interference; this is the formula followed by all successful people." Clearly, Wang Hai is an outstanding example among these successful people.

Well, what kind of person can be called entrepreneur? Peter Drucker, once the adviser of American president, father of modern management has defined in *Innovation and Entrepreneurship* that "entrepreneurs are those who are willing to consider change as an opportunity, and strive to pursue it." According to this definition, Wang Hai deserves the title of entrepreneur.

In 1987, China named 20 outstanding entrepreneurs for the first time, who were met by state leaders in Zhongnanhai. While nowadays, they are facing different destinies. Wang Hai is the only one among them who is still active in the reform of state-owned enterprises as a pioneer, doer, risk-taker, as well as a survivor. As director of former Qingdao Ninth Rubber Factory and president of Double Star Group, Wang Hai earns names of "general market" and "long life president." Wang Hai says he votes for himself just for two achievements: one is that he solved the employment problem of thousands of people as an outstanding party member; the other is he created the brand of Double Star for China as a professional entrepreneur. He acts out the meaning of that title and is selected as "president for life" by employees. He is worth up to 32.142 billion RMB Yuan as an entrepreneur, becoming the first person of such a great value among Chinese entrepreneurs.

"Take myself as the backbone of the company"
   - Strong personal initiative

Who forced Wang Hai to make all positioning of himself and Double Star? Who urged him to achieve such a position and goal? From 30 years of successful experience of Wang Hai, we can learn that the answer is neither his leaders nor his staff, but himself. Then, why he perseveres to do so? Maybe the words from the world famous master of the success can give us some clue.

Andrew Carnegie, founder and first representative of Success, King of Steel once told Napoleon Hill that "There are two kinds of people who will never succeed. One is those who will never take the initiative to do things unless someone pushes him. Another is those who cannot do things well even when there is someone to urge him. Those who strive to do things that should be done rather than be forced to and do them well without giving up half way will sure to succeed." The last kind of people expect more of themselves and do more than other people expect. In a word, these people have personal initiatives.

Well, then what is personal initiative? Napoleon Hill, second generation master of Success says that it is the sense that one will do what needs to be done with no push from others. It is the best personality, also the one that is easiest to forget. Initiative is an extremely rare virtue, which can drive a man to take the initiative to do things before he is told to."

From the forefront, the reason why Wang Hai makes and achieves his own position and goals is that he has strong personal initiative. The sentence he always says, "Take myself as the backbone of the company." is a concentrated expression of this personal initiative.

Relation of individual initiative and human is like that of steam and locomotive. It is a main driving force of action. Individual initiative is the inherent power which can turn ideas to actions by motivating and promoting all actions. In a word, individual initiative is in fact a self-motivated force. Once you own the power, you can put a variety of dreams, ideals, hopes, desires, and goals in your heart into practical actions. Moreover, you will insist to carry them out till you get what you pursue. Wang Hai is one such outstanding example.

Nearly 50 production plants of Double Star, including 30 thousand employees throughout the country follow the same system of management. For example, in early stages, Double Star challenges itself and create the brand; in difficult times, People of the company take themselves as the backbones and get through crisis; in the face of setbacks, they adjust their attitude and feel confident; in achievements, it sets goals for itself and gains further development; with famous brands, it drives itself to be successful.

Again, Double Star develops in the third industry and forms a comprehensive enterprise group. The street where the old plant lies is famous for its bad public security. When the plant is moved from that place due to the plan of Big Double Star Group, there are nearly 7 thousand former workers who lost their jobs. They again act out beliefs of taking themselves as backbones by adjusting the industrial structure of their own accord. They make use of the former plant to build up the Double Star City where services like dining, entertainment, and saunas can be found. It gains a reputation in Qingdao, which is also the first success modification of a state-owned company even in China. Double Star faces a comprehensive and multi-level pattern of development.

"We need a set of practical theory to guide the development of state-owned enterprises"
   - To attach importance to both practice and theory

Lenin, leader of former Soviet Union has said that "There will be no revolutionary movement without guiding theory." Wang Hai believes this is true to run business. It can be proved from dialogue between him and a radio host.

Host: It is the most critical moment for reform of state-owned enterprises now. Then what do you think China's state-owned enterprises need most now?

Wang Hai: I believe it is theory. We need a set of practical theories to guide the development of state-owned enterprises. Practice has proven that Double Star's achievements come mainly from the theory made during its development. Theory summarizes essences of social sciences and natural sciences, which not only guide the development of natural science, but also promote the progress of the whole history. In every historical period there should be a corresponding theory for guidance. Theory plays an immeasurable role in social progress.

Host: Many state-owned enterprises are not yet completely out of the woods, while Double Star Group works very well in the market economy. What does it mainly depend on according to you?

Wang Hai: I think the most important thing is reverse thinking; a unique "Double Star Market Theory" comes from the actual situation of the company. Its development aims to meet the market request, or we may say it is forced to come up with by the market.

There are in general, two common modes of thinking among a large number of entrepreneurs in China. One is to follow the usual rules and regulations at every time, in which case they dare not go one step beyond the prescribed limit. The other is doing what one thinks is right, which means they only act according to personal experience. The former is what usually state-owned companies will practice, while the latter most exists in private enterprise. As a leader of state-owned enterprise, Wang Hai dares to do reverse thinking. He points out the importance of theory and stresses the guidance of theory. Therefore, "Double Star Market Theory" is developed and used in business practice to create the miracle of "Double Star Kingdom." Its highlights are as follows:

Market is the driving force and source of enterprise development.
The user is God and the market gives gold medal.
All strategies taken are for occupying the market.
Market is the top leadership of the enterprise.
Market tests all work in enterprise.
Market is the best balance of business.
The company will produce what the market needs.
There is market a for shoes as long as there are humans.
It is better to fight on one's own rather than to depend on others.
There is no weak market, only weak products.
To produce, adjust and change following the market.
To aim at market positioning, species changes, and competitors.
Market is a never-ending battle.
Entrepreneurs in the market are generals on the battlefield.
To go to the market instead of the mayor.
An enterprise gets no further development without upgrading market theory.
And so on.

These highlights once made some economic theorists stare in amazement. Wang Hai says that "I will walk my own way since I wear my own shoes.

There is only one way for survival and development of the company, which is market. We treat market as the top leadership and the standard to test our achievements. If a company cannot survive in a market, everything done is in vain." He asserts that "Practice has proven that Double Star's achievements come mainly from the theory made during its development."

Wang Hai is a thoughtful entrepreneur who not only creates the "Double Star Market Theory," but also gets many other theoretical results. They all serve as parts of Wang Hai's management system, as well as the main contents of corporate culture of Double Star. Ideas determine ways out. So in every critical juncture, Wang Hai always comes up with new ideas or new concepts to make Double Star grow in a healthy and stable way for 30 years.

"Think of how the company should develop in 10 years"
 - To be farsighted and win with strategic planning

World renowned company strategy expert John W. Dizi has said that "The task of a strategist is not to see what a company is like today, but rather to see what kind of company it will be in the future."

Another world-renowned Strategist Frederick Geroke indicates that "A strategist must make the balance between wideness and depth of information he obtained. An eagle has to fly high enough to find a hare from a widened point of view; meanwhile, it has to fly low enough to target and attack it. A strategist acts like that in continuous balancing, which is the task for him or her alone."

World-renowned futurist Alvin Toffler warns clearly that "A company without strategy is just like an aircraft flying in a hostile climate, which is tossed and tortured in the storm, resulting in loss. If a company has no long-term plan and clear guidelines, it will lose its living conditions in the revolutionary technology and economy change no matter how large it is or how stable a position it holds. "

These experts tell us that we must first become a strategist and innovator before being a successful entrepreneur. So we must strive to focus on the future, have global visions, look forward, design good strategy, dare to change and be good at innovation.

In *Art of War*, plans are made first in a warfare, "Thus the highest form of generalship is to balk the enemy's plans; the next best is to prevent the junction of the enemy's forces; the next in order is to attack the enemy's army in the field; and the worst policy of all is to besiege walled cities. The rule is, not to besiege walled cities if it can possibly be avoided. "

Wang Hai has "general complex" since his childhood. He was determined to grow up to be a general to serve the motherland. But fate gave him no choice but to abandon general dream. Strange combinations of circumstances transferred him to be a civilian and made him create the famous Double Star, being the general of market. His general dream came true. A military career made him understand the art of war, and apply strategic and tactical skills of "military warfare" to "commercial war" with impressive results.

For example, Wang Hai has already commanded many business wars on the battlefield. He used strategies and planned to explore the shoe market. Among them, the most typical three are as follows:

First Battle: Wang Hai makes major breakthroughs to find market step by step. As early as the end of 1983, he correctly predicts that business sectors would not be possible to buy all products out according to plans facing so many shoe factories in the country. Therefore, he decides to put all staff to exploring the market for development and takes actions to support. He sets strategic goals of "entering the market in the plain areas and even the country based on Shandong." Taking advantage of leading technology, Double Star begins to grow in cities like Zhengzhou, Beijing, Xuzhou, Wuhan, Shenzhen, and Shanghai, and then in the whole country. Depending on its excellent product quality and sincere service, Double Star stands firmly in the shoe market within just a few years. In1994, the national market survey indicates that market share of Double Star shoes has reached 33% of the total, ranking first in the country.

The second battle: Wang Hai dares to explore overseas markets. Wang Hai gradually learns situations in the world after overseas study. He understands that two thirds of the market lies in other countries, with a total amount of 3 billion shoes demand. In order to develop in a larger market, he makes plans to gain orders relying on the high quality goods with low prices and good reputation. Meanwhile, in order to create an international brand, Wang Hai takes use of the opportunity of cooperating with the U.S. Bu Ruike Company. They work out 5 technical difficulties within 4 months and spend

20 days to build a special production line, which takes more than 6 months for similar U.S. manufacturers. All these productions are qualified to be sold in the U.S. and European markets, millions of pairs each year. Since then, Double Star gets into U.S. supermarkets through efforts to design the first generation of high-end sports shoes.

The third battle: Wang Hai changes its focus to poor areas. In 1992, when Double Star grows well in both domestic and overseas markets, Wang Hai decides to develop in developing areas. He believes that it is consistence with the international trends of transferring labor-intensive enterprises from developed regions to less developed regions. He specially stresses that "We should think of how the company should develop in 10 years rather than just in recent years. We also shall take the initiative other than be forced to do so." Then he chooses Yimeng Mountain, Shandong province as target market. A new city of shoes, Double Star Lu Zhong Company is set up within 3 months in the poor mountainous area. It also changes thousands of farmers to new Double Star workers with a totally new appearance. Chen Junsheng, leader of The State Council Leading Group Office of Poverty Alleviation also prizes this kind of action after seeing investigation report about Double Star.

In addition, Wang Hai often makes advanced strategic decisions in critical moments when the business is rising and people are confused. For example, brand strategy, out of the city strategy, countryside strategy, uphill strategy, going west strategy, diversification strategy, car "shoes" strategy, and so on. It is under the guidance of these strategies that Double Star grows into a large company group with a "big double star" strategy pattern.

"Honesty is the standpoint for brand building"
    -to be honest and trustworthy to build brand

Deng Xiaoping, a reformer and leader of China, says that "We have to develop our own leading products and create our own national brand." After 30 years of commercial warfare, Double Star grows from small to large, from weak to strong, and gains steady development as a state-owned company. This is partially due to its brand strategy.

Among many strategies of Double Star, brand strategy is a top priority. Wang Hai first proposes a slogan "to create a national brand in order to revitalize national industry with national spirits." When people in China are not aware of the concept of famous brand, Double Star has already taken it as the goal and outlined the company and stimulates its staff to work for that.

However, to create a famous brand does not mean a slogan, but requires a lot of practical work; of them the most important thing is credibility and quality. Wang Hai stresses that "The market economy is not only the interests of the economy, but also the credibility of the economy. Credibility is the key to success of Double Star in the market economy and is the image of the brand. Sense of the achievements of the binary, as binaries in a market economy the key to success, but also a binary image of the brand. Sense of integrity and Honesty lays the foundation for brand building and quality is fundamental to a credible brand. "

In order to implement these ideas of quality and credibility, in 1997, Double Star burns shoes with problems, which is worth more than 100 thousand RMB Yuan. People of Double Star begin to have a profound understanding of what quality means to market and to the survival of the company. Besides, Double Star also attaches importance on raw materials it used to produce shoes. For this purpose, it builds up test center to check raw materials and half-finished products. As the sense grows deeply in people's minds, Double Star establishes a strict management system to realize the institutionalization and standardization of quality management rules.

In 1995, after the Double Star wins its first title of "Famous Chinese Trademark," its professional sports shoes, sneakers, leather shoes, Tires all gain the title of "Chinese famous brand." Double Star becomes the first company that has four products with the Chinese famous brand title in the Chinese rubber industry. Its brand value reaches 50 billion RMB Yuan.

"Dare to be the first"
    - to dare to reform and excel at innovation

Peter Drucker points out that "Entrepreneurs must take a variety of resources from low-income or declining-revenue areas to high-income or increasing-revenue areas. They have to give up the past, no matter what they have got and known, and create the future. Entrepreneurial spirit is to create enterprise in the future, which is bound to innovation."
Another management guru Peters warns, "Innovate or perish!"

There is a banner sent by Professor Guan Dongsheng on Wang Hai's office wall. It reads "Dare to be the first." It is the real description of Wang Hai's personality. He always says that "Personality is a sign of entrepreneurs. Personality is different with personal worship and without personality; there is no development and creation. "

The implementation of the planned economy in China for decades makes people used to fixed systems. As a state-owned enterprise, Double Star starts with being market-oriented. It tries to change its management and mechanisms on its own, rather than according to red tape documents.

Hai claims himself as "an ordinary shoemaker." However, with his spirit of "dare to be the first," he achieves extraordinary performance that an ordinary shoemaker cannot make. Under his leadership, Double Star achieves several "firsts."

> The first to product and sell goods all by itself.
> The first to realize horizontal integration of enterprises.
> The first to hold a national order meeting in name of an enterprise.
> The first to reform structure of the company according to market needs.
> The first to show at the World Expo in name of an enterprise.
> The first to hold cultural display and performances of Chinese shoes in other countries.
> The first to establish own national world famous brand in China.
> The first to get access to capital market as a listed shoemaker enterprise.
> The first to engage in other industries like tires and machineries other than shoes.
> And so on.

All these "first" interpret Wang Hai's personality. Wang Hai faces a brighter future for he steps earlier by making leading decisions. It creates more room for Double Star to develop. It also enables the enterprise to seize the opportunity to win in the market.

Until now, the people of Double Star keep on working. They know there is no final standard for the constantly changing market. Wang Hai often says that "We will change in the way how the market changes. We need to produce, adjust and change following the market." He continues that "You will fall behind if you do not innovate today, while you will be eliminated if you still don't do that tomorrow." Due to this, he tries every way to encourage both managers and staff of Double Star to create in order to contribute to its development.

"Party committee's decision must be executed immediately"
  - To break through the resistance of decisions

Reform is the re-adjustment of vested interests. While someone whose interests are violated could become a resistance to change. Whether or not to break through the resistance to carry out the reform is a serious test of courage and working style of an entrepreneur. It is also the most important guarantee for the success of the reform to break through the resistance.

Wang Hai says that "The essential problem of the reform is human resources. You can really achieve something only when you can work that problem out." Therefore, he proposes that "the largest enterprise management function is to serve the market."

To meet the needs of the market and solve urgent problems, Wang Hai decides to conduct a comprehensive package of institutional reforms. His first target is the Safety Section. However, the first conversation brings no results because the tough attitude of its staff. 20 employees in the department are all relatives of some leaders and managers. They occupy an entire floor of office buildings, with an office for each person but not that much work for them. The factory intends to let them move to leave room for other departments. They refuse to move due to their relationship with leaders and managers. But Wang Hai clearly states that "Party committee's decision must be executed immediately. If you don't move to the planned location before 6 o'clock pm tomorrow, chief and deputy chief will be fired for not doing job well." Then all staff of the company is shocked by this statement. They all look forward to know the results. The next day, the Security Section still doesn't move until 12 o'clock. Then Wang Hai holds a meeting with party committee members to make new decisions, which is to relieve the two chiefs of their posts. Then the Safety Division begins to move.

After that, institutional reform of the whole company is carried out smoothly. Through the reform, Wang Hai combines four original departments Armed Section, Security Section, Safeguard Section and Vehicle Management Department into one, and combines two departments of Technology Section and Quality Test Section into one, so does Office of the factory and of the party. In this way, the original 27 departments decrease to 17, administrative staff accounts from former 11.8% to 7.8%.

"There is only enterprise that is not managed well, no company that cannot control."

- Management is the eternal subject to improve development of an enterprise

Capital, technology, labor, management are the four elements of wealth creation. But they play various roles in respective positions. Management takes the position as a commander in chief, playing a leading role; while capital, technology, labor take the position as followers, playing a supporting role. Without management, capital, technology, labor are just potential but actual productivity that cannot create wealth. So only with the lead of management, these four elements can become an organic combination, form a real productivity, and create wealth. Therefore, management is the most important elements of wealth creation and the eternal subject to improve development of an enterprise.

Double Star realizes in the market that gap lays Chinese enterprises and foreign enterprises are not so much in technology than management. Therefore, Double Star takes management as the base of its survival and development. People of the company firmly believe that "There is only enterprise that is not managed well, no company that cannot control." Then they do much to improve management in details, using quantitative methods in order to find out enterprise management mode suits for Chinese companies.

With 30 years of practice, review, and sublimation, Double Star creates a unique management mode that is in line with China's national conditions, and the actual manufacturing and processing industries. American people have once evaluated "Double Star has the world's best-managed factories," Japanese people come to learn experience, and Korean companies want to hire Wang Hai as president. With excellent management, Double Star wins recognition of the market, respect of the industry, and admiration of foreigners.

Over 30 years, China is transferring from a planned economy to a market economy. Double Star gives up all traditional and unpractical ways of management. Instead, it creates a variety of feature management, including strict management, fine control, contract management, credit management, money management, and emotional control. People of Double Star also realize that management is source of survival, development and competitive for success. All enterprise activities depend on this source to create new glories.

"I am Chinese, and I have to do for my country!"
   - National spirit, national brand, and national entrepreneur

In 1992, Mr. Allen, ZTE's president, has insisted to hire Wang Hai as general manager of his company. He also offers three tenths of the share capital and salary of $ 3,000 monthly. But Wang Hai refuses, "I am Chinese, and I have to do for my country!"

Wang Hai states that "A true entrepreneur should first be a politician. He has his own thoughts, theories and ideas, and can apply them to the enterprise. Spirit is always needed in commercial wars, which is the soul of a person, a company, a state and even a nation, especially national spirit. Loss of spirit will directly lead to the loss of the company, losing in development goals and directions."

In face of global economic integration, some experts and scholars, even individual officials claim that "China could only become the world's factory instead of encouraging national industry. For the latter will inevitably affect the process of internationalization of enterprises. And only by approaching and getting into the international market can we meet customers' needs." Wang Hai opposes this kind of wrong standpoint and advances the significance of national spirit, national brand, and national entrepreneur. He advocates inspiring the national spirit, to create a national brand, and to foster national entrepreneurs in order to develop national industries and revitalize the national economy. It is cited as new version of "Three People's Principles" by the media in the new era. It has profound practical significance and far-reaching historical significance on China's current ideological guidance and long-term economic development.

Wang Hai considers that "On this planet, no matter how does the economy integrate, national interest should always be the bottom line of a country, which should by no means be given up." He claims that "First of all, national entrepreneurs shall show patriotism, being proud of their nation and having strong national sense of responsibility. National entrepreneurs serve as generals on the battlefield, who can lead the companies of the nation to win the commercial war representing interests of the nation. "

Wang Hai frequently says that "I do not believe Chinese people can do no better than people of other countries. Instead, Chinese people can do and even do better." 30 years of practice has proved his words. The famous brand he creates "Double Star" and "the world's best-managed shoe factories with first class scale, management, quality and service" indeed win honors for Chinese nation.

"Do not put in the wrong pocket, and don't go to the wrong bed"
   - To protect oneself through self-discipline

On the opposite wall of Wang Hai's desk, there hangs a couplet written by Zhao Puchu, president of China Buddhist Association. It writes that "fame is as light as water while career is as heavy as a mountain," which is the true portrayal of Wang Hai's mind and character.

During 30 years of reform and development, a few entrepreneurs in China sacks in the middle. Although each of them may have their own specific reasons, there are four main common reasons: First, poor health which may lead to death. Examples are Peng Zuoyi of Qingdao Beer, Wang Junyao the 38-year-old private entrepreneur and so on. Second are major decision mistakes, causing major losses as well as dismissal, such as Lu Qunsheng of Qingdao Aukma. Third is expansion of personal selfishness which hit people like "sugar-coated bullets." The so-called "sugar-coated bullets" here means money and women. Fourth is being doubted, framed or falsely accused by his followers and being embarrassed, knocked and dismissed by the higher authorities.

The reasons why Wang Hai can be a long living president for 30 years lie in the followings: first, he is healthy and positive. His staffs all praise him as president with age of 60, body of 40 and thought of 20 years old. Second is he makes series of correct decisions. Third is he doesn't be picked off by "sugar-coated bullets." Fourth is he excels at turning to superiors for understanding, help and support him, which make it easier to protect him and promote the work.

Wang Hai admits that "In China, it depends in order to find faults and overthrow a reformer. According to my experience, there are two aspects that I think are very important. That is, as entrepreneurs, whether you can resist the lure of money and whether you can deal well with women. In short, do not put in the wrong pocket, and don't go to the wrong bed. I never overstep the bounds in terms of these two aspects."

Wang Hai always says that "The responsible persons of companies should be moral to examine themselves. They shall often consider the victims of greed and the sense of self-discipline." He refuses the hiring invitation of companies of other countries, and announces his unchangeable principles of following the Communist Party, acting as a Chinese shoemaker and devoting to his wife.

Wang Hai regularly educates managers that it won't work to enter the market using products with a world famous brand without a group of excellent managers. In addition, corrupt managers train no good followers. So as long as we control ourselves not to be corrupt, we can catch up with world famous brand and reach the world-class level of products.

"Cultural management is top management"
   - To attach importance to corporate culture

Thomas Watson, former chairman of the board of IBM, says that "I firmly believe that any company, in order to survive and succeed, must have a set of sound and reliable beliefs; and on this basis, make its own various strategies and various actions. I think that the most critical factor, in the process of gaining access to success is always adhering to these beliefs. "IBM's history and achievements in the past century is the best proof of this passage.

Zhang Ruimin, president and CEO of Haier Group also states that "Haier's achievements of ten years are not because of tangible reasons, instead, intangible thing, that is Hai culture. A company without culture is just like a person without a soul."

Wang Hai also says that "An enterprise without personality and culture is doomed to be a hopeless enterprise. That is not only true to an enterprise, but also to a country and even to a nation. Without the support of an excellent culture, the future of this country or nation is unthinkable. "

Enterprises become the players in the market competition since reform and opening up. New concept of thinking has impact on the old one, which pays less attention on the importance of public interests than personal interests. All these are testing the wisdom and courage of enterprises and entrepreneurs. In this regard, Wang Hai proposes that "It is a difficult job to manage people depending on leaders, while easy to guide their souls relying on corporate culture." He believes "Cultural management is top management," and establishes principles of "to carry on outstanding traditional culture, to learn foreign advanced experience and to create own unique spirit" in market economy.

Over 30 years, people of Double Star continue to practice and create cultural theory in new eras. These new corporate cultures are summed up as a corporate culture system with nine series of cultures (market competition culture, brand culture, ideas management culture, moral culture, quality management culture, cost management culture, innovation culture, technical standards culture, and implementation culture) and more than 3,000 concepts. These new theories, new ideas inherit essence of traditional Chinese culture, including Confucianism, Taoism, and Buddhism, adhere to core principle of "seeking truth from facts" of Marxism-Leninism, Mao Zedong Thought, and Deng Xiaoping Theory and reflect cultural identity of the new era. It is corporate culture belonging to Double Star, as well as to the Chinese nation and China's new industrial civilization.

"I believe I am right"
  - To strengthen the confidence of victory

Wang Hai states that "Why I have the courage to march forwards though a large number of people find faults on me for decades? That is because I believe I am right." Yes, confidence of victory is the first thing we should hold and strengthen in order to change our lives.

Napoleon Hill points out that "With confidence, you can move a mountain. As long as you believe you can succeed, you will. Approach to test your faith is to see whether you can use it in your most difficult times, especially in the most needed times."

Behind each successful people, there is a strong force - confidence to support and promote them toward their goal. Confidence is an important factor in all the great achievements; it is important for people who determine to succeed as the engine of success.

Confidence is a state of mind, a positive attitude, the source of the soul, and a great cornerstone. In all aspects that people have effects on, confidence can create miracles. Confidence may double the power of people to enhance their ability.   But people without it will accomplish nothing. Wang Hai can make fully and completely use of power of confidence to get rid of all the constraints in mind, make plans and achieve goals; that is the reason why he succeeds.

In short, entrepreneurs tested by the market are the real entrepreneurs. Wang Hai summarizes that "The real entrepreneurs are market oriented entrepreneurs. They will do their jobs in any time, whether the market is in depression or in prosperity. They can make the company survive in depression and grow in prosperity. They can appeal to people with spirits spiritual to follow him; they dare to break the routine to do what other people believe is impossible; they are well aware of unknown market risk." There is no doubt, Wang Hai is a truly market oriented entrepreneur.

Source: This case describes entrepreneurial thinking of Wang Hai based on author's in-depth observation and Wang Hai's practice and experience in the past 30 years. It is written to commemorate the 30th anniversary of China's reform and opening up, taking invitation of *Chinese Companies* and the Double Star Group. It has been put in to *Market Economy and Theory Innovation - Thoughts of the National Excellent Entrepreneur Wang Hai's,* published by China Social Sciences Publishing House, first edition in February, 2010.

Review

There must be an outstanding entrepreneur in an outstanding enterprise. Double Star Group develops from the edge of bankruptcy under the leadership of Wang Hai step by step. No one can deny that there will be no Double Star without Wang Hai, who serves as the soul and core of leadership of the group.

A reporter once asks Wang Hai "In your opinion, what qualities should a qualified entrepreneur have?

Wang Hai answers that "An entrepreneur has to treat the enterprise as his home and be really market oriented. An entrepreneur represents a spirit, as well as the soul of the state and the nation. He must have wisdom of thinkers, astuteness of politicians, and flexibility of diplomats and strategy of strategists. That all because outcome of a company, no matter success or failure, gain or loss, are often associated with fate of an excellent entrepreneur." Wang Hai answers well, more importantly; he truly practices it out, acting as model of all domestic entrepreneurs.

Questions

1. What is entrepreneur's strategic thinking? What are its characteristics?
2. What are the typical characteristics of entrepreneur's strategic thinking? Why opportunity goes the first?
3. What are characteristics of strategic analysis?
4. What are the basic contradictories of enterprise strategic management? What are their natures? Which is the main contradictory?
5. What is the general thought of guiding enterprise strategic management?

Notes

(1) Mao Zedong, "Strategic problems of Chinese revolution wars," the first volume of *Elected Works of Mao Zedong, 2en Edition*, People's Publishing House, June, 1991, p. 176.

(2) Deng Xiaoping, *Elected Works of Deng Xiaoping,* the second volume, *2en Edition*, People's Publishing House, October, 1989, p. 82.

(3) Mao Zedong, "Strategic problems of Chinese revolution wars," the first volume of *Elected Works of Mao Zedong, 2en Edition*, People's Publishing House, Beijing, June, 1991, p. 176.

(4) (U.S.) Fred. R. David, *Strategic Management*, Li Kening trans., 1st edition, Economic Science Press, June 1998, p.16.

(5) (U.S.) Fred. R. David, *Strategic Management*, Li Kening trans., 1st edition, Economic Science Press, June 1998, p.123.

(6) (U.S.) Peter Drucker, *Management: Tasks, Responsibilities, Practice*, China Social Sciences Press, June 1987, p.62.

(7) (U.S.) Peter Drucker, *Management: Tasks, Responsibilities, Practice*, China Social Sciences Press, June 1987, p.65.

BIBLIOGRAPHY

Mao Zedong, *"Elected Works of Mao Zedong,* four volumes, People's Publishing House, Beijing, 1966.

Deng Xiaoping, *Elected Works of Deng Xiaoping,* the second volumes, People's Publishing House, October, 1994.

〔U.S.〕Peter Drucker, *Management: Tasks, Responsibilities, Practice*, 1st edition, China Social Sciences Press, June 1987.
〔U.S.〕Fred. R. David, *Strategic Management*, Li Kening trans., 1st edition, Economic Science Press, June 1998.
〔U.S.〕Stephen P.Robbins, *Management*, 4th Edition,China Renmin University Press, 1998.

Li Xiyan, *Study of Modern Strategy*, 1st edition, Sichuan People's Publishing House, October, 2000.

Liu Jisheng ed, *Company Operation Strategy*, 1st edition, Tsinghua University Press, April 1995.

Chiang Yuntong ed, *Company Operation Strategic Management*, 1st edition, Company Management Press, April 1996.

〔U.S.〕Napoleon Hill, *Everyone Can Be Successful*, 2nd edition, Hubei People's Publishing House in February 2001.

Zhang Xiuyu, *How to be successful*, 1st edition, Enterprise Management Press, January 2005.

Sun Qingguang, *Run to Success*, 1st edition, Enterprise Management Publishing House, January, 1997.

CHAPTER 5
Overall Strategy Models

Abstract

This chapter first states the concepts, positions and importance of enterprise overall strategy. Then, it introduces four types of enterprise overall strategy, namely growth strategy, stable strategy, shrink strategy and complex strategy. At last, it has appendix of cases and comments of "Zong Qinghou's Art of War" and "Wahaha mode."

Learning Objectives

- To make it clear the concepts, positions, objects and importance of enterprise overall strategy.
- To master four types of enterprise overall strategy.

Introduction

Overall strategy or corporate strategy is the outline of a company's strategies, which stipulates what should top managers do to lead and control the company. Overall strategy is targeted at companies as a whole. In the large and medium sized companies, especially in those with various businesses, it is the one at top level among all enterprise strategies. There are four types of overall business strategy, namely growth strategy, stable strategy, shrink strategy and complex strategy, as shown in Figure 5-1.

Figure 5-1 Overall Business Strategy Models

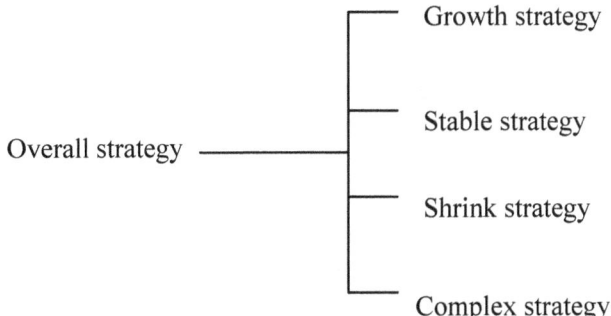

Overall strategy —
- Growth strategy
- Stable strategy
- Shrink strategy
- Complex strategy

Lesson

I.   Growth Strategy

Growth strategy is a strategy that makes the firm to grow from the current strategic level up to a higher level. Taking growth as target, this strategy leads the firm continuously to explore new products and new market and to introduce new production and management models so as to enlarge the firm's scare of production and sales, to increase its competitive capacity, and to enhance the firm's competitive strength. Using growth strategy correctly will make a firm gain continuous growth and development from small to larger and from weak to strong.

Generally speaking, growth strategy has following basic models (see Figure 5-2). They have been proved by business practices to be realizable in operations.

Figure 5-2 Growth Strategy

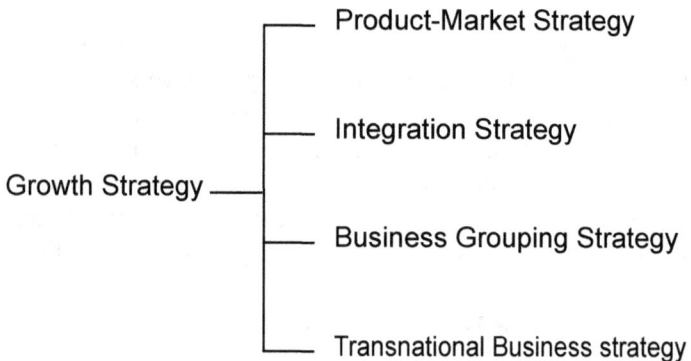

(I) Product-market strategy

Product-market strategy is the basic growth strategy; other growth strategies are derived from it. It can be shown as a 3X3 matrix (see Table 5-1). In the matrix, "interrelated market" refers to entering into market of other companies; "interrelated products" refers to producing products that other firms are producing and marketing.

Table 5-1 Product-Market Strategy Matrix(1)

Market\Products	Original Products	Interrelated Products	New Products
Original Market	Market penetration strategy	Product development strategy	Product renovation strategy
Interrelated Market	Market growth strategy	Multiplization strategy	Product invention strategy
New Market	Market transfer strategy	Market creation strategy	Total creation strategy

(II) Integration strategy

"Integration" means to put or combine individual parts together into one body. It is often used when a firm is implementing concentrated development strategy. It is because a company has to consider how to enlarge and where to grow when it gains more market shares and competitive strengths resulting from concentrated development strategy.

There are three basic forms for integration strategy: vertical integration strategy, crosswise integration strategy, and mixed integration strategy.

1. Vertical integration strategy

Vertical integration strategy, or perpendicular integration strategy, is a strategy that combines production and raw material supply, or production and product marketing into one body. Based on directions of integration, vertical integration strategy can be classified into backward integration and forward integration; based on levels of integration, it can be divided into wholly integration and partially integration. Its strategic goal is to consolidate the marketing position, to increase the competitive advantage, and to enhance the strength of the firm.

2. Crosswise integration strategy

Crosswise strategy is a strategy applied when firms expend business and gain more profits by directly buying competitors or by making an alliance with competitors. Its purpose is to enlarge the firm's business strength scope and to increase its competitive capacity.

3. Mixed integration strategy

Mixed integration strategy is the one that combines the above two strategies simultaneously. This strategy is especially suitable for large companies. Although it has distinct impacts on modeling large firms, it is relatively difficult to implement with relative high risks. Therefore, companies must be very careful in implementing it.

(III) Business grouping strategy

1. Implication of business group

The concept of business group is introduced from Japan. According to the explanation by the Japanese *Economical Dictionary*, business group refers to a collective business unit of many firms that keep their independency when behave coordinately, hold each other's stocks, and establish closed relationships in financing, staffing, raw material supplying, product marketing, and production technology, and so on.

Business group is a complex economic organization that features with capital combination but multiplied ownership. Its essential attribute should be a joined business alliance of two or more legal person companies.

2. Characteristics of business group

Characteristics of business group can be listed as following:

(1) Multiple levels. There are two types of connection tires for business group: one is capital connection by joint stock system, another is contractual agreement connection with long term favorable treatment. Based on this, business group can be divided into four levels, namely core level, stock control level, stock holding level, and fixed coordination level. The first three are established on the basis of stock holding system and are the formal members of the group. The fourth one is based on agreement with legal render service, and usually is not a formal group member but is just within the influential scope of the group.

(2) Non-legal man. Business group is consisted of four parts, that is, parent company, subsidiary companies, related companies, and other firms connected with agreements. From the legal perspective, the first three are all independent legal man business firms, while business group is legal men

partnership based on shareholding and stock control system. It is not an economic body that takes integrative tax responsibility or shares profits and lost together, nor does it has a whole legal man position.

(3) Shareholding and manager exchanging based on business legal men shareholding system. There are two kinds of situation in terms of the way of shareholding relationship among its members: one is pyramid shareholding model, in which core firms of the group hold shares of certain amounts of lower position companies and control them, see Figure 5-3. Another is unbalanced circulated shareholding model, in which member firms of the group hold shares of each other, see Figure 5-4.

Figure 5-3 Vertical Integration Business Group

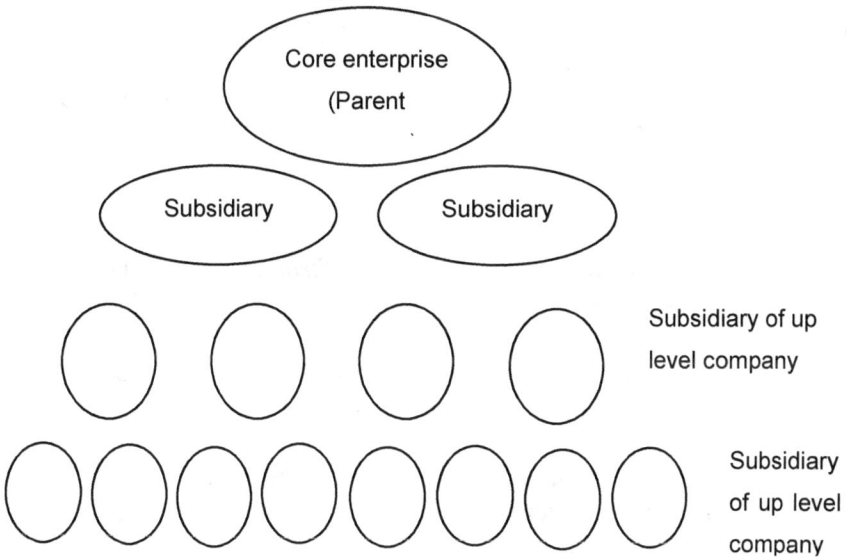

Source: Liu Jisheng, *Company Operation Strategy*, Tsinghua University Press, 1995. p. 182.

Figure 5-4 Cross integration Business Group

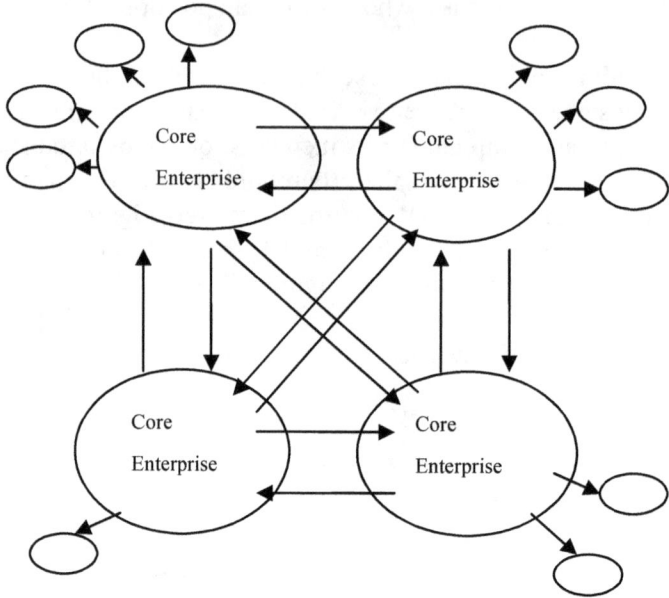

Source: Liu Jisheng, *Company Operation Strategy*, Tsinghua University Press, 1995. p.181.

Exchange of ownership with each other leads change of operators, i.e., managers exchanges based on stock controls. When one firm become another firm's large legal man shareholder, it will use its power of shareholder to dispatch director or chairman of the board, who will manage the internal business in order to assure the maximum benefits of its capital.

(4) A leadership and management system that combines board of directors of the group and its parent company. For those groups that featured with vertical or pyramid shareholding model, the core position of parent company is sticking out, which naturally determines the top leading position of its board of directors. Through stock control, board of parent company is able to control and influence the decision made by boards of subsidiary companies and other related firms in order to unify the whole group's behavior.

In the business groups with no clear pyramid shareholding feature, no single firm can have the core position since there are many strong companies.

136

Therefore a group board of directors is formed by directors of member companies. It mainly plays the role as a coordinator who internally coordinates member firms' economic interactions, market division, market price, implementation of guiding plans; and connector who externally takes the responsibility to maintain the relations with non-member firms, industrial associations, and related government institutions, as well as to accept supply contract of the state on behalf of the whole group.

(5) Taking the firm that has very strong competitive strength as the leading firm, and operating multiple business and series products. Business group develops series products and multiple business operations in related fields. It is a significant symbol that separates the group from other general business units and series in product structure.

(6) Establishing joint investment company. Group has joint capital from companies with internal economic relationship. And financing firm plays an important role in it. Therefore the group can set up an investment company internally. It can on one hand concentrate to use collected capitals, and lend series loans to member firms, and on the other to invest to companies which have close relationships with development of the group.

(7) Owning strong and large marketing channels. A business group must have strong operational function; therefore it needs its own marketing channels. There are three functions: a) to organize internal member firms to exchange materials; b) to purchase raw materials for member firms from outside; and c) to be responsible for marketing the products of member firms and market information feedback.

(8) Owning the common trademark and symbol that are consistent with the group name. Because the business group implements multiple business strategy, it is better to use common trademark that is consistent with group name when introduce new products to the market. It cannot only increase the popularity of the whole group, but also increase competitiveness of the products. Business group is not a legal person, due to that, the board of directors of the group takes trademark management very serious to avoid poor product quality of any individual member firms to destroy the brand.

(IV) Transnational business strategy

Transnational business strategy is the highest level, the most difficult and most complicated strategy among business development strategies. It covers lots of contents with large scopes. In fact it is an independent management science. In this book we mainly discuss a few points as follows:

1. Characteristics of transnational business

(1) Definition of transnational business

Transnational business refers to firms conduct resources transportation and transformation beyond one national sovereignty scope in terms of goods, labor, capital, and technology.

Line between transnational and domestic business operations is whether or not related firms directly involved in the transportation and transformation of goods, labor, resources, and technology cross national boundaries.

(2) Specified characteristics of transnational operation

From the perspective of crosswise comparing of transnational and domestic operations, transnational operation has the following specified characteristics:

    1. Transnational business operation not only needs to face domestic environmental   factors, but also need to face these in the world and in the host country.
    2. Although transnational operation does not require changing the basic functions of   management, it increases contents of each function broadly and profoundly.
    3. There are great potentials in terms of exploring business potentials, increasing business economic effectiveness, and accelerating the business growth. It is due to the fact that under various economic conditions in various related external hosting country and international environmental factors, transnational operations involve people from various value systems and institutions, have larger geographic areas and industrial array to develop. In that case, markets it lays in are very different in terms of capacity, population, and area. Nevertheless, it means risks that firms meet with are relatively much higher than that faced by the simply domestic operations, which makes a higher requirement for managers.

(3) Forms of transnational operation

There are many forms for business transnational operations, and new forms come out from time to time. The most basic forms are the followings:
1 Direct import and export.
2 Special permission to foreign firms.
3 Contractual manufacturing.
4 Turnkey project.
5 Joint venture.
6 Independent operation.

In addition, cooperative operation, international contract, and international leasing are all transnational operational activities. And there are some business activities that more or less have some transnational operation characteristics, such as compensative trades.

(4) Focal points for transnational business strategic decision

Transnational business strategy is a very comprehensive and highly difficult strategic decision. In order to enter into a target country for business operation, the firm needs to conduct overseas operation research, to select a hosting country, and to make evaluation on overseas investment project. However, the decision focal point is to balance and solve the following three problems: first, what is the specific motivation for the firm to conduct transnational operations? Second, where is the target country in where the motivation can be realized? Third, which form should be taken to get into the target country?

1. Entering motivation

It, at certain level, can be viewed as the specific one of the firm's international development strategic motivation. Due to the difference for individual firms in terms of industries, scales, product contents, technological levels, and management levels, their motivations for entering target countries are not the same. Generally, their motivations can be:

First, market oriented. "Market oriented entering" takes it as its goal to occupy and enlarge overseas product market. It includes leading to enter the market, striving for and enlarging new market, and following up.

Second, labor oriented. This motivation aims at taking advantages of relatively lower labor cost in host country.

Third, natural resources oriented. It means to gain stable raw material sources whose prices are relative low. There are a few types of this kind of motivation: one is to search for domestic disadvantageous resources in overseas; another one is to maintain stability of raw material resources; the third one is to use advantage of production regional position.

Fourth, avoiding trade barriers oriented. Higher tariff tax, lower quota for import, and import control are major means of protectionism. The purpose of a nation country to set up trade barrier is to protect its national industry, which is not only suitable to some developing countries, but also for some developed ones. Through transnational operation, a company can cross over the trade barriers in target country and thus promote its domestic business development.

Fifth, internationalizing production and marketing. Its holders are mainly large transnational firms. These firms usually are with sufficient capitals, advanced technologies and higher level of management. They implements global strategy and multiple operations based on these advantages, which determines there are many characteristics of their transnational operations, for instance, diversification, global optimization and with tactics. Except for above motivations, others are included, for example, to establish international production bases, to identify internal labor divisions horizontally and vertically, as well as to conduct multiple operations.

2. Target country

Because there are many countries in the world with various regional conditions, furthermore, resources a firm possesses are limited, the company should select a country to enter reasonably, which should has the greatest potential to contribute to its lone term development.

Focus and standard for selecting are not the same due to various purpose of entering. In addition, strengths and products of individual firms are different, which determines their separate requirements for risk and demand. Some would take high risks for large demand in the market; while others prefer rather lower demand for avoiding risks. In real practice, selection of the target country can usually with aids of matrix with three factors, competitive advantage, attractiveness, and risk. It can be seen in Figure 5-5.

140

Figure 5-5 Three Factors for Selecting Target Country(2)

		Attractiveness				Risks
		High	Middle	Low		
Competitive advantage	Strong					
	Middle				Low	
	Weak					
	Strong					
	Middle				High	
	Weak					

Note: Among these three factors, attractiveness is the motivation of the company, risk is the restriction and competitive advantage is the basis for the company's choice.

3. Entering way

After the company selects its target country, it has to consider how to enter it with a combination of resources like product, equipment, technology, trade mark and management. There are three available types for firms to extend internationally:

The first is entering by trade. The company enters the target country through export, whether in direct or indirect way. The so called indirect export refers to export with middle distributors. The so called direct export refers to export directly to customers.

The second is entering by contract. It refers to the firm enters by signing long term, throughout, non-investment intangible assets transferring and cooperating contract with a legal man firm in the target country. It mainly has the following forms: foreign empowering, empowering monograph, technology agreement, service agreement, manage agreement, turnkey project, contractual production, and international sub-contract.

The third is entering by investment. It means to enter the target country via direct investment. The company will transfer capital, along with management techniques, marketing, financing, and other expertise into the target country. It will set up branch company or subsidiary company that under the firm's control through independent operation, joint venture, newly build and merger, etc.

Focuses of above three strategic decisions can be summarized as in Figure 5-6.

Figure 5-6 Transnational Operation Strategy

```
                                              ┌─ Market oriented
                                              │
                                              ├─ Labor
                                              │   oriented
                         ┌─ Entering          │
                         │  motiva-  ─────────┼─ Natural resources
                         │  tion              │   oriented
                         │                    │
                         │                    └─ Avoiding trade barriers
                         │
                         │                    ┌─ Internationalizing
                         │                    │  production and
Transnational            │                    │  marketing
business strategy ───────┤                    ┌─ Competitive
                         │  Target            │   advantage
                         ├─ country  ─────────┼─ Attractiveness
                         │                    │
                         │                    └─ Risk
                         │
                         │                    ┌─ Trade
                         │  Entering          │
                         └─ way      ─────────┼─ Contract
                                              │
                                              └─ Investment
```

II. Stable Strategy

Stable strategy means that a company keeps its expected outcomes equal to scope and level of strategic starting point due to business environment and its own condition. The so called strategic starting point refers to real situation of key strategic variables when the firm makes new strategy. Among them, the most important ones are business direction, products and market areas, scale of production and marketing, as well as market position of the company in its business field. "Equal" here means no or few increase or decrease in market position and share in former or adjusted business field.

(I) Specific Characteristics of Stable Strategy

Stable strategy has the following specific characteristics:

1. To be satisfied with economic effectiveness in the past time and to continuously pursue the same or similar economic effectiveness goal.
2. To continuously use the same products or services to satisfy the present customers.
3. To Make effort to keep the present market share with present production and marketing scale or with small growth, and to stabilize and enhance the firm's present competitiveness.
4. Within the strategic period, the expected annual achievement keeps growing at the same growth ratio.

It is clear that stable strategy basically depends on previous strategy. It upholds the previous selections of markets and products, taking the previous strategic achievements as its expected goals of present strategic period. Thence, the premise for adopting stable strategy is to have a successful previous strategy. In this way, as long as the company continues to implement the strategy, the company is able to avoid threatens and explore the opportunity to make the firm stably develop.

(II) Types of stable strategy

Due to different external environments, internal resources conditions, and competitive positions, firms that adopt stable strategies have different choices in terms of strategic goal, strategic focus, and strategic countermeasures. Accordingly, stable strategy can be divided into four types from different perspectives, which is shown in Figure 5-7.

Figure 5-7 Stable Strategy

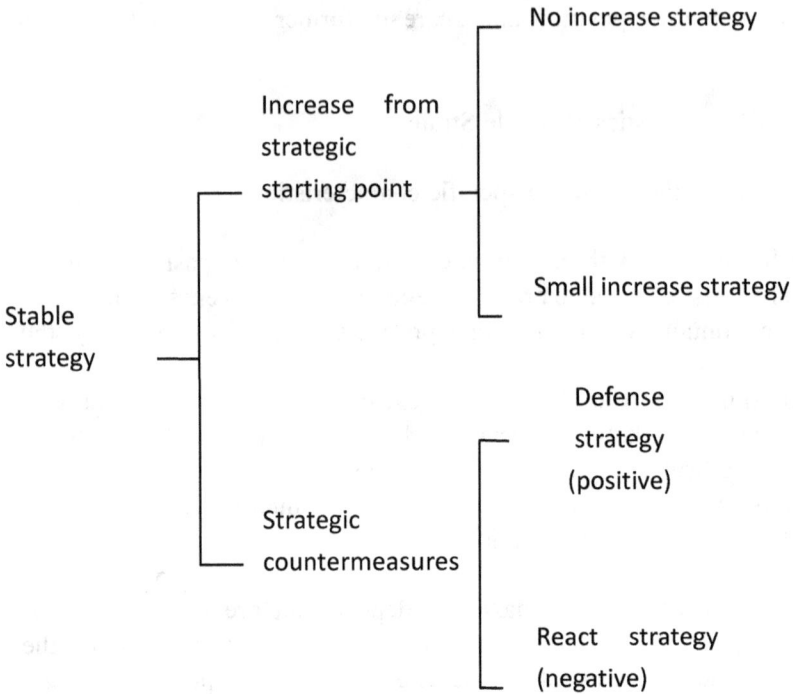

```
                                            ┌─── No increase strategy
                        Increase   from
                        strategic
              ┌───────  starting point  ──┤
              │                            │
Stable        │                            └─── Small increase strategy
strategy  ────┤
              │                            ┌─── Defense
              │         Strategic          │    strategy
              └───────  countermeasures  ──┤    (positive)
                                            │
                                            └─── React   strategy
                                                 (negative)
```

III. Shrink Strategy

Shrink strategy refers to the firm shrink or withdraw from its present strategic business areas and operation levels with a larger deviation from the strategic starting point. Compared with development and stable strategies, it is a kind of passive development strategy. Usually firms implement shrink strategy temporarily to switch to other strategic choices when the company gets through difficulty times. Sometimes a company can defend competitors' attack only by implementing shrink and withdraw strategic steps, which allows the company to avoid threatens from environments and take action quickly to effectively allocate resources. So shrink strategy is a strategy that takes withdraw as attack.

144

(I) Specific Characteristics of Shrink Strategy

Unlike development and stable strategies, shrink strategy has the following specific characteristics:

1. To take actions to shrink, adjust, and withdraw the firm's present products and market   areas, to reduce market coverage of some products, to give up some products, till the   company entirely withdraws from its present business.

2. Step by step to shrink the firm's scale of production and marketing, to decrease market   share, and at same time to lower relatively some economic index level.

3. Key point of shrink strategy goal is to improve the firm's cash flow, and to gain larger benefits as well as higher capital values. Therefore, the company shall make every effort   to control and reduce cost and to input least operational resources in terms of capital   spending.

4. Shrink strategy has the nature of transition. Usually, a firm only implements this   strategy in a short period of time with basic purpose to let it get rid of crisis with   preserved   strength,   or   remove   operational burdens to concentrate resources to take   alternative strategies.

(II) Types of Shrink Strategy

The practices have demonstrated that firms have different reasons to adopt shrink strategy. They face different internal and external conditions, pursue different purposes, select different strategic ways and display different strategic characteristics. Accordingly, we can classify shrink strategy taking anyone of above differences as standard. It is shown in Figure 5-8.

IV.   Compound Strategy

It is the combination of the above three strategies. Majority of aforementioned strategies can be adopted independently or combined. In fact, most business firms do not implement one single strategy. However, the possible strategic combination formats are not many, they are:

Figure 5-8 Shrink Strategy

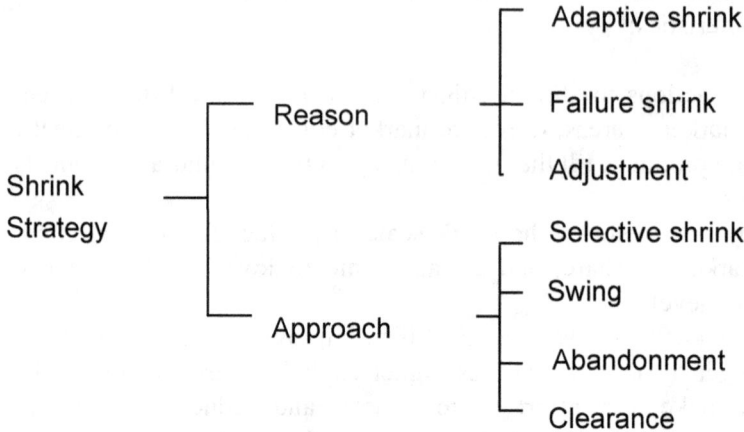

```
                                           ┌─ Adaptive shrink
                                           │
                        ┌─ Reason  ────────┼─ Failure shrink
                        │                  │
                        │                  └─ Adjustment
Shrink      ───┤        │
Strategy                │                  ┌─ Selective shrink
                        │                  │
                        │                  ├─ Swing
                        └─ Approach  ──────┤
                                           ├─ Abandonment
                                           │
                                           └─ Clearance
```

(I) Simultaneous strategic combinations

1. To simultaneously add another one when withdraw a strategic business unit, a product   series, or operating department.
2. To simultaneously apply shrink strategy to some domains or products and development strategy to some else.
3. To adopt harvest strategy to some products and development strategy to others.

(II) Sequential strategic combinations

1. To implement development strategy in one specific period and stable strategy in another.
2. To adopt stable or shrink strategy at first, and development strategy when situation turns to better.
In short, for most leaders and managers, there are plentiful and broad options of available strategies, whether in amount or in type. But how to identify these adoptable strategic plans is the first decisive step for choosing a proper one for a specific firm.

Case Study

"Zong Qinghou's Art of War" and "Wahaha mode"
   -Business strategy of Chairman of Hangzhou Wahaha Group

Zong Qinghou spends 15 years in the farm in Zhejiang since he is 16 because of the Cultural Revolution. In 1979 he comes back to the city and works in a school-run factory. He sells popsicles on the street at the age of 42, pulling three wheel delivery vehicles, while sets up the largest beverage company - Wahaha Group after 15 years. In 2002, Wahaha Group has sales revenue of RMB Yuan 8.8 billion and net profit of 1.2 billion. Zong Qinghou holds 29.4% of its shares and his personal assets reach RMB Yuan1.64 billion. It makes him rank 58th in the list made by Forbes China. When he talks about the mystery of his success, Zong Qinghou says peacefully that "No myth of the modern company exists today because we are long away from the success relying on an idea or an operation. Comprehensive strength and strategic advantage are what companies compare. Unusual way and usual mind are needed to run a business in this era when myth fades.

Differentiation strategy lays the foundation
   - From the "popsicle" to "Wahaha"

In 1979, Zong Qinghou is lucky to return to Hangzhou to replace his mother in the factory. Being penniless, he has to pull the three wheel delivery vehicle to sell textbook and popsicles from one school to another. In his delivery process, he has noticed that many children lose their appetites and have malnutrition problems which bother the parents mostly.

At his age of 47, he feels that "there should be a prospect future of children nutritional drink." His personality of reclamation formed in early years makes Zong Qinghou decide to take this opportunity.

In many people's eyes, he is forcing himself on a "dead end": to give up a stable life, determining to develop new nutrient solution product. Facing all kind persuasions of his friends, Zong Qinghou still seems so stubborn by saying "have you tried to understand the feeling of a 47 year old middle-aged man in the face of the last opportunity of his life?"

In 1988, Zong Qinghou runs the school-run company to develop the first nutritional drink specifically designed for children - Wahaha child nutrition.

He raises a loan of RMB Yuan 140 thousand and invites experts and researchers.

Wahaha then is just a school-run factory with only 3 people and 50 square meters of business space. At that time, there are more than 3,000 health care products companies and 38 kinds of nutrient solution in the Chinese market. Facing the cruel competitive environment, researchers suggest withdrawing from the market for the market saturation. While Zong Qinghou decides to start from nutrition for children to compete in a different field and succeeds.

According to the survey of 38 kinds of nutrient solution on the market, they are fit for all ages with wide range of common nutritional effects. In China, "one child policy" inspires the idea to develop children nutrient solution as children become the core of families and consumptions. Nevertheless, children's anorexia and partial eclipse problems has made their parents headache. Among 38 species of nutrient solution on the market, there is no one that is specifically designed for children, and further for the address of their appetite problems that bother their parents. "

Zong Qinghou says that "based on this discovery, I go to hire the Head of the Department of Nutrition, Zhejiang Medical University to develop nutrient solution and to solve their appetite problems. Wahaha nutrient solution immediately gets popular as soon as it is introduced to the market. Its advertising song 'have Wahaha and have good appetite is well-known. Some children can remember and sing these words, or even turn it into a jingle. "

As the spread of the ad throughout the country, Wahaha nutrient solution quickly becomes popular. Its fourth annual sales revenue reaches RMB Yuan 400 million, and its net profit is more than 70 million. Then Wahaha completes its initial primitive accumulation.

Strategic merger leads to its growth
    -small fish eats big fish

In 1991, sales of Wahaha child nutrition soar and it is soon in short supply on the market. Even so, the Zong is still very well aware of Wahaha's situation. He says, "I feel that if Wahaha doesn't expand its production scale, it is likely to miss market opportunities; but if it develops according to the traditional way, that is to project, acquire land and build infrastructure, it at least should spends two to three years, which may makes the good products be not marketable.

There are three ways lie in front of Zong Qinghou, association, leasing, and paid mergers. Obviously the former two paths are stable and the latter one is risky. But in front of a sound one, and paid a large merger and bear risk, but Zong Qinghou ultimately decides to spend large sums of RMB Yuan 80 million to try the last one.

He chooses old state-owned Hangzhou Canned Food Factory as the target. At that time, the factory has more than 2,200 employees and is insolvent; while Wahaha only has 140 employees and several hundred square meters of production space.

Wahaha's act like small fish eats big fish shocks the whole nation. At first, all people including workers of original factory are opposed to this initiative. It is Zong Qinghou final against all the odds. Wahaha quickly activates the fixed assets of the factory and expends itself taking use of the factory's plant and employees. The canned factory turns to make profits within 3 months and its sales and profits doubled in the next year.

The merger in 1991 lays the foundation for subsequent development of Wahaha and makes Zong Qinghou understand the good of mergers and acquisitions. After that, merger almost becomes the main method for Wahaha to expend in different places. By the end of 2002, Wahaha has established 30 production bases in 21 provinces and cities in addition to Zhejiang. By 2002, it produces a total 3.23 million tons of drinks, accounting for 16% of beverage production in China.

Innovative joint venture helps it be stronger
    -Project Joint Venture

If the earlier merger lets Wahaha expand rapidly, then its strategy-based cooperation with Danone help it be stronger.

In 1996, Wahaha products have grown extensive from a single children's nutrient solution to three series including added milk drinks and bottled water.

Zong Qinghou once again feels the crises for its small size makes the business vulnerable. He says that "Except for our flagship product nutrient solution, other two series of products encounter competitors of almost the same strength and brand popularity with Wahaha."

He makes a long-term investment plan amounting to several hundred million RMB Yuan for this issue. At that time it is hard to get that amount from banks and domestic private financing, so finally Wahaha turns to foreign capital.

"Before the joint venture with Danone in 1996," he says, "we have already understood its ambition of fully controlling the China's food industry. And now, it reaches its goals." He further explains that "Although Wahaha has a certain size then, its managers show some rigidity and its staff enjoys the security of average lives. I stick in the middle for several days because I have to develop the company by taking use of foreign funds, and to ensure it will not be merged as well. "

"I think twice and finally decide to share joint venture with Danone. Furthermore, it's not a joint venture of the entire group, but just projects. And Wahaha wants to uphold four cardinal principles, namely unchanged brand, unchanged chairman, unchanged treatment of retired workers and unchanged post of workers over 45. Wahaha Group spends its brand and 300 million out of 1.2 billion of total assets to always take the major shareholder position in the course of joint venture projects.

Wahaha begins to cooperate with Danone in 1996. After it sets up 5 joint venture companies, Wahaha starts to take use of external funds in wider range of business fields and invests nearly 100 million U.S. Dollars by now.

According to Zong Qinghou, "Almost every year, several billion of external funds are available for Wahaha. That enables the company to maintain a high growth rate."

With joint venture as a good basis, Wahaha can seize and meet needs of foreign investors who want to make profits. Meanwhile, it keeps the control of business operation.   Therefore, Wahaha's joint venture with Danone gets a win-win instead of failure of many other domestic and foreign joint venture projects.

Focus transfers from brand building to multi-line operation

Wahaha attracts many critical comments since it starts to engage in popular consumer goods such as green bean paste and mixed congee. Some people even believe that it undermines the purity and professional of children's products. They consider diversification as a wrong way. However, Wahaha ultimately proves its choice using its good sales.

Zong Qinghou says that "I think diversification is what every company has to do through in its development in a certain period of time."

"As the time passing by, competition will go more intense, industry background will change, and the average profit will shrink sooner or later. In that case, it is a good way for survival that keeping the company's cash flow changes in different fields. It is really a serious cut-throat competition of Chinese companies in the beverage industry. Wahaha now has enough financial strength and technical strength to develop new product but to follow up. So creation of independent product with a new concept is where Wahaha will go to.

He further explains that "I mainly use three criteria to measure whether a company can conduct diversified operations. First is its actual situation which determines the necessities; second is its own financial strength which affects the possibility; third is its overall capacity which decides the continuity of the project."

As for the future growth of Wahaha, Zong Yuanqing expresses that "we will invest more than a billion RMB Yuan spare money to two areas. First is area of food, health products, and pharmaceuticals; second is the product for children. "

Deal with the defects of stronger rivals
    -myth of challenging two kinds of Cola

Success of Wahaha Cola is essential for the growth of Wahaha Group. It has been more than 100 years since Coca Cola and Pepsi Cola appeared in the world. They have absolute advantages in the world market. In the late 1970s, these two kinds of Cola enter the China market and soon occupy half of China's beverage market with irresistible forces.

In the communication with their distributors, Zong Qinghou finds there are two defects in their market operations. One is decision-making of these two kinds of Cola overly depend on data mode analysis. It makes it longer in process and hard to develop in the vast rural areas. And actually they haven't entered the rural market since they entered China 20 years ago. The other is the conflict between their endless pursuit of high profits and less market profits for their unconsolidated dealers. Along with the establishment of their leading market position, these two kinds of Cola pay more attention to the in-depth terminal distribution mode in big cities, which leaves little room for their dealers to earn profits.

Zong Qinghou foresees the opportunity once again.

When Zong Qinghou decides to launch Wahaha cola, many people cannot understand because there are so many lessons lay ahead. Someone even says pessimistically that Wahaha Cola is doomed to fail with a short life.

In 1998, Wahaha cola comes out, challenging these two kinds of Cola officially. It aims to develop in China's vast rural areas. People in the vast rural areas are not quite aware of these two kinds of Cola, and can accept the low price of Wahaha cola. Meanwhile, Wahaha Group leaves enough profits to its dealers and Wahaha cola is soon put on a conspicuous position on dealers' counters.

It is because Wahaha cola makes up the blank of these two kinds of Cola that it soon springs up. In 2002, Wahaha series of carbonated beverages production and sales reach 620 thousand tons, accounting for about 12% of carbonated drinks market shares. In terms of individual product, it is approaching the sales of Pepsi cola in China. Although these two still have absolute advantages in cities and developed regions, Wahaha cola firmly holds the vast rural beverage market.

This is an overwhelming offensive. Even some markets in China see no more these two kinds of Cola. Drinks in hotels and restaurants also are changed into Wahaha cola. Only notice the powerful offensive does Coca Cola begins to take actions. It rarely increases ads and requires bottle factories with which it cooperates not to supply products for Wahaha. But all of these are in vain for it is too late to stop Wahaha's growth. By 2001, Wahaha cola has already ranked the top three among these two with production and sales of 620 thousand tons. At that time, these of Pepsi Cola are up to 900 thousand tons and Coca Cola reach 1.3 million tons. From 2002, Wahaha cola begins to develop according to its plans and achieves a growth rate of 61% in its first month. Then competition of two kinds of cola truly turns into that of three.

When Wahaha cola is first introduced to the market, Coco Cola once is arrogant and says carelessly that "such challengers are encountered everywhere every year in the market." While just after the Lantern Festival in 1999, Coca Cola has to openly admit in Shanghai that competitive challenges it faces in China are domestic companies.

Now people all say Wahaha cola is very successful. But Zong Qinghou stays calm, saying "I feel badly for the poverty of Chinese farmers. Otherwise, Wahaha cola can do more."

Pragmatic innovation in a reasonable manner
    -multinational corporations can be paper tigers

In the WTO environment, business managers are always talking about the U.S. business models and Welch of GE. Similarly, in the international trend, multinational corporations are overstated in China.

In fact, it is partly because Chinese companies attribute their failures to the multinational while on the contrary, their desire to expand is indeed what they should blame for. Take Jianlibao as an example, its reputation in previous years comes from its unrealistic expansion. But what is the sense of building a company in Manhattan or ranking among the world's top 500 without profit? Its tragedy actually lies in its rapid expansion. As a former state-owned company, it hasn't totally changed in some aspects and keeps the management level. Finally, due to investment mistakes and slow reaction to the market, it breaks down. This is a common problem of many companies in China, and also the reason Wahaha mode is put forward.

In this era, slogans like "learn from multinational corporations" and "reach WTO standards" come into peoples' eyes. There are some extreme Chinese companies which only imitate others. A lot of failure cases happen, such as that McKinsey defeats Shida and that founders of Robust are forced to resign, etc. We can learn lessons from them that one can never succeed without critical learning from existed international experience.

Wahaha does better than Robust in the international thinking and vision. It has completed the first round of joint venture with Danone in 1996, four years before Robust begins to do that. At that time, Wahaha grows well but comes into troubles like others and Zong Qinghou plans to take use of international capital to run his business. But when Danone shows its willing of holding, Zong Qinghou insists four cardinal principles, namely unchanged brand, unchanged chairman, unchanged treatment of retired workers and unchanged post of workers over 45. After negotiation, Wahaha Group spends its brand and RMB Yuan 300 million out of 1.2 billion of total assets, while Danone Group and Peregrine Hong Kong spends 45 million US Dollars to build 5 joint venture companies. Thus Wahaha takes the biggest shareholder position with 49% of the total shares. Although Donone takes in charge of the shares sold by Peregrine Hong Kong after its withdraws, becoming a major shareholder, its share is still only 40% of Wahaha Group. In 1999, Wahaha improves its corporate governance structure through restructuring and shareholding of leaders and managers.

Another experience of Wahaha comes from reasonable study and use of multinational management modes and marketing practices according to its own advantages. Senior team of Wahaha is extremely stable and open-minded. They never stop learning with the continuous changes of the environment for decades. Wahaha introduces less people return from overseas and less fashionable brand manager system than other Chinese companies. In the marketing, Wahaha tries to build channels before brand and prefers market in rural areas than in cities. It leads the company steps away from core advantages of the multinational in marketing.

It even will not totally satisfy what the world-renowned AC Nielsen market research firm demands in their international cooperation. Once people of a Shanghai company visit Wahaha and propose a question that "will related Wahaha people refer to media data provided by AC Nielsen in making strategy and budget?" People of Wahaha answer that they will consider more about their media data, however, they prefer sales data collected by themselves because samples of sales selected by AC Nielsen are mainly cities, far from Wahaha's products coverage. So Wahaha must complete that on its own. This indicates Wahaha's pragmatic attitude towards the new instruments.

A competitive company that can compete with multinational corporations never comes out of the government protections or imitation of multinational companies. It grows in its practice in China's market economy, and gets improvement from competition and innovation it goes through. The problems lie in that they don't master the strategies and methods to compete with international giants. Similarly, Chinese companies blindly resort to experience of multinational corporations but learn in a critical way and make use of their own imagination and innovation. The success of Wahaha mode is comprehensive strategy based. It relies on two aspects; one is the understanding of Chinese customers and integration ability of market resources. It accelerates Wahaha to stand equally with multinational in the market. Another is reasonable choice of modern development under circumstance of international. It allows Wahaha to leave other domestic companies behind and take use of advanced foreign management and technical experience. All these lead Wahaha to be a model of mature and strong competitor in the international competition.

The success of Wahaha also tells us that as a competitor, multinational corporations also have their limitations along with advantages. In that case, a competitive wolf can turn into a paper tiger that we should not be afraid of.

Problem that should always try to solve
 - ensuring cheap goods with high quality.

A lot of marketing guru who concern the growth of Wahaha point out that there are three problems that Wahaha should always try to solve. First is ensuring popular daily goods provided to dealers. Second is ensuring reasonable profits of dealers. Third is ensuring powerful market management capability that requires not passing pressure of market management and advertising to dealers.

But Zong Qinghou has his own understanding.

"A company will continue to encounter new problems in its development process. So tactics are temporary but permanent. "

"As for the above three points, I have my own views. All Wahaha products stand close to the daily lives of customers. Although not every kind of product is popular, the brand Wahaha will gain a very wide popularity. We also keep on providing reasonable profits to dealers. Only with acceptable returns, can dealers try their best to build marketing network to sell the products. The company cannot live long without dealers. What dealers to the company is what water to fish. Moreover, Wahaha does a lot for dealers in its actual operations, including warehouse management, public relations and sales promotion. It never passes the pressure of market management and advertising to dealers.

"In my opinion, problem that Wahaha should always try to address is ensuring cheap goods with high quality. It will lead manufacturers, distributors and consumers to create win-win situation. Furthermore, ecosystem of the food industry can keep healthy development.

Source: Dang Ning, History of How Chinese Rich Families Emerge, Harbin Press, 2004.

Review

Zong Qinghou sets up the largest beverage company - Wahaha Group in China after 15 years of struggle. In 2002, Wahaha Group has sales revenue of RMB Yuan 8.8 billion and net profit of 1.2 billion. Zong Qinghou holds 29.4% of its shares and his personal assets reach RMB Yuan1.64 billion. It makes him rank 58th in the list made by Forbes China. Wahaha Group is the sole current national drink group that can compete with strong companies in the world industry.

When he talks about the mystery of his success, Zong Qinghou says peacefully that "No myth of the modern company exists today because we are long away from the success relying on an idea or an operation. Comprehensive strength and strategic advantage are what companies compare. Unusual way and usual mind are needed to run a business in this era when myth fades."

The case "Zong Qinghou's Art of War" and "Wahaha mode" gives a detailed introduction to business strategy of Zong Qinghou, chairman of Hangzhou Wahaha Group. It is also a typical example in which strategies and tactics are combined technically and vividly.

Questions

1. What is growth strategy? What are types of it?
2. What is multiplization strategy? What are its types? What should be paid attention to in implementing it?
3. What are different types of product-market strategy?
4. What are basic forms of integration strategy?
5. What is business group? What are its characteristics?
6. What are characteristics and main forms of transnational operation?
7. What the focal points for transnational business strategic decision?

8. What are features of stable strategies? What are the types of them?
9. What are features of shrink strategies? What are the types of them?
10. What are the possible strategic combination formats?

Notes

(1) Liu Jisheng ed, *Company Operation Strategy*, 1st edition, Tsinghua
    University Press,   April 1995, p.161.

(2) Wang Chao ed, *Transnational Strategy: International Business
    Management,*1st   edition,   China   International   Business   and
    Economics Press, January, 1999, p. 294.

BIBLIOGRAPHY

〔U.S.〕 Arthur A. Thompson Jr. & A. J. Strickland, *Crafting and executing strategy: the quest for competitive advantage concepts and cases*, 10th ed, Duan Shenghua, Wang Zhihui trans., Xu Erming revision, Peking University Press, 2004.

〔U.S.〕 Fred. R. David, *Strategic Management*, Li Kening trans., 1st edition, Economic Science Press, June 1998.

〔CAN.〕 Henry Mintzberg, *Strategy Safari*, 2nd edition, Machinery Industry Press, June 2006.

Liu Jisheng ed, *Company Operation Strategy*, 1st edition, Tsinghua University Press, April 1995.

Xu Erming ed, *Company Strategy Management*, 1st edition, China Economic Publishing House, May 1998.

Wang Chao ed, *Transnational Strategy: International Business Management*, 1st edition, China International Business and Economics Press, January, 1999.

Si Yan ed, *Win by Strategy—Key to Business Success*, 1st edition, China Citic Press, July, 1994.

Chiang Yuntong ed, *Company Operation Strategic Management*, 1st edition, Company Management Press, April 1996.

CHAPTER 6

Establishment of Enterprise Overall Strategy

Abstract

This chapter begins with the process of constituting the strategy and then introduces basic procedures of overall enterprise strategy, the main components of overall strategy and guarantee measures of formulating a strategic plan. At last, it has an appendix of cases and comments in "Eleventh-Five Year Overall Strategic Plan of Beiren Group Corporation (2006—2010)."

Learning Objectives

- To make it clear the basic procedures of formulating a strategic enterprise plan.
- To master the main concepts of strategic enterprise plan and its formulation procedures.
- To understand and master the concept, main points, contents of enterprise objectives, as well as steps and regarding problems in defining it.
- To understand and master the concept, functions, contents of strategic target, as well as basic requirements for making it.
- To master the basic contents and methods for environment analysis.
- To master the basic contents and methods for industrial environment analysis.
- To master the basic contents and methods for enterprise resource analysis.
- To make it clear the purpose of environment analysis and enterprise resource analysis.
- To understand, master and properly apply principles to select the business direction for the enterprise.
- To understand and master the analysis of five competitive industrial elements, SWOT analysis and Boston Matrix.
- To understand and take measures to formulate a strategic plan.

Introduction

An overall strategy for an enterprise is the highest level and most important strategy as well as the most difficult strategy to lie out. It determines vital issues of the enterprise, such as the developmental direction, objectives, purpose, organizations, and source allocations and so on; meanwhile, it has a rather long time limit. Therefore, no matter if it is correct or not, it relates to the prospering or declining of an enterprise directly. The process of establishing the overall strategy is shown as in Figure 6-1.

Figure 6-1: The Process of Constituting the Strategy

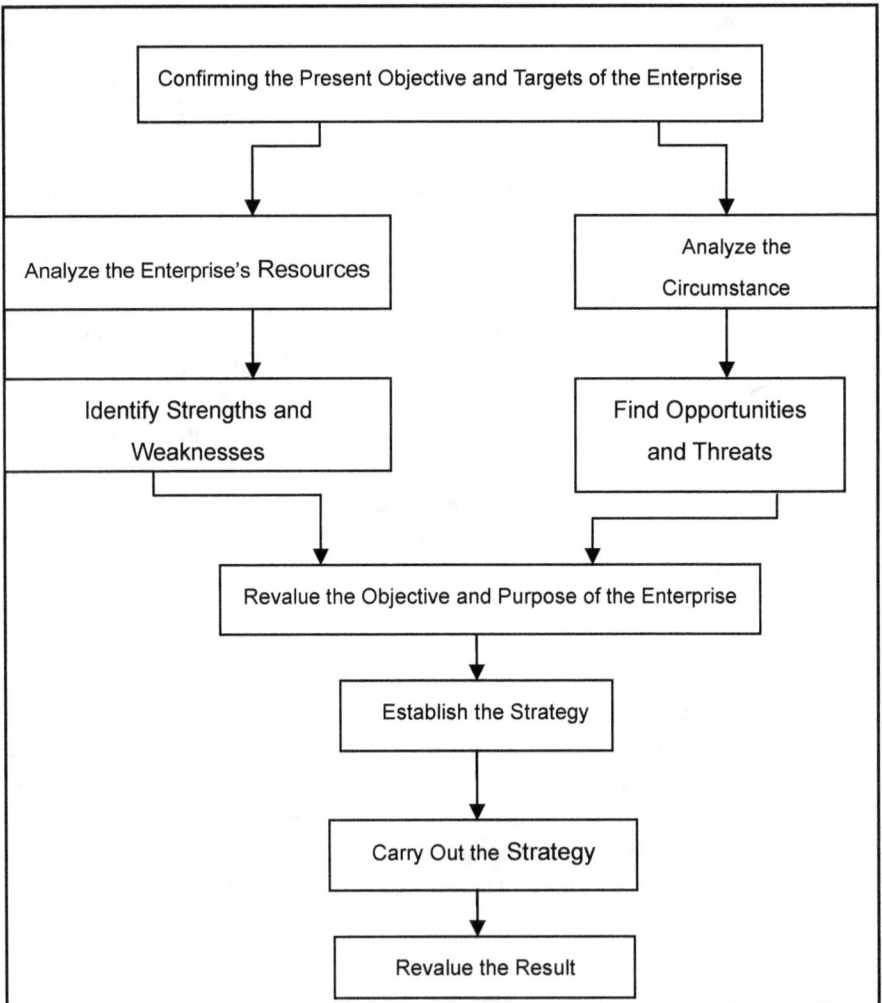

Lesson

I. Constituting Objective and Target of an Enterprise

(I) Constituting objective of an enterprise

The famous America management expert Peter Drucker has suggested that to know a company, its objective, which exists outside the company, should be known first. As a matter of fact, since industrial and commercial enterprises are cells of society, their objectives must exist in the society. And the objective of a company is solely defined as to create customers. (1)

The main points of Drucker's statement are as follows:

- The objective of an enterprise is the primary sign to make it different from others.
- The objective of an enterprise lies outside the enterprise, to put it clearly, it exists in the society.
- The objective of an enterprise is solely defined as to create customers.

In order to comprehend the concept concretely and deeply for confirming the objective of a company, we will focus on the following issues:

1. Concept and main points of the objective of an enterprise

The objective of an enterprise is an exposition to its task. It determines the activity the enterprise is carrying out or plans to carry out, and the organization type the enterprise has at present or expects to have.

The main points of the enterprise objective are:

- Who are the existing customers?
- Who are the potential customers?
- Is the business of the enterprise appropriate? And should it be changed?

This concept tells us that objective is the task of the enterprise. It should work out two issues: one is the activity or business the enterprise is carrying out or plans to carry out; and the other is the organization type the enterprise has or expects to have. For example, should the enterprise be managed into a famous enterprise with a high reputation both at home and abroad, or an enterprise similar to others?

It is obvious that, to confirm the objective of an enterprise, the precondition is to confirm its customers. Only when the customers are confirmed, could the business of a company be ensured. Generally, there are two kinds of customers: one is existing customer--who purchases products of the enterprise and enjoys the service the enterprise offers at present; and the second is potential customers--who is not the customer of the enterprise, but may become in the future with the enterprise's efforts.

2. How to confirm the existing customer?

The following questions need to be answered:

(1) Who is the customer? Where is the customer? Why does the customer buy? How to close to the customer?
(2) What does the customer buy?
(3) What are the value of the customer (i.e. what does the customer expect to gain while they purchase)?

Among the three questions mentioned above, the first two are obvious, easy to be understood and achieved, and the third question is vital to comprehend. The "Customer Value", in a word, is the value that the customer expects to realize through buying the commodity. Buying a watch, for example, one may buy an electronic watch or a common stem-winder, and the other may purchase a Rolex. The former buys the watch for knowing time accurately and having the convenience; while the latter purchases watches to symbolize his or her social identity and status. After understood different values of customers, enterprises, aiming at different customer requirements, can satisfy various customers with various products and services.

3. How to confirm the potential customer?

The following questions need to be answered:

(1) How are the development trend and potential of the market?
(2) What changes on the market structure may happen, along with the development of economy, changes of consuming fashion and the force of competition?

(3) Which kind of reform may change the customer's purchasing habit?

(4) At present, what requirements of the customer cannot be fully satisfied through existing products and services?

(5) Is the business of the enterprise appropriate? Should the enterprise change its business?

The potential customer is the potential market for the enterprise. The requirement of the potential market is sometimes the requirement which the consumer does not pointed out definitely, i.e., "the obscure requirement which cannot be satisfied by the existing goods or services." To satisfy this requirement, enterprises need to develop new products. At this aspect, the development of Ya Du Moistener is a successful representative.

Aiming at people's revolt against the sensation of dryness as well as the thirst for wetness, "Ya Du" described the dryness as an unbearable co. At the same time, it propagandized repeatedly that wetness is indispensable to human health just like sunshine, air and water. Under the campaign, the company presented Ya Du Moistener and made it come into thousands of families, and thus created a big market.

4. How to confirm the objective of the enterprise

The following questions need to be answered:

(1) Which kind of business we should involve in?
This is to select the business direction for the enterprise. It reflects the decision-maker's judgment towards changes of environment in future, and expectations towards the future development of the enterprise.

(2)Which kind of enterprise should we become?
This is to confirm the status of the enterprise in the business and its image in society. It reflects the value of the strategy maker.

Whether these two questions can be answered correctly relates to the result that the decision maker can make the objective of the enterprise right or not. How to answer these two questions shows the basic essence, ability as well as the value of the decision maker of enterprises. Therefore, to deicide the objective of enterprises, actually, is the concrete reflection of the purpose of the life of the enterprise decision maker. Consequently, the competition among enterprises, after all, is the competition among decision makers on their basic essence, ability, value and personality. As a result, it is very hard for a decision maker to confirm the objective of the enterprise if they don't pay attention to improve their learning and culture.

Then, what contents should be involved in the objective of enterprises?

5. Contents of the objective of enterprises

Professor Mike Chris, America Scholar in Management, suggests that five principles should be followed by the statement of good objectives.

(1) It should be clear that what the enterprise is and what the enterprise is expected to be.
(2) Permit the enterprise developing itself creatively at the aspect of strategy, while limit the enterprise taking risks at the aspect of tactics.
(3) Make a difference between the enterprise or organization and other enterprise or organization in the same type.
(4) The framework, which is used for evaluating current and future activities of enterprises, should be confirmed.
(5) In order to be understood easily by the whole enterprise or organization, the statement should be accurate and clear.

Basing on above principles and practice experiences of many enterprises, the contents of the enterprise objective can be summed up as follows:

Leading products, markets and important technologies

- Purposes of the enterprise
- Corporate culture
- The self-evaluation of enterprises
- The social responsibility of enterprises.

The explanation, which is to help readers to comprehend the connotation of the content mentioned above accurately, is as follows:

Leading products, markets and important technologies

The objective of an enterprise is a statement which distinguishes the purpose of the enterprise from purposes of other enterprises in the same type. The objective of an enterprise must give a clear definition of its product, market and important technologies, as they are the clearest differences among enterprises.

Purposes of enterprises

As an economic organization, what fundamental purposes should the enterprise pursue? This is a vital question every enterprise must answer definitely. One point of view believes that-the basic purpose of enterprises is to pursue the biggest profit. We disagree with this point of view as it will bring two disastrous effects to enterprises: one is that it will mislead enterprises to pursue the profit maximization unscrupulously; and the other is that it will mislead enterprises to put the cart before the horse on the pivot of enterprise works. So, how to answer the question correctly? The points of view of two enterprises may worthy to be read as references.

The objective of Haier

"Pursuing profits is a target instead of a purpose of the enterprise. The basic purpose of enterprises is to drive society developing. Enterprises contribute themselves to society and the target of pursuing profits will generate during the process. To pursue profits, some companies produce counterfeit and shoddy products; however, the profit, even obtained, cannot for long."
    -Zhang Ruimin, CEO for Haier

The Profit Opinion of Panasonic (Beijing)

Panasonic (Beijing) contributes itself to society, and gains corresponding rewards from society as well. The rewards are the profit of the company.

In addition, another question should be noticed, namely, the relationship between the short-term earning and the long run development of enterprises. Sometimes, the short-term earning is emphasized while the need of the long run development is ignored during the management practice of enterprises. The strategic decision, which is only made for pursuing short-term earning, is not only short sight, but extremely dangerous. Only the long run development, in nowadays environment which is full of changes and challenges, is the vital guarantee of the permanent survival of enterprises.

Corporate culture

Corporate culture is a general name for the enterprise concept, spirit and image. It reflects the basic belief and value of an enterprise and is the spiritual pursuit and behavior principles of all employees. Once the culture of an enterprise is founded and upgraded to mainly manage the enterprise, the above-mentioned culture will become an important invisible assets and priceless treasure for the enterprise. The successful practice by Haier Group, who adopts "Haier Culture" to merge "Shock Fish", is one typical embodiment of this aspect.

Self-assessment of the Enterprise

In order to find its own position under the circumstances of competition, an enterprise must assess its advantages and disadvantages in an objective, practical and realistic way, which requires that the enterprise should have a correct assessment for itself, and pay particular attention to eradicating the bad habit of "report only the good but not the bad."

Social Responsibility of the Enterprise

An enterprise cannot only consider its own interests in the production and management activities but also the social benefits and social obligation as well. It is a crucial task among the objective of an enterprise. In view of the current international situations, the social responsibilities of enterprise is increasingly emphasized in the whole country, which is not only the requirement of society, but also a demand for establishing a good image for the enterprise itself and getting victory in competitions. On the whole, social responsibilities that an enterprise should take on are: paying taxes according to regulations; protecting the interests of consumers; protecting the ecological environment; and making contributions to regions and society.

To sum up, an enterprise should reflect all the above-mentioned aspects in a comprehensive, brief、coordinated、refined way to indicate a unified direction for its strategic actions and guarantee its healthy and sustainable development.

6. Regarding problems on defining the objective for an enterprise

(1) Defining the enterprise objective in agreement with the demand of the consumer

When making the objective, an enterprise should not define it only according to its own products or technique; instead, it should follow the consumers' demands. As products and technologies will be out of date one day; however, some of the consumer's basic demands won't be changed, some of which will last for a long time. For instance, an enterprise which produces slide rulers considers providing slide rulers for consumers as its objective——namely, defines its mission based on products——when a new product emerges (such as the electronic calculator) on the market, the enterprise will be easily bogged into a passive position in operation. If it defines providing calculating tools for consumers as its objective in the first place, it will be more likely to adapt to the market changes, thus win initiative in operation.

(2) Enterprise objective must have binding forces on the enterprise

The binding force mentioned here has requirements in two aspects: One is not only to define explicitly what an enterprise should do in operation, but also point out what shouldn't do in order to specify its task and concentrate all resources it has to fulfill the task. For instance, the mission of Bell System (AT&T——American Telephone & Telegram Co.) designed by the famous American scholar Toffler is: The purpose of Bell System is not to product equipment or to operate a network, neither to provide a second or third phone for every family, nor to satisfy needs of every communication required by someone who is willing to pay. The right mission is by providing customers with those products and services (and only those) that other corporations cannot supply to them with the same cost, quality and social benefits to ensure that USA possesses the most advanced communication system at the aspects of audio and data technology. The other one is the promise that an enterprise would like to make to the public in its objective, such as "to provide the excellent service for its clients etc." The enterprise must carry them out firmly in behavior, and mustn't say one thing but do another or deceive its clients.

(3) Enterprise objective must be agitational

If an enterprise can make out some contributions to public in its objective, the so-called objective will bear an agitational feature. For instance, the objective of Haier Group is "to promote social progress." TDK company in Japan advocates "creation——makes contributions to the world

167

culture industry and strives for TDK of the whole world." Such kinds of objectives are more noble to people. In addition, the agitational effects of an enterprise objective are: on the one hand, the enterprise will establish a good image of serving for society and public; on the other hand, its staff will be stimulated to have a sense of mission, honor, pride, and thus consciously work even harder to carry out the objective.

(4)Frequently examining the enterprise objective
Once the environment of an enterprise changes, or the operating/management orientation undergoes great changes, the enterprise should adjust or modify its objective in time.

All in all, if an enterprise wants to survive and further its development and prosperity, it must be just and necessary to define its objective and continuously examine it and make some adjustments as well. Otherwise, it will probably go bankruptcy. Just as what emphasized by Peter Drucker, "such a unique operating objective is the only principle leading to management failure for an enterprise or an institution, and also is the foremost reason." Therefore, when making strategies, the enterprise must give its first priority to define a correct objective.

An enterprise can set down its strategic target after making its objective. Objective determines the target which embodies objective and realizes it.

(II) Defining strategic target

1. Conception and function of the strategic target

Strategic target is the expected effect for an enterprise to realize its objective. It is the core of an enterprise strategy.

The functions of the strategic target are: it reflects the management idea of an enterprise, points out its striving orientation in a long period and provides evidences for choosing strategic plan.

The strategic target is a long-term target. In order to implement and carry it out, the short-term target should also be made.

2. Conception and basis of a short-term target

A short-term target is the executive target, with a general time limit within one year. It is used for the manager to guarantee the realization of long-term target.

The short-term target should be originated from the in-depth evaluation to the long-term target, and this kind of evaluation ought to be carried out according to the respective target in the orders based on the degree of importance and emergency. Once the orders are fixed, the enterprise can establish its short-term target and thus realize its long-term target.

3. Contents of strategic target

The Strategic Targets are multiplex, including both economy target and non-economy target. Under normal circumstances, an enterprise should establish its strategic target from the aspects below:

- Profitability: It is represented by profit, rate of return on investment, average return per share, sales profit rate and so on.
- Market: It is represented by sales volume and market share.
- Productivity: it is represented by ratio of input and output or unit product cost.
- Production: it is represented by the product line or sales volume for products and profitability and the finishing period to develop its new product.
- Competitiveness: It stands for the status, technical level, quality ranking of an enterprise in industry and its image in the mind of consumers.
- Social responsibility: It means how to protect the interests of consumers, protect environment, save resources, and participate in various undertakings and activities that are beneficial to society and regions.

It is necessary to explain here that the content of strategic target do not have any legal requirements. Different industries or enterprises may have different demands, and the contents mentioned here apply to most enterprises in most industries.

4. Basic requirements for making strategic target

(1) Fix the term of target explicitly

As long as an enterprise knows the term of target, it is able to examine and check the implementation of the target on time and by stage, master the completion degree of the target and take necessary measures toward the weak link, thus guarantee its realization. When defining the target term, an enterprise should attach great importance to suitable time length and taking all factors into consideration. In principle, the target term should keep accordance with planning term.

(2)Target level should be advanced and reasonable

The target made by an enterprise should be strategic on one hand and practical on the other. It should be slightly above the capability of the enterprise together with individual, and at the same time avoid unattainable/too high to reach. An approach of integrating progressiveness and rationality is, to confine the realization of target within the allowable scope of subjective and objective conditions. Only by this can people make the target come true through their efforts.

(3) Specification and qualification of the target as much as possible

The general target of an enterprise should be decomposed into some specific, measurable concrete targets through Purposes——Means Chain, then carried out to each level, department and even each employee within the enterprise step by step. In this case, the target of a certain level will become the means of target in last level, thus a target system is formed. In the meantime, the target should try to be quantitative during the process of specification in order for examination and evaluation.

(4) Index of target should be more than two sets

One set is the "index to be surely guaranteed." The so-called "index to be surely guaranteed" is, once this set of index has been confirmed, it has to be accomplished desperately and falls through at no time. Two points are worth the notice when establishing this set of index: one is "considering from the worst point", try to take various possible risk in strategy period into account and also make some relevant precautionary measures; the other one is to leave some leeway when confirming the index level. Do not set the index level too high.

The other set is the "index that tries to be fulfilled through efforts." The so-called "index that tries to be fulfilled through efforts" means that after confirming this set, an enterprise doesn't have to accomplish it. Instead, it should try its best to fulfill the index when condition allows. The "condition" mentioned here is mainly "opportunity for development" under circumstances. While making strategy, it always has two cases due to a long time of the strategy term normally: one is that some risks cannot be predicted; the other one is some opportunities cannot be predicted either. The "index to be surely guaranteed" mainly applies to the first case and the "index that tries to be fulfilled through efforts" mainly applies to the second case. Its level can be higher.

II. Analysis of Environment

Environment is the space for survival and development of an enterprise. It is also the major restrictive factor of its strategic and management behavior. Analysis of environment is the key element to make the strategy. Why do we say so? For the environment of an enterprise, to a large extent, determines the possible strategic choice for its manager. All successful strategies are mostly those which can adapt to the environment.

The analysis of environment includes many contents. To sum up, it mainly involves three aspects below:

(I) Analysis of macro-environment

Why do we have to analyze the macro-environment? Because it is the ultimate origin to influence the strategic choice for an enterprise——without research and analysis for macro-environment, it is even hard for the enterprise to make correct strategic policy.

The macro-environment of an enterprise includes policy and law environment, economic environment, technical environment, social & cultural environment and natural environment. The natural environment involves factors such as geography, climate, resource distribution, ecology etc. in regions or market where the enterprise locates. Owing to smaller or slower changes in each factor about natural environment in general and bigger possibility for changes in political、economic、technical and social & cultural environment, therefore, the latter has a more noticeable impact on the management strategy of the enterprise.

An approach to analysis of macro-environment in an enterprise is called the PEST analysis. Figure 6-2 shows the relation of macro-environment to an enterprise.

Figure 6—2 PEST analysis

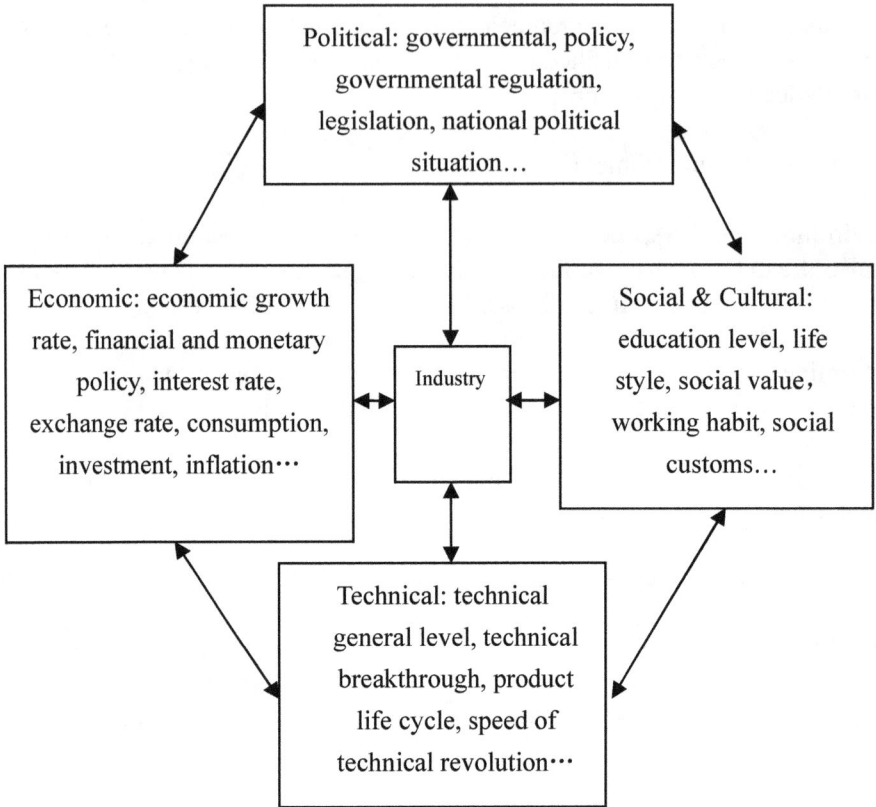

Political: governmental, policy, governmental regulation, legislation, national political situation…

Economic: economic growth rate, financial and monetary policy, interest rate, exchange rate, consumption, investment, inflation…

Industry

Social & Cultural: education level, life style, social value，working habit, social customs…

Technical: technical general level, technical breakthrough, product life cycle, speed of technical revolution…

Source: Editing group of required MBA core courses, *Business Strategy*, 1st edition, China Transnational Radio Press, September 1997, p.28.

(II) Analysis of mid-environment

The mid-environment is in fact the environment in the region of an enterprise. Why should we analyze the mid-environment? For it is an important source to influence the strategic choice of an enterprise. Without the research and the analysis of mid-environment, the strategic choice would probably alienate from regional practice, so it will be hard to make correct strategic policy. The analysis contents of mid-environment are more or less the same as that of the macro-environment. However, it should be emphasized here that the analysis for mid-environment should focus on two main points: the first one, what are the characteristics in this region? The second one, what are the advantages in this region? Besides, the strategic choice of an enterprise should be established on the basis of the characteristics and advantages of this region, but should never be copied from other regions blindly.

(III) Analysis of industry environment

Figure 6-3 shows the contents of the analysis of industry environment

Figure 6-3 analysis of industry environment

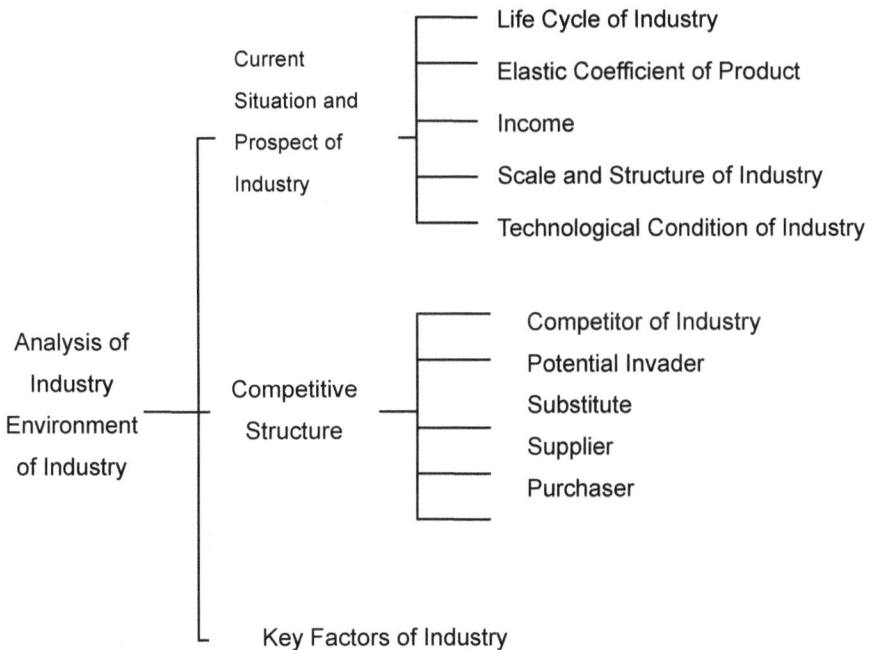

The analysis of industry environment is not only the main point in environmental analysis, but the difficult one as well, for the industry environment is the direct source to influence the strategic choice of an enterprise. Therefore, without the study and the analysis of the industry environment, the developmental strategy of the enterprise cannot be made at all.

1. Analysis of current situation and prospect of industry

To make out the current situation and prospect of an industry, we should focus on the following several aspects to analyze:

(1) Analysis of life cycle of industry
(2) Conception

The life cycle of an industry refers to the period of an industry from its emergence to complete withdrawal from the social and economic activities where it went through. It includes four developing stages of infant period i.e. growing period、 mature period and recession period (see Figure 6-4). The curves of the life cycle of industry reflect its wants and needs condition by society.

Figure 6—4 The Life Cycle of Industry

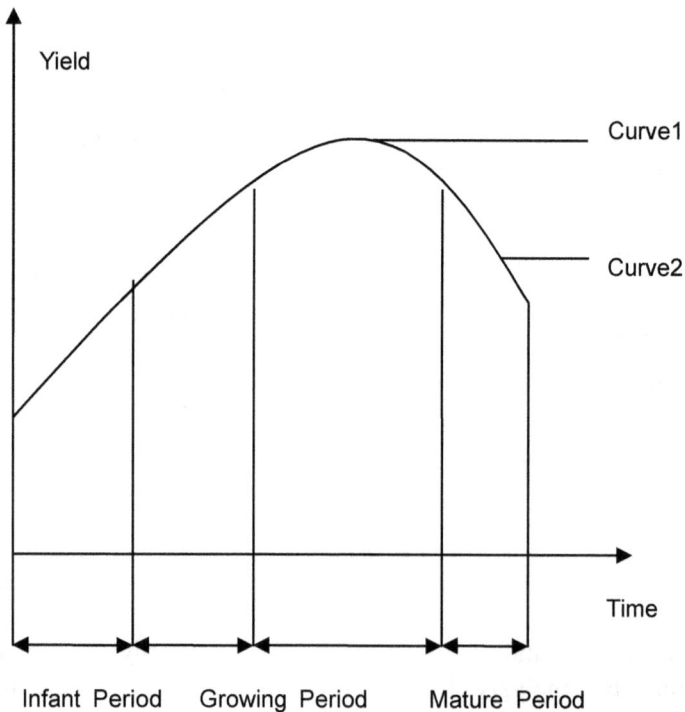

Source: Liu Jisheng, *Company Operation Strategy*, Tsinghua University Press, 1995, p.33.

Characteristics of life cycle at each stage

Infant period: with a higher market growth rate, faster increase of demand and comparative big change in technology, the enterprise of an industry focuses mainly on opening up new consumers, occupying market. However it has a great uncertainty in technology in this period but a large room in strategy such as product, market, service etc. It doesn't have enough information about the industry characteristics, situation of industry competition and consumer characteristics etc., and therefore, the entry barrier for the enterprise is quite low.

Growing period: with a quite high market growth rate, fast-speed increase of demand, gradual stable in technology, the situation of industry characteristics and competition has been clear comparatively. Besides, the entry barrier has been improved, and the varieties of product and numbers of competitors have been increased.

Mature period: with a not high market growth rate and not high increase of demand, the technology has been mature, and the industry characteristics condition, industry competition and consumer characteristics are both very clear and stable. Meanwhile, with the formation of purchaser's market, and the industry profitability decline, the exploitation of new products and their new applications become even more difficult, and the entry barrier is high for the enterprise.

Recession period: the market growth rate and demand are declining and the varieties of product and numbers of competitors are decreasing.

Main signs to identify the life cycle of industry at each stage

The main signs to identify the life cycle of industry at each stage include growth rate of market sales, growth rate of market demands, product varieties, numbers of competitor, entry & exit barriers, technological revolution and purchasing behavior of consumer etc. Among them, the growth rate of market sales, growth rate of market demands, product varieties, and number of competitors are the most important ones.

Generally, these four signs will take on the following trends:

Let's look at the growth rate of market sales and growth rate of market demands first, both of which are basically synchronic: relatively slow increase in infant period; very fast increase in growing period; slow or even stagnant increase in the mature period and gradual decline in recession period.

Now let's look at the product varieties and numbers of competitor, both of which are not all completely synchronic: both are low in numbers in infant period. In growing period, the product varieties increase fast but are not the period of its most, while the number of competitors increase enormously and are the time of its most. In mature period it has the most product varieties, but the number of competitors begins to decline. In recession period, both of them tend to decline.

1. Significance of analysis of industry's life cycle

The analysis of life cycle of an industry enables an enterprise to have a basic understanding to the current situation and prospect of the industry and help choose a better period to enter into a certain industry.

Then, what time is better for an enterprise to enter into an industry in normal condition?

The first one is the infant period. Once it is successful in this period, the enterprise will be the leader of a certain industry and can get high profit in a longer time. However, it requires a relatively high cost to enter into the industry at this period, and also has relatively more risks

The second one is the growing period. If an enterprise which has entered into an industry can crush into the first several tops or even the top one of the industry, it is destined to be successful. However, it also has risk in this period, because it is also the golden time for other competitors to enter. Once there are too many competitors in this industry, it will aggravate the competition fierceness in it and thus lead to a declining profit rate or even experiencing loss in the whole industry.

Then, should the enterprise enter into an industry in the mature period? It is believed that it's not the right time either because the entry barrier and risk are too high at this period or the possibility of success is little.

2. Elastic analysis of product income

The income elasticity of product can prove an industry's status in social economy. The formula is as follows:

Elastic coefficient of product income in an industry=growth rate of product demands/growth rate of per capita national income

If the elastic coefficient is more than 1, it shows that this kind of industry can account for a bigger share in the industry structure, thus has a wider room for development.

3. Analysis of industry scale and structure

The purpose for an enterprise to analyze the scale and structure is, to make out the relationship between industry development and social demand, which is significant in confirming the business scope and scale of the enterprise.

- Analysis of total demand for product or service
  - How much is the total demand for product or service of this industry required by society? Is it at an increasing or reducing trend?
- Analysis of comparison between production capacity and total demand of industry
  - How much is the current aggregate production capacity (design capacity 、 practical ability) of this industry? Compared with the demand for product or service of society and this industry, the production capacity of this industry is surplus or insufficient?
- Analysis of industry concentration degree
  - The industry concentration degree refers to the sum total of market shares occupied by the four big enterprises within the industry. The more its sum total is, the higher the industry concentration degree will be and vice versa.
- Analysis of development trend of enterprise scale and industry scale
  - Whether the development trend of the enterprise scale is consistent with that of the industry scale? Is the current scale of enterprise suitable? Should it be enlarged or reduced?

- Analysis of product type structure in industry and enterprise
  - Do the product types within an industry (such as raw materials, parts and components, complete machine and various final products) have reasonable structures? Whether the proportion is suitable? How is the development trend? What kinds of product types does the enterprise belong to? According to the industry collectivity, should the enterprise be enlarged or reduced?
- Analysis of industry scale and structure
  - Does the enterprise of an industry belong to the type of greatest disparity or the balance type in scale? It should attach particular importance to the analysis of the management condition, management strategy, and technology level and product feature of the first several tops of intra-industry big enterprises.

4. Analysis of technological condition of industry

In a rapid development of science and technology age, the technological condition has a great impact on the industry development. Therefore, it's advantageous to make out the technological condition to the analysis of industry prospect.

To analyze the technological condition of an industry, several aspects can be focused on to spread out problems.

- What stage of technological life cycle is the industry technology at?
- How is the technological level of the industry? Does it belong to the advanced technological industry or the backward one?
- How about the variability of the technology? It means the rhythm of technological change is fast or slow. Some industries are advancing very fast, such as the electronic industry, aerospace industry and pharmaceutical industry etc., while some are advancing quite slowly, such as steel industry, building material industry, textile industry etc.
- What direction is the technology of today's industry heading for?
- What is the position of the current technological level of an enterprise in the whole industry? Is it in a leading position, or in a middle or backward position?

5.   Analysis of intra-industry strategic groups

The enterprises within an industry will take different competitive strategies on one hand and on the other, they are likely to have something in common and work cooperatively with each other to some degree, thus form the strategic group. Generally speaking, there are several strategic groups in an industry, or only one in some industries.

The enterprises in a same strategic group may vary in the aspects of production sales and market share etc. However, their natures are the same, so they take the same response to some situational changes. Likewise, different strategic groups may take different attitudes and actions towards changes to the same situation. For instance, to confront the entry of new enterprises to participate in the competition, the whole industry will join up together and set up entry barriers. Meanwhile, each strategic group also sets up their respective entry barriers, which not only prevents enterprises of external industries from entering into this industry, but also other intra-industry groups from moving into this group.

Due to the different economic benefits among various intra-industry strategic groups, the strategies they adopt have an opposing relation. Therefore, knowing the structure of intra-industry strategy groups and their interrelation among them is beneficial to the analysis of industry condition.

By analysis of the above-mentioned aspects, we can have a basic understanding for the overall condition and prospect of industry, which is also the prerequisite for an enterprise to make management strategy.

2. Analysis of competitive structure of industry

The competitive structure of an industry is a fundamental factor to determine the competition rules and fierceness degree in the industry, thus the analysis of it is crucial for an enterprise to make the strategy. The analysis of competitive structure is not only the main point in the industry analysis, but the difficulty as well.

The famous American strategic management expert, Michael Porter points out: in any industry, domestic or abroad, not matter it produces a kind of product or provides a kind of service, all the competition laws are embedded in the following five competition power: namely, the entry of new competitors、 threat of substitutes、 bargaining ability of purchasers、 bargaining ability of suppliers and competition among the current competitors (shown in Figure 6-5).

Figure 6-5 Competition power to drive industry

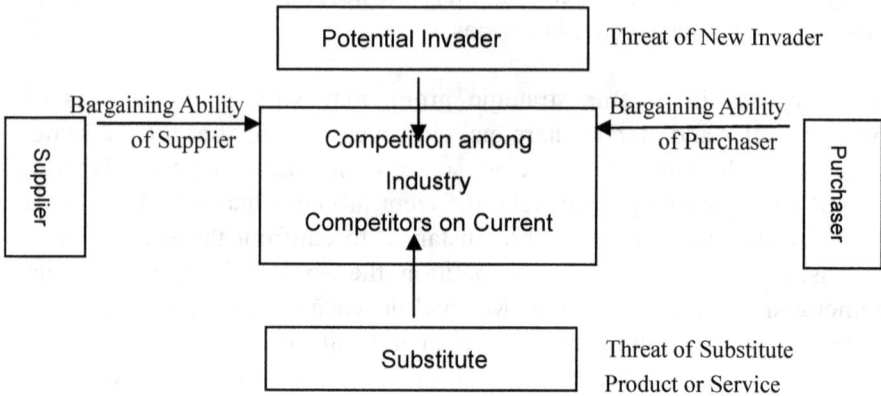

Figure 6-5 shows five competition forces in the industry, which is the fundamental factor to drive the industry competition. Among the five factors, each competitive force has to be determined by some important factors. Now, let's give a brief description for the decisive factors in each competition force.

(1) Threat of new invader
The new invader includes a newly-established enterprise or an enterprise that adopts diversification strategy and engaged in other different industries before. The degree of its threat to industry depends on the obstacle it needs to conquer and the cost it pays (namely the entry barrier) when entering into a new industry, as well as the fierceness degree reflected by the old enterprises after entering into a new industry. The entry barrier includes:

- Scale economy
- Product differentiation
- Demand for capital
- Switching cost
- Distribution channel
- Cost disadvantage that is Irrelevant to scale
- Governmental policy

- The reaction of the existing enterprises
- Competition among existing competitors

Industry competitors are existing enterprises in the trade. The competition among existing enterprises in the trade usually adopts means which people are already familiar with to strive for market position. These means are as follows: the price competition, the advertising war, the products' introduction, the increase of services to customers and so on. The competition occurs because one or more competitors realized pressures from other enterprises or saw opportunities which can increase market share. Enterprises are interdependent in many trades, so competitive activities raised by one enterprise will certainly influence other rivals prominently and give rise to counterattacks or struggles which reject this kind of behavior. This kind of behavior and reaction pattern may bring advantages or not to the enterprise and the entire trade which raised the competition. But if this kind of behavior and rejecting activities are upgraded further, then all enterprises in the trade will be deeply hurt and the whole status of the trade will get worse rapidly.

Some competition methods such as the noticeable price strategy, is a kind of extremely inadvisable strategy because it can easily result in the descending earning power of the entire trade. Price reduction can be adopted by rivals easily. Benefits of all enterprises will reduce if rivals adopt the price reduction strategy unless the price elasticity of demand of the trade is high enough. On the contrary, the advertising war can enlarge demands or raise the degree of product differentiation, thus it benefits all enterprises in the trade.

The competition in some trades is "militant", "painful" or "brutal"; but in some other trades, it is "complaisant" or "gentlemanly." The severity degree of competition is the interactional result of a series of structural factors. These factors are:

- Numerous or Counterbalanced Competitors
- Slow Growth Rate of the Trade
- High Fixed Cost and High Inventory Cost
- Lacking Product Differentiation or Conversion Cost
- Vast Scale Expanded Production Capacity
- Various Competitors

- High Strategic Interests

- High Withdrawal Barriers

Withdrawal barriers refers to the economic, strategic and emotional factors which make the enterprise have to hold its ground in an industry competition, even though the enterprise could only gain rather low or even minus income from its investment. Sources of withdrawal barriers are mainly as follows:

Specific Assets: It is the highly specialized assets which are used for specific businesses or places. Its liquidation value is comparatively low while the cost of transformation or reconstruction is rather high.

Fixed cost of exiting: It contains labor agreements, relocating cost, and the maintenance capacity of spare parts.

Contacts among Internal Strategies: Refers to the interaction and interrelationship between a certain operating unit and other operating units of the company at aspects of the enterprise image, marketing ability, approaches for entering the financial market, common facilities and so on. These factors make the company believe that it is strategically important to stay in the industry, so as to block the operating units to exit from these businesses.

Emotion Impediment: The administrators are unwilling to make the economical and reasonable decision of exiting because of the mark of a special business, loyalty to employees, anxiety about personal future, sense of pride and so on.

Restrictions of Policies and the Society: It includes the government rejects or discourages the enterprise to exit due to the government's attention to the unemployment and the impact of regional economy.

When the withdrawal barriers are very high, the surplus production capacity in the industry cannot be released and the enterprises which failed in competition cannot withdraw, and have to hold the line. However, as they are weaker than other enterprises, they have to adopt extreme strategies which result in long term low earning power of the entire industry.

(2) Pressure of substitutes
Broadly speaking, all enterprises of some industry participate in the competition with the trade which produces substitutes. When enterprises of

the industry price profitable products, the existence of substitutes limits the price; so as to restrict the potential profit of the industry. The more attractive the price of the substitute is, the more serious the restriction of industry profits is. The pressure of substitutes is mainly laid on the following factors:

- Earning power of substitutes
- Strategies adopted by enterprises which produce substitutes
- Transformation cost of users
- Pressures of buyers

Buyers are also competing with intra-industry enterprises. They force enterprises to reduce the price, to supply high quality products and more services and to make intra-industry enterprises oppose mutually. All of these will reduce the earning power of the industry. The bargaining capability of each important buyer group in the industry is laid on the characteristics of its market status and the importance of the purchase compared with its all business activities. Pressures of buyers mainly include the following aspects:

- The degree of concentration of buyers.
- The proportion of the product in the buyer's product cost.
- The standardization degree of the product.
- Conversion cost.
- The earning power of buyers.
- Possibility of buyers' backward integration.
- The Influence degree of the industry's products to the quality of buyers' products.
- Information seized by buyers.
- Pressures of Suppliers

Suppliers may bargain with enterprise in certain industry about the price through threatening that increasing the price and reducing the quality of products or services. The exit of strong suppliers sometimes increase enterprises' purchasing costs and the enterprises have to cover the increasing cost via increasing the price of their products. The pressures of suppliers include the following aspects:

- The concentration degree of suppliers and the concentration degree of the industry.
- The substitution degree of the supply.

- The significance of the industry to providers.
- The significance of the supply to the industry.
- The supply's characteristics and the conversion cost of the supply.
- The possibility of provider's forward integration.
- The effect of the governmental power in industry competition

We have discussed governmental impact in the issue of Entering the Barrier ahead. In many industries, the government, purchasers or suppliers can affect the industry competition via the policy it adopted. For instance, governmental regulations can restrict the behavior of suppliers or purchasers. The government can also impact the status of the industry through regulations, subsidies, substitutes or the other measures. The government can also impact the competition among enterprises in the industry through impacting the growth of the industry, and the cost structure of the industry via related regulations. Consequently, how policies of governments at all levels now and in the future will impact the structural condition must be analyzed and judged while one processes the structure analysis. Meanwhile, when processing the strategy analysis, it is more instructive to think over how the government impact competition via five kinds of competition powers rather than to consider the government itself as a competition power.

3. Analyses on the key factors of a successful industry

The key factors of a successful industry refer to some specific factors which determine whether the industry is successful. These factors are distinguished in different industries.

The purpose of finding key factors of a successful industry is to concentrate all resources of the enterprise and devote them into these key factors to form the competition advantage and thus achieve the success on management.

Each industry has key factors for its success, and the enterprise could achieve its success easier in the competition, if it finds out these factors accurately and uses them skillfully. Therefore, finding out the key factors of a successful industry is the cross cut to the success of the enterprise.

There are two ways to find out the key factors of a successful industry:

(1) Comparison Method

The comparison method is to compare successful enterprises with failed enterprises in the same industry and analyze these differences and causes of the differences—they are just key factors of a successful industry. Since the successful enterprise, without saying, must have some outstanding aspects on the status and strength, and the disparity on these aspects between the winner and the looser is just the reason why the failed enterprise loses. Consequently, the disparity must be the key factor for being success. And thus a complete, delicate and serious analysis on these factors must be carried on to avoid the omission.

There are two clues for the analysis: the first one is to compare and analyze each link of the managing and producing activities of the enterprise, from raw material purchase, design, production, marketing to after-sale services and so on. The second one is to comparatively analyze each managing and producing element of the enterprise, namely, the capital, devices, technologies, managements, talents and so on, without omissions.

After the above mentioned comparison and analysis, find out the differences, then the enterprise could find out the key factors of a successful industry favorably.

(2) Methods of market analysis

The method of market analysis uses market segmentation principles to anatomize the entire market of the industry, finding the vital, strategically important market and product, progressing economic arguments, analyzing economic benefits, predicting required resources, as well as confirming products the enterprise plans to develop, the market the enterprise plans to occupy and measures the enterprise plans to adopt in competitions. This is also a rather effective way to find out key factors of a successful industry.

III. Finding Opportunities and Threats

After analyzing the circumstance, administrators need to evaluate the opportunities the enterprise can find out and use, and the threats the enterprise may possibly face.

Analyzing the starting point and foothold of the circumstance is to find out opportunities and to avoid threats. Then, are there opportunities in the circumstances on earth? Let us have a look at answers of several outstanding entrepreneurs first.

Chen Rongzhen, the president of Royalstar, says the following philosophical words with sharp insights: the sun is owned by all, but questions that everybody receives are various. The one, who accommodates itself well, is the one, who accepts more. To put it clearly, "there are only unmarketable products and no saturated markets."

Zhang Ruimin, the CEO of Qing Dao Haier Group, explains and deducts his innovative philosophy repeatedly: only the weak product, without the weak market; only the thought of a slack season, without the slack season of the market; small differences between products, big differences in market.

Besides, there are other warnings, such as "only non-profitable enterprises, no non-profitable business." "Opportunities can be caught by the well-prepared mind and the market is just inside."

Why we cannot see opportunities if there are plenty of them in the circumstances? It is because that we lack the thinking and the vision for finding opportunities. Just as what Zhang Ruimin says, "No thinking, no outlet; having thinking, having outlet." He suggests that Haier should have "three eyes": "The first eye is to look at staff within the enterprise for maximizing the satisfaction of them; the second eye is to look at the market outside the enterprise and consumers for maximizing the satisfaction of consumers; the third eye is to look for external opportunities." The situation that Haier gain many opportunities and successes is directly contributed by the leading thinking and the acuminous vision of Haier.

Opportunities exist in the circumstance and penetrate into every aspect. This is so-called "opportunities can be caught by the well-prepared mind and the market is just about."

In addition, what should be explained is that the same circumstance may bring opportunities to some enterprises, and threats to the others.

For example, the circumstance of tight money, reduced investment and economic depression is a prodigious threat to distressed enterprises, which are in bad management, heavy losses and close to bankruptcy; but to strong and big enterprises, which are in good management, it is a good opportunity to expand their market with a lower cost, and thus develop themselves stronger and bigger. Another example, the introduction of natural gas into Beijing provided a good development opportunity to chemical enterprises in Beijing. But it also brought a severe threat to the coal industry in Beijing.

186

It is obvious that, whether changes of the circumstance are opportunities or threats to an enterprise depend on resources the enterprise controlled. So resources controlled by the enterprise must be analyzed, after analyzed the circumstance.

IV.   Enterprise Resources Analysis

To analyze the resources of an enterprise one should examine the internal conditions of the enterprise. The major criteria used in this analysis are narrowed down to five points as follows:

(I) Analysis on components

The chief element of an enterprise is technology, which is the foundation of the enterprise. It includes the production technology and the management technology. Next is the resource. The most important resources are human resources and capital. Resources are the foundation of an enterprise. Enterprises can produce products with technology and resources. Products consist of the software, hardware, and services. Value is created after products are produced. However, the created value cannot be kept in stock in the warehouse and cannot be realized unless the product has been sold. So the element of marketing is required. The created value can only be realized by the selling of products through effective marketing. Then enterprises can gain an economic advantage. The essence of marketing is the distribution channel and its core is the end user.

Figure 6-6 Four Important Component Elements of an Enterprise

Technologies ──────▶	──────▶ Products
Production Technology Management Technology Resources ──────▶	Software and Hardware Service ──────▶ Markets
Human Resource Capital	End User Distribution Channel

(II) Analysis on the incremental processes of an enterprise

An enterprise is like a big box; at one end is the input and the other end is the output. The input includes: laborers, materials, technologies, and capital management. While the output includes: excellent products, the increase of profits and business, the satisfaction of users and staff (shown as in Figure 6-7). The input and output are different in material form and quantity of value, and the output quantity of value is greater than the input quantity of value. That is to say, the quantity of value of elements inputted is increased via processes of the enterprise, such as the processing, and manufacturing. The process of making the input quantity of value greater than the output quantity of value is called the increment process. It includes: research and development, production manufacturing, marketing, delivery and installation, and after-market service. At the same time, in order to make the incremental processes go smoothly, enterprises need some support processes such as personnel management, financial administration, administrative management, quality control and the information management (shown as in Figure 6-8).

Figure 6-7 Increment Process of an Enterprise

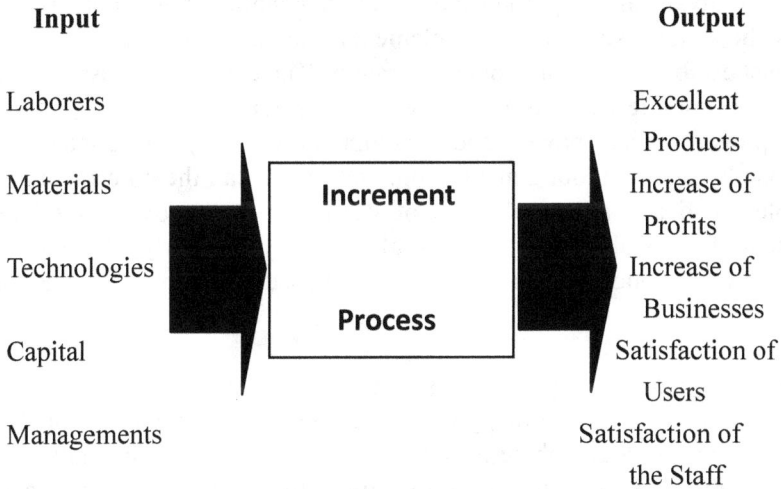

Input   **Output**

Laborers   Excellent
                                                        Products
Materials | **Increment** | Increase of
                       | | Profits
Technologies | | Increase of
                       | **Process** | Businesses
Capital | | Satisfaction of
                                                        Users
Managements   Satisfaction of
                                                        the Staff

Figure 6-8 Main Processes of an Enterprise

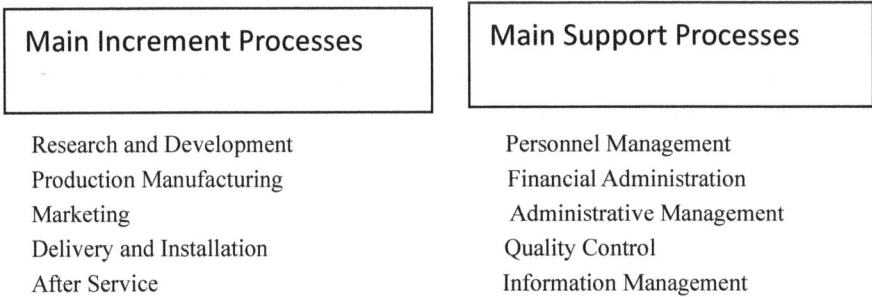

Main Increment Processes	**Main Support Processes**
Research and Development	Personnel Management
Production Manufacturing	Financial Administration
Marketing	Administrative Management
Delivery and Installation	Quality Control
After Service	Information Management

Different kinds of enterprises have different kinds of incremental processes. For example, the incremental process of an R&D enterprise is obviously different from that of the enterprise which specializes in production manufacturing or marketing. The purpose of analyzing the enterprise incremental process is to understand fully what kind of incremental process

189

the enterprise should have, and then set up the enterprise's strategy on the basis of the incremental process

(III) Analysis on comprehensive economic benefits of an enterprise
Besides the enterprise component elements and the increment processes, firms must establish the firms' overall strategy. The enterprise must evaluate the firms' economic benefits objectively. The enterprise must evaluate its earning power, service power, and development capacity and contribution ability one by one, without generalizing. Only then, can the enterprise have a complete and accurate evaluation of itself and thus provide a reliable foundation for establishing its overall strategy properly. Indexes of comprehensive economic benefits of an enterprise are shown as in Figure 6-9.

(IV) Analysis on competitive position of an enterprise
The core of the enterprise strategy is the strategic objective, and the premise of determining strategic objectives for an enterprise is to understand its position in the line of business at any given time. The main criteria for judging the competitive position of an enterprise are the sales volume and market share. The enterprise should pay more attention to its market share because it is a major sign of the enterprise strength.

(V) Analysis on comparative advantages of an enterprise
When competing with rivals, an enterprise will naturally have more chances to achieve its success if it has absolute advantages; and the enterprise should seek comparative advantages, if it does not have absolute advantages. The comparative advantage refers to the strength possessed by an enterprise in some aspects comparing with rivals.

Figure 6-9 Indexes of comprehensive economic benefits of an enterprise

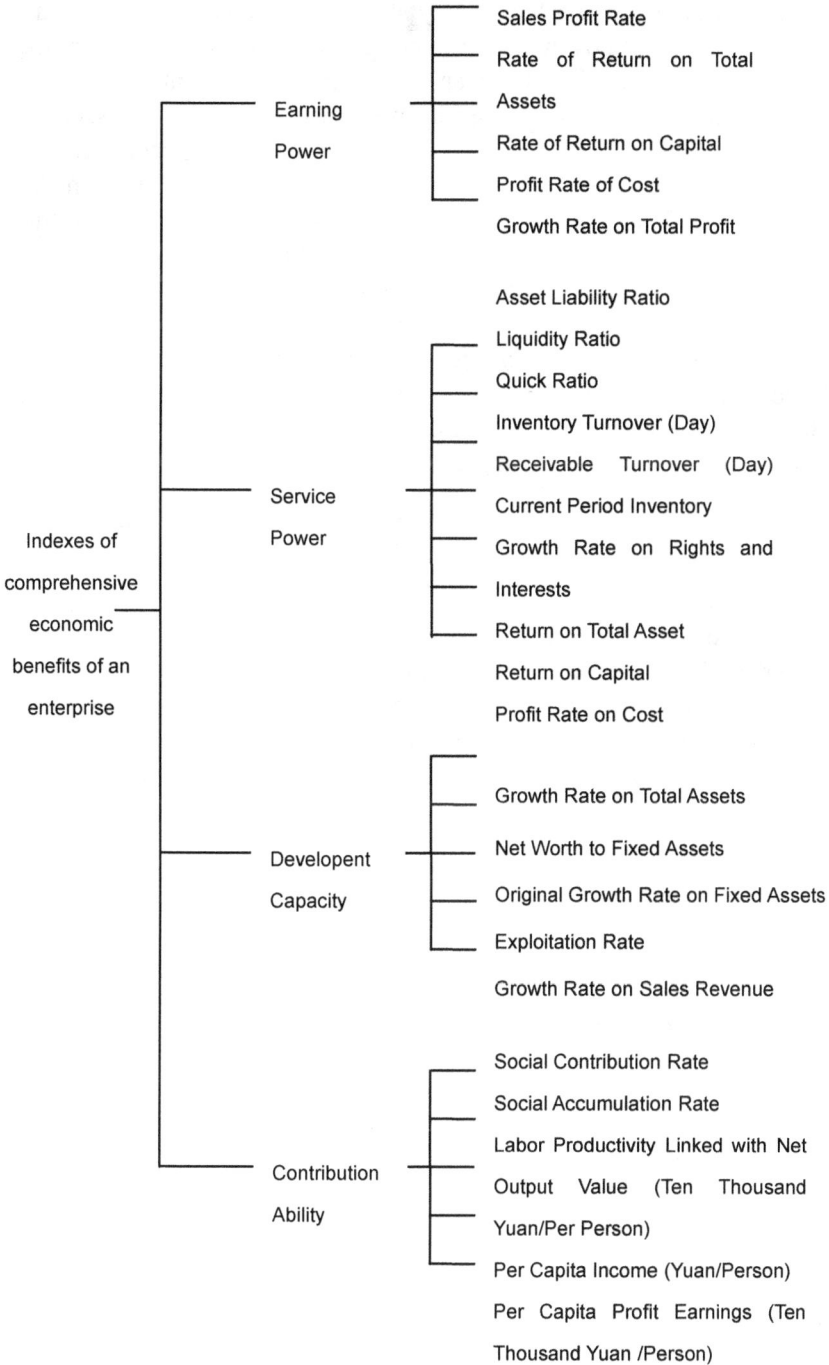

Indexes of comprehensive economic benefits of an enterprise

Earning Power
- Sales Profit Rate
- Rate of Return on Total Assets
- Rate of Return on Capital
- Profit Rate of Cost
- Growth Rate on Total Profit

Service Power
- Asset Liability Ratio
- Liquidity Ratio
- Quick Ratio
- Inventory Turnover (Day)
- Receivable Turnover (Day)
- Current Period Inventory
- Growth Rate on Rights and Interests
- Return on Total Asset
- Return on Capital
- Profit Rate on Cost

Developent Capacity
- Growth Rate on Total Assets
- Net Worth to Fixed Assets
- Original Growth Rate on Fixed Assets
- Exploitation Rate
- Growth Rate on Sales Revenue

Contribution Ability
- Social Contribution Rate
- Social Accumulation Rate
- Labor Productivity Linked with Net Output Value (Ten Thousand Yuan/Per Person)
- Per Capita Income (Yuan/Person)
- Per Capita Profit Earnings (Ten Thousand Yuan /Person)

For example, if the cost of an enterprise is lower than that of its rival, then it has the cost advantage; if its technology is more advanced than its rival, then it has the technical advantage. It is certainly fabulous if an enterprise has absolute advantages. However as a matter of fact, enterprises are usually unable to possess advantages in every aspect. Therefore, seeking comparative strengths the enterprise has in one or several aspects becomes the key factor for the enterprise to grasp successes in competition. In the horse race between Tianji and the King of Qi, the method that helped Tianji beating the King of Qi is that Tianji adopted comparative advantages or relative advantages, instead of absolute advantages.

Of course, the evaluation of the interior circumstance of an enterprise does not only contain the above five aspects. We can evaluate other aspects as well. But it is unnecessary to deal with analyses and evaluations redundantly or trivially, from the angle of the overall strategy.

V. Identify Strengths and Weaknesses

Through analyzing its resources, the enterprise should be able to identify its strengths and weaknesses, affirm its competencies which differ from those of other enterprises, and carry it's competence out in its strategy. The purpose of analyzing the resources of an enterprise is to make the enterprise be able to develop its strengths and overcome its weaknesses. When establishing its strategy, besides making use of the opportunities the circumstance provided fully, the enterprise must make use of its advantages and bypass its disadvantages ---- the strategy, which bands opportunities in

the circumstance and the strengths of the enterprise together, is an effective strategy.

What needs to be emphasized here is that, when establishing the strategy, the strengths should be affirmed, but the enterprise should never avoid or cover up its weaknesses. The attitude of "reporting the good news but not the bad" is not only wrong, but also dangerous when the enterprise establishes its strategy.

VI. Reevaluating the Objective and Purpose of an Enterprise

It will lead to the revaluation of the enterprise opportunities if combining Step Three and Step Five together. This is usually called SWOT analysis (shown as in Figure 6-10). SWOT is the abbreviation of English words which combines strengths, weaknesses, opportunities and threats together for analyzing them synthetically. By doing so, the enterprise can revalue its objective and purpose, and confirm its appropriate orientation, namely, confirm the management direction of the enterprise and constitute the strategy of the enterprise.

Figure 6-10 SWOT Analysis

Interior Conditions of the Enterprise	Exterior Circumstances of the Enterprise
Strengths 1. Advanced Technology 2. Good Quality Control 3. High-quality Employees 4.Good Administrative Foundation	Opportunities 1. Possibility to be exported 2. Price Fall on Raw Materials
Weaknesses 1. Capital Scarcity 2. Ageing Equipment 3. Small Enterprise Scale	Threats 1. Increase of Rivals 2. Credit Squeeze

According to the requisite of SWOT for analyzing and recognizing enterprise opportunities, administrators need to reconfirm the objective and purpose of the enterprise: Are they in accordance with the reality? DO they need to be modified? Establishing the process of strategy needs to be started at the beginning if the management direction of the enterprise needs to be changed and the objective of the enterprise needs to be modified. Administrators should embark on establishing the strategy if the main direction of the enterprise does not need to be changed.

At this time, one task should be done; confirming the firm's orientation—the management direction of the enterprise. Then select the managerial principles? At the conclusion of the above mentioned statements, eight principles can be generalized:

Making market orientation the first choice and combining the market orientation with the resources orientation.

Acting in accordance with long-term development programs, industrial policies, technology policies, environmental policies and so on, issued by the state government or local governments.

- Life cycle of the business
- Coefficient of resilience of products revenue of the business is bigger than "one"
- Degree of association of the business
- Characteristics of the business (entry barriers and exit barriers, degree of concentration, key factors to success)
- Strengths and weaknesses of the enterprise
- Interest and preference of the enterprise leaders

In the light of the above principles, the management direction of the enterprise can be confirmed. And the next step is to establish the strategy.

VII.   Establishing the Strategy

To establish the strategy, is to establish the strategic plan. As the overall strategy of an enterprise, the procedures for the formulation of the strategic planning are as follows:

(I) Establishing the appropriate business portfolio
To "establish the appropriate business portfolio" is to carry the management

194

direction of the company into each actual business of the company, and drive for a comparative ideal combination among these businesses. The enterprise overall strategy i.e. the corporate strategy, is the highest level strategy of the enterprise. A sizeable enterprise, especially a mega enterprise, sometimes manages not only one business, but several, a dozen or dozens of and even more. Facing various items of businesses, enterprises cry for the information that: businesses can keep up appearances of the enterprise but provide positive economic returns. What businesses can earn money though they are unattractive, what businesses should the company persist in all the way, and what businesses should be given up. At the same time, enterprises also need to pay attention to new businesses opportunities which develop in the marketplace. In a word, the strategic planning of an enterprise must finally prove its usefulness in products and the market development.

During the time of planned economy, the launch and withdrawal of projects of the state-owned enterprises are mostly decided by government instructions and leaders' hotheaded thoughts and so on. However, under the condition of market economy, enterprises must make decisions by themselves and take responsibility for its success or failure. So, it is obviously necessary to analyze business portfolio in a scientific way. In this aspect, Boston Matrix--- a portfolio analysis method which is provided by Boston Consulting Group (BCG) to a paper making company in the consultation in 1960 is a scientific and effective method comparatively.

1. Basic principles

Boston Matrix is also called Four-quadrant analysis, configuration management of product line and so on. This method analyzes all the products or the business portfolio the enterprise produced and operated as a whole. It is often used to analyze the issue of the balance of the cash flow among related operations of the enterprise. Through this method, the enterprise can discover the origin of the enterprise resources and find out its units which can optimize these resources.

2. Matrix Illustration

In Figure 6-11, the horizontal axis of the matrix represents the relative market share of the enterprise in the trade. It is the ratio of market share between a certain business of the enterprise and its strongest rival in market. The division of the relative market share is 20%, marking off two areas: the higher one and the lower one. A business or product, which has more relative market share, shows that it is in a strong competitive position, and keeps ahead in the market; inversely, it is in a weak competitive capacity and in a subordinate position in the market.

Figure 6-11 Boston Matrix

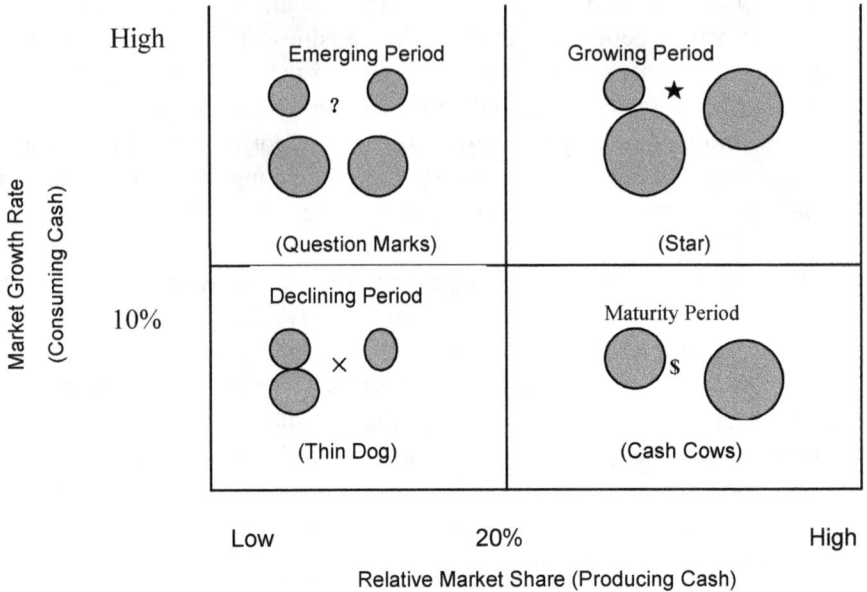

The vertical axis represents the market growth rate which is the ratio of the increase on the sales volume of some business in the trade the enterprise engaged in before-and-after two years. This growth rate demonstrates the relative market attractiveness of each business. In the analysis, average growth rate of 10% is usually used as the division for the high rate of increase and the low rate of increase: the business with an average growth rate over10% in the last two years is the high-growth business and the business with an average growth rate under 10% in the last two years is the low-growth business.

In the Figure, the cross point of vertical and horizontal coordinates represents one business or product of the enterprise. And the area of the circle represents the ratio between the income of the business or product and overall income of the enterprise.

3. Analytical methods

According to the market growth rate of the related business or product in the trade and the relative market share standards of the enterprise, Boston Matrix can locate the overall businesses of enterprises into four regions. They are as follows

(1) Question Marks are businesses, with a high growth rate and in a weak competitive position. This kind of business is usually in the worst state of cash flow. On the one hand, the market growth rate in its trade is high and enterprises need plentiful investment to support its producing and operating activities; on the other hand, the position of its relative market share is low and thus produces few capital. Therefore, towards the further investment on the Question Marks, enterprises need to deal with issues such as analyzing the business, and thus estimating the quantity of investment to be transferred to Stars, analyzing its future profits and studying whether it is worthy to be invested on and so on.

(2) Stars are businesses which have high growth rates and are in a strong competitive position. Stars have a long term opportunity in development and profit making among all businesses of the enterprise; however, they are the main consumers of enterprise resources and need large amount of investments. In order to protect or extend the leading position of Stars in the growing market, enterprises should provide the resources they need primarily in a short term for driving them to develop continuously.

(3) Cash Cows are businesses which have low growth rates and are in strong competitive positions. This kind of business is in a mature market which grows in a low rate. The business has a positive position in market and a high rate of return, and does not need to be invested; instead, it provides plentiful capital to the enterprise which can be used to support other businesses.

(4) "Thin Dogs" are businesses which have low growth rates and are in a weak competitive position. This kind of business exists in a saturated market where competition is severe and only low profits can be gained. So this kind of business cannot become the source of the enterprise capital. If this kind of business still can maintain by itself, its scope of business should be reduced and its interior management should be strengthened. If the business has already failed completely, enterprises should take steps as soon as possible to settle the affairs of the enterprise or to withdraw from the

business.

4. Revelation of Boston Matrix

The purpose of Boston Matrix analysis is to help enterprises confirm their overall strategies. It makes two important contributions to the selection of enterprises' overall strategies:

(1) The matrix points out the status of each business in competition, thus the enterprise can understand its function or task, and use the preferential assets selectively and intently.

For example, the enterprise should consider "Cash Cows" as an important source of assets, and place it in preferential position. Similarly, the enterprise can also concentrate assets on promising "Stars" or "Question Marks", and give up "Thin Dogs" and hopeless "Question Marks" selectively as the circumstances may require. If the enterprise does not distinguish its businesses, and adopts a sweeping approach, stipulating the same purpose, distributing assets by the same proportion, and equipping machines and staffs averagely, consequently, the "Cash Cows " and "Thin Dogs" are usually invested overfull assets; while "Stars" and "Question Marks" are invested inadequately. And as a result, it is very difficult for the enterprise to develop itself lastingly.

(2) Boston Matrix, collecting different businesses of the enterprise into one matrix, is brief and clear.

On the premise of the other strategies being unchanged, an enterprise can judge its opportunity and threat, strength and weakness, and find out the major strategic problem it is facing currently and the enterprise's status in the future competition through Boston Matrix. Comparatively, the perfect investment combination is that the enterprise has more "Stars" and "Cash Cows", less "Question Marks" and very few "Thin Dogs."

(II) Determining strategic business units
The so called strategic business units refer to units that are in charge of constituting and implementing strategies under corporate-level. One of essentials of constituting the strategic planning is "how many and what kind of strategic institutions should be an enterprise divided into." So partition of strategic business units is a major issue that should be solved by the strategic planning.

Generally, a strategic business unit should possess features as follows:

- It is an integration of one or several related businesses.
- It has a clear definition of the business.
- It has its own competitors.
- It has a special manager.
- It is composed of one or more planning units or functional units.
- It can benefit from strategic plans.
- It can be independent of other institutions.

Determining strategic business units is to put each business managed by the corporate-level into effect according to the requirement of the strategy. After determining strategic business units, there is a need to study and decide the type of the strategy.

(III) Studying and Determining the Strategy Type

There are four types of enterprise overall strategies, shown as in Figure 6-12:

Figure 6-12 Enterprise Overall Strategy

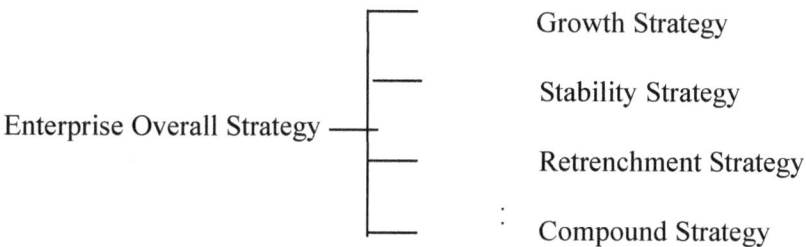

Enterprise Overall Strategy
- Growth Strategy
- Stability Strategy
- Retrenchment Strategy
- Compound Strategy

Then as to an enterprise, how should it choose its strategy type?

Generally, it can adopt SWOT strategy option Figure (as shown in Figure 6-13) for its selection.

Figure 6-13 SWOT Strategy Option

Opportunities

From Stability   Growth Strategy
To Growth

Retrenchment Strategy   Strategy of Diversification

Threats

The enterprise can judge which type of strategy it should adopt according to SWOT analysis. The enterprise, which has mighty internal superiority and plenty of environmental opportunities, belongs to Type I, and it is a good choice to adopt Growth Strategy, such as developing market, increasing output, and so on. The enterprise of Type II has opportunities outside, but its internal condition is not so good. It should adopt Torsion Strategy, i.e. turning stability to growth in order to change its internal superiority. The enterprise of Type III, which has threats outside, and bad internal conditions, should try to avoid threats, eliminate weaknesses and adopt Retrenchment Strategy. The enterprise of Type IV, which has both internal superiorities and outside threats, should make use of its strength to develop diversified businesses, disperse risks, seek new opportunities and adopt the Strategy of Diversification.

For some enterprises, with a large scale and having various operations, it is very hard to judge its strategy type intuitively, then SWOT matrix analysis Figure can be adopt as an reference. Germen Volkswagen supplies a good example for how to apply SWOT matrix analysis Figure, shown as in Figure 6-14.

(IV) Selecting the mode of strategy constitution
Constituting and selecting a management strategy for an enterprise is the primary duty of the top executive level of the enterprise. Currently, common methods of constituting strategy are as follows:

Figure 6-14 Example of German Volkswagen applying SWOT matrix analysis method

Internal Factors of the Enterprise　　External Factors of the Enterprise	Internal Strength (S)　　1.Strong ability on study and development, and high level in technology　　2.Owning the net of global sales and services　　3.High production efficiency in automatization	Internal Weakness(W)　　1.Non-diversified products　　2.High production cost in Germany and loss incurred in enterprises　　3.Lacking experience of making contact with American company unions
Opportunity Outside(O)　　1. Increasing demands for limousines　　2. The condition to build auto assembly plants in America is mature　　3. Chrysler and American Motors Corporation demand plenty of small engines.	Strength + Opportunity (SO)　　1. Developing and producing multilevel sedans (according to S1, S2, and O2)　　2. Building auto assembly plants in America (according to S1, S3, and O2)　　3. Developing and producing small engines (according to S3 and O3)	Weakness + Opportunity (WO)　　1. Producing many car models of different prices (according to W1 and O1)　　2. Employing experienced American staffs (according to W2, W3, and O2)
Threats Outside (T)　　1. US Dollar is devaluated compared with Mark.　　2. Competitions from American and Japanese carmakers are fiercer.　　3. Fuel is lack and its price is high	Superiority + Threat (ST)　　1. Building factories can offset impacts of the exchange rate (according to S1, S3, T1, and T2).　　2. Produce Rabbit cars to oppose American cars and Japanese cars (according to S1, S2, T1, and T2).　　3. Developing oil saved diesel engines (according to S1 and T3)	Weakness + Threat(WT)　　1. Diversification of products (according to W1 and T2)　　2. Cooperating with Chrysler or American Motors Corporation in the way of joint venture(according to W2, W3, T1, and T2)

1. The executive level decides the direction of the strategy and the strategy will be constituted from top to bottom progressively.

Generally, the high level administrative supervisors of enterprises discuss the strategy and appoint the secretary or related professionals to draft the overall strategy of the enterprise and then administrative supervisors of each level constitute the strategy progressively on the basis of their own practical situations and requirements of business opportunities. The advantage of this mode is that the administrative level puts a high value on the strategy, and has time to concentrate its energy on thinking about the direction of the strategy.

2. The leader level establishes the business unit for constituting strategic projects

The planning department of the enterprise or "Enterprise's Tiptop Staff Department" of the enterprise, which has certain authority on business, and has the right to balance each business unit, takes charge of constituting the strategy. The advantage of this mode is that it has a professional business team, which is familiar with its enterprise's situation and understands intentions of leaders.

3. Strategic business units will be the core for constituting the strategy

When using this method, the high administrative level does not give any advice to each strategic business unit at first, but requires them to submit their strategic plans. The high administrative level only examines, balances, and replies to the plans. The advantage of this method is that each strategic business unit is constrained slightly, and can constitute a practical strategic plan, on the basis of features of its own field and in favor of competition.

4. Mandating the organization with some advantages to constitute

The mandated organization should be an authoritative consulting firm or planning department outside the enterprise, which can bear legal liability,

keep secrets of the enterprise, and submit more than one selective strategic project to the enterprise's leaders.

5. Cooperating with consulting firms

The cooperation can offset the weakness of the above mentioned method and learn strong points to offset its weakness. Whether organizing and cooperating well or not determines the success of the method.

(V) Compiling strategic planning

The final result of constituting a strategy is to compile a strategic planning. Then, what is strategic planning? Henry Mintzberg, a well-known Canadian strategic management expert, indicates, strategy planning, as in the practice, is actually strategy designing, i.e. those existed explanations and particular descriptions of strategy or strategic vision. (2)

The overall strategy of an enterprise usually includes the following parts:

- Strategic positioning and business objectives
- Strategic Environmental Analysis;
- Assessment of business conditions;
  Guiding ideology of the strategy
- Enterprise's mission and strategic purpose
- Strategic emphasis
- Strategic phase
- Strategic measures

In addition, besides the text, there usually should be some attachments in strategic planning. Contents of attachments are determined completely by the enterprise on the basis of its practical needs. But generally, the following attachments are necessary:

1. Feasibility demonstration reports of major projects for deciding the investments in the strategic planning;
2. The concrete implementation program of major projects which are to be put in force right away in the strategic planning;
3. The suggestion or plan about the enterprise resource allocation corresponded with the requirement of the strategic plan.

(VI) Improving strategy system

The enterprise's strategy is a complete system. After the constitution of the overall strategy, the enterprise has still to constitute its business-level strategy and functional-level strategy. Only through these constitutions, the overall strategy can be assured to implement.

After the strategic planning is written, related experts will proof it, and then the board of directors or the enterprise decision-making level will examine and approve it. After all these are done, the strategic plan will be promulgated and implemented.

VIII. Measures for Strategic Planning

- Great importance should be attached in mind.
- Agenda should be made in plan
- Implementation should be ensured in company
- Funds should be guaranteed
- Guidance should be invited
- Innovation should be made actively
- Opinion should be exchanged fully
- Decisions should be made decisively

Liu Chuanzhi, chairman of Lenovo Group has made a good points that "The so-called formulation and implementation of strategies and tactics can be interpreted into a more simple way. That is, first to determine the long-term goals; Second to divide their achievements into several stages; Third to find out the most recent goal; Fourth to choose a road to get there; fifth to consider whether or not to adjust the goal."

Case Study

Eleventh-Five Year Overall Strategic Plan of Beiren Group Corporation (2006—2010)

Since the implementation of Tenth Five Year plan, under the guidance of scientific development concept, Beiren Group Corporation (use Beiren hereinafter for short) tries to be market-oriented, to pursue independent innovation and development, and to make fully use of its brand advantages. Its product chain has expanded from offset to pre-press and post-press areas, as well as related products. Its core competitiveness and benefits are growing rapidly. Compared with 2000, in 2005, industrial output value (current prices) increases by 1.28 times, with an average annual growth rate of 17.94%; sales revenue increases by 0.9 times, with an average annual growth rate of 13.72%; profit grows by 1.43 times, with an average annual growth rate of 19.42%. It also continues to maintain a leading position in domestic printer industry.

"Eleventh Five-Year Overall Strategic Plan is especially made in order to make full use of brand advantage and overall advantages of internal and external resources to further improve core competitiveness. Besides, it is designed to maintain its leading position in the printer industry and create international brand and to make more contributions to economy and national industry.

(I) Strategic Positioning

Consider printing machinery manufacturing as main business and develop downstream products in a positive and steady way. In particular, it includes:

1. Group Corporation (Headquarter)

Group Corporation will do the following but not limited to these. Focus on developing diverse, high-end automatic printing equipment. Introduce strategic investors to achieve investment diversification. Develop post-press finishing products following the international development trend. Emphasis to the development of new, high-end, international level post press finishing and packaging products. Moreover, develop and produce CTP and digital inkjet. Apply computer control technology to printing in order to address automation and intelligence issues of post press finishing equipment. Integrate the whole process of printing production at one digital and network platforms (CTP Technology includes the three concepts, namely, computer to paper, computer to plate and computer to press). Developed countries have successively developed mass products based on CTP techniques, including direct CTP plate setter, direct proofer, digital presses, and inkjet printers.

2. Stock Company

Make effort to take use of brand advantages, to develop new printing technology and new products, as well as to focus on production of high-end multi-color sheet-fed offset press and roll offset products. Moreover, it should improve independent intellectual property of products and core competitiveness of the enterprise.

(II) Objectives of Beiren

Continue to create the perfect printing equipment, provide the global users with the best service, strive to disseminate human culture, make the landscaping and colorful world better, and improve the quality and standard of living of human beings

Main points of the objectives are as following:

1. Beiren's value-added activities: continue to create, which means that:

A. Beiren is engaging in creative activities, such as research, design, development, manufacturing, sales, and service of printing equipment.
B. This kind of creative activities last a long time in a continuous way but a short term. It requires "keeping making progress and innovation."

2. Beiren's industry or product: perfect printing equipment, which means that:

A. Beiren is engaging in the printing equipment industry. So it provides printing equipment other than specific printing equipment products.
B. Beiren seeks to provide perfect but general printing equipment.

3. Beiren's customers or markets: global user or market, and it means:

Beiren aims not only to develop in the domestic market, but also to explore in the international market in order to create international famous brand.

4. Beiren's contributions: Continue to create the perfect printing equipment, provide the global users with the best service, strive to disseminate human culture, make the landscaping and colorful world better, and improve the quality and standard of living of human beings, which means:

(1) Direct contributions: provide users in the global printing industry with the best services, including both the best hardware and software services.
(2) Indirect contributions: strive to disseminate human culture, make the landscaping and colorful world better, and improve the quality and standard of living of human beings.

II.   Strategic Environmental Analysis of the Company

(I) Status and trends of the global printing machinery industry

1. Market Status and Trends

The printing industry is one of the world's largest manufacturing industries. However, its development in western countries is stagnant and declining, while rapid in developing countries, especially China. Therefore, many of the world press manufacturers are coming to the Chinese market.

The world printing machinery manufacturers are mainly distributed in Germany, Japan, the United States, Britain, France, Switzerland, and India, so are main printing machinery brands, such as Germany's Heidelberg and MAN Roland, the United States' Gaussian, Japan's Komori, Mitsubishi, Hamada, and Rota UK, France's MEGTEC, Switzerland's Martini and Bobst, and India's East. Most of the products are exported except for meeting the domestic market demands. Meanwhile, they are also large consumption countries of printing machinery and equipment, whose import volumes are huge.

In recent years, due to the saturated, slowing economic growth in the printing machinery market in Western developed countries; foreign manufacturers begin to set up wholly owned enterprises and joint ventures to develop the Chinese market. Scale of the imported equipment is also increasing, which reaches 60% of the market share in China.

These enterprises continuously grow in size through assets merger and restructure. Leading world-class printing enterprises, represented by Heidelberg, adjust development strategies by transferring focus to the manufacture of sheet-fed offset press to pursuing professional development in depth. Meanwhile, major companies like the U.S. HP, Gaussian, Kodak are expanding their business scales and product areas by through acquisitions, mergers and other ways. Thus the global printing market is still growing steadily. According to forecast of Rochester Institute of Technology, this growth trend will continue till 2040-2050 year.

2. Technical status and trends

In printing technology, high-techs such as flexo, color inkjet, digital, network and information have a profound impact on the traditional printing industry. They have become the hot field of printing technology, developing rapidly.

However, the offset printing process technology is still the mainstream, and will not change in the next decade, although its may turns slower. At the same time, new technology revolution based on digital, network and information technology will increase rapidly, becoming a new growth in area of short vision and personalized printing. However, from the perspective of a

larger filed of printing, printing technology is shifting from analog to digital technology, which will last in parallel for a long time.

The main current trends of printing technology in the world are:

(1) Integration of printing production process, management process and sales process, forming a digital chemical process;
(2) Popularization pace of CTP plate setter is accelerating;
(3) Color management system gains more and more attention;
(4) Rapid development and applications of digital quick printing;
(5) Automation level of offset Printing is increasing;
(6) Huge development potential of ink jet technology;
(7) Improvement of supporting equipment such as post press finishing equipment;
(8) Conditions of printing environmental protection are taken more seriously.

3. Competitive situations and trends

Printing machinery market is a global market with trends of growth. In recent years, manufacturers are rapidly engaging in the printer industry, especially Chinese companies, with rise fast in the printer industry. However, compared with high technology products with international competitiveness, these of Chinese companies are lack of independent intellectual property rights. Moreover, Chinese companies cannot match these in Germany, Japan, and the United States in term of manufacturing strength. Nevertheless, through active joint venture, technology transfer, self-development, innovation, etc., Beiren has had impact on international brands with increasing influence.

4. Regional market conditions and trends

From a global perspective, the printing press market development can be divided into two regions. There are two trends of them:

First, in developed countries such as the United States, Europe and Japan, the printer industry faces a recession, becoming a "sunset industry. " Therefore, the printer industry is declining in those countries, reflected by slow development, fewer sales and profits, downsizing and other business development difficulties.

Second, in developing countries like Russia, China, India, Vietnam, Indonesia, Egypt and Brazil, especially China, it has just entered the development period as a "sunrise industry." There are strong demands for printing machinery, great potential printing markets and continuous growing trends. Therefore, the world's leading manufacturers of printing machinery generally feel optimistic about the Chinese market.

(II) Statuses and trends of the domestic printing machinery industry

1. Market statuses and development trends

In the world's printing industry, China is the market with fastest growth, best prospects and greatest potential. Large number of domestic printing enterprises helps to form three printing industrial bases, that is, the Pearl River Delta, Yangtze River Delta and Bohai Economic Zone.

In the next five years, the printing industry will continue to maintain a rapid growth rate, of which packaging and printing will grow most rapidly. Meanwhile, the development imbalances still exist, including differences between various markets all over the country.

In 2010, China aims to build the world's major printing base. total output value of the printing industry is expected to reach 400 to 450 billion RMB Yuan, accounting for 2.5% of GDP, with an average annual growth rate of up to about 8%. it fits for needs of national economic development and people's material and cultural life improvement .

2. Level and trend of industrial growth

In recent years, the Chinese printing industry grows at a rate of more than

10% annual growth, which is 2-4 % of that of economic development. It is predicted that the average annual growth rate of China's printing industry in 2010 will be around 9%, of which, that of packaging and printing is 13%, of newspaper printing is around 12%, and of books printing is about 5% -7%.

To measure a country's pace of the printing industry development, the production and consumption of paper and paperboard is an important indicator. At present, that of China ranks second in the world after the United States, and is growing at a high speed. However, per capita paper consumption is still less than that of developed countries.

Chinese printing machinery industry association studies 56 key domestic printing machinery enterprises on their completion of main indicators. According to the statistics it gets, printing machinery market is still growing.

3. Amount and function of printing firms

According to statistics of Printing Industry Association, there are around 106 thousand printing companies in 2005 in China. It includes 6 thousand or about publication companies, with an increase rate of about 3%, 39 thousand packaging printing enterprises, with about 10% of annual growth, round 57 thousand enterprises of other matters with an annual growth of about 3%, and 4000 specific products printing companies with an increase of about 3%. There are a total of 164 domestic professional manufacturers of printing presses, and 600 or so non-professional manufacturers.

Total industrial output value in 2004 is 258 billion RMB Yuan, accounting for more than 2% of GDP. By 2005, there co-exist printing enterprises of all sizes and grades. In the printing industry, different products can be found in terms of target customers, products quality, products features and so on.

4. Levels and gap of product technology

Driven by the rapid development of the printing industry in recent years, the domestic printing machinery industry is in rapid growth with continuous improvement of manufacturing levels. Among them, folio multi-color offset press N300 of the Beiren Printing Machinery Co., Ltd represents the highest level of domestic multi-color offset press. Of course there are others that stand for the current high level of domestic manufacturing printing presses. For instance, BT Series Multi-color offset press produced by Shanghai

Guanghua Printing Machinery with Japan Akiyama technology, commercial web offset press M300 of Beiren, SSC web offset press produced by Shanghai Goss Graphic Systems with imported U.S. Technology, etc..

However, the domestic high-end products market is still almost occupied imported equipment, accounting for almost 2 / 3. According to information provided by Customs, the annual growth rate of imports of printing equipment is about 12%.

5.   Statuses and trends of post press finishing equipment

In the face of the rapidly growing market of post press finishing equipment, traditional ways of manual folding, binding cannot meet the needs for competition in China. Meanwhile, high-end printing equipment is relied mainly on imports, such as bookbinding flow-line production, folding machines, saddle stitching, paper cutter, and hot stamping machine. But due to the high prices, general printing factories are facing financial pressure. Middle and low grade post press finishing equipment cannot fulfill the quality demands of users although they are produced in China. This situation indicates that in the "Eleventh Five-Year" period, post press finishing products with high performance cost ratio will be in hare demand in the domestic market.

It is also because of seeing the huge demands in Chinese post press finishing printing market that the world's well-known printer companies, such as Heidelberg, MBO, Muller Martini have invested in China and build factories. As for the international market, post press finishing product market is also a large one. In various large printing presses fairs, post press finishing products by no means take account of less than 1/5 of the total area, showing its large export potential.

In the past decade, China imports many machines such as high-end newspaper printing presses, commercial web and books printers, as well as sheet-fed offset press with a speed of 16 thousand sheets per hour. At the same time, imports of CTP also increase to more than 500 sets in 2005 from less than 100 in 2002. Its application in large printing companies with strength make printing materials with features of short fast, personalized, low-cost become a new economic growth point. Moreover, State Press and Publication Administration make some requirements on quality and safety control, prompting the rapid development of post press finishing printers. All these form the peak of the third time printing transformation in China.

(III) Development policies and objectives of the printing machinery manufacturing industry

1. Development policy

China's printing machine manufacturing industry is the basis for the development of printing industry. Its future development can be summarized as follows:

Digital and networking pre-press;

Multi-color and high efficiency of printing;

Diverse and automation of post press finishing;

High-quality and serialization of equipment.

2. Development goals

According to development plan of the printing machinery manufacturing industry, development goals by 2010 are:

(1) Focus on the development of the sheet fed offset press is multi-color offset press. Products of key enterprises in the industry should be close to or reach the international
advanced level. Besides, quarto multi-color offset printing press and digital press should be developed according to the market demand.

(2) Focus on the development of web offset press is newspaper color web offset press as well as middle and high grade commercial web offset press. Main objectives are: to develop different types of folio newspaper color web offset press of single 60 thousand per hour, and to make to the middle and high grade commercial web offset press approach or reach the international advanced level.

(3) Other printing presses
- Focus on the development of flexo printing press is narrow machine set flexo printing press.
- Focus on the development of gravure printing machine is middle and high grade multi-color gravure printing machine;

(4) To apply a variety of techniques and equipment to improve the quality of post press finishing products, to develop large-format, high speed,

multi-functional and fully automated post press finishing equipment and to enable post press finishing products to become diversify.

(IV) Advantages and disadvantages of major competitive teammates in the industry

1. Advantages and disadvantages of international competitive teammates

There are both outstanding advantages and distinct disadvantages.

(1) Main advantages: large scale, long history, large amount of capital, high level of technology, brand recognition and high reputation, extensive sales network, sound and fast service system and so on. For example, Heidelberg, Germany, is the world's largest supplier of sheet-fed printing press. Its acquisition of the U.S. Harris fills the supply gap of web press equipment; its acquisition of Jie Lasi makes it become one of suppliers of flexible printing machine. Besides, it also acquires cutter manufacturers, binding machine manufacturers, folding machine manufacturing enterprises. Moreover, it cooperates with Kodak and Creo to launch multiple output machine, CTP and digital presses, thus becoming able to provide super provider of variety of printing solutions. Its sales in Chinese printing industry have been growing, with an average annual increase of 12%.

2. Advantages and disadvantages of domestic teammates

Domestic teammates among professional manufacturers of printing press mainly concentrate in coastal areas including Shanghai, Jiangsu teammates, Zhejiang, Shandong and so on.

(1) Main Advantages: These teammates are foreign joint venture enterprises or private enterprises, with convenience to raise funds, flexible operation mechanisms, high level of technology, product variety, higher quality, higher exports, less burden on enterprises and rapid growth in profits, and so on. For example, Shanghai Electric Group Printing and Packaging Machinery Co., Ltd. and its affiliated enterprises have four advantages: first is its advantage of raising capital as listed companies; second is flexible mechanism as joint venture companies; third is export-oriented economy mode and large exports; fourth is full range of products.

III.　Future development opportunities and potential risks of the company

(I) Development opportunities

1. In the 21st century, with the rapid development of electronic, network and digital technology, traditional printing machinery manufacturing industry is facing new challenges. With the sustained rapid growth of China's socialist market economy and comprehensive national strength, development of printing industries, such as news publishing industry, book publishing, advertising and decoration industry, packaging industry, trademark, office printing, forms and ticket industry are promoted. As the increasing of market demand for the printing industry and continuously expanding of printing fields, the demand for printing machinery and equipment is growing fast.

For a long time afterwards, China is the world's most economically dynamic region. With large potential market demands, China's printing industry shows a growing trend, attracting the world's leading manufacturers of printing machinery. China's rapid development of economy, culture and education will inevitably drive the fast development of the printing presses manufacturing industry. As the leading printing press manufacturing company, Beiren faces more opportunities for development.

2. in the United States, Europe and Japan and other developed countries, the printing presses manufacturing industry comes to its recession through the infancy, growth, maturity of its development, becoming a "sunset industry. " However, in China, it is still in a growth stage as a "sunrise industry" with limitless future. As the leading printing press manufacturing company, Beiren will certainly get more opportunities than the others.

3. China has established a national development strategy of building an innovative country. The main indicator of innovation-oriented country is to have a large number of world-class science and technology and world-renowned brands. Therefore, China is now vigorously promoting enterprises to make independent innovations, to create national brands. Besides, it gradually introduces a number of preferential policies to support national brands. As the only national brand in the printing press industry, Beiren offset naturally enjoy the preferential policy support, which is bound to bring better opportunities.

4. Beijing treats high-tech industries as its pillar industries. Printing

machineries widely use technologies of computer equipment, numerical control, fiber optic, laser and other contemporary advanced technology. A series of integration of high-techs enable them to be high-tech products. It not only is consistent with the development principles of Beijing, but also brings new economic growth points for expanding the city's information industry chain. Therefore, it will certainly gains strong support of the Beijing municipal government, which also brings development opportunities to Beiren.

5. Positioning of Beiren's leading products is applicable middle and high grade. It meets needs of almost every market in developing countries. Especially in South-Eastern Europe, Asia, Africa and Latin America, there are huge potential markets, which provides tremendous market opportunity for exports of Beiren's products

6. Duty-free policy for foreign companies on the import of high-end printing products has been discontinued which greatly weakens the competitiveness of imported products. It stimulates Beiren to research and develop high-end products with independent intellectual property rights, to catch up with international strong opponents, and to create a world famous brand.

(II) Potential risks

1. International large-scale printer giants enter the Chinese market

The world's leading manufacturers of printing machinery generally feel optimistic about the Chinese market due to its potential demands and growth trends. They do much such as to improve competitiveness, to integrate prepress and post press manufactures and to expand business scales. They become supper suppliers of a variety of printing solutions. Following them, a large number of companies jointly enter China to enlarge their sales, which also forms a tremendous threat to Beiren.

2. Strong followers in domestic printer industry are trying to catch up Beiren

There are about 700 to 800 professional and non-specialized press manufacturers in China. They are struggling to catch up on Beiren in their own respective areas of strength.
It passes Beiren enormous pressure.

3. Potential intruders will reach the printer market at any time

There is huge surplus of capital in international and domestic capital markets. This kind of capital can be invested in any potential profitable market. As a "sunrise industry", there is still a huge potential market capacity, so are attractive investment returns. Therefore, the huge social hot money may be used in the printer market at any time. Formation of new invaders is a huge threat to the Beiren.

4. Product replacement cycles are getting shorter for increasing update of new technologies and new products

High-end printing machinery products, especially the CTP products are co-developed by the world's largest companies through industrialization of recapitalized and horizontal joint approach. It makes these high-tech products in a monopoly position. China is still in infancy of its development period, but with the cultivation and development of high-tech products market, China will face the second peak of imports. This serious situation is also a great threat to Beiren.

5. Beiren also has some inner problems, such as less capital, smaller scale, weaker independent research and development capacity compared with world-class companies. Moreover, there are also a number of shortcomings in its business structure, mechanism and management.

IV.　Analysis of advantages and disadvantages of the company

(I) Main advantages

1. Scale advantages

Beiren is currently China's largest printing machinery manufacturer. It has fixed assets of 20 billion RMB Yuan, with annual sales exceeding 1 billion. Its products are introduced to six printing markets, including press publishing, publications printing, packaging, financial bills, office machinery, advertising and trademark printing. It manufactures eight series of products with a total of more than 140 different specifications, including sheet-fed offset press, web press, gravure printing machine, corrugated printing machine, flexo printing, forms printing, hot stamping machine, binding equipment and a variety of printing press ancillary products.

2. Brand advantages

Beiren, as one of the first batch of standardized share system experimental companies, goes public in Hong Kong. It is the only one listed company in domestic printing machinery industry. With the famous printing press trademark of "Beiren," it has high brand recognition and intangible assets of 2 billion RMB Yuan.

3. Wide coverage and large market share of leading products

Over the years, Beiren provides twenty thousand high quality and efficient printing machines to all over the country, some of them are even exported to other countries.

Manufacturing of its leading products such as sheet-fed press of monochrome, two-color press, and perfectos achieves industrialization by using assembly lines. Its domestic market share reached 60% due to high quality, sound sales service system and good reputation among users. In this way, similar products of foreign enterprises have been withdrawn from the market in China.

Through reforms and adjustments, Beiren sets nine offices (stores) , 60 sales outlets, and more than 50 service outlets in China.

4. Technical advantages

Over 50 years, Beiren has successfully developed several offset printing press products, filling the blank in domestic market.

Beiren establishes a state-level enterprise technology center, which enable it with strong product development capability. By the mid-90s, it independently develops the first folio four-color offset printing printer that with intellectual property rights and reaches the international advanced level in China.

It has 900 senior technical personnel of all variety, more than 30 patents, and dozens of awards at all levels of science and technology.

It also own modern factory, stereoscopic warehouse, complete sets of processing equipment at the world's advanced level. They all provide guarantees for the production of first class products.

5. Large resources strength and low assets and liabilities rate

According to the overall requirements of Beijing Urban Planning, Beiren transfers the original site and builds a new one in Beijing Economic and Technological Development Zone. It raises a lot of money with a low assets and liabilities rate of 34.8%.

6. Industry management advantage

As the leading enterprise in the printer industry, Beiren is responsible for industry management work of trade associations, standards committees, information center, measurement center, and printing machinery institute. It is also director unit of the Chinese printing machinery industry association and director unit of China Printing Machinery Standardization Committee. All these industrial management functions and information resources means a lot for Beiren.

7. Geographical advantages

Located in the Beijing, Beiren engages in manufacturing of integrated modern machineries, which is consistent with Beijing's industrial policies. Moreover, there are relative concentrations of so many universities, research institutes, and large companies large companies with strength in press, publication and printing business. All these bring unparalleled geographical advantages to Beiren.

V.   Guiding principles and development strategies

(I) Guidelines

Beiren Group Corporation aims to achieve scientific development, independent innovation and institutional mechanistic improvement under the guidance of Deng Xiaoping Theory and "Three Represents."

It will make full use of brand advantage and overall advantages of internal and external resources to further improve core competitiveness. Besides, it will try to maintain its leading position in the printer industry and create international brand. In addition, it will strive to make more contributions to economy and national industry.

(II) Development strategy

To use digital technology to enhance the level of the traditional printing press manufacturer in order to maintain leading position and create international brand of its leading product offset press. Moreover, the company also pursues integrated development in related industrial upstream and downstream, even related industries. It tends to serve as systemic supplier of the printing press industry to be adequate at product and capital operating and to achieve its extraordinary development.

VI.　Development goals and ways to achieve them

(I) Development goals

1.　Overall development goals

(1) Sales income: in 2010 up to × ×. × hundred million RMB Yuan, with an average annual increase of ××.×%, maintaining the first of domestic sales volume.
Of which: Group Corporation (headquarter) ×. × hundred million RMB Yuan
Stock Company × × hundred million RMB Yuan
(2) Total profit: in 2010 up to ×. × hundred million RMB Yuan, with consolidated sales revenue margin of × ×%.
Of which: Group Corporation (headquarter) 0. × hundred million RMB Yuan
Stock Company × hundred million RMB Yuan
(3) earn foreign exchange through export: in 2010 up to ×. × hundred million dollars.
Of which: Group Corporation (headquarter) 0. × hundred million dollars.
Stock Company × hundred million dollars

2.　Development goals of Group Corporation (headquarter)

(1) In 2010, sales revenue reaches ×. × hundred million RMB Yuan.
(2) In 2010, profit reaches × × × × hundred thousand RMB Yuan.
(3) In 2010, earn foreign exchange through export reaches hundred thousand dollars.
(4) In 2010, return on net assets reaches ××.×%。

3. Development goals of Stock Company

(1) In 2010, sales revenue reaches ×. × hundred million RMB Yuan.

(2) In 2010, profit reaches × × × × hundred thousand RMB Yuan.

(3) In 2010, earn foreign exchange through export reaches hundred thousand dollars.

(II) Ways to achieve these goals

1. Stock Company

Make effort to take use of brand advantages, to develop new printing technology and new products, as well as to focus on production of high-end multi-color sheet-fed offset press and roll offset products. Moreover, it should improve independent intellectual property of products and core competitiveness of the enterprise.

(1) Sheet-fed offset press values × × hundred million RMB Yuan. Revenues of Multi-color sheet-fed offset account for × ×% of that of sheet-fed offset production and sales of BR200 and BR300 reach separately × × × units.

(2) Web offset press values × × hundred million RMB Yuan. To form large scaled manufacture of newspaper rotary press (75 thousand sheet / hour) and commercial rotary machines, accounting × ×% of web.

(3) Sales revenue of gravure press reaches × hundred million RMB Yuan.

(4) Sales revenue of Quarto single-color and multi-color offset press reaches × hundred million RMB Yuan.

(5) Sales revenue of form printing press reaches × hundred million RMB Yuan.

(6) Sales revenue of flexographic printing press reaches × hundred million RMB Yuan.

2. Group Corporation (Headquarter)

(1) Focus on developing diverse, high-end automatic post press finishing equipment and improving new, high-end, international level post-press printing and packaging machinery products.

(2) Co-development and production of CTP, and digital inkjet. Applications of computer control technology in the press area work out automation and intelligence issues of post-press finishing equipment and

achieve the integration of digital and network platform in the whole process.

VII.　Strategic states

(I) The first phase (2006-2008)

Group Corporation (headquarter):

In 2008, sales revenue reaches ×. × hundred million RMB Yuan, profit × × × × hundred million, and per capita sales × × hundred million.

Stock Company

In 2008, sales revenue reaches ×. × hundred million RMB Yuan, profit × × × × hundred million, and per capita sales × × hundred million.

(II) The second phase (2009-2010)

Group Corporation (headquarter):

In 2010, sales revenue reaches ×. × hundred million RMB Yuan, profit × × × × hundred million, and per capita sales × × hundred million.

Stock Company

In 2010, sales revenue reaches ×. × hundred million RMB Yuan, profit × × × × hundred million, and per capita sales × × hundred million.

VIII.　Strategic focus

(I) Leading strategy

The fundamental requirement of the leading strategy is to maintain and strengthen leading position of Beiren in the same domestic industry. That means every series of products of a leading enterprises should be the leader in domestic industry and leading company's products are the best in China. Otherwise, it is not commensurate with its status as a leading enterprise, not to mention to create an international brand.

(II) Export strategy

Beiren's goal is to participate in international competition, and to create a world-renowned brand. This requires the implementation of export strategies. Priority is to develop export strategies, to further clarify the guidelines and export work objectives in order to establish export strategy management system and to implement management of unified planning, policy and image, as well as regional division. It will help to realize the goals set in its "Eleventh Five-Year Plan."

(III) Strategic sharing of favorable resources

Beiren's advantages in brand, technology, management strengths and network are intangible assets accumulated over the years. Its brand value alone is worth 2 billion RMB Yuan, which is a tremendous wealth. Values of these resources can be achieved only in practice rather than put them in the shelf. To share favorable resources will enable Beiren to make use of its advantages, to turn its resource advantages into competitive advantage, to reduce repetitive tasks and costs, to save time, as well as to strengthen competitiveness and to accelerate development of the enterprise.

(IV) Capital management strategy

Beiren is the only company in printing industry that gets listed in both Hong Kong and Shanghai stock company. In addition to issuing shares to raise funds through securities markets, acquisitions, and mergers in order to achieve low-cost expansion, Beiren can pick appropriate means of capital operation among a large amount of selections to achieve extraordinary development.

(V) Quality engineering strategy

To strengthen management and to provide customers with satisfying products are basic requirements of quality engineering strategy. It shares similar objectives with creating international brands. It is not only a workable approach, but also an assurance measure. Quality engineering is affected by Beiren's management, quality, technology and quality of workers. The strategy can promote basic work and exports of the enterprise; it is also a long term fundamental task.

IX.   Strategic measures

(I) Establishment of R & D centers and marketing company overseas

1.   To explore in the international market. In 2010, earn foreign exchange through export reach × ×% of income;
2.   To create international brand;

3. To establishing overseas marketing networks and agencies;
4. To establish overseas R & D center.

(II) Establishment of post-press packaging production base

In the period of its "Eleventh Five-Year Plan", the company will build research and development center, sales center, training center and production base of post-press packaging equipment; besides, it will set up research and development centers and incubators of digital work flow, as well as digital color printing and digital printing press production base. It also will form a stable strategic cooperative partnership with HP Company.

(III) Completion of Tender Program of State Science and Technology

That is the successful development of digital workflow. It includes:

1. Acceptance of CTP equipment;
2. Digital transformation of quarto four-color offset press;
3. Digital transformation of post press folding machine;
4. Successful development of digital workflow software.

(IV) new progress in cooperation with HP

1. Establishment of digital color printing production base and sales service centers. Digital printing machinery earns foreign exchange up to × × × × hundred thousand dollars by 2010;
2. Formation of a production base of digital presses.

(V) Substantial progress made in the reform of state-owned enterprises

1. Achievement of the planned split share structure step by step, which gradually changes the dominant situation of state-owned shares;
2. A selective and controlled introduction of strategic investors, which makes Beiren change from state-owned company to enterprise with diversified equity;
3. Optimized enterprise operation mode, which contributes to the formation of pattern features in "large group, small company, professional and market oriented."
4. Further improvement of the corporate governance structure.

Opportunities and challenges come together in the next five years. Under the leadership of Beijing government and Beijing Electrical and Mechanical Company, Beiren will adhere to principles and policies of the arty and state and make use of its own advantages. Facing opportunities and challenges, it fells confident to strive to become a stronger group, especially with direction specified in its "Eleventh Five Year Overall Strategic Plan."

Note: Beiren's strategic plan is drafted by Zhang Xiuyu, chairman and general manager of Beijing Successful Key Consulting Co., Ltd. and approved by Zhu Wuan, party committee secretary, chairman and CEO of Beiren Group Corporation. To maintain confidentiality of corporate business, the specific data is expressed with "× ×" , and some of the contents is replaced with "...."

Review

Main leaders of a company in the market economy should first be a strategist. He has to study, predict, and control the future of the company. Only in this way can a business stand firmly and make progress in a fierce competitive market.

What are the tasks for business strategists? John W. Diz indicates that "The task for strategists is not to find out what the company is now, but to predict what it will become in the future." According to the international

convention, the so called "what it will become" refers to appearance of the company after 5 years, 10 years, or an even longer time.

To fulfill this task, entrepreneurs need to learn the skills of eagles. Strategist Frederick Geroke indicates that "A strategist must make the balance between wideness and depth of information he obtained. An eagle has to fly high enough to find a hare from a widen point of view; meanwhile, it has to fly low enough to target and attack it. A strategist acts like that in continuous balancing, which is the task for him or her alone." The primary requirement to complete the task is the formulation of an overall strategy of the company.

Overall business strategy or corporate strategy is the outline of a company's strategies, which stipulates what should top managers do to lead and control the company. Its rightness directly determines the success of a company, and vice versa.

Just as Jiang Xipei, chairman of Jiangsu Far East Cable Co., Ltd. has said "A company cannot plan for just one step. Despite that it is difficult to predict trend in later decades, yet it is possible to make a 5 to 10 years plan through careful research and thinking. In fact, company without this kind of sense can get no way out, no matter how good it is now. It has already been summarized in an old Chinese saying, worries will soon come if one gives no thought to a long-term plan."

Beiren Group has always attached importance in strategic development for 50 years. All its other management activities serve the implementation of strategy. It introduces Beiren offset, which creates the only national brand Beiren and grows to be the leader in domestic printing press industry. In order to build a more brilliant tomorrow, Beiren formulates its "Eleventh Five Year Overall Strategic Plan," which could also serves as reference for other companies.

Questions

1. What are objectives of an enterprise? What do they mean?
2. How to determine objectives of an enterprise? What problems should be considered?
3. What is strategic target? What are its contents?
4. What are the requirements to develop strategic goals? How should an enterprise   determine its profits target properly?
5. What kinds of contents does environmental analysis include? What is the purpose of analyzing environment?
6. What are the main contents of the analysis of industrial environment? What is the industry product life cycle and industry income elasticity? What is concentration?
7. What is the industrial competition structure? What are the factors that determine the profitability of an industry?
8. What are the contents of enterprise internal evaluation? What's the purpose of that?
9. How to choose business direction of the company correctly?
10. What are the procedures to make a strategic plan? What are the

contents of enterprise overall strategic plan?

11. Try to analyze SWTO of unit you are working for.

12. Retell the procedures of formulating enterprise overall strategy and design an overall strategy for your own company or unit.

Notes

(1) Luo Ruiren, Zeng Fanzheng, *Business Strategy and Principles*, 1st edition, Red Flag Press, October, 1997, p.69.

(2) 〔U.S.〕 Michael Porter & Gary Hamel, *The Future of Strategy Management*, 1st Edition, Sichuan People's Publishing House, April 2000, p.56.

BIBLIOGRAPHY

〔U.S.〕 Michael Porter, *Competitive Strategy*, 1st edition, Huaxia Publishing House, January 1997.

〔U.S.〕 Michael Porter, *Competitive Advantage*, 1st edition, Huaxia Publishing House, January 1997.

〔U.S.〕 Michael Porter & Gary Hamel, *The Future of Strategy Management*, 1st Edition, Sichuan People's Publishing House, April 2000.

〔U.S.〕 Jack Trout, *Trout on Strategy*, 1st edition, China Financial and Economic Publishing House, October 2004.

〔U.S.〕 Arthur A. Thompson Jr. & A. J. Strickland, *Crafting and executing strategy: the quest for competitive advantage concepts and cases*, 10th ed, Duan Shenghua, Wang Zhihui trans., Xu Erming revision, Peking University Press, 2004.

Luo Ruiren, Zeng Fanzheng, *Business Strategy and Principles*, 1st edition, Red Flag Press, October, 1997.

Editing group of required MBA core courses, *Business Strategy*, 1st edition revision, China International Radio Press, 2000.

Liu Jisheng ed, *Company Operation Strategy*, 1st edition, Tsinghua University Press, April 1995.

Xu Erming ed, *Company Strategy Management*, 1st edition, China Economic Publishing House, May 1998.

CHAPTER 7
Types of Enterprise Competitive Strategy

Abstract

This chapter starts with a brilliant expositions on "Attack by Stratagem," *The Art of War*. Then it states the concepts and main points of competitive strategy, and introduces its main types. Later, it explains in detail the specific forms of each competitive strategy. Finally, the appendix discusses the three cases with commentary.

Learning Objectives

- To master concepts and main points of competitive strategy.
- To master main types of competitive strategy and their specific forms.
- To learn to choose a right enterprise competitive strategy through the combination of The Art of War and modern enterprise competitive strategy theories.

Introduction

Sun Tzu says that "In the practical art of war, the best thing of all is to take the enemy's country whole and intact; to shatter and destroy it is not recommended. Also, it is better to recapture an army rather than destroy it, capture a regiment, a detachment or a company rather than to destroy them. Hence, to fight and conquer in all your battles is not supreme excellence; supreme excellence consists in breaking the enemy's resistance without fighting. Thus the highest form of generalship is to balk the enemy's plans; the next best is to prevent the junction of the enemy's forces; the next in order is to attack the enemy's army in the field; and the worst policy of all is to besiege walled cities. The rule is, not to besiege walled cities if it can possibly be avoided. "Principles in military are applicable for an enterprise to compete in the market".

Competitive strategy is the most effective weapon that a company can resort to acquire an advantageous position varying with industries, products (services), rivals and situations, to highlight its distinctive features, to strengthen its competitive advantage, and in summary, to maximize its business competence. Four essentials points are included:

1. The essence of competitive strategy is to acquire an advantageous position, in other words, to position the enterprise;
2. The purpose of competitive strategy is to differentiate one enterprise from others, in other words, to be "unique";
3. The core of competitive strategy is to build competitive advantage;
4. The primary goal of competitive strategy is to maximize business competence.

Competitive strategy is really hard to categorize, due to its diversity and variety in operation and classification standards. This book ventures to divide competitive strategy into three kinds according to the company's competitive posture toward its rivals: confrontational competitive strategy, anti-counterattack strategy and wining without fighting strategy.

Lesson

I. Confrontational Competitive Strategy

Confrontational competitive strategy, as its name suggests, refers to an open competitive campaign designed to defeat rivals by giving full play to one's own distinctiveness. This strategy manifests itself in many ways. Besides three general competitive strategies, special competitive strategies are adopted on varied occasions, such as competitive strategy for different industries, statuses and business scales. (See Figure 7-1)

Figure 7-1 Confrontational competitive strategies

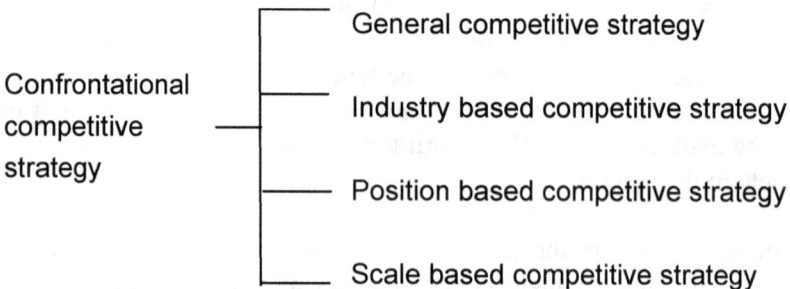

Confrontational competitive strategy
- General competitive strategy
- Industry based competitive strategy
- Position based competitive strategy
- Scale based competitive strategy

(I) General competitive strategy

The core problem of competitive strategy is a company's relative status in the industry, which determines the company's profitability, above or below the industry average. An enterprise that sets a proper status can still earn higher profits even if the industrial structure is comprised of a low or average level of profitability.

It is essential to keep a lasting competitive advantage for an enterprise that wants to maintain a profit higher than the average. One enterprise may have numerous good and bad points, among which, two basic competitive advantages, i.e. low cost and differentiation are necessary. These two basic strategic advantages, combined with business scope for an enterprise to acquire a competitive advantage, bring three general strategies, with which the enterprise can earn a profit higher than the industry average. They are cost-leading strategy, differentiation strategy, and concentration strategy. Concentration strategy is shown in two forms: cost concentration and differentiation concentration. Three general strategies are shown in Figure 7-2.

Figure 7-2 Three General Strategies (2)

Competitive strength

Cost-cutting   Differentiation

Competitive scope	1.Cost Leadership	2. Differentiation
Wide target	3A.Cost Concentration	3B.Differentiation Concentration
Narrow target		

Combining type options and strategic goals for competitive advantages together, results in different ways to realize the competitive advantage in each general strategy. Cost-leading strategy and differentiation strategy aim to acquire a competitive advantage in an extensive industrial scope, while concentration strategy focuses on taking a leadership position in cost (cost concentration) or in differentiation (differentiation concentration) in a narrow industrial scope. It is required that specific measures in conducting each general strategy are different between industries. However, although it is not easy to select and conduct a general strategy, it is the necessary way for each enterprise to develop its competitive advantage.

The basic concept of general strategy is that the competitive advantage is the core of all strategies. Each enterprise must make a decision if it wants to craft a competitive advantage. In other words, if an enterprise wants to acquire a competitive advantage, it must decide on which competitive advantage it shall take and in what scope it can be achieved. The idea that "keeping ahead in everything and everything shall satisfy everyone." can only result in a third-class strategy with low profit, which usually means that an enterprise has no competitive advantage at all.

In order to conduct a general strategy successfully, enterprises must have different financial forces and skills. Different organizational structures, control procedures and innovation initiatives are also required for these general strategies. As a result, it is a basis for success to set one of three general strategies to be the basic goal. Some common meanings of general strategies in these regions are shown in Table 7-1.

1. Cost-leading strategy

   (1) Definition

   Cost-leading strategy requires the enterprise to keep a cost leadership among peers in the long term. (For details, please see Case Study: Galanz: From National No.1 to Global No. 1)

Table 7-1 Three General Strategies (3)

General Strategies	Skills and Financial Forces Generally Required	General Requirements on Organization
Cost-leading Strategy	Persistent input of funds and the way to attract funds; Processing techniques; Strict labor supervision; Design of products that are easy to make; Low-cost distribution system;	Strict cost control; Regular and detailed control report; Structured organization and distinctive responsibility; Stimulation based on basic target to meet strict quantitative goals;
Differentiation Strategy	Powerful marketing capability; Product processing design; Creative insight; Solid capability of basic research; Reputation in quality and leading technology; Unique combination of tradition and new skills from other enterprises; Strong cooperation between distribution channels;	Strong cooperation in research and development, product development and market; Replacement of quantitative measurement with subjective measurement and stimulation Comfortable environment to attract skilled labors, scientists or innovative talents;
Concentration strategy	Combination of above policies according to specific strategic goals.	Combination of above policies according to specific strategic goals.

(2) Significance

Cost-leading strategy can guarantee the enterprise gains a profit higher than the industry average. With the cost being lower than the average, it can earn more benefits than others even if its price is as same as or lower than the average one.

(3) Points for success

Following are points necessary to be understood in order to guarantee the success of cost-leading strategy:

Cost-leading strategy requires the enterprise be the cost leader, instead of just a member of several vendors fighting for the position.

Success of cost-leading strategy depends on the perseverance of implementation day after day.

An enterprise with a cost leadership strategy shall not overlook its basis of product diversity.

2. Differentiation strategy

(1) Definition

Differentiation strategy refers to an enterprise that strives to be unique in some aspects of the industry to which customers pay extensive attention (For details, please see Case Study: Haier Color TV Plays the Strong Voice of "Personalization".)

(2) Significance

Differentiation strategy is to select one or multiple characteristics in the industry that is recognized by many customers, and oriented to meet these requirements uniquely for a premium. The margin, which is equal to the premium less the extra cost and basis of differentiation strategy, is the source of profit, and can be expressed as the following formula:

Profit=Premium-Extra Cost

The root of differentiation strategy is just as what Zhang Ruimin, CEO of

Haier Group, has said "It is not to launch a price war, it is to launch a value war! Even under new economic conditions, the value of enterprise is to find and maximize the customer's personal demands, making the goods have the value equal to or even higher than the money they pay. " Haier is a good example in applying differentiation strategy."

(3) Points for success

The following points are necessary to be understood in order to guarantee the success of differentiation strategy:

Ways of differentiation vary in different industries; therefore a same method can't be used blindly in two industries. For instance, the architecture device industry shall focus on durability service, components resource and outstanding sales network; the air transportation industry shall focus on safety, comfort and convenience; and the cosmetic industry shall focus on product packaging and counter location.

Differentiation strategy requires the enterprise to select the features that make it unique but different from others.

When conducting a differentiation strategy, an enterprise shall not overlook its cost position, which is because the margin from this strategy must be higher than the cost.

3. Concentration strategy

(1) Definition

It is a strategy to do the selection based on a narrow competitive range in the industry (For details, please see Case Study: King of nylon yarn - Ma Jianbo).

By selecting partial or a segmented market in one industry, the strategy only serves selected markets while paying no attention to others. Such a strategy can be conducted in two ways:
First, the enterprise achieves a cost advantage in the target market, which is called cost concentration strategy.

Second, the enterprise achieves a differentiation advantage in the target market, which is called differentiation concentration strategy.

(2) Significance

The two types of concentration strategy are based on the differences between target markets and other markets of the same industry. But the sources of profit for the two strategies are different. The profit of cost concentration strategy comes from the differences of cost actions in partial market, while the profit of differentiation concentration is made by meeting the customer's special demand in certain market. Concentration strategy is an effective strategy that is frequently adopted by most domestic and foreign enterprises, especially medium and small-sized ones.

(3) Points for success

The following points are necessary to be understood in order to guarantee the success of a concentration strategy:

The target market, in which a company adopting a concentration strategy has chosen must be different from others, otherwise, it won't be successful.

If the enterprise can create a sustainable cost leadership (cost concentration) or a differentiated image (differentiation concentration) in partial markets, the enterprise adopting concentration strategy will reach a level higher than the industry average.

As long as the enterprises adopting a concentration strategy have different target markets, there will be enough space to keep several markets of steady concentration in each industry. That is to say, each industry has different customer demand, different optimized production or segmentation with different delivery systems, all of which are candidates for a concentration strategy.

4.   The dilemma

If the enterprise adopts every one of the general competitive strategies but accomplishes nothing, then the firm is in a predicament.

There is no competitive advantage in obtained by being in the dilemma. The enterprises in this situation can only make substantial profits when its industrial structure is much superior to its competitors or its competitors are in the same condition. However, the profits it earns are generally much less than those made by vendors adopting a general strategy.

5. Risk of general competitive strategy

There are 3 general competitive strategies that are effective in conveyance, however there is no a strategy that has no risk at all. Therefore, each of strategy has its own potential risk, shown as Table 7-2.

Table   7-2 Risk of General Strategy (4)

Risk of Cost-leading Strategy	Risk of Differentiation Strategy	Risk of Concentration Strategy
The cost-leadership can't prevent: ●Imitation of competitors ●Technical reform ●Other bases of cost leadership being weakened ●Position of differentiation is lost correspondingly ●Vendor of cost concentration gain lower cost in partial market	The differentiation image can't prevent: ●Imitation of competitors ●Importance of differentiation base being decreased ●Lost of cost position ●Vendor of differentiation strategy wining partial market	The structure of target market will not be attractive: ●Concentration strategy is easy to be copied by others ●Destroy of structure ●Loss of demand ●Partial market being occupied by competitors with extensive targets ●Less difference between the target market and others ●Prominence of diversified production increased ●New vendor with concentration strategy making the industrial market more segmented.

(II) Competitive strategies for companies with different scales

The enterprise is the main body of strategic management. According to business size, it can be classified as large-sized, medium & small sized enterprises. Now we are going to discuss business features and strategy options of these two types of enterprises.

Business features

- Business features of large-sized enterprise

1. Strong in capital
2. Capable of operating large sized enterprises in large demand of funds
3. Capable of increasing market share, monopolizing the market and setting the price relying on a large amount of sales

4. Capable of setting large sized formal organization with solid foundation and various talents;
5. Generally adopting a production scheme of streamline working, automatic operation in large batch and single brand;
6. The expenditure is much higher because of large sales;
7. A contracted distribution system is formed taking the core enterprise as the nucleus and attracting a lot of medium and small sized enterprises;

- Business characteristics of medium and small sized enterprises

1. Normally being monopolized by one person and the success of the enterprise is rested on the owner's personal capability;
2. The funds available are limited, and the raising capability of external fund is not strong. The scope of business is only limited to what the small amount of funds can afford.
3. Whether an enterprise can develop or not is influenced by its dependence;
4. A lot of new competitors will rush in, thus causing an excessive competitive situation;
5. The differences between the enterprises' adaptability to environmental change is challenging;

Strategy options of large-sized enterprises

In general, there are two strategies for large-sized enterprises: one is Product Portfolio Management or PPM system, another is diversified operation. Here the article makes a brief introduction to these two strategies:

(1) PPM of large-sized enterprise product composition

- Definition, content and background of PPM

PPM, an abbreviation of Product Portfolio Management, means to conduct a balanced style of management according to the product composition.

Contents of PPM: to adopt different counteraction to keep a balance between each other in accordance with various factors, such as profitability, capital turnover and development prospect, meeting the business target as much as possible in whole.

- Mode of PPM

Just as the name indicates, the base of PPM is the concept of investment classification management. It is a method to comprehensively optimize the company's target through increasing or return of investment with limited funds and labors. The PPM method can be expressed as Figure 7-3. Each point on the four or nine- celled matrix represents one element of business. The location is decided according to 1) their attraction (generally equal to the growth rate and total scale) to each competitive market (Vertical) and 2) their competency in the market over the competitor in the market of each business. To set a basic target of the enterprise following the comprehensive classification, the risk and benefit can be balanced properly, with a special point representing a kind of special strategic meaning on the matrix (Figure 7-3).

Figure 7-3 Instances of Nine Standard Strategies

Market attraction	Low	Middle	High
High	Trial Entry Tentatively enter to test the market growth ability and withdraw when no potential sustainable growth	Selective Growth Select areas with sustainable growth trend and invest in them	All-out Struggle Concentrate to keep power and maintain profit structure by investing if necessary
Middle	Limited expansion or retreat Seek expansion ways with less risk and retreat in time if things don't go smoothly	Selective Expansion Concentrate to invest and only expand to segment market with best profit and less risk	Advantage Maintenance Cultivate the ability to fight back competition and to enhance profitability by increasing productivity, avoiding large-scale investment
Low	Less Losses Take preventive measures such as reduce investment and reduce fixed costs, and withdraw if loss is inevitable	Full Harvest Shift from fixed costs to variable costs and enhance profitability through the application of value analysis (VA) and value engineering (VE) method	Limited Harvest Minimize risks in some segment markets in order to maintain profitability even if the market position has been shaken

Company Strength

Source: Editing group of required MBA core courses, *Operation Strategy*, 1st edition, China Transnational Radio Press, September 1997, P.303.

- Example: PPM of GE

The strategic scheme of GE in 1969 is made according to the management of main products list. Figure 7-4 shows the list, on which one end is the potential of GE's technology, sales force, market share and enterprise image etc., another is its industry attraction reflected by market scale, grow rate and competitive condition of each product, which forms the matrix.

Figure 7-4 PPM of GE

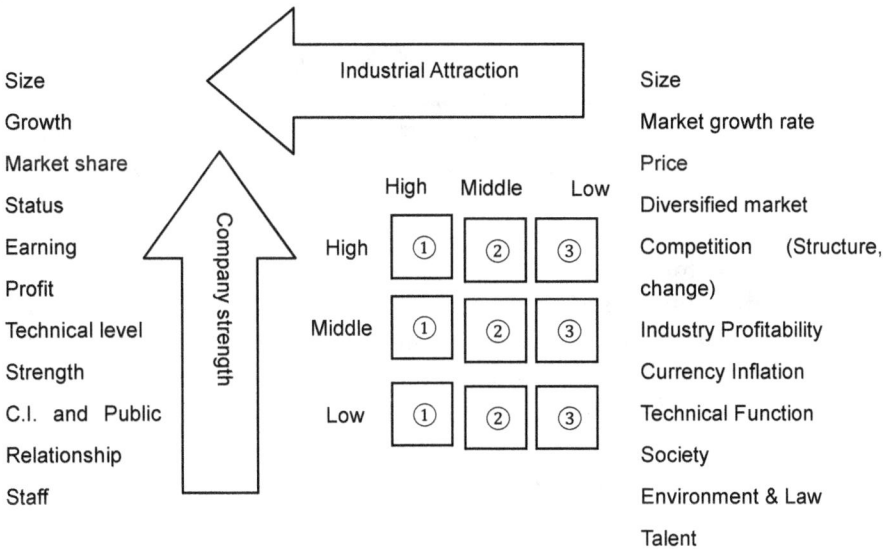

	High	Middle	Low
High	①	②	③
Middle	①	②	③
Low	①	②	③

Size
Growth
Market share
Status
Earning
Profit
Technical level
Strength
C.I. and Public Relationship
Staff

Industrial Attraction
Company strength

Size
Market growth rate
Price
Diversified market
Competition (Structure, change)
Industry Profitability
Currency Inflation
Technical Function
Society
Environment & Law
Talent

① Investment/Growth type ②Selection/ Income type ③Withdrawal/Stop type

According to the matrix, a company can select its business strategy according to three levels as follows:

(1) Comprehensive input of all resources, including personnel, technology and fund;
(2) Selective investment;
(3) Investment reduction or withdrawal.

(2) Diversified operation of large enterprises

Diversified operation strategy is worked out under joint efforts of new

241

product development and new markets. That is to say, it is generated as a result of increasing new product category and new markets. It is generally adopted by large-sized enterprises.

Strategy options of medium and small-sized enterprises

There are five strategies for Medium and Small sized Enterprises. The introduction of each strategy is as follows:

(1) Concentrating on one point—"Small but specialized, small but precise" strategy

This strategy is designed for small-sized enterprises with limited resources. Being inferior in strength, small –sized enterprise can't manage multiple products to transfer risks. By concentrating the forces, it can select one segment to develop its strong point and develop its specialized business.

(2) Seeking a gap—"seizing every opportunity" strategy

It is intended for small-sized enterprises with features of flexibility and strong adaptability. Based on the principle that "I have what the others don't have and I don't have what the others already have", small-sized enterprise seeks all opportunities to enter a new market and build success relying on its quickness and flexibility.

(3) Making a difference ----featured business strategy

It is formed due to the fact that small enterprises are closer to customers. Generally, a small sized enterprise cannot compete effectively using a cost leadership strategy. However, they can still take advantage of many aspects. For example, operation scope of small-sized enterprise is narrow and distance between customers and them are shorter, what's more, their products and services can attract customers rely on their different features.

(4) Allied competitive strategy

It is designed for the small-sized enterprise based on its features of inadequate funding and limited production technology, as well as a lack capability to take use of economies of scale. On a basis of equality and mutual benefit, small-sized enterprises can try to learn from each other's strong points to offset own weaknesses, and develop the market together, creating conditions for their survival and development.

(5) Contracted business strategy

It is recommended for the small-sized enterprise based on features of limited market share and a single product. When the firm decides its direction of production, a small-sized enterprise doesn't develop new products but refers to the production system of large-sized enterprise. It accepts long-term orders from one or several enterprises and becomes their contractor. That is so called contracted enterprise strategy. Small-sized enterprise adopting this strategy also called contracted enterprise or entrusted enterprise.

As mentioned above, enterprise of different business size shall adopt different competitive strategy. An overview of all the strategies is shown in Figure 7-5.

Figure 7-5 Competitive strategies for Company of different scale

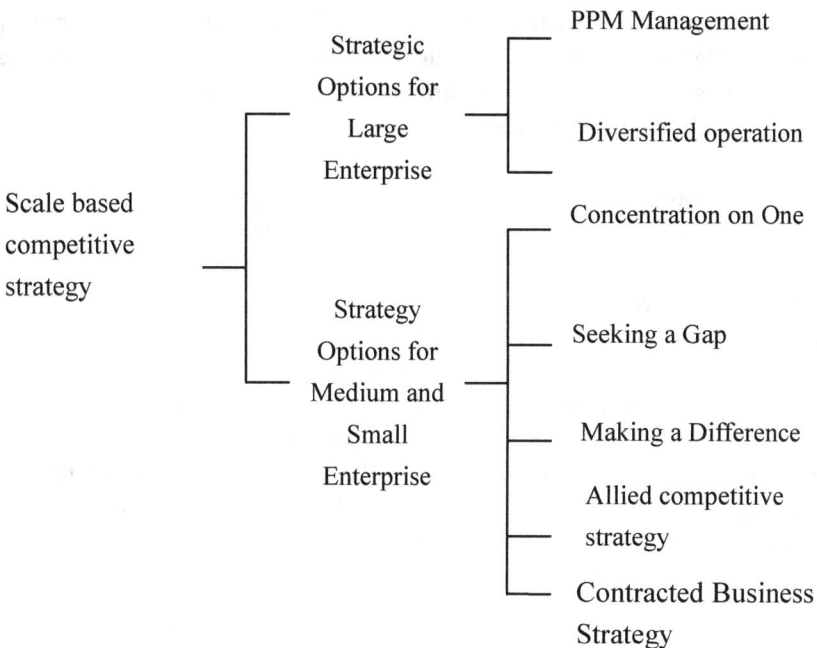

```
                          Strategic           ┌── PPM Management
                          Options for         │
                          Large       ────────┤
                          Enterprise          └── Diversified operation

Scale based                                   ┌── Concentration on One
competitive                                   │
strategy         ──┐                          │
                          Strategy            ├── Seeking a Gap
                          Options for ─────────┤
                          Medium and          ├── Making a Difference
                          Small               │
                          Enterprise          ├── Allied competitive
                                              │   strategy
                                              │
                                              └── Contracted Business
                                                  Strategy
```

II. Anti-counterattack strategy

Anti-counterattack strategy mainly aims to deflate the competitors' desires of counterattack, and to set barriers that make them hard or unable to do, even if they have the desire. Generally, there are three typical situations:

(I) To make the competitor be passive and unable to launch counterattack

The competitor gets into passive condition because of the effects caused by the counterattack; therefore the desire of counterattack is weakened sharply because of the dire consequences resulting from the counterattack.

(II) To launch attack first to make the competitor unable to counterattack

Limited resources necessary for operations puts constraints on the competitor's resource supply. It includes hiring skilled workers and excellent technicians, signing long-term supply contracts with raw material supplier, applying for patent technology and attracting investments, and so on. Whoever obtains those resources can develop first and set barriers to its competitor. Besides, whatever measures one enterprise takes first will lead to a lot of wastes for followers to imitate, which weakens the competitor's desire to launch the counterattack.

(III) Revealing sufficient preparation and capability for defeating a counterattack making it difficult for rivals to counterattack

For example, when finding a competitor is going to invest in a new initiative, the enterprise shall disclose the news intentionally or announce through news or press conference that it is considering about lowering prices. Or it announces the completion of equipment investment to stop the competitor's attack. Other counterattack methods can also be used, for instance, sending capable sales person to the area where the competitor has the strongest counterattack desire to make statement concerning the enterprise's strength and the competitive measures in preparation, showing that it is ready to defeat the competitor.

The three conditions can be summarized in Figure 7-6.

Figure 7-6 Anti-counterattack Strategy

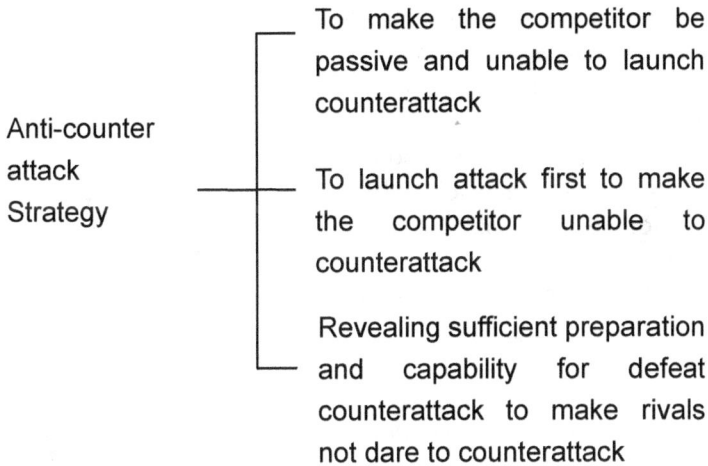

Anti-counter attack Strategy

- To make the competitor be passive and unable to launch counterattack

- To launch attack first to make the competitor unable to counterattack

- Revealing sufficient preparation and capability for defeat counterattack to make rivals not dare to counterattack

III. Winning without Fighting Strategy

Sun Tzu has mentioned in "Attack by Stratagem," *The Art of War* that "Hence to fight and conquer in all your battles is not supreme excellence; supreme excellence consists in breaking the enemy's resistance without fighting. " It means that in the operation of war, the highest form is to defeat the enemy without bloody battle and no damage to nation power; while the battle won through bloody battle and waste of nation power is not so good. Therefore, fighting and conquering in all battles is not supreme excellence; supreme excellence is to break the enemy's resistance without fighting. This can be called the supreme and most ideal strategy. "Win without fighting" is also the supreme excellence in competition strategy. Under any condition the enterprise shall consider this strategy first as much as possible. It can be realized in the practical operation to avoid the potential competitor to become real one. "Winning without fighting" strategy is divided into 3 types:

(I) Coexistence in individual segment

Competitors taking the strategy of coexistence in individual segments to avoid the crossover by selecting their own segmented markets. In social economy life, large-sized enterprises with strong power and medium and small-sized enterprises with relatively weak power can coexist in the competitive. Even in the advanced capitalism country, in which the capital indicates a kind of concentration trend, a lot of medium and small-sized enterprises still have sufficient life force to survive. The reasons for this phenomenon are various, of which the most important one is that although a big difference exists in the power between each competitive party, each of them has formed a strong position in the competitive that is suitable for their survival in their own environment. Ways to practice the strategy include:

1. To invest in undeveloped areas
2. To attack the weakest part of the competitor

(II) Cooperative action

Cooperative action can be classified into 3 groups:

1. Cooperative action in resource

Enterprises in competition can be cooperative in talent, fund, raw material and technology to
get a good result for each party.

2. Cooperative action in production

It is a requirement of socialized production and science & technology development for enterprises in competition to cooperate in production. With the development of science & technology, the machinery becomes large sized and modernized, and the production process becomes automated and consecutive. All these require enterprises of similar industries to cooperate to realize economies of scale, and to further cut production cost.

3. Cooperative action in marketing

Enterprises in competition can cooperate with enterprises engaging in railway, roadway, waterway and airway to solve the problem of goods transport. Meanwhile, they can work with sales departments in different markets to promote wholesaling, which can be done through the cooperation in market planning, market testing, product exhibition and market development. They can also cooperate with foreign trade departments to develop international marketing together.

"Cooperative action" virtually is to establish an "enterprise strategic alliance". Enterprise Strategic Alliance is a bi-lateral or multi-lateral cooperation agreement that promotes the realization of a common target. Based on the share of market, fund, technology and management, it aims at consolidating the enterprises' advantages with a view of development of markets and the stability of the enterprise for a longer term, keeping a sustainable development.

(III) Extra-leading innovation

Among "winning without fighting" strategies, "extra-leading innovation" strategy is the optimal choice. The so called "leading innovation" strategy requires the enterprise to stay ahead of the customer's demand, to continuously "create new markets and customer" and to bring the user "unexpected surprise" and " super-valued enjoyment". It also requires the enterprise to stay ahead of the competitor and itself, to continually "defeat and surpass itself" and to remain a leader in the industry. No competitor will appear in the course of conducting this strategy, therefore it is named "winning without fighting" strategy.

The three modes mentioned above can be shown as Figure 7-7.

Figure 7-7 Winning without Fighting Strategy

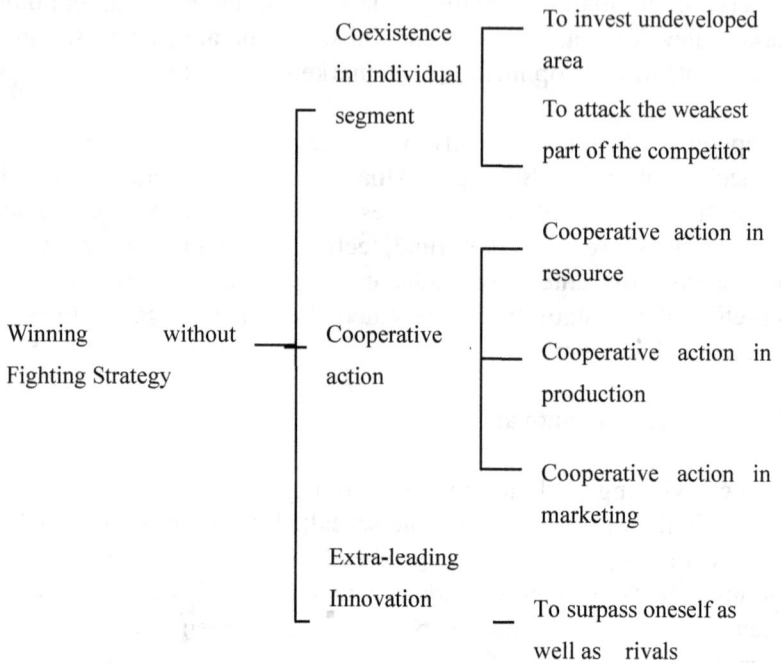

Winning without Fighting Strategy

- Coexistence in individual segment
  - To invest undeveloped area
  - To attack the weakest part of the competitor
- Cooperative action
  - Cooperative action in resource
  - Cooperative action in production
  - Cooperative action in marketing
- Extra-leading Innovation
  - To surpass oneself as well as rivals

Case Study:

Galanz: From National No.1 to Global No. 1

From one small township factory producing feather clothing to China's No.1 in electronic appliance, Galanz illustrates a wonderful millennium story, which is named "Galanz Phenomenon" by the economist.

In 1992, when Liang Qingde, the founder of the company, decides to use the word Galanz found in dictionary, he has set a goal: to be an international giant in global stage. In the following years, Galanz achieves his goal.

How can a weaving enterprise shoulder such a responsibility to develop a new space in the electronic appliance industry? It is compelled by a sense of nationality mission. In 1991, after one year of market investigation, Liang Qingde, GM of Galanz, finds that the domestic microwave market is occupied by imported brands while local ones are in a terrific downturn. In order to build up China's own brand in the microwave market to compete with imported ones, he invites famous experts to the company and at the same time, prepares for project approval and imported equipment. In Sept. 1992, with the most advanced automatic production line imported from Toshiba, it starts to construct Galanz Enterprise Co.Ltd. to have the trial production. In 1993, the company has an adjustment on the industrial construction, transforming from a textile company into an electronic appliance company. In the same year, it produces 10,000 sets of microwaves for a trial.

During the growth and expansion stage, dozens of multi-national companies keep eyes covetously on Galanz. With big differences in comprehensive strength and disparate industrial policies, Galanz institutes a CI strategy, which opens a way to generate large scale production with specialized technology and produces many advantages even under substandard conditions. Corporate culture advantage is the basis for the prosperity of Galanz. Centered on the personnel, Galanz cultivates a strong culture atmosphere around the enterprise by combining the faith, moral and psyche to form a force of self-guidance, self-discipline and self-excitation that communicate and promote each other. Everyone in Galanz will consciously work towards the goal and honor at a higher level, because "Galanz is in every staff's Galanz".

Inside Galanz, all business factors are based on quality. The concept of "To be honest to the customer, to consider the benefit of customer and to make the customer's money earned from hard work is worthy" has been incisively and vividly defined by Galanz, which enjoys popular support now. Backed with the quality, guided with the technology and based with the service, Galanz introduces extra-value products with extra-value service. By using the strategy of "small profits but quick returns," it delivers high quality technology products at a low price. By now, the brand Galanz has won popular support from the customer. Whenever microwave is mentioned, Galanz will come to the customers mind.

Concentrating limited resources and standing firm in the microwave market, Galanz creates a record in scale that other brands can't copy. By now the annual output of Galanz microwave has reached 6 million, with the market share being still increasing. Since 1995, with a market share of 25.1% in domestic market, Galanz has become No. 1 in sales. Its market share in domestic market is also No.1 5 years in a row and it has taken more than 70%

of domestic market share by now. Simultaneously, Galanz is successful in international markets also. It has earned many qualification certifications, namely ISO9001 qualification system, American standard (UL), Germany Standard (GS) and EU standard (CE) etc. Galanz's products have covered nearly 60 countries and areas in five continents today. In 1998, Galanz has 15% share of global markets and by now, has 20% share of EU market, with the market share in France and Argentina both reaching 30%. It is reported that the export of Galanz reaches above 85% of the microwave industry. Another report shows that the export of Galanz in the first half year has increased by 300% compared with the same period of last year. The foreign exchange earned through exports is over $70 million, setting a solid foundation for accomplishing the export task of this year. It is expected that the foreign exchange earned through exports will exceed $100 million, hopefully being No.1 at earning foreign exchange through exports in the domestic electronics appliance industry.

"Either to be the No.1, or to be nothing." By now, Galanz has realized the strategic target ahead to be No.1 in one aspect in 3 or 5 years. Directed by the strategy of internationalization in market, talent and brand, Galanz has established and run a production base with a turnout of 12 million sets to develop a global sales network omni-directionally, through which Galanz becomes an international brand and the king of electronic appliance kingdom.

Source: Kong Ming, *China Companies*, 15th, Nov., 1999

Taking a comprehensive view on the competitive market, we can tell the winners are usually the leaders in cost. With low product cost, they can have enough space to do product development, advertising and cutting price promotion, making the competitor lag far behind.

Galanz adopts is cost-leading strategy. Galanz enters into microwave industry, a new industry for it in early 1990s, and matured very quickly. By turning down a diversified operation strategy, it concentrates all resources on the development, production and sales of the microwave for developing economies of scale, which lies on a solid base for the formation of cost-leading strategy.

Since 1996, whenever Galanz goes into a new stage, it will decrease the price with a range over 30%. Therefore, the manufacturers of small size, slow development and no technical differentiation go into deficit one after another and over time are force out of business. On the contrary, Galanz operates at peak performance, creating a sensation in the electronic appliance industry with a market share exceeding 60% with over 1 million sets exported.

Facts show that low cost is the sharp weapon for market development. Since at any time, a product of low price but high quality can be favored by the customer. There are words of wisdom in Marketing Management, written by Philip Kotler, the founder of Marketing, that there is no a brand loyalty that two cents can't kill. Therefore, in the situation that little difference in product quality and service exist between domestic products today, those who focus on cost leadership by attracting the customer with a price advantage can gain the competitive advantage.

Haier Color TV Plays the Strong Voice of "Personalization"

In June, 1999, when the price wars goes on like a raging fire in China's Color TV market, Haier which has always kept silent shows its secret weapon at that time. Instead of taking the price war that is seriously criticized, Haier introduces a personalization strategy which is really a delightful surprise.

The exhibition of Personalized Products in Digital Times held by Haier really makes the customer appreciate the charm of its personalized Color TV. New products in internationally advanced level strike a pose on the stage with more than 60 types of 8 series, named Health, FPD, Digital, Plasma, TFT, Wangshen, Big Screen and High Sensitive series. It includes Integrated Media Digital color TV developed by German Haier Design Center, ultra-thin TFT color TV developed by Haier Silicon Design Center, HDTV developed by Haier Los Angel D & R Center, the first set of connected FDP digital TV in China co-developed by Haier and Toshiba and wide range voltage TV for rural customers, as well as big screen TV with breakthrough in technology, 42 inches plasma non-radiant TV and healthy TV. All products are featured with personalization that is customized for the customer in different layers, which symbolizes that Haier takes a leadership role in a digital age, and also leads in the personalization era.

"Personalized products are the demand of time development". "Have personalized idea first, then comes personalized market."

Haier's concept of personalization is originated from its recognition to the market and emphasis on the customer. Haier thinks that the saturation of some products doesn't mean the saturation of the whole market. The potential of the market exists everywhere. The color TV market today in China is relatively but not absolutely overstocked, and it is a relatively overstocked and insufficient in efficient supply. In another words, there is an overstock while there is also under-stock and even shortage. That is to say, the market has the potential to create consumption, and the key for the operator is to understand and develop the market correctly.

Where to create the consumption hot spot? Haier thinks it shall start with the formation of consumption hot spot and the representation of market.

Compared with the seller's market, the formation of consumption hot spot and the representation of the buyer's market have new features as follows: In 1980s, the storm of electronic appliance purchase comes like hundreds of bricks. Undoubtedly, the crazy action of irrational customers is the driver to make it become the hot spot. Nowadays, there are more and more goods for the customer to choose, their purchase action becomes much more rational. Therefore, the customer's demand is the main driver for the formation of consumption hot spot, which slows down the temperature of consumption hot spot. Second, the consumption hot spot changes from being concentrated to being relatively de-concentrated. In the past, the hot spot was concentrated on several or even a single product. Today, with the diversification of consumption demand and difference between purchase levels, the consumption hot spot of different classification and force will co-exist. Third, the consumption hot spot is not a flash in the pan any more, instead as one hot spot falls, another rises. In the past, the consumption hot spot comes fast and goes fast. Nowadays, the multilayer of consumption hot spot may make it appear one after another in different places and customer groups.

Products of diversified categories and personalization are the best practice to respond to the three changes of consumption hot spots mentioned above. It is the concept of personalization that promotes the formation of Haier's personalized product.

The personalization of the Haier Color TV is much more representative market segmentation strategy. Haier recently introduces eight series of products and each of them has its own characteristics. The digital integrated media TV of perfect voice and image effects is prepared for fans seeking for entertainment. The streamline mode which in the past was used on the plane and automobile is successfully migrated to color TV now. RGB Royal TV which represents local European design style meets the demand of the customer pursuing a dignified, graceful and unique appearance. Wide range voltage TV is specially designed for the rural customer. And the thinnest TFT TV in the world by now, which is as thick as one book, represents the future of color TV.

Service is always the strong point of Haier. The service of Haier TV is much more featured with personalization. At the beginning, they introduce a "San Quan Service," in another words, " 7x24 hours service, omni-directional door to door service and free charged service," which had its features already. Then, the service is upgraded to "Happy San Quan(Three all) Service," which adds two items of "Globalized Internet Service " and "Door to door Debugging Service ," giving prominence to the globalization and affection. Thus, their services become much more different.

Professor Zhang in Jilin University recently buys a set of "Yingyinwang" color TV. At the beginning, he doesn't know how to operate the TV and wants someone to give a door to door training but he forgets the hotline number. Fortunately, he remembers the address of "Happy Website" mentioned in the "Happy Sanquan Service" and just has a try by sending one email. What surprises him is that within 2 hours two workers of Haier go to his home and do the training.

Guided by such a service sense, Haier color TV positions its products to bring the customer not only material satisfaction but also spiritual satisfaction, making the customer feel like a god when he/she buys the product.

Source: Haiyang, "Economic Daily," Aug. 11, 1999

In a competitive market, a company can succeed by adopting cost-leading strategy, such as Galanz and can win by adopting differentiation strategy, like Haier Color TV. As the offspring of color TV industry, Haier introduces its secret weapon—"Personalization" strategy instead of "Price War" strategy, with which it wins the first battle and becomes the leader in personalization times.

"Personalization" is to be characteristic, in other words, to be differentiated.

Adopting personalization strategy must have a personalized idea first, and then a personalized market. Simultaneously, remember the foundation to be personalized is the technology, product and service. Haier establishes a good example for us in doing this.

King of nylon yarn - Ma Jianbo

In the 2010 trade fair of Jie-Da Company, there are dozens of executives of toothbrush manufacturers whose domestic market shares account for 80% of the whole. Ma Jianbo, chairman of CiXi Jie-Da nanometer compound materials Co., Ltd., announces that their tooth brush wires have occupied more than 50% of the domestic market share. Moreover, its series of products have been exported to more than 20 countries and regions like Asia, Europe and South America. It breaks the long-term monopoly of DuPont Company (USA), Rhodia (France) on the Chinese market. Due to this, Ma Jianbo also wins a nickname - King of nylon yarn.

Engage in trade for unwilling to be mediocre

In the mid-1980s, CiXi City is still a remote poor country on the south bank of Qiantang River estuary where water and electricity resources are deficient and traffic is problematic. Its available cultivable land per person is less than 0.5 mu. People there make their living cotton planting and salt production.

Ma Jianbo is just a senior school graduate then. In the fall of 1984, everyone is engaging in business in CiXi. At that time, Ma Jianbo's father works for diversified business office of Canton Town and his mother acts as a primary school teacher. They never expect him to be a businessman being under 20. But his uncle, deputy secretary of Canton Town comes to ask him to work in the local agricultural machinery plant.

Canton agricultural machinery plant is a cooperative enterprise manufacturing parts of agricultural machinery. It has big advantage in both product quality and sales channels. Although Ma Jianbo is engrossed by the new experience, he decides to work for himself after working only 9 days. He gets his first wage of 36 RMB Yuan and hides it in a box quietly.
Ma Jianbo discloses that he is just excited by the booming development of private enterprises in CiXi City.

Get defeated in his first business

One night, a colleague of his father talks about two military products manufacturers named 755 and 760 factory in Xinxiang, Henan Province. They yield large amounts of products with many cheap scrap materials. Hearing this, Ma Jianbo tells his father he wants to go Xinxiang alone to have a look, but is denied the opportunity.

He still wants to go and by asks his third grandfather who tends to support him. Unexpectedly, he gets 100 RMB Yuan as travelling expense as well as support from his third grandfather. In addition, his mother also gives her savings of 50 RMB Yuan to him being moved by his son's persistence. Then Ma Jianbo goes to Xinxiang by caravan with 186 RMB Yuan, including his wage in the box without informing his father.

However, his first business is ended up in a complete failure. No wonder, as a green hand, he is unfamiliar with the place and the people, besides, he is short of capital. Ma Jianbo has to turn back to CiXi broke because these two manufacturers don't trust him.

Never give up by continuing his business

Ma Jianbo goes to Xinxiang again after a few days. He suffers more than before this time. Of course, he also fortunately makes it possible to earn his first fortune. He then travels between CiXi and Xinxiang many times for a very long time.

At that time it takes 60 hours to arrive Xinxiang. He sleeps in the train car aisles and freight cars, eats one bowl of noodle which is worth 1 RMB Yuan twice a day as meals, and lives nowhere by spending 2 RMB Yuan in staying in a collective bathroom and wonders the streets until 12 o'clock at night. Because there are various kinds of people in the bathroom, Ma Jianbo has to be extremely careful of watching his belongings, making him be cautious even nowadays.

He has to sort, bag and carry all goods by himself for he has no helper. In addition, he has to sleep on piles of goods, risking his life in order to manage back to CiXi over 1200 km away.
Ma Jianbo's excessive physical exertion also causes permanent physical damage; even now, his lumbar muscles will hurt whenever it rains or is cloudy.

Make his first fortune with empty hands

Ma Jianbo gets his first goods of 1 ton of plastic waste from 755 plants. But he doesn't have enough money to pay. So he goes back to grant a loan of 1000 RMB Yuan in Zhengzhou, of which 30 RMB Yuan is charged as a monthly interest rate on the spot and goes back at night. Early next morning, he hands over it to the treasurer.

At last, two tons of goods are loaded on the train after they are transported to the station, so does Ma Jianbo. And he has to stand by the seatback for there is no seat on the train. A few days later, the consignments arrive on schedule. Ma Jianbo uses a four-wheel tractor to transport them back home in twice.

Without a plant, Ma Jianbo cleans his own yard; without washing equipment, he fills salt water into a vat instead; without workers, he seeks some neighbors to help by offering wages. His mother and sister who come back from school on weekends also join them to sort, rinse and dry waste plastics, which are finally sold to local waste plastic processing plants as raw material.

Although he only earns a few thousand RMB Yuan for his first pot of gold, he is encouraged to do more. Moreover, he earns supports from his family in both spiritual and financial aspects.

Be fond of dream and innovation

Fang Bailing, secretary of Kandun street party committee in CiXi says that Ma Jianbo is an excellent representative of private entrepreneurs. In fact, many of them experience unlimited hardship and bitterness in their entrepreneurial processes. But it also cultivates their unique tenacity and courage.

Young Ma Jianbo understands clearly the difficulty of starting a business when he runs between Xinxiang and CiXi, but also tastes the joy of growth. By the late 80s, waste plastics acquisition business of Ma Jianbo extends from Xinxiang to other places in Sichuan, Jiangxi, Anhui and so on. Ma Jianbo has also become one of the directors of some big companies like Sichuan Changhong, Ariston Refrigerator Factory in Jingdezhen in Jiangxi and Hefei Meiling

Electrical Appliance Co., Ltd., Anhui. It makes him earn enough profits for his original capital accumulation.

Ma Jianbo also met his wife Lu Qunying during the process of selling treated waste plastics to plastic processing companies. Lu Qunying's father takes charge of a local collective company, who is also an important client of Ma Jianbo. He always invites Ma to talk for a while in his office when Ma delivers goods to him. It makes Ma meet and get familiar with his daughter Lu who then becomes Ma's supportive and couple.

Be taken in when he starts his own company

During the process of selling raw materials to plastic processing companies, Ma Jianbo begins to think of opening his own.

He tells his idea to a friend who does work in plastic processing in northeast China. This friend claims to sell his own set of equipment at a price of 20 thousand RMB Yuan. Ma Jianbo transfers the money to his friend's account without thinking and transports the equipment back to CiXi using a local truck.

Back in CiXi, Ma Jianbo invites local experienced instructors to install the equipment at the fastest speed. Then he recruits a dozen skilled workers to set up his own company, CiXi Storm Nylon Yarn Factory.

But no product comes out after raw materials are added to the hopper. Ma Jianbo takes the train to Shanghai on the next day to ask advice from experts of Shanghai Chemical Fiber Institution. And then he goes to plead with Huaiyin public wires plant in the northern Jiangsu to send a technician person to his company. Experts from these two units tell him it is a set of waste machines that cannot be used any more after they test it.

Phone calls to his friend in northeast China are not answered. Ma Jianbo problem is not resolved and goes to visit him, but no one there. In this case, hard-earned 20 thousand RMB Yuan is lost. But from this, Ma Jianbo seems to understand the cruelty of the competition for the first time.

Suffer greatly after being cheated again

But Ma Jianbo is not deterred and he starts over by purchasing new equipment. After repeated installations and tests, he opens CiXi Storm Nylon Yarn Factory.

Unfortunately, bad events follow, which suddenly pushes him into the lowest period of his life and career!

In October 1996, a friend Xiong Guangjun asks Ma Jianbo to make a 30 thousand loan guarantee for his company. And Ma Jianbo agrees. But because of the lesson of his northeastern friend, Ma Jianbo personally inspects the goods in Xiong's storage yard, carefully checks the memorandum provided by the audit and signs his name on letter of guarantee produced by the bank.

Two weeks later, on his arrival, Ma Jianbo is informed by the bank and the Public Security Bureau that Xiong runs off with money. It means that Ma Jianbo has to pay back all loans and interest up to 1.5 million within the time limit for Xiong's cheating behaviors.

Ma Jianbo appeals to the higher authorities and the court for help again and again over the next three years in vain. Meanwhile, Wuhan toothbrush wire factory, the main downstream customer of CiXi Storm Nylon Yarn Factory declares bankruptcy due to poor management.   It's accumulated more than 1 million in bad debt.

At that time, Ma Jianbo is in the middle of a crisis and including ongoing lawsuits, unprecedented financial pressures, corporate reputation loss, complains of family members, abandoned production and poor sales.

Find another way to stand up again

By autumn that year, Ma Jianbo convinces his family to start again as Jie-Da Company. This time Ma Jianbo goes to Pingdingshan City. It is not only rich in coal resources, but also has China ShenMa Group, which is famous for its chemical products in the domestic market and manufactures products like nylon 66 salt, nylon 66 resin, nylon 66 industrial yarn, chlor-alkali and so on. Ma Jianbo hopes to expand his business with China ShenMa Group based on their many years of good quality relation. He wants to expand his product line from producing a simple nylon-based consumer product in order to maximize the company's in order to expand the business within the shortest amount of time.

Ma Jianbo tells Zhao Qilin, the director of marketing of China ShenMa Group, that Jie-Da hopes to begin using ShenMa's leading product diaminocyclohexane as raw material and is willing to try to sell Shenma's products. It makes Zhao Qilin very happy. And Zhao says bluntly that although the quality of diaminocyclohexane is the best because its production line is just introduced from Japan, yet its market visibility and market share need to be further improved. ShenMa welcomes Ma Jianbo, who has a strategic vision as a partner and is willing to provide Ma Jianbo with the most favorable conditions for collaboration.

With ShenMa's strength and technical support, CiXi Storm Nylon Yarn Factory goes through its hard times. After several years of adjustments, it has developed a long-term supply and marketing relationship with China Shenma Group. Jie-Da Company has officially become ShenMa's chief distributor of Nylon 66 hexanediamine products in East China, occupying half sales.

Research and development of new materials

In order to make his own competitive products such as nylon 66 chips and tooth brush monofilament and to be the leader in domestic level production, Ma Jianbo imports advanced processing equipment from Germany, Italy and other countries. He also recruits top talent from the domestic spinning industry, and cooperates closely with the laboratories of engineering plastics, and works with the Chinese academy of sciences, which is the most authoritative organization domestically.

The laboratory who contributes its technology becomes a shareholder and helps Jie-Da Company research and produce nylon 6 / clay composite materials and improves the international competitiveness of Chinese plastic fill materials.

In just 4 years, the obscure CiXi Jie-Da nanomater compound materials Co.,Ltd. has 6 national patents in high-tech composite materials field. In 2004, nylon corrugated grinding wire wins Second Prize of CiXi Scientific-technical Progress Prize and is selected as the country-level key new product project by Department of Science and Technology, Ministry of Commerce, General Administration of Quality Supervision, Inspection and

Quarantine, and State Environmental Protection Administration. In 2005, another leading product imitation bristle brush wire is selected as country-level new product. High performance negative ion health protection brush wire wins Third Class Prize of Ningbo Scientific-technical Progress Prize and is selected as country-level torch program. The company is also awarded the title of CiXi Scientific-technical Progress Enterprise. Its production line grows from one to 15, and its products develop from single nylon 610 to dozens of varieties and specifications.

The introduction of talent and a think tank

The cooperation with laboratory and engineering plastics lets Ma Jianbo realize the importance of technology and talent. He often says that Jie-Da needs nothing more than talent, especially those who can contribute to the rapid and sustainable development of the company.

In order to maximize the advantage of talent, Ma Jianbo adopts a modern enterprise management system, provides excellent treatment and development platform for personnel, and employs more than 20 people with advanced management and technical experience from all over the country. On one hand, Ma Jianbo applies the latest technologies of research institutes in Beijing and Shanghai, and invites well-known experts to guide the enterprise in technology and management; on the other hand, he invests special funds to the staff training and accepts outstanding college students from Ningbo Institute of Technology as interns and employees. It strengthens the foundation for future development of his company.

The outstanding performance of Jie-Da attracts attentions of some large companies home and abroad such as Colgate, Liangmianzhen, Chengxin, Sunstar, etc. They send senior managers to the production line of Jie- Da for inspection and establish good supplier relationships which lead to increased demand. In addition to a large share of the domestic market, Jie-Da's products have been exported to some European, South Asia and American countries and regions, achieving more than 4 million dollars of annual export sales.

Be kind to customers and strategic partner

In order to further strengthen the supply chain, Jie-Da continues to improve its full-service marketing program for downstream clients. The company can adjust specifications and colors of single-wire at any time according to customers' demands. It also opens all parts of its production lines to downstream customers and accepts inspection and supervision responsibility for them. Jie-Da Company's quality control measures earn the trust of investors at home and abroad, and bring orders of a variety of products. Its rivals DuPont (USA) and Rhodia (France) completely withdraw from the Chinese market.

In 2007, he comes up with the idea of using six steadfast rules as a development strategy. That is, a promise of implementing an expansion strategy; promise of pushing project construction; promise of cooperating with large domestic enterprises and implementing internationalization strategy. Promise of implementing technological innovation and introduction of the talented; Promise of stressing economic benefits and industrial control ability; and the promise of building a corporate culture and corporate brand. In addition, he sets a new goal of realizing the integration of technology, industry and trade businesses.

Rapid development of Jie-Da Company also wins strong financial support from a number of banks. Moreover, its new collaboration model with China ShenMa Group provides a fresh momentum. Lv Qinghai, party secretary and chairman of ShenMa believes that there are broad prospects for their collaboration in the area of business operation, so are other aspects like the construction and communication of enterprise culture.

Success and social returns

Jie-Da Company grows to be a local leading company with more than 400 employees engaging in technology, industry and trade from a small plastics processing factory with only 20 staff members. It earns more than 300 million RMB Yuan annually and continues to grow.

Ma Jianbo never forgets to pay back to society when he is successful in his career.

Since 2004, Ma Jianbo volunteers to assume the health insurance of the elderly above 70 in his village and sets up fund with 50 thousand RMB Yuan in his name. In 2007, Jie-Da Company establishes a 500 thousand million benevolence fund to help staff work out family difficulties as well as to improve their circumstances. Moreover, the company also actively takes part in a variety of enterprise cultural activities held in the streets of Kandun. It sponsors literary awards and writers' forums conducted by

October, a magazine run by the Beijing Publishing House Group and initials the long-term collaboration agreement.

Ma Jianbo decides to continue the development principle of "Base in Zhejiang, thrive in the whole country, go out of Asia and march to the world." In order to strive to be a flagship company in China's plastics industry and be a "little giant" following DuPont in terms of the international nylon yarn business.

Sources:

(1) Materials provided by CiXi Jie-Da nanomater compound materials Co.,Ltd.;

(2) Gu He, Sunshine after the storm - stories of chairman of CiXi Jie-Da nanomater compound materials Co.Ltd.. *October,* No. 5, 2007. Beijing Publishing Group. p.192-200 .

Review

Nylon yarn business is one big company that does not hesitates to do what a small company is unable to do. Ma Jianbo controls more than 50% of the market share and earns 400 million RMB Yuan of annual sales. He is also known as King of Nylon Yarn. It can be said that every profession produces its own leading authority.

Why can a small company which produces and sells nylon yarn become a giant within its industry and maintain a positive reputation in the community? The reason is that he adopts the competitive strategy of focus.

You can win in the competitive market depending on cost advantage, unique products or focus. The key to a focus strategy is to maintain focus, pursue excellence, and build a brand. In this regard, Ma Jianbo sets a good example for us.

Questions

1. What are the types of enterprise competitive strategy?
2. What are the types of confrontational competitive strategy?
3. What are the kinds of general competitive strategies? What is so

called "Being in the dilemma"?

4. What are the definition, significance and points for success of a cost-leading strategy?
5. What are the definition, significance and points for success of a differentiation strategy?
6. What are the definition, significance and points for success of a concentration strategy?
7. How many industrial types are there? And what are the main options of an enterprise competitive strategy in each industrial type?
8. How many kinds of industrial categories does the enterprise have? How does a firm choose the competitive strategy for each enterprise in the different categories?
9. How many strategies are there for large-scaled enterprise in general?
10. How many strategies are there for small and medium-scaled enterprises in general?
11. How many types of strategy can make rivals hard to counterattack?
12. How many types of strategy can achieve "winning without fighting"?

Notes

(1) Sun-Tzu(the original), Kung-sun Daoming ed, *Art of War and Thirty-Six Stratagems*, 1st edition, Guangxi Ethnic Publishing House, July 1995, p.31.
(2) Editing group of required MBA core courses, *Business Strategy*, 1st edition, China International Radio Press, September 1997, p.147.
(3) Editing group of required MBA core courses, *Business Strategy*, 1st edition, China International Radio Press, September 1997, p.148.
(4) Editing group of required MBA core courses, *Business Strategy*, 1st edition, China International Radio Press, September 1997, p.175.
(5) Sun-Tzu(the original), Kung-sun Daoming ed, *Art of War and Thirty-Six Stratagems*, 1st edition, Guangxi Ethnic Publishing House, July 1995, p.31.

BIBLIOGRAPHY

Art of War commentary group of War Theory Research Department of Academy of Military Sciences, CPLA, *New Commentary of Art of War*, 1st edition, Zhonghua Book Company, January 1977.

Sun-Tzu(the original), Kung-sun Daoming ed, *Art of War and Thirty-Six Stratagems*, 1st edition, Guangxi Ethnic Publishing House, July 1995.

Editorial board of Art of War and Strategy for Business and Politics, *Art of War and Strategy for Business and Politics*, 1st edition, Blue Sky Press, May 1997.

Guo Jixing, Li Shijun, *Romance of the Three Kingdoms and Business Strategic Management*, 1st edition, Guangxi People's Publishing House, June, 1988.

Yao Youwei, *Strategies in the Three Kingdoms and Tips for Commercial War*, 1st edition, Donghua University Press, August, 2006.

〔U.S.〕 Michael Porter, *Competitive Strategy*, 1st edition, Huaxia Publishing House, January 1997.

〔U.S.〕 Jack Trout, *Trout on Strategy*, 1st edition, China Financial and Economic Publishing House, October 2004.

〔U.S.〕 Arthur A. Thompson Jr. & A. J. Strickland, *Crafting and executing strategy: the quest for competitive advantage concepts and cases*, 10th ed, Duan Shenghua, Wang Zhihui trans., Xu Erming revision, Peking University Press, 2004.

Editing group of required MBA core courses, *Business Strategy*, 1st edition, China International Radio Press, September 1997.

Editing group of required MBA core courses, *Business Strategy*, 1st edition revision, China International Radio Press, 2000.

Liu Jisheng ed, *Company Operation Strategy*, 1st edition, Tsinghua University Press, April 1995.

CHAPTER 8
Enterprise Competitive Strategy Formulation

Abstract

This chapter begins with brilliant expositions of modern Chinese strategist Mao Zedong's *On Protracted War* and ancient Chinese strategist Sun Tzu's *Art of War*. It reveals laws of "If you know the enemy and know yourself, you need not fear the result of a hundred battles" and points out that the central task of formulating competitive strategy is to understand and analyze competitors. Then by referring to the classic exposition of "In all fighting, the direct method may be used for joining battle, but indirect methods will be needed in order to secure victory." and "Attack him where he is unprepared, appear where you are not expected" in *Art of War*, it explains the goal of formulating competitive strategy is to make a company to become the unique one and emphasizes the extreme importance of innovation and uniqueness in formulating competitive strategy. Subsequently, this chapter introduces processes to formulate competitive strategy and basic tools for shaping competitive advantage - the value chain. Finally, it has an appendix of cases and comments in "How does Haier freezer force to open the U.S. market" and "Three kinds of cola with three strategies."

Learning Objectives

- To define the central task of formulating competitive strategy is to understand and analyze competitors.
- To grasp four diagnostic elements of competitor analysis.
- To understand and grasp processes to formulate competitive strategy.
- To understand and grasp value chain, the basic tool for shaping competitive advantages.
- To formulate innovative and unique company competitive strategy combining *Art of War* with Porter's competitive theory.

Introduction

Modern Chinese strategist Mao Zedong has stressed in *On Protracted War* that "The law of Sun Tzu,' know yourself as well as the enemy ' is still scientific truth." (1) Sun Tzu has said in Art of War that "If you know the enemy and know yourself, you need not fear the result of a hundred battles. If you know yourself but not the enemy, for every victory gained you will also suffer a defeat. If you know neither the enemy nor yourself, you will succumb in every battle." (2) it means that when one knows the situations of the enemy and oneself, one will not fail conducting many operations; when one knows the situations of oneself but the enemy, one may have half the possibility to defeat; when one knows none of the situations of neither the enemy nor oneself, one will lose every battle. Therefore, the central task of formulating competitive strategy is to understand and analyze competitors.

Lesson

In *Art of War*, there are sentences of "In all fighting, the direct method may be used for joining battle, but indirect methods will be needed in order to secure victory. Indirect tactics, efficiently applied, are inexhaustible as Heaven and Earth, unending as the flow of rivers and streams; like the sun and moon, they end but begin anew; like the four seasons, they pass away to return once more. There are not more than five musical notes, yet the combinations of these five give rise to more melodies than can ever be heard. There are not more than five primary colors (blue, yellow, red, white, and black), yet in combination they produce more hues than can ever been seen. There are not more than five cardinal tastes (sour, acrid, salt, sweet, bitter), yet combinations of them yield more flavors than can ever be tasted. In battle, there are not more than two methods of attack--the direct and the indirect; yet these two in combination give rise to an endless series of maneuvers. The direct and the indirect lead on to each other in turn; it is like moving in a circle--you never come to an end. Who can exhaust the possibilities of their combination?"(3) and "Attack him where he is unprepared, appear where you are not expected. These military devices, leading to victory, must not be divulged beforehand." (4)

That is to say in almost all warfare, the direct method may be used for joining battle, but indirect methods will be needed in order to secure victory. Therefore, for generals good at using these two methods, tactics are inexhaustible and changeable. And nobody can exhaust the possibilities of their combination. In that case, attacks should be launched where enemy is unexpected and when he is unprepared. These are secrets of strategist for victory and cannot be specified in advance.

"The direct method may be used for joining battle" in *Art of War* is to compete with competitors by adopting the usual strategy; while "indirect methods will be needed in order to secure victory" means to win by adopting an innovative strategy. The main indicator of innovative strategy is unique, or to be different.

I.   Goals of competitive strategy

(I) The goal of competitive strategy is to enable companies to become unique

On June 18, 2004, Michael Porter describes the essence of his competitive strategy that he has studied for more than twenty years to a large number of Chinese entrepreneurs in "2004 Michael Potter Strategic Forum." He believes that a company should not consider competition just as striving to be the first in the industry. Perfect competitive strategy is to create uniqueness of the company, so it cannot be copied in this industry. (5)

In price competitive industries in our country like household appliances, he thinks it is not the best to compete on price. In his opinion, there must be a good competitive strategy. In fact, competition is not to be the best, but to make you unique. From a strategic point of view, there are many aspects of competition. As a company, you should find a way to make yourself to make you different in the industry rather than find the only panacea. If the company can think in this way, then the competition it faces will not be destructive and will not cause malicious price wars. Do not put the competition in a position to compete on prices but become more unique to the competition. (6)

"If all you've done is relied on experience, your competitors may also implement the same highly developed experience and techniques, so, it is not enough to merely have some experience. What happens if this expertise is implemented in the whole industry? Then all companies seem to look the same. This is the worst case scenario. In this case, you eventually will compete on price and have difficulty in maintaining a long-term advantage. Strategy is not trying to be the best; being different and unique allows you to compete in various ways." (7)

(II) Effective competitive strategy must have five key points

How can a company uncover a unique strategy to make oneself stand out? In Porter's opinion, an effective competitive strategy must have five key points:

1. To have a relatively unique value orientation compared to competitors

This includes three important aspects: What types of customer are you going to service? What needs of these customers will be met? What are the relative prices you would expect or seek? These three points could form your values orientation.

2. To have a distinctive value chain which is carefully designed for potential customers?

If your competitive advantage is the same as others', then it is of little value. Strategy is to choose a different operating model, which reflects a different value chain for sure.

3. To make a clear choice, doing some things and leaving some things undone

Strategy needs to make a clear choice, doing some things and leaving some things undone. Mistakes that companies often make are to try to do too much without preferences. Strategic choices will make the strategy more durable and not easy for competitors to imitate.

Management master Peter Drucker puts it well that "No company can do everything. Even if there is enough money, it will never have enough talent. It must prioritize something for the worst is to do all but a little, which will accomplish nothing. To have a focus that is not the best is better than to have none." (8)

4. Activities in the value chain must be shared to promote each other.

5. Must have perseverance

A good strategy must have perseverance; otherwise it cannot be regarded as strategy because the implementation of any strategy will take three to four

268

years to implement. Perseverance of a strategy is very important for maintaining a competitive advantage. To update and adjust directions frequently costs too much and confuses customers easily.

II. Processes to formulate competitive strategy

Michael Porter has said that "Essentially, developing a competitive strategy is developing a broad formula for how a business is going to compete, what its goals should be, and what policies will be needed to carry out those goals." (9) Processes to formulate competitive strategy are shown in Figure 8-1.

Figure 8 —1 Processes to Formulate Competitive Strategy

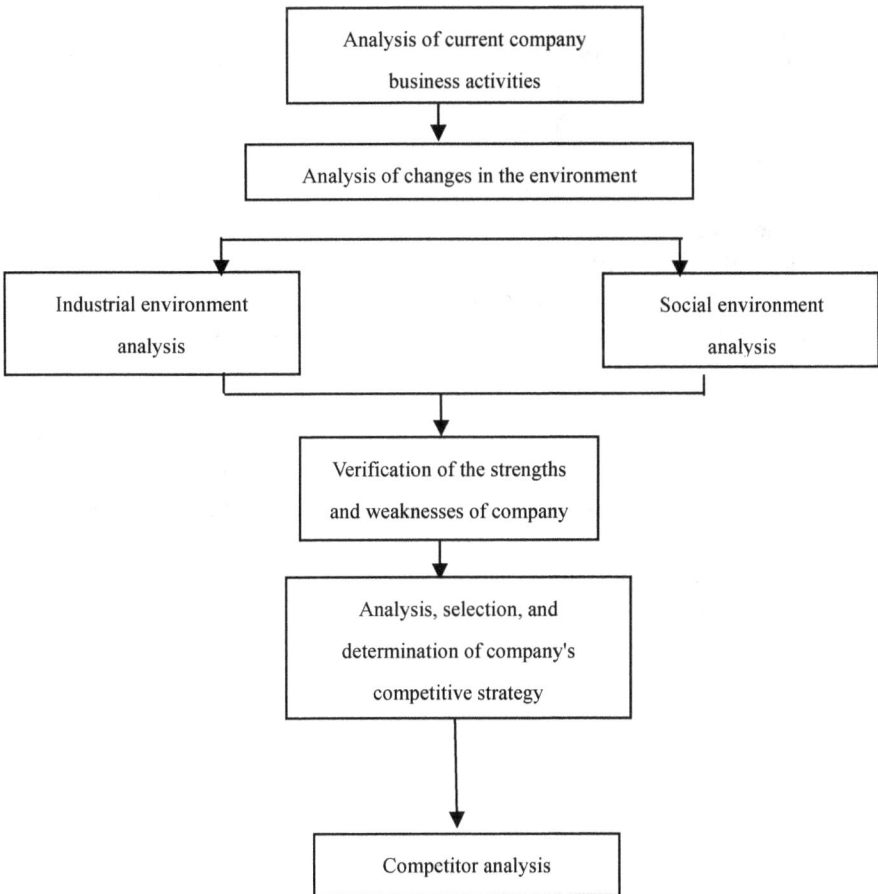

```
            ┌─────────────────────────────┐
            │ Analysis of current company │
            │      business activities    │
            └─────────────────────────────┘
                          │
                          ▼
        ┌───────────────────────────────────────┐
        │ Analysis of changes in the environment │
        └───────────────────────────────────────┘
                          │
         ┌────────────────┴────────────────┐
         ▼                                  ▼
┌────────────────────┐            ┌────────────────────┐
│ Industrial         │            │ Social environment │
│ environment        │            │ analysis           │
│ analysis           │            │                    │
└────────────────────┘            └────────────────────┘
         │                                  │
         └────────────────┬─────────────────┘
                          ▼
            ┌─────────────────────────────┐
            │ Verification of the strengths│
            │ and weaknesses of company   │
            └─────────────────────────────┘
                          │
                          ▼
            ┌─────────────────────────────┐
            │ Analysis, selection, and    │
            │ determination of company's  │
            │ competitive strategy        │
            └─────────────────────────────┘
                          │
                          ▼
            ┌─────────────────────────────┐
            │     Competitor analysis     │
            └─────────────────────────────┘
```

Main elements included in various procedures are:

(I) Analysis of current company business activities

1. Identification
    What are the current businesses? What is the existing strategy? Is this strategy implicit or explicit?

2. Assumption
    What are the assumptions made of the company's relative positions, strengths, weaknesses, competitors, and industry trends in order to make the existing strategy effective?

(II) Analysis of changes in the environment

Michael Porter has said that "The essence of formulating competitive strategy is relating a company to its environment. Although the relevant environment is very broad, encompassing social as well as economic forces, the key aspect of the firm's environment is the industry or industries in which it competes. Industry structure has a strong influence in determining the competitive rules of the game as well as the strategies potentially available to the firm. Forces outside the industry are significant primarily in a relative sense; since outside forces usually affect all firms in the industry, the key is found in the differing abilities of firms to deal with them." (10)

Figure 8-2 shows that at the broadest range, four key factors have to be considered in formulating competitive strategy. The strengths of a company are assets and technologies relative to competitors, including financial resources, technology conditions and trademarks visibility. Personal values of a company are incentives and demands of implementation managers and other certain strategies implementers. Strengths and values determine internal boundaries for a company to use competitive strategy successfully. Industry environment and wider external environment determine outer boundaries of the strategy. Opportunities and challenges within the industry determine industrial competitive environment, associated risks and potential benefits. Social expectation reflects the impact of government policies, social concerns, changing practices and other factors to the company. In forming a set of realistic, achievable goals and policies, companies must consider these four factors in advance.

Figure 8-2 Environment for formulating competitive strategy

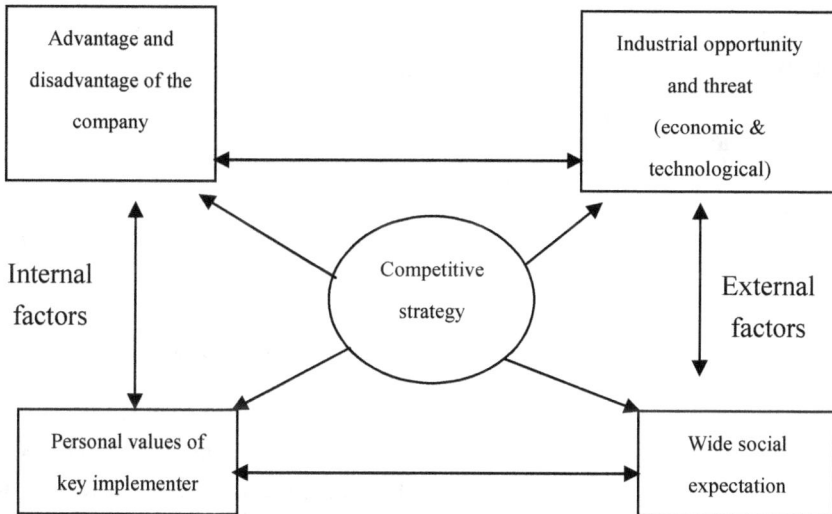

Source: Editing group of required MBA core courses, *Business Strategy*, 2001 edition, China International Radio Press, September, p. 215.

1. What are the key factors of competitive success in industrial environmental analysis? What are important opportunities and serious threats in the industry? (Contents of industrial environment analysis have been told in Chapter 6).

2. Competitor analysis - What are the capabilities and limitations of existing and potential competitors? What are the actions they could take? (Contents of competitor analysis will be explained in detail in the third question.)

3. Social environment analysis - What are the important social and political factors that will bring opportunities and risks? (Contents about social environment or the macro and micro analysis have been described in Chapter 6.)

(III) Verification of the strengths and weaknesses of company

Based on analysis of the industry and competitors, what are the company's strengths and weaknesses relative to its current and potential competitors? (Contents of company's internal assessment have been told in Chapter 6.)

(IV) Analysis, selection, and determination of company's competitive strategy

1. Strategy analysis

Compare changes in the environment with the company's resources and assumptions in order to see whether they are consistent. Focuses of analysis are:

(1) To compare changes in the environment and to study how the company's assumptions embody the current strategy?

(2) Whether this strategy can sustain the "Tests of Consistency," including test of environmental adaptability, Resource fit and internal consistency?

A. Environmental fit test
Do the goals and policies exploit industry opportunities?
Do the goals and policies deal with industry threats (including the risk of competitive response) to the degree possible with available resources?
Does the timing of the goals and policies reflect the ability of the environment to absorb the actions?
Are the goals and policies responsive to broader societal concerns?

B. Resource fit test
Do the goals and policies match the resources available to the company relative to competitors?
Does the timing of the goals and policies reflect the organization's ability to change?
Are the goals well understood by the key implementers?
Is there enough congruence between the goals and policies and the values of the key implementers to insure commitment?
Is there sufficient managerial capability to allow for effective implementation?

C. Internal consistency test

> Do the goals and policies exploit industry opportunities?
> Does the timing of the goals and policies reflect the ability of the environment to absorb the actions?
> Are the goals and policies responsive to the broader societal concerns?

(3) Is the strategy well understood by the key implementers? Is there enough congruence between them? Are there sufficient resources to implement effectively?

2. Strategy choice

In above analysis, what are the strategy choices viable for the company? Decide whether the current strategy has been adopted by one of them?

3. Strategy determination

Which strategy choice can establish the best contact between the company's situation and the external opportunities and risks?

III. Competitor analysis

Michael Porter has said that "Competitive strategy involves positioning a business to maximize the value of the capabilities that distinguish it from its competitors. It follows that a central aspect of strategy formulation is perceptive competitor analysis. The goal of a competitor analysis is to develop a profile of the nature and success of the likely strategic changes each competitor might make, each competitor's probable response to the range of feasible strategic moves other firms could initiate, and each competitor's probable reaction to the array of industry changes and broader environmental shifts that might occur." (11)

In Art of War, there is saying "If you know the enemy and know yourself, you need not fear the result of a hundred battles." Although two aspects here talked about "your enemy" and "yourself", from the perspective of strategy formulation, both focus the difficulty in "knowing your enemy", that is to analyze and understand one's competitor. Well then, how do we analyze competitors? There are four diagnostic elements for competitor analysis (shown in Figure 8-3): future goals, current strategies, assumptions and abilities.

Figure 8 - 3 Contents of competitor analysis

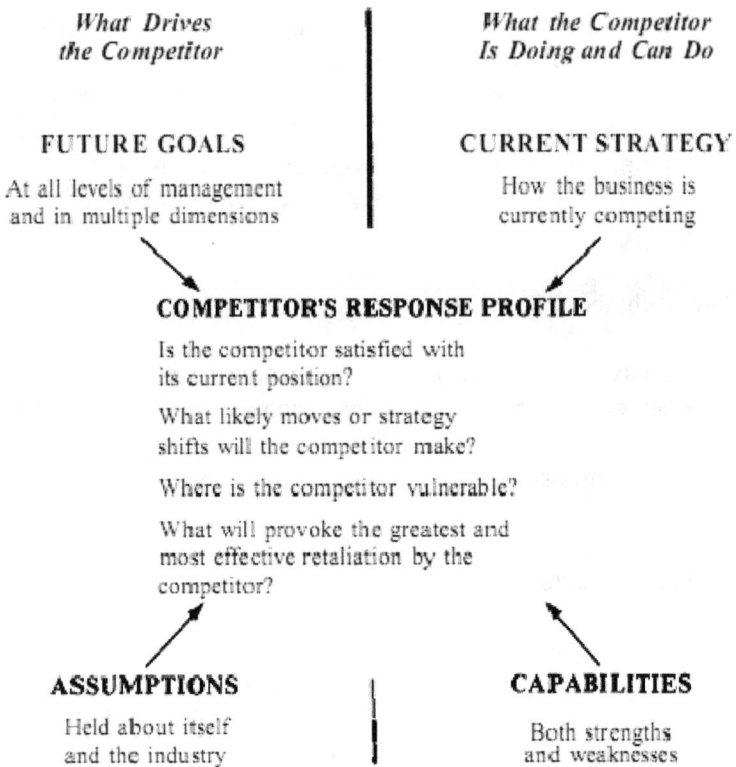

What Drives
the Competitor

What the Competitor
Is Doing and Can Do

FUTURE GOALS

CURRENT STRATEGY

At all levels of management
and in multiple dimensions

How the business is
currently competing

COMPETITOR'S RESPONSE PROFILE

Is the competitor satisfied with
its current position?

What likely moves or strategy
shifts will the competitor make?

Where is the competitor vulnerable?

What will provoke the greatest and
most effective retaliation by the
competitor?

ASSUMPTIONS

CAPABILITIES

Held about itself
and the industry

Both strengths
and weaknesses

(U.S.) Michael Porter, *Competitive Strategy*, Huaxia Publishing House, 1997, p.49.

Understanding of these four elements can make a company have a broad understanding of its competitors' reactions in advance, as key issues listed in Figure 8-3. Most companies have some intuitive sense about competitors' current strategies, strengths and weaknesses (seeing Figure 8-3 on the right), but pay far less attention to those on the left, that is to understand what is driving competitors, which includes their future goals and their assumptions of own conditions and industrial nature. Observation of these motives is more difficult than that of the actual behavior of competitors. But these motives often decide how competitors should act in the future. Therefore, competitor analysis should focus on diagnosis of competitors' goals and assumptions.

(I) Factors of competitor analysis

Competitor analysis includes four elements:

1. Future goals

The future goals of a competitor are the first element of competitor analysis. First, through understanding of goals a company can predict satisfaction status of competitor on its current position and financial condition. And thus can predict whether it will change its strategies and react to external events such as the economic cycle or to other company's strategic actions. Second, understanding of the competitor's goals can also help predict its response to changes in strategies. It means the possibility of retaliation when a competitor is under a threat of certain strategic changes. Finally, it can also help to explain the seriousness of a competitor's initial actions.

Most people are concerned about the financial goals. While a comprehensive study on the competitor's goals should normally include a number of qualitative factors, such as it goals in the aspects of market, technology position, social performance and so on. Goals study should also investigate multi-level management, including company level, business unit level, even individual functional departments and key managers. It is because high-level goals can guide low-level goals, but cannot completely determine the:

Future goals analysis includes four aspects:

1. Goals of the business unit
2. Goals of the parent company and business unit
3. If the competitor is a unit of a larger company, its parent company will likely have   restrictions or requirements. To understand such restrictions or requirements is critical for predicting its behaviors.
4. Business portfolio analysis and competitor's goals
5. When the competitor is part of a diversified company, a business portfolio analysis of the   parent   company   will   be   very enlightening for the answers to above questions.
6. Goals and strategic positioning of competitor

Porter pointed out in a creative way that "One approach in formulating strategy is to look for positions in the market where a firm can meet its goals without threatening its competitors. When competitors' goals are well understood, there may be a place where everyone is relatively happy."

This conclusion is extremely important. If a company can do so, it can do in its place avoiding vicious competition situation like millions of soldiers seizing the single-plank bridge. Of course such positions do not always exist, particularly when one takes into account that new entrants may be tempted into an industry where existing firms are all doing well. In most cases the firm has to force competitors to compromise their goals in order for the firm to meet its goals. To do so it needs to find a strategy it can defend against existing competitors and new entrants through some distinctive advantages.

Analysis of competitors' goals is crucial because it helps the firms avoid strategic moves that will touch off bitter warfare by threatening competitors' ability to achieve key goals.

2. Assumptions

- The second crucial component in competitor analysis is identifying each competitor's assumptions. These fall into two major categories:
- The competitor's assumptions about itself
- The competitor's assumptions about the industry and the other companies in it

Every firm operates on a set of assumptions about its own situation. For example, it may see itself as a socially conscious firm, as the industry leader, as the low-cost producer, as having the best sales force, and so on. These assumptions about its own situation will guide the way the firm behaves and the way it reacts to events. If it sees itself as the low-cost producer, for example, it may try to discipline a price cutter with price cuts of its own.
A competitor's assumptions about its own situation may or may not be accurate. Where they are not, this provides an intriguing strategic lever.

Just as each competitor holds assumptions about itself; every firm also operates on assumptions about its industry and competitors. These also may or may not be correct.
3. Current strategies

The third element of competitor analysis is to list current strategies of each competitor.

Every competitive company in an industry has its own competitive strategy. A company can either formulate a clear competitive strategy in planning process, or formulate a subtle strategy through activities of various functional departments.

However, if various functional departments act on their own, their strategies are inevitably affected by their professional characteristics and the incentives of management. What's more, the sum of these sector strategies is also not the best strategy.

A useful strategy is to view competitors' strategies as key operating principles in various functional areas and to understand how they link with various functions. This strategy may be explicit or may be implicit and always exists in one of these two forms.

4. Abilities

Realistic assessment of the strength of competitors is the final step of competitor analysis. Goals, assumptions and current strategies of competitors will affect the possibility, time, nature and intensity of their response. And their strengths and weaknesses will determine their abilities to take strategic action and to deal with events in the environment or industry. These abilities include core competencies, growth capacity, rapid response capabilities, ability to adapt to changes and endurance.

(II) Summary of fighting competitors back

If you have analyzed competitors' future goals, assumptions, current strategies and abilities, then, you are able to raise some key questions after combining these four elements. These questions will constitute a summary of how to react on competitors.

1. Attack

Step one: to predict strategic change may be initiated by competitors

① The degree of satisfaction rivals feel about their current positions.

To compare goals of competitors and their parent companies with their current positions, then you may predict whether competitors may proceed to initiate strategic changes?

② Possible actions competitors may take. According to competitors' goals relative to current positions, their assumptions and abilities, what kind of strategic changes do competitors most likely initiate?

③ Intensity and seriousness of competitors' actions. Analysis of competitors' goals and abilities can be used to assess the expected strength of these possible actions. Meanwhile, it is needed to estimate benefits that competitors can get from these actions. Combination of

possible benefits and goals of competitors will help to judge competitor's seriousness of their actions when facing resistance.

2. Defense capabilities

Step Two: to list a series of possible strategies and possible changes of a certain company in the industry. These are available to estimate from the following criteria to determine the defense capabilities of competitors and from conclusions obtained previously.

3. Selection of the battlefield

Assuming that competitors will retaliate to firm initiatives, its strategic agenda is selecting the best battleground for fighting it out with its competitors. This battleground is the market segment or dimensions of strategy in which competitors are ill-prepared, least enthusiastic, or most uncomfortable about competing. The best battleground may be competition based on costs, centered at the high or low end of the product line, or other areas. There are three options:

First, ideal choice. The ideal is to find a strategy that competitors are unable to react given their present circumstances. The legacy of their past and current strategy may make some moves very costly for competitors to follow, while posing much less difficulty and expense for the initiating firm. For example, when a small coffee company attacks a very large coffee company adopting price-cutting strategy, the cost will be enormous for the large company who has a larger market share to cut prices.

Second, general choice. Another key strategic concept deriving from competitor analysis is creating a situation of mixed motives or conflicting goals for competitors. This strategy involves finding moves for which retaliation, though effective, would hurt the competitor's broader position. For example, as IBM responds to the threat of the minicomputer with its own minicomputer; it may hasten the decline in growth of its large computers and accelerate the changeover to minicomputers. Placing competitors in a situation of conflicting goals can be a very effective strategic approach for attacking established firms that have been successful in their markets. Small firms and newly entered firms often have very little legacy in the existing strategies. Firms reap great rewards from finding strategies that penalize competitors for their stake in these existing strategies.

Third, forced to choose. Realistically, competitors will not often be completely unable to move or even torn by mixed motives. In this case, the questions posed above should help to identify those strategic moves that will put the initiating firm in the best position to fight the competitive battle when it comes. This means taking advantage of an understanding of competitor goals and assumptions to avoid effective retaliation whenever possible and picking the battlefield where the firm's distinctive ability represents the most formidable artillery.

(III) Establishment of intelligence systems for gathering information about competitors

Answering these questions about competitors creates enormous needs for data. Intelligence data on competitors can come from many sources: reports filed publicly, speeches by a competitor's management to security analysts, the business press, the sales force, a firm's customers or suppliers that are common to competitors, inspection of a competitor's products, estimates by the firm's engineering staff, knowledge gleaned from managers or other personnel who have left the competitor's employment, and so on. It is unlikely that data to support a full competitor analysis could be compiled in one massive effort. The data to make the subtle judgments implied by these questions usually come in trickles rather than rivers and must be put together over a period of time to yield a comprehensive picture of the competitor's situation.

Compiling the data for a sophisticated competitor analysis probably requires more than just hard work. To be effective, there is the need for an organized mechanism-some sort of competitor intelligence system-to insure that the process is efficient. The elements of a competitor intelligence system can vary according to the particular firm's needs, based on its industry, its staff capability, and its managements' interests and talents. Figure 8-4 diagrams the functions that must be performed in developing the data for sophisticated competitor analysis and gives some options for how each function might be performed. A manager is needed to be in charge of gathering competitors' intelligence.

Each of the functions can also be performed in a number of different ways, as noted in Figure 8-4. The options shown cover a range of degrees of sophistication and completeness. Whatever the level of sophistication, the importance of the communication function cannot be stressed enough. Gathering data is a waste of time unless they are used in formulating strategy, and creative ways must be devised to put these data in concise and usable form to top management.

Whatever the mechanism chosen for competitor intelligence gathering, there are benefits to be gained from one that is formal and involves some documentation. It is all too easy for bits and pieces of data to be lost, and the benefits that come only from combining these bits and pieces thereby foregone. Analyzing competitors

IV.   Basic tool for shaping competitive advantage - Value Chain

If competitive advantage is the core of any strategy, then where is its source? Porter has said that competitive advantage comes from values a firm creates for customers and the benefits outweigh its cost. (13)

After a long research, Porter creates a tool of "value chain" for analyzing sources of competitive advantage. He believes that to take the company as a whole cannot unit a firm will not be able to understand the competitive advantage.

Figure 8-4 Functions of intelligence system for gathering about competitors

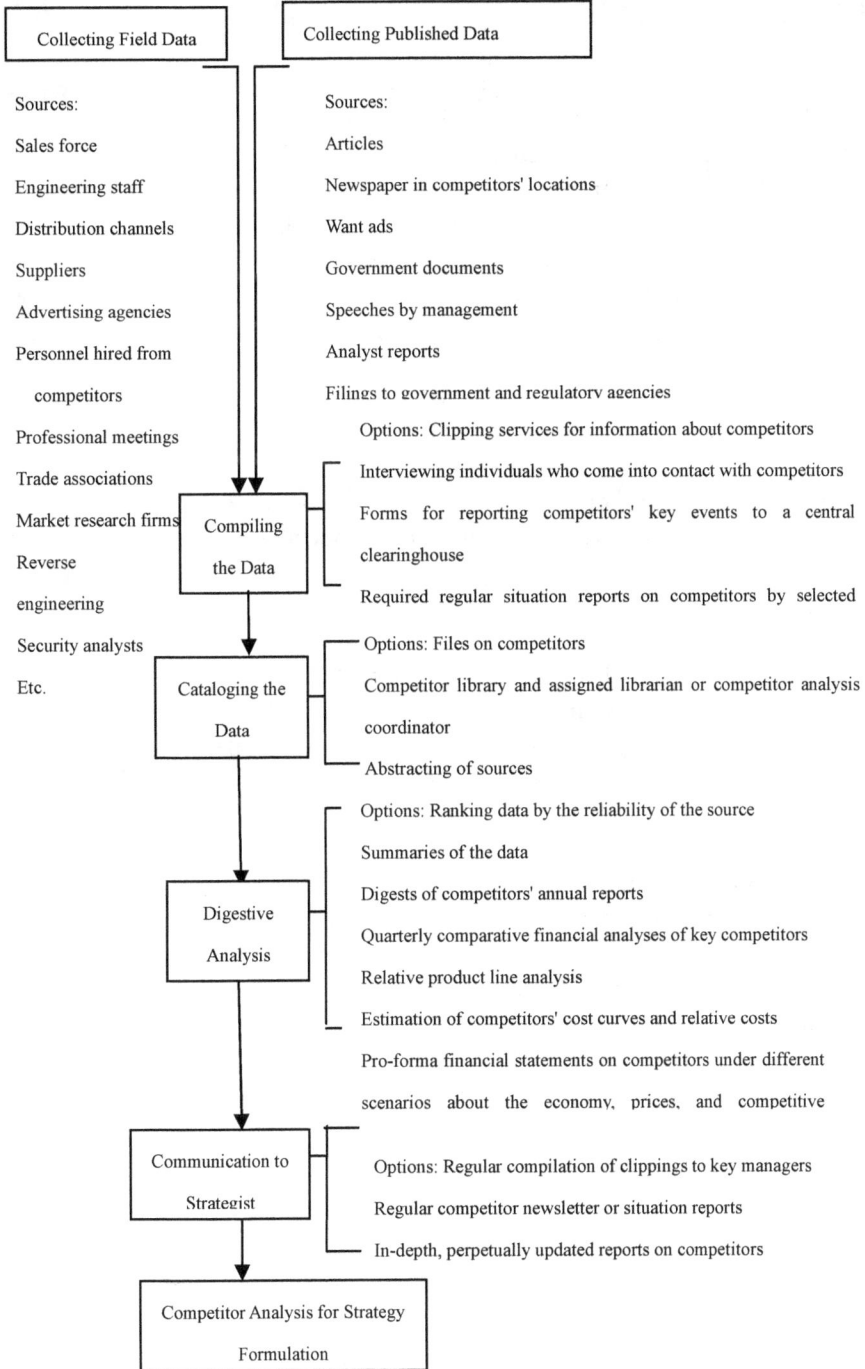

Collecting Field Data	Collecting Published Data

Sources:

Sales force

Engineering staff

Distribution channels

Suppliers

Advertising agencies

Personnel hired from

   competitors

Professional meetings

Trade associations

Market research firms

Reverse

engineering

Security analysts

Etc.

Sources:

Articles

Newspaper in competitors' locations

Want ads

Government documents

Speeches by management

Analyst reports

Filings to government and regulatory agencies

Compiling the Data

Options: Clipping services for information about competitors

Interviewing individuals who come into contact with competitors

Forms for reporting competitors' key events to a central clearinghouse

Required regular situation reports on competitors by selected

Cataloging the Data

Options: Files on competitors

Competitor library and assigned librarian or competitor analysis coordinator

Abstracting of sources

Digestive Analysis

Options: Ranking data by the reliability of the source

Summaries of the data

Digests of competitors' annual reports

Quarterly comparative financial analyses of key competitors

Relative product line analysis

Estimation of competitors' cost curves and relative costs

Pro-forma financial statements on competitors under different

scenarios about the economy, prices, and competitive

Communication to Strategist

Options: Regular compilation of clippings to key managers

Regular competitor newsletter or situation reports

In-depth, perpetually updated reports on competitors

Competitor Analysis for Strategy Formulation

Source for Figure 8-4: (U.S.) Michael Porter, *Competitive Strategy*, Huaxia Publishing House, 1997, p. 74.

Competitive advantage comes from company's mutual separated activities in design, production, marketing, delivery, and auxiliary processes. Each of these activities contributes to company's position of relative cost, and lays the basis for differentiation. For example, cost advantage comes from a number of different resources, such as low-cost goods distribution system, high efficient assembly process or excellent sales team. Differentiation depends on similar factors, including the procurement of high-quality raw materials, ordering systems with fast response or excellence product design. (14)

(I) Value system

A value chain will divide a company into a number of strategic-related activities. It is through carrying out these important strategic initiatives cheaper or better than its competitors that a company gains its competitive advantage.

Value chain is embodied in a broader series of activities which are called value systems, as shown in Figure 8-5. Providers have value chains for purchases used which can create and deliver a company's value chain (upstream value). Suppliers not only deliver a product, but also affect many other aspects of the company.

In addition, many products reach the hands of buyers through value chains (channel values) of a number of channels. Additional activities of channels affect buyers, as well as companies' own activities. A company's products eventually become part of the value chain of its buyers. Basis of differentiation is the function that a company and its products have in its buyers' value chain, which determines buyers' needs. To obtain and maintain a competitive advantage depends not only on the company's understanding the value chain, but also depends on how a company adapts to fit the understanding of a certain value system.

(II) Composition of value chain

Every company is the collection of various activities like design, production, marketing, product delivery and other activities that play supporting roles. All of these activities can be represented by the value chain, as shown in

Figure 8-5 Value system

Diversified Firm

Firm Value Chain

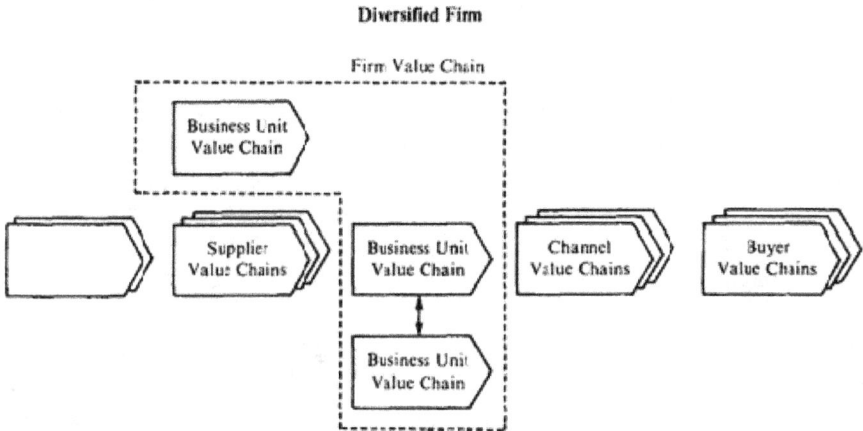

Figure 8-6 Basic value chain

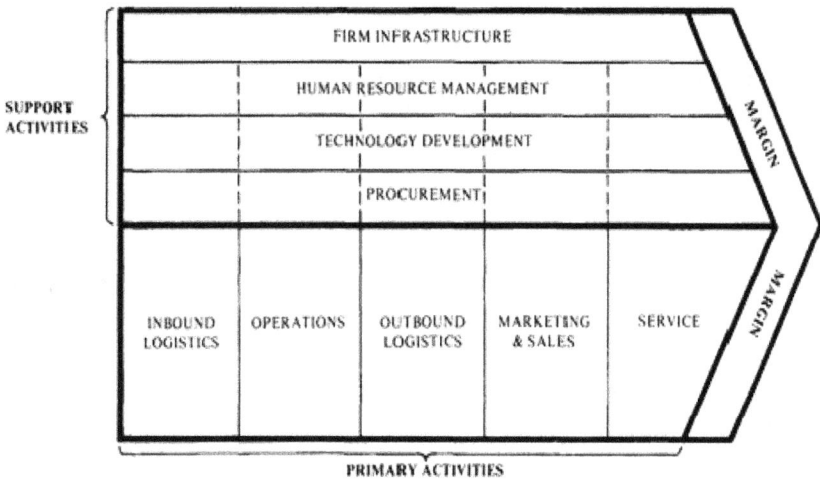

Source: 〔U.S.〕Michael Porter, Competitive Advantage, Huaxia Publishing House, 1997, p. 34-37.

Figure 8-6. A company's value chain and single activity it engaged in reflect its history, strategy, approach to implement the strategy and the fundamental economic benefits of these activities themselves.

Value chain at a certain level is the combination of various activities of the company in a particular industry. Although value chains of companies in same industry are similar, value chains of the competitors are often different. Differences in the value chains of competitors are a key source of competitive advantage.

Each value activity exerts its effects by using procurement inputs, human resources (labor and management) and certain technology. Each value activity uses and creates information, such as buyer data (order registration), performance parameters (evaluation) and waste statistics. Value activities can also create assets such as inventory and receivables, or liabilities and accounts payable.

Value activities can be divided into two categories: basic activities and auxiliary activities. Basic activities, as shown in the bottom of Figure 8-6, involve activities in product creation, marketing, transferring to buyers and after-sales service. Various basic activities involved in the competition within any industry can be divided into five basic types, as shown in Figure 8-6. Auxiliary activities support basic activities, and provide procurement inputs, technology, human resources and various functions within scope of companies. Dotted lines reflect the fact that procurement, technology development and human resource management are linked with a variety of specific basic activities and support the entire value chain. Although the company's infrastructure is not linked with a variety of specific basic activities, it supports the entire value chain as well.

Therefore, value activities are composed of various separated activities of competitive advantage. Combinations of each value activities and economic effects will determine the level of a company's cost competitiveness. Implementation of each value activity will determine its contribution to meet buyers' needs and may be unconventional. And comparison of the value chains of competitors reveals the reason that causes differences in competitive advantage.

(III) Value activities

(1) Basic activities

Various basic activities involved in the competition within any industry can be divided into five basic types, as shown in Figure 8-6. Each of them can be divided into a number of significantly different activities based on industry's characteristics and company's strategy:

Internal logistics. Various activities associated with receiving, storage and distribution. For example, raw material handling, storage, inventory control, vehicle scheduling and return to the supplier.

Manufacturing operations. Various activities related to turn inputs into final products, for example, mechanical processing, packaging, assembly, equipment maintenance, testing, printing and facilities management.

External logistics. Various activities related to concentration, storage and sending products to buyers. For example, finished goods inventory management, raw material handling, delivery vehicle scheduling, order processing and production scheduling.

Marketing and sales. Various activities related to provide buyers with a way to purchase products and guide them to purchase. For example, advertising, promotion, sales force, quoting, channel selection, channel relations and pricing.

Services. Various activities related to provision of services in order to increase or maintain the product value. For example, installation, maintenance, training, parts supply and product adjustment.

According to conditions of the industry, each type of activity may be crucial for competitive advantage. For wholesalers, logistics management of purchase and delivery is most important; for companies that provide services like restaurant or retail, external logistics may be largely non-existent, while operation is the key; for a bank that is committed to business loans, efficiency of collection personnel, loan packaging and pricing play a vital role in competitive advantage; for a high-speed copier manufacturers, service will become a core source of competitive advantage. However, in any company, all types of basic activities exist to some extent and play a role in competitive advantage.

(2) Ancillary activities

Various ancillary activities involved in the competition within any industry can be divided into four basic types, as shown in Figure 8-6. Same with basic activities, every type of auxiliary activities can be divided into a number of significantly different value activities according to specific circumstances of the industry. For example, in the technology development process, various independent activities may include component design, feature design, field testing, and process and technology choices. Similarly, procurement can be divided into various activities such as audits of new suppliers, procurements with different combinations of inputs and continuous monitoring of suppliers' performances.

Procurement. Procurement refers to activities purchasing inputs for the value chain, rather than inputs for purchasing them. Inputs for purchase include raw materials, reserve materials and other consumables, as well as a variety of assets, for example, machinery, laboratory equipment, office equipment and buildings. Although inputs for purchase are associated with basic activities in general, it exists in all value activities, including auxiliary activities.

Procurement often occurs throughout the company. Some objects, such as raw materials are purchased by the traditional purchasing department, and other things are purchased by the plant manager (such as machines), division managers (such as temporary workers), sales personnel (such as rations and quarters), and even president (such as strategic advice). Here procurement is used instead of purchase because the latter is usually limited to managers and too narrow. Dispersion of the procurement function often leads to vagueness of the total purchases. It means that many purchases are rarely studied in detail.

A specific procurement activity is usually associated with a specific value activity or activities it supports, although usually, a purchase department services many value activities and purchasing policies apply to the entire company. The cost of the procurement activity itself is often considered only a small part, but it often has great impact on the company's overall costs and operating diversity. Improved procurement activity will have a strong impact on inputs for procurement, costs and qualities that receiving and using these inputs, and will interact with suppliers. For example, in the chocolate production industry and supply industry, procurement of cocoa and fuel is done separately even though it is the most important factor in

286

determining its cost position.

Technology development. Each value activity has a technical component, whether it is technical ability, procedures, or technology embodied in process equipment. Technologies are widely adopted by most companies, from technology for the preparation of documents and transport of commodities to technology reflected by the product itself. In addition, most technologies used in value activities are combinations of different technical disciplines of different branches. For example, machining includes technical disciplines of metallurgy, electronics, and machinery.

Technology development is composed of a range of activities, which occur in many departments in the company. Technology development process may play a supporting role in a variety of value activities, including electronic communication technology in the registration system, or office automation of accounting departments. It not only applies to technology which is directly related to the final product. There are also many forms of technology development. Technology development related to products and their characteristics can play a supporting role in the entire value chain, while others are related to specific basic or auxiliary activities.

Technology development is important for competitive advantage in all industries and even plays a central role in some industries. For example, in the steel industry, technology is the most important factor for competitive advantage.

Human resources management. Human resources management includes recruitment, hiring, training, development, remuneration and other activities of all types of staff. Human resource management not only plays a supporting role in a single basic and auxiliary activity, such as employment of engineers, but also supports the entire value chain, such as labor negotiations. Various activities of human resource management happen in different parts of companies and the cumulative cost of human resource management must be correctly understood.

Human resource management impacts the company's competitive advantage through its role in decision of employees' skills and enthusiasm, as well as the costs of hiring and training. In some industries, it will have a key impact on the company's competitive advantage. Human resource management has a profound consequence on the whole company's working methods, which not only makes the company more efficient, but also greatly enhances the company's services for customers.

Company infrastructure. Company infrastructure is composed of a large number of activities, including overall management, planning, finance, accounting, legal, government affairs and quality management. Infrastructure is different from other auxiliary activities because it plays a supporting role through the entire value chain rather than individual activities. Based on whether the operation of company is decentralized, the company's infrastructure can be self-supporting or shared between business units and the parent company. In the company of decentralized operations, activities of the infrastructure typically has a far reaching impact among business units and companies, for instance, financial management is carried out in the company, and quality management in the business unit. However, many infrastructure activities are carried out within business units and the companies at the same time.

Company infrastructure sometimes is only considered as indirect cost, but it is an important source of competitive advantage. For example, in a telephone business company, negotiations with old buyers and maintenance of lasting relationships may be one of the most important activities for competitive advantage. Similarly, appropriate management information systems will make a significant contribution to the company's cost position, and senior management in dealing with the relationship with buyers is essential in some industries.

(IV) Types of activities

In each category of basic and auxiliary activities, there are three types of activities which have different influences on competitive advantage:

Direct activities. It refers to the various activities directly related to create value for the buyer. For example, assembly, spare parts processing, sales, advertising, product design, recruitment and so on.

Indirect activities. It refers to the various activities making it possible for direct activities to continue. For example, maintenance, scheduling, facilities management, sales management, research management, sales records, and so on.

Quality assurance. It refers to the various activities ensuring the quality of other activities. For example, supervision, inspection, testing, review, verification, adjustment and rework. Quality assurance and quality management are not synonymous, because a lot of value activities contribute to quality.

Any company has value activities of direct, indirect and quality assurance. These three types of activities exist not only in basic activities, but also in various ancillary activities. For example, in technology development, the actual experimental team is engaged in direct activities, and research management falls under indirect activities.

Roles of indirect activities and quality assurance activities often are misunderstood, which makes identification of these three forms of activity an important factor in determining competitive advantage. In many industries, the cost of indirect activities is considerably high, and its proportion of the total cost grows rapidly. Indirect activities play a decisive role in operating diversity by impacting direct activities. However, managers still link indirect activities and direct activities together when studying the company, although these two activities have completely different economic effects. There are often trade-offs issues between indirect activities and direct activities. Indirect activities are often classified as subject of "management fees" and "indirect costs", which leads to the confusion of their costs and contributions to operating diversity.

Quality assurance activities exist in almost every part of the company, even though few people realize this. Detection and monitoring are associated with many basic activities. Quality assurance activities except for manufacturing operations are wide-ranging, but they are not so obvious. According to studies, the cumulative cost of quality assurance activities may be very large. Quality assurance activities often affect the cost or efficiency of other activities, while other activities will in turn affect the needs and means of the quality assurance activities.

(V) Determination of the value chain

In order to determine the competitive advantage, it is necessary to define the company's value chain. To analyze starting from basic value chain and individual value activities in a particular company are recognized. Each basic type can be separated into a number of activities, as shown in Figure 8-7. An example of a complete value chain is shown in Figure 8-8, which is the value chain of copier manufacturers.

289

Figure 8-7 Decomposition of a basic value chain

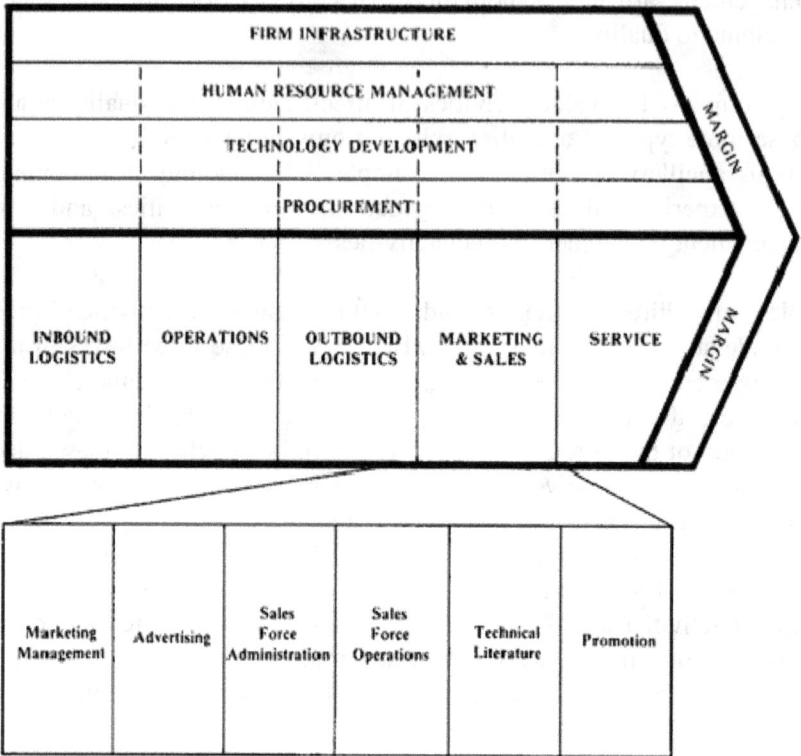

FIRM INFRASTRUCTURE					
HUMAN RESOURCE MANAGEMENT					MARGIN
TECHNOLOGY DEVELOPMENT					
PROCUREMENT					
INBOUND LOGISTICS	OPERATIONS	OUTBOUND LOGISTICS	MARKETING & SALES	SERVICE	MARGIN

Marketing Management	Advertising	Sales Force Administration	Sales Force Operations	Technical Literature	Promotion

The definition of related value activities requires less significant activities whose technical and economic effects are separated. Functions such as production or marketing must be further subdivided into a number of activities, which are to some extent independent from each other. For example, each machine in the factory can be seen as a separate activity. In this case, the number of potential activities will usually be very huge.

The breakdown degree depends on the economic efficiency of these activities and goals of the value chain analysis. The basic principles are: to have different economical efficiencies, to have a huge potential impact on the differentiation, and to occupy a large proportion or a rising proportion of the cost. When value chain is used to analyze and reveal different effects on competitive advantage, some activities are broken down, while others are combined.

Figure 8—8 Copier manufacturer's value chain

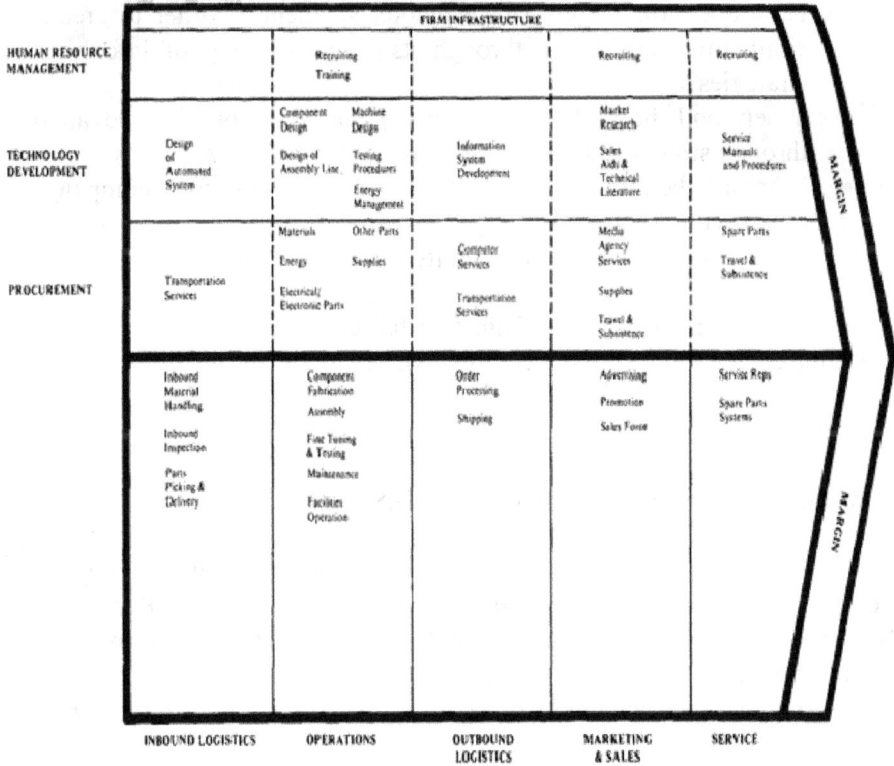

	FIRM INFRASTRUCTURE				
HUMAN RESOURCE MANAGEMENT		Recruiting Training		Recruiting	Recruiting
TECHNOLOGY DEVELOPMENT	Design of Automated System	Component Design, Machine Design Design of Assembly Line, Testing Procedures Energy Management	Information System Development	Market Research Sales Aids & Technical Literature	Service Manuals and Procedures
PROCUREMENT	Transportation Services	Materials, Other Parts Energy, Supplies Electrical/Electronic Parts	Computer Services Transportation Services	Media Agency Services Supplies Travel & Subsistence	Spare Parts Travel & Subsistence
	Inbound Material Handling Inbound Inspection Parts Picking & Delivery	Component Fabrication Assembly Fine Tuning & Testing Maintenance Facilities Operation	Order Processing Shipping	Advertising Promotion Sales Force	Service Reps Spare Parts Systems
	INBOUND LOGISTICS	**OPERATIONS**	**OUTBOUND LOGISTICS**	**MARKETING & SALES**	**SERVICE**

(MARGIN)

Source: 〔U.S.〕 Michael Porter, *Competitive Advantage*, Huaxia Publishing House, 1997, p. 46-47.

(VI) Value of the value chain

Porter has said in the preface of *Competitive Advantage* that "Competitive advantage is at the heart of a firm's performance in competitive markets. After several decades of vigorous expansion and prosperity, however, many firms lost sight of competitive advantage in their scramble for growth and pursuit of diversification. Today the importance of competitive advantage could hardly be greater. Firms throughout the world face slower growth, so do domestic and global competitors that are no longer acting as if the expanding pie is big enough for all."[15]

- How can a company create and maintain its competitive advantage? How to implement these general theories in practice? For example:
- How can a company get long-lasting cost advantages?

- How can a company make a differential advantage compared with competitors?
- How does a company select market segment in order to create a competitive advantage through its own gathering of information strategies?
- When and how does a company gain competitive advantage through strategic coordination in related industries?
- What are the impacts of uncertainty in the process for a company to pursue competitive advantage?
- How can a company to protect its competitive position?

For such questions, the value chain is a basic and effective analysis tool, and is the basic tool of shaping competitive advantage.

Case Study

How does Haier freezer force to open the U.S. MARKET?

Haier Refrigerator has sold more than ten thousand units in only two months in New York. It makes Mr. Bob, U.S. agents of Haier Refrigerator distribution puzzled. In the United States, refrigerators of Whirlpool, GE and other large household appliances have been good enough and there is excess supply in the U.S. refrigerator market. Then why does the Haier refrigerator break into the U.S. market and sell well?

Yang Chuanxin, general manager of Haier refrigerator, has said that "We are making a piece of cake that we can enjoy ourselves in accordance with the concept of Haier's market development." Haier's staff believes that if the market is compared to a piece of cake, Haier cannot excessively "eat" the existing cake, but should make another cake to enjoy alone. Even if the cake is smaller; pieces they received will be much larger than pieces shared with the crowd. To make a cake one needs to study the process to do so, study the market and create the need.

Before entering the U.S. market, Haier's staff makes a detailed investigation and comprehensive study of the U.S. refrigerator market. They find that, although refrigerators of Whirlpool, GE and other U.S. companies occupy very large market shares, they are all large ones more than 200 liters in size and there are few small refrigerator under 160 liters. However, small refrigerator has its market. With the changes in American family structure, family size becomes smaller, and many people begin to prefer smaller refrigerators. Some students studying abroad and bachelors also prefer to use small refrigerators. This is a potential market, a "new cake" that can be made bigger.

Haier Refrigerator Corporation makes preparations in advance after getting the information of a new cake that can be made bigger. First of all, it has passed the ISO9001 international certification, U.S. UL certification, the German CE, GS certification and other international certifications, which are the pass checks to get access to anywhere in the world market. Then, according to the characteristics of the U.S. market, they specialize in the development of small refrigerators of various sizes from 60 to 160 liters. In appearance, the design pays attention to beauty, and functionality; the design combines high-tech, and product quality, and pursues excellence.

With the "pass," superior product quality and market demand, it is still not easy to enter the U.S. Market. Haier also researches extensively before choosing a strategy to enter the market. Through active participation in international fairs and product exhibitions, Haier displays and promotes its products in order to draw the attention of foreign investors. Also, through participation in the worldwide selection of refrigerator hosted by the World Health Organization, the UNESCO and the World Bank, Haier wins their confidence and shows the world the high quality of its refrigerator line. Confident, Haier then contacts the U.S. distributor, and Mr. Pope agrees to try to sell the line. The first dozens of refrigerator are sold out in less than a week. Mr. Pope sends an urgent telegram quickly to order ten thousand Haier refrigerators, which are sold out in only two months in the United States. Recently, he signs a contract with the Haier Refrigerator Corporation to order 25,000 units. Currently, these freezers have been transported to the United States.

Source: Wen Yan, *Chinese Companies*, June 3, 1998.

In the United States, refrigerators of Whirlpool, GE and other large household appliances have been good enough and there is excess supply in the U.S. refrigerator market. Then why does the Haier refrigerator break into the U.S. market and sell successfully?

Abiding by the marketing concept of "learning to make a cake for ourselves, rather than taking away that of others," Haier's staff makes a detailed investigation and comprehensive study on the U.S. refrigerator market. They find that, although refrigerators of Whirlpool, GE and other U.S.

companies occupy very large market shares, they are all large ones that are larger than 200 liters in size and there are few small refrigerators under 160 liters. However, small refrigerator has its market. With the changes in American family structure, family size becomes smaller, and many people begin to prefer small refrigerators. Some students studying abroad and bachelors also prefer to use small refrigerators. This is a potential market, a "new cake" that can be made bigger.

According to the characteristics of the U.S. market, they specialize in the development of small refrigerators of various sizes from 60 to 160 liters. In appearance, the design highlights attention to beauty, function; the design combines high-tech, and in product quality, and pursues excellence. Coupled with a successful sales strategy, it finally breaks into the U.S. market.

Michael Porter, father of competitive strategy has said that "One approach in formulating strategy is to look for positions in the market where a firm can meet its goals without threatening its competitors. When competitors' goals are well understood, there may be a place where everyone is relatively happy." If a company can do so, it can avoid a vicious competitive situation similar to millions of soldiers seizing a single-plank bridge.

The fact that Haier freezers forced itself into the U.S. market illustrates a successful experience to many companies.

Three kinds of cola with three strategies

Competition between two kinds of cola is long-standing, and has existed for a century. In 1886, Pemberton, a pharmacist concocts kind of red syrup in a hospital in the United States, which later becomes Coca-Cola. 12 years later, Brad, also a pharmacist develops Pepsi. Thus, in the history of commercial warfare in the 20th century, unparalleled wars between Coca-Cola and Pepsi occur over and over.

Since Coca-Cola and Pepsi have entered into China's beverage market or more precisely, the carbonated beverage market it has become a battleground of competition between these two cola giants. Both firms have equal skills, although Coca-Cola has a time advantage. It arrived in China 3 years prior, and its soft drink output is double that of Pepsi, but it still has not overtaken Pepsi.

China had no cola but only soft drinks originally. Since reform and opening its borders, there have been many China-made types of cola, such as Shaolin Cola, Tianfu Cola, Blue Sword Cola, etc. 1998 is an important year for the Chinese cola drink industry, since Hangzhou Wahaha and Guangzhou FenHuang Company have launched their own colas. In 2000, Ali Chinese Cola and Yanjing Cola are added to the new generation of cola brands. In 2001, Jianlibao Hua Ting Cola is launched. The increase of the brands explains in part that the intensity of competition in the cola industry, adding to the competition of Coca-Cola, Pepsi and Chinese Cola.

From the illustration above, we can see that China's cola market has challengers everywhere and wars frequently with its competitors. It is worthy to note that, in this cola war, though there are three kinds of colas to competing in the Chinese market, the competitive strategies adopted are different due to their different competitors' ad strengths.

Coca-Cola casts it net all over. According to Sinomonitor monitor Coca-Cola consumer market reaches 20 major cities nationwide. Coca-Cola, with its "dragnet" attack strategy in the market, casts nets nationwide and promotes by level. Its market penetration rate (ratio of number of consumers drinking a certain cola brand and the number of total cola consumers) has been far ahead of Pepsi. In 1999 and 2000, the penetration rates in the 20 cities are respectively 83.9% and 85%; Pepsi's are only 65.5% and 67.9%. For the "dragnet" strategy, Lu Bingsong, director of external affairs of Coca-Cola China Limited has a wonderful strategy. First, he chooses Chinese cities with populations of more than a million and who own computers and then distribute its products there; then, to list those more than 500 thousand ... and so on. Relying on this market strategy of being everywhere and wanting for everyone to be exposed to their soft drinks, Coca-Cola invests 1.2 billion in China to set up 28 bottling plants, making the red cyclone sweep across China.

Pepsi Cola makes significant breakthroughs. According to data of Sinomonitor, Pepsi's market performances in each city have significant polarization. Those with higher market penetration rate are even more than Coca-Cola, while those with lower penetration are less than 40%. This is precisely the results what Pepsi would like to see, because its goal is to seize the strategic weaknesses of Coca-Cola and to make significant breakthroughs concentrating superior forces. Finally, Pepsi stands out in wars of Cola and Pepsi in Shanghai, Chengdu, Chongqing, Wuhan, Shenzhen and other cities.

Chinese colas march into the countryside. Under the attack of two types of cola, Chinese carbonated drinks lose again and again, and Shaolin Cola, Tianfu Cola, etc., have disappeared, while Fenhuang Cola and Wahaha Cola have lost significant market share. In 2000, market the penetration rate of Fenhuang Cola and Wahaha Colaonly are separately just 15% and 10.6%. Now, Chinese colas seem to have found some "feelings," that is, to be unrefined and rural and to find a breakthrough in small cities and rural areas where Coke and Pepsi pay less attention. However, Chinese colas have a long way to go in order to fundamentally change positioning of its cola selection in people's minds. To have a firm foothold in the bottom of the market where Coke and Pepsi apply minimal efforts, and to finally form their own brand positioning is most likely its best strategy.

Source: Jiang Lifeng, "Cola market: fighting frequently," *China Business*, October 16, 2001.

Review

In *The Art of War*, article "Weak Points and Strong" tells that "Water shapes its course according to the nature of the ground over which it flows; the soldier works out his victory in relation to the enemy he is facing. Therefore, just as water retains no constant shape, so in warfare there are no constant conditions. He, who can modify his tactics in relation to his opponent and thereby succeed in winning, may be called a heaven-born captain." (17)

The original meaning of this passage is that water flows based on its terrain, military forces for winning should be determined according to the enemy situation. Therefore, there is no fixed way in devising tactics for battles, just as there is no fixed shape of water.
You should change according to the enemy situation, that is, to deploy military forces with great skill.

Therefore, companies' strategies and tactics have no fixed formula, so its formulation must be based on market conditions, advantages and disadvantages of both sides. It means to make a concrete analysis of a concrete problem.

That's the reason why three kinds of cola in the Chinese market formulate three different competitive strategies. Practice has proven that despite their competitive strategies each one employs a completely different approach, but they are suitable for themselves.

Questions

1. What is the central task of competitive strategy formulation? What are the four elements of competitor analysis?
2. What are the goals of competitive strategy? What are the principles and methods to achieve the goals?
3. What are the processes of competitive strategy formulation?
4. What is the core competitive strategy? Where is the source of competitive advantage?
5. What is value chain? What practical value does value chain has for shaping competitive advantage?
6. Try to analyze a company's product or service competitors referring to knowledge and methods of competitor analysis.
7. Try to formulate a competitive strategy for a company's products or services referring to processes and methods of competitive strategy formulation.
8. Try to formulate innovative and unique company competitive strategy combining the *Art of War* with Porter's competitive theory.

Notes

(1)Mao Zedong, Selected Works of Mao Zedong, four volumes, People's Publishing House, Beijing, 1966, p. 480.
(2)Sun-Tzu(the original), Kung-sun Daoming ed, Art of War and Thirty-Six Stratagems 1st edition, Guangxi Ethnic Publishing House, July 1995, p. 32.
(3) (U.S.) Michael Porter, Competitive Strategy, Huaxia Publishing House, January 1997, p. 6.
(4) (U.S.) Michael Porter, Competitive Strategy, Huaxia Publishing House, January 1997, p. 57.
(5) China Business, June 28, 2004.
(6) China Business, June 28, 2004.
(7) China Business, June 28, 2004.
(8) Cited in (U.S.) Fred. R. David, Strategic Management, Economic Science Press, 1998, p. 16.
(9) (U.S.) Michael Porter, Competitive Strategy, Introduction, Huaxia

Publishing House, January 1997, p. 3.

(10) (U.S.) Michael Porter, Competitive Strategy, Huaxia Publishing House, January 1997, p. 2.

(11) (U.S.) Michael Porter, Competitive Strategy, Huaxia Publishing House, January 1997, p. 48.

(12) (U.S.) Michael Porter, Competitive Strategy, Huaxia Publishing House, January 1997, p. 58.

(13) (U.S.) Michael Porter, Competitive Advantage, Introduction, Huaxia Publishing House, January 1997, p. 2.

(14) (U.S.) Michael Porter, Competitive Strategy, Huaxia Publishing House, January 1997, p. 33.

(15) (U.S.) Michael Porter, Competitive Strategy, Huaxia Publishing House, January 1997, p. 1.

(16) (U.S.) Michael Porter, Competitive Strategy, Huaxia Publishing House, January 1997, p. 58.

(17) Sun-Tzu(the original), Kung-sun Daoming ed, Art of War and Thirty-Six Stratagems, 1st edition, Guangxi Ethnic Publishing House, July 1995, p. 74-75.

BIBLIOGRAPHY

Mao Zedong, *Selected Works of Mao Zedong*, four volumes, People's Publishing House, Beijing, 1966.

Art of War commentary group of War Theory Research Department of Academy of Military Sciences, CPLA, *New Commentary of Art of War*, 1st edition, Zhonghua Book Company, January 1977.

Sun-Tzu (the original), Kung-sun Daoming ed, *Art of War and Thirty-Six Stratagems*, 1st edition, Guangxi Ethnic Publishing House, July 1995.

Editorial board of *Art of War and Strategy for Business and Politics*, *Art of War and Strategy for Business and Politics*, 1st edition, Blue Sky Press, May 1997.

Luo Guanzhong, *Three Kingdoms*, 1st edition, Changjiang Literature Press, January 1981.

Guo jixing, Lee Shijun, *Three Kingdoms and Business Strategy*, 1st edition, Guangxi People's Publishing House, June 1988.

Yao Youwei, *Strategies of Three Kingdoms and Tips for Commercial War*, 1st edition, Donghua University Press, August 2006.

〔U.S.〕Peter Drucker, *Management Practice*, 1st edition, Mechanical Industry Press, January 2006.

〔U.S.〕Michael Porter, *Competitive Strategy*, 1st edition, Huaxia Publishing House, January 1997.

〔U.S.〕Michael Porter, *Competitive Advantage*, 1st edition, Huaxia Publishing House, January 1997.

〔U.S.〕Fred. R. David, *Strategic Management*, Li Kening trans., 1st edition, Economic Science Press, June 1998.

Liu Jisheng ed, *Company Operation Strategy*, 1st edition, Tsinghua University Press, April 1995.

Xu Erming ed, *Company Strategy Management*, 1st edition, China Economic Publishing House, May 1998.

Chiang Yuntong ed, *Company Operation Strategy Management*, 1st edition, Company Management Press, April 1996.

CHAPTER 9
Transnational Operation Strategy Formulation

Abstract

This chapter starts by proposing a global mission with objectives for a company, and then introduces a transnational operation strategy for formulation steps and policy. It concludes with an appendix of cases and comments in "Haier: to create a global company."

Learning Objectives

- To make clear transnational operation strategy formulation steps and policy.
- To understand the mission of transnational companies.
- To understand the characteristics of strategic objectives of transnational companies.

Introduction

The world we live in seems to become smaller and smaller. The global economic integration and the development of transnational trade tells us that the economy of the future will be global and without borders.

Brian Dumaine has said that globalization will change this catchphrase into a widespread reality. Companies will have to meet transnational standards in all aspects of product quality, design, price and service. (1) Fred. R. David has also said that global strategist seeks to meet the global needs of users with the lowest cost and highest value. This means producing products in countries with the lowest labor costs or rich natural resources and to research and carry out complex engineering experiments in countries with scientists and engineers, as well as to conduct marketing in countries closest to its target market. It also includes meeting the global needs in design, production and marketing of products other than merely to consider the needs of certain individual countries.(2)

A transnational operation strategy is one in which a company develops strategies with the highest potential, the most challenges and the most complexity. It is an independent management subject which includes a great many implications and covers a wide range of topics. This chapter focuses on the steps and policies of transnational operation strategy formulation.

Lesson

I.   Proposing of global mission and objectives of a company

(I) Mission of a company

The mission of economic organizations provides their responsibility in the social and economic existence. The mission of a transnational operations company is conveyed in the overall portrayal of its operating intentions, providing the reason of its existence, explaining the reason why it engages in some industries, markets, regions and countries rather than in others, and reflects its operating philosophy, image and self-awareness it pursues. The description of the mission of a transnational operations company distinguishes the company from other competitors in the world. This self-knowledge and self-identification helps it continue to recognize its global market position, key technologies and resources.

Particular operating philosophies embodied in the mission of transnational operation companies specifies a company's internal characteristics, guiding principles and ideological basis, provides company functions, services, transnational operations and points out long-term direction, basic objectives and the profit motive for transnational operation companies. The operating philosophy and mission of a transnational company should highlight its transnational operation focus.

To establish the right mission is the foundation to formulating a company strategy. But the company must first have a realistic perspective on its specific technologies required to achieve its mission. Every company must have its own characteristics. The company's mission expressed in words is also known as the prospectus. A prospectus not only describes a transnational operation company's products, customers and markets, it also stipulates its transnational operation characteristics, identifies its profit center, and establishes relationships among headquarters, branches, main strategic operating units and associated companies of various countries. The

302

mission of a transnational operation company should include the following:

1. Provide basic products or services;
2. Identify the customers in need of services;
3. Cover national or regional markets;
4. Identify the technology used in the production and marketing of products or services;
5. Show how to maintain the survival of a transnational operation company with growth and profitability objectives;
6. Demonstrate the management philosophy, including the basic tenets, values and vision, and company guiding principles;
7. Illustrate the Public image the company needs;
8. Classify the beliefs the employees should adopt for the company;
9. Understand and recognize the best interests and legal rights of the company
10. What are the parameters of Social responsibility for transnational operation company?

It is necessary to specify that the company needs to revise and improve its mission continuously. The modification is based on comprehensive surveys of circumstances of both its current resources and interests of the company over time.

(II) Strategic objectives

Strategic objective is a concrete manifestation of the company purpose, which provides the direction and process of the development of company, and is usually indicated by some qualitative and quantitative indicators.

Strategic objectives of transnational operation are basically the same as a domestic operating, but there are three different characteristics:

1. To highlight the economic objective of earning foreign exchange;
2. To strive to create an transnational brand;
3. To emphasize the contribution to the global marketplace.

The basic functions of company's objectives:

1. Provisions of the relationship between company and the environment;
2. Coordination of decision and decision makers;

3. Provisions of company operational performance assessment criteria;
4. Objectives provided that are more specific than that of mission. If the objective is the   objectives that company should hit, then mission is an explanation that how does the company attempt to hit in the objectives.

II.   Global environmental assessment

Global environmental assessment of transnational operation company is relatively more diverse and complex compared with domestic environmental assessment. Therefore, the importance of company to acknowledge environment will be more prominent.

(I) Transnational operation environment framework

In terms of geographical space, transnational operations environment consists of home country environment, host country environment, and transnational environment.

1. Home country environment

Home country environment consists of domestic indirect and direct environmental factors, which are known best by domestic managers. These factors affect not only the domestic operations, but also overseas business. Home country's economic, political and social conditions force government to take measures to encourage or restrict foreign investment or exporting. For example, when the government is facing a shortage of foreign exchange, it may limit the outflow of funds, which will limit the overseas expansion of transnational companies based in the country. Conversely, if the domestic unemployment rate is high, transnational companies owing overseas production bases may have import restrictions.

2. Host country environment

Host country environment is all local direct and indirect environmental factors faced by a company when operating in a foreign market. The same factors also exist in the home country, but in other countries, their conditions may be different from the home country.

In the domestic environment, managers face a number of unchanged factors like the single currency, homogeneous and familiar culture, common language, and familiar infrastructure. Managers grow up, live and work in this environment and can expect, accept and make instinctive reactions to the environment; therefore, they often ignore it.

While in transnational operations, there are few factors with such features. Of course, specific conditions in different host countries are not the same, so as there are various types of environmental, opportunities and threats. There might be big differences between environmental conditions of the host country and home country, while small differences exist among host countries. Thus, despite environmental differences among some countries, compared with domestic environment, the differences become very small. For example, for Western transnational companies, when operating in the former Soviet Union and Eastern countries, they may find that their political environments are very different; but when operating in Africa and Asian countries, they may find that their cultural differences are greater.
Another feature of host country environmental factors is difficult to evaluate and predict. Unfamiliar environment and lack of information often impose an incorrect evaluation and prediction. In a foreign environment, political and legal factors may be two factors that are most difficult to grasp. The Iran revolution is an example, which surprises many analysts. Political instability in some countries makes a government agree with foreign investment by being replaced overnight by the one that is against it.

Those transnational operation managers are unfamiliar with the local environment and a high degree of uncertainty and diversity of these environmental factors will cause their decision-making processes to become more complex.

3. Transnational environment

When a company conducts transnational operations, its operating activities will involve resources and operating flows between different countries. There are Environmental interactions between the home country and host country, as well as between host countries form the globe operating environment. The Global environment contains a series of diverse political, legal and economic factors, and the World Bank, the World Trade Organization, the International Monetary Fund and international agreements constitute the main body of transnational environment. Policies and activities of global organizations like the United Nations and its agencies, regional organizations such as the European Union, and the global industrial organization as Petroleum Exporting Countries Organization will affect company's transnational operation activities directly or indirectly. These organizations are generally formed on the basis of industrial, regional or global transnational agreements.

(II) Steps and methods of global environmental assessment

Information source

Information needed to assess the global operating environment can be obtained from internal and external sources, and in oral or written form. Written information can be derived from the company's management information system, competitors, suppliers, trade associations, banks, customers, government, embassies, transnational organizations, particular research institutions, magazines, newspapers and other channels. Studies show that most companies make decisions based on internal and external information, whose reliability can be tested.

Environmental prediction

The primary responsibility of transnational operation companies' strategists is to ensure the survival of the company by predicting environmental changes and seeking opportunities among these changes. Thus, strategic researchers need to use techniques to predict environmental changes. The following steps may be taken to predict the environment, and explore opportunities and threats in the future:

1. To select essential environmental factors;
2. To choose sources of important environmental information and collect necessary information;
3. To use predictive techniques to forecast future environmental conditions;

4. To put predicted results into a company's strategic management process;
5. To control the accuracy of these predictions.

Selection of key environmental factors by a transnational operation company depends on its experience in transnational operations, breadth and depth of transnational business activities, company operating characteristics, industry characteristics, company's product and service lines, and company's customers and markets. It also depends on choice of business types that the company has started or plans to expand.

4. Prediction techniques

There are a lot of methods and techniques used for transnational operation companies to choose for predicting environmental circumstances. They can be divided into three types: qualitative analysis, quantitative analysis and expert opinion quantitative analysis.

5. Anatomy chart of environmental opportunities and threats

Environmental assessment is designed to help strategists better understand complexity and constraints faced in formulating strategies for transnational operation companies to expand opportunities and reduce threats in a highly competitive market. Such transnational operations strategic management allows strategists to have time to anticipate significant opportunities and to plan on taking advantage of these opportunities. In addition, environmental assessment also plays a role in an early warning system, which helps keep a lookout for threats, develop strategies to reduce their impacts, or transfer these threats into operating advantages.

An important aspect of environmental assessment is to assess differences between the existing environment and future environment. Strategists look for positive opportunities and negative threats that the environment provides. If a strategy formulated in the first phase is used, then assessment starts based on the most likely circumstances in the future. If strategy is formulated in the second phase, it is needed to assess the best, the worst and the most likely situations in the future. This generates several sets of reports related to the future environmental opportunities and threats. Strategists should work out different strategies to deal with different environmental conditions in the future.

In this respect, strategists need to present key opportunities and threats to managers by using a systemic approach in order to attract their attention. Environmental Threats and Opportunities Prospects (ETOP) is one of the more commonly used methods. It is a document outlining key opportunities and threats and their impacts on transnational operation companies. For a variety of transnational operation companies, multiple sets of environmental threats and opportunities are needed to provide, one set for the whole company, and one set for each various strategic operating units.

6. Establishment of a management information system

Management Information System (MIS) can provide transnational operation companies with information on economies, government intervention, social development, market conditions, etc. of countries in which they operate.

III.   Organizational analysis of transnational company

Organizational analysis is similar to environmental assessment. The difference lies in transferring focus from the external environment to the internal environment. Based on analysis and conclusions, strategists draw a strategic advantages anatomy chart to show the company's strengths and weaknesses.

Transnational operation companies should be able to validate its competitive advantage or relative strength that is better than its competitors and take advantage of it in strategic implementation in a particular country and in the market. Organizational analysis of a transnational operation company at level of strategic operating units should consider the following issues:

1.   To identify and evaluate each operating unit's relative strengths and weaknesses;
2.   To assess each strategic operating unit's competitive market position;
3.   To assess current strategic operating performances and reasons for each operating layer and functional layer;
4.   To identify respective specific strategic issues of transnational companies and its strategic operating units.

IV.   Formulation of transnational operation objectives

For most companies, the ultimate objective of a transnational operation is not just to survive but to achieve a higher growth and return on investment. Therefore, companies must first determine their long-term objectives, and then refine them into short-term annual objectives. Strategists have a clear understanding of current and future situations based on works done in the first of several phases, so the strategic objectives they established should reflect the company's strengths and weaknesses.

308

(I) Objectives formulation process

Objectives are formulated by strategic decision makers at the company level, the strategic operating unit level and functional level. The choice of objectives reflects a range of factors, which are:

1. Environmental forces. The primary factors affect objectives formulation are current situations of the external environment and external power relations, which restrict objectives. Current environmental situations are shown in the environmental assessment. External power relations refer to requirements, rights and expectations of external stakeholders.

2. Competitors actions. Competitors' expected behavior and actual behavior in the transnational market is the key to formulating strategic objectives. Strategic objectives must be realized in the opposite strategy of competitors. In fact, competition is the core of any strategy. However, what effective transnational operation management strategy seeks is to guide companies, to reduce unpredictable adjustment and to act responsibly to activities of competitors.

3. Current situations of transnational companies' resources and power relations. Companies with abundant resources and high levels of profits can better withstand environmental threats and seize opportunities better than firms with less resources and low levels of profit. Power struggles within the company determine the choice of objectives. If the various views are evenly matched, it is difficult to form an authoritative opinion, and the choice of objectives can only be a compromise. Conversely, if a view is dominant, then the choice of objectives will be determined based on this view.

4. Value systems and objectives of top managers and strategist. Personal value systems and objectives depend on the individual's cultural background, education, past experience and insight gained through work. These values and objectives are philosophies about what is desirable or not, and what is good or bad. They affect views of certain strategic actions and the choice of objectives. Strategic planning groups of transnational operations companies is composed of a staff with different value systems and objectives, therefore in large diversified transnational operation companies, personal factors impact the objectives formulation processes and objectives

5. Previous objectives, strategies and development trajectories of transnational operation companies. Most objectives are not coming out of thin air, but are based on past objectives, successes and failures and experiences drawn from achieving those objectives. In objective formulating, strategists make adjustments of existing objectives considering current environmental conditions, future trends and requirements of parties with conflicting interests. Unless there are big changes or a crises, objectives in the past will not completely change. Just as the big ship takes time to change route, large transnational operation companies also need enough time to make a major reorientation. Therefore, achievement of these changed objectives and strategies is often impacted by previous objectives and their achievements.

(II) Types and characteristics of objectives

Objectives of the company can be divided into abstract objectives and specific objectives. Maximal profits and maintenance of survival are abstract objectives. Such objectives are basic, long-term, non-time-bound, thus, in a sense, these kinds of objectives can never be reached naturally. For example, the survival of a company is under threat all the time. Specific objectives are different and contain four elements: abstract objectives pursued, scales to measure progress to reach objectives, objectives, and time to reach the objectives. Therefore, specific objectives need to be expressed as accurately as possible and its constituent elements must be thoughtfully selected to establish single and unambiguous next objectives within a time period with simple statements, for example, to achieve 10% of the net profit within two years.

Transnational operation companies must determine specific objectives of the company, strategic operating units and functional departments. Objective of all departments at all levels must be an interrelated balance. To this end, once the company's objectives are established, senior managers of transnational operations companies need to do the followings:

1. To check whether the selected objectives are interrelated. Whether these objectives can be achieved simultaneously? If not, they need to be adjusted to enable synchronization;
2. To collate objectives;
3. To resolve each objective into sub-objectives for different strategic operating units;
4. To check internal objectives compared with the existing business

strategy, environment condition and organizational strength to see if they can be achieved. If not, new strategies or objectives and adjustments are required.

Similarly, various departments and strategic operating units are required to repeatedly do the job.

(III) Specific strategic objectives

After different levels of management in the company collate objectives, the specific objective that ranks first at each level is the specific strategic objective of this level. Strategic objectives at different levels often reflect profits, sales, investment income, market share, productivity, employee relations and social responsibility. Only when the transnational operation company runs a single business, can market share become the company's general objectives. If the company is diversified, its market share cannot be added up to one meaningful objective.

V.   Choice of transnational operation strategy

Determination of transnational operation strategy and its parts aims at ensuring the company's effect (to achieve the desired objectives) and efficiency (to gain maximum output with a minimum input). Similar to formulating objectives, a transnational operation company should formulate different strategies to achieve objectives for different levels. In order to achieve transnational operation objectives; the key to propose transnational operation strategy is to employ advantages and avoid disadvantages, or to seize opportunities using the company's strength to meet challenges.

Transnational operation companies usually can plan an exceptional future for strategic operating units after assessing their relevant environmental factors and making appropriate organizational analysis. Of course, many diversified transnational operation companies should apply complex combination methods at the company level. They allocate resources among business areas and among strategic operating units based on priorities. At this time, strategists at the company level must consider the following issues: what is the scope of our businesses and markets? Should we devote more resources to businesses and markets with great growth potential? Can our existing businesses and markets generate sufficient funds to meet future investment needs? Do we need to find additional businesses and markets? Do we invest too much in a certain business and market? Do we involve too much in a country with a high degree of political risks and financial risks? Should we withdraw or reduce the resources from these businesses, markets or countries?

(I) Global competitive strategy

Global competitive strategy is divided into two kinds: high share global competitive strategy and place global competitive strategy. High share global strategy is usually adopted by giant transnational companies, who see themselves as parts of the global industry, pursue a larger share in the global market, and make their products, pricing, distribution and marketing strategies using a segmentation global market mix. Although research and development costs of these companies are very high, that is very low compared to its sales, and is even much below that of the industry average.

The basic philosophy of global strategy is the global coordination of company resources around global objectives. Many transnational operation companies obtain a competitive advantage using a global strategy. For instance, scale economies and experience brought by large production in the world reduce costs; various agents and customers get services through branch networks all over the world; the ability to organize worldwide cheap materials, labors and other resources; cross-border transfer of experiences; build of a global company image; capability to gaze global resources; maintenance of portfolio of global strategic operating units.

Place global competitive strategy pursues a professional road, and is mostly used by smaller transnational companies. Internationalization of these companies is motivated by one or more global competitive advantages through specialization. Companies using this strategy can avoid head-on collisions with larger transnational companies pursuing a larger global share. Their specialized areas can be one segment of a product offering, services, technologies, product life cycle stage, market segments, production stage, and so on. Finnish Wasilla Shipbuilding Company is an example. When big Japanese and European shipbuilding companies compete fiercely in segment of large capacity dry cargo and tanker products, Wasilla Company, targeted the luxury cruise ships and icebreakers markets and other specialized markets that were not attractive for large transnational companies and, successfully occupy a "place" through rapidly researching and meeting the needs of customers.

(II) Country of origin competitive strategy

Country of origin competitive strategy for transnational operation companies is divided into two kinds; large share country strategy and place country strategy.

Transnational operation companies that pursue a high share country strategy capture a large share country market by adopting a high share country strategy. The marketing and production strategies they designed aim at occupying larger market share and lower costs than other competitors. The main disadvantages of this strategy lie in the fact that their economies of scale and productions cannot match that of transnational companies pursuing global strategies.

Transnational operation companies that pursue large share country strategy often rely on country entry barriers to deal with global competitions. Such barriers include tariffs, quotas, subsidies and other unfavorable laws for country competitors. In addition, the host country's communication transports barriers and institutional preferences barriers.

Transnational operation companies that pursue place country strategy use country specialized strengths to prevent domestic competitors and global competitors crowding the market. The target market size of companies adopting this strategy is usually not big enough to attract large transnational companies. Country entry barriers are used to deal with global competitors like a large share country strategy. This strategy is more popular in the industry dominated by country preferred products, such as food, clothing, and small-scale handicrafts.

Large transnational companies will usually use these strategies together, and take a series of such strategies with the expansion of their transnational business. For example, American Express begins as a domestic shipping company. On its way to being international, it adopts the place country strategy in professional financial services based on traveler's check. Since then, it uses a series of global place strategy in businesses like credit cards, travel agencies, investment banks, and so on.

(III) Strategy of strategic business units

Choices of strategic business units is a process of selecting a scheme that not only meets this level's specific objectives, but also makes the greatest contribution to achieve the company's global strategic objectives. The process includes the development of metrics, use of these metrics to evaluate all strategic options and decisions of a final choice. Finally, the selected strategic scheme should be reported to company headquarters to receive approval and authorization. There are five main factors in decision-making strategic choice of this level: transnational operation companies' dependency on the environment; strategists' attitudes for risks, values and decision-making approaches; previous strategies of transnational operation companies and their strategic operating units; transnational operation companies' internal power relations, cultural and organizational structures and resources; attitudes and cooperation conditions of lower managers.

Managers at lower levels play an important role in transnational operation strategy. Strategic management of transnational operations is not a top-down one-way process, which means that its decision is not made by top managers alone, but a two-way process. That is, information comes from the lower layers of the organization, strategic decisions are made at the top of organization, and then strategic decisions are assigned to lower managers for implementation. In some companies, middle managers are sometimes also involved in the strategic decision-making activities. They filter the information strategists get, thus some information may never be sent to top managers. In addition to this filtering process, workers' representatives of some countries, such as some European countries can also influence strategic choices. For example, Sweden's Volvo Car Corporation has intended to set up factories in the United States, but it runs aground because of workers' resistance to close factories in Sweden. Strategic choices of Germany Volkswagen AG to re-allocate its resources are affected by Germany's workers'.

Case Study

Haier: to create a global company

In 2009, as the world's fourth largest household appliances manufacturer, China's most valuable brands, Haier Group enters the fourth year of implementing a global brand strategy. Haier grows and develops into a transnational corporation with a good reputation at home and abroad from a small plant which is now on the verge of bankruptcy. A big question in the industry concerning Haier refrigerators is when it decided to "go out" into the world in 1990, and the "Haier" brand became a world famous name as a home appliance brand, and how it was able to continue accelerating the pace of overseas development and expanding overseas for all those years. Another question is how does Haier build its own "foreign kingdom" around the world and achieve to create a Chinese world famous brand? Today, a reporter interviews Haier Group to explain the global experiences of Haier and how it serves as a successful example for Chinese companies "go out."

Implementation of local development strategy

Investment in any country and region, and creation of localized famous brands has become a difficult challenge for Haier.

For any transnational companies, designing products to meet local customers' demands and sell according to local operating customs with acceptable trading practices has the potential to keep a foothold in the local market and maintain growth patterns. Haier is familiar with these principles and has always adhered to the "three-merge and one-create" strategy in the course of the market globalization. This strategy is to merge intelligence, finance, and culture and to create localized famous brands. Using this strategy, Haier establishes trinity marketing systems, including localized design, production and marketing. Haier establishes 29 manufacturing bases and processing plants and 16 industrial parks, to achieve localized manufacturing in the United States, Europe, and the Middle East; It builds 8 design centers to achieve localized design in Tokyo of Japan, Milan of Italy, and New York of the United States; and set up 61 global trading companies, of which 19 are overseas, and 58 800 sales outlets to achieve localized marketing. In the United States, Europe, South Asia, the Middle East ... trinity centers are finished one after the other, it makes Haier complete its phased overseas distribution and lays the foundation for "going out."

To meet the local needs and realize the localization of its products is an important factor for Haier to succeed in entering overseas markets and win among the global appliance companies in the increasingly fierce competition. With constantly enhanced technical development and product innovation, Haier launches mainstream products in connection with local customers' characteristics. For example, regarding the voltage instability, frequent power cuts and high temperatures in Nigeria, Haier researches and develops a refrigerator that does not thaw within 100 degrees. Facing the reality in the Middle East that there are generally large families and people prefer to wear large gowns, Haier designs a washing machine to wash large gowns. It can wash 12 kg clothing one time and can wash clean with low wear, so it is popular in the Middle East. Considering Indian religious beliefs and current status of loving to go vegetarian, Haier develops a refrigerator which is mainly for cold storage and needs no stop when using. For small residential areas of young Japanese, Haier designs a small washing machine named "personal laundry room" ... Based on local cultural and economic situation, Haier designs and sells products starting from birth. No wonder people say Haier does not sell products, but life.

It is a necessary condition for success of "going out" strategy that requires every one of Haier's staff to visit local agencies and identify its management style and values. There is a story about Haier in the United States. According to Haier's management, employees should be released whether doing good or bad. It does not work in the United States where they only announce who is doing well because firing people with poor work habits is a violation of human rights. But Haier requires the co-existence of positive incentives and negative incentives. Finally, the manager of U.S. Company solves this problem in a very clever way. He uses a teddy bear to show superiority and a toy pig to illustrate inferiority, and gives teddy bears to those doing well while giving toy pigs to those doing badly. American workers are willing to accept this approach. Haier's harmonious management style is to make the staff of both cultures accept its management approach by using an inclusive and constructive culture, and transnational concepts. It is also the key to Haier's success.

To achieve development by innovation

It is has been proven that development and growth of the Haier Group, both domestically and abroad, are inseparable from innovation, which has become the key for companies to become bigger and stronger.

Facing the current conditions of reduced global demands, in order to fight for market share, to meet local needs, and to reduce the impact of the financial crisis, Haier accelerates innovation, and forms a complete and effective innovation system. It includes product innovation, which provides customers with solutions, an operating model innovation, which can distribute just in time inventory and mechanism innovation, which creates the autonomous body matching people with orders.

In terms of product innovation, Haier needs to provide users with solutions to the problems. Haier divides users into "fellow" and "foreigner," the former refers to the user in the domestic market and the latter refers to the users in the foreign market. According to situations at home and abroad, Haier helps users solve problems grassroots problems in rural and urban communities. Because of the information age companies should provide the fastest services to meet the practical requirements of users. For this reason, Haier explores the operating model of "just in time inventory" in 2008. In order to solve problems caused by accounts receivable and inventory, Haier has implemented accounting on a cash basis in the Chinese market since 1998. Since July 2008, Haier proposes to prevent "two more and two less," that is to prevent more inventories, more receivables, less profit, and less cash. Because of the financial crisis last year, a lot of companies have closed down due to poor cash flows. It is this predictable operating model that makes Haier still have a healthy cash flow and achieve a sustained development while under the global market pressure. It can create an autonomous body combining people to orders, motivate employees match their income with company's market objectives and values, and stimulate the staff's creativity and enthusiasm.

Timely strategic transformation

Starting with the customers' needs, to change from a product manufacturer to a services provider and to provide customers with solutions for living a better life has become the current ultimate objective for the Haier Group.

At the annual meeting in 2008, Zhang Ruimin, chairman of the Board announces a new development plan for Haier Group. "Haier's future positioning and objective should be to become the first competitive solution company offering a better life." This speech shows that the Haier Group is in a rapid development stage undergoing a strategic transformation, shifting from a large products manufacturer to a large service provider. It does not provide customers with products, but s0lutions to solve problems. A senior leader of Haier tells reporters that "At the information age, in a sense, products do not making money, and what really makes money is bringing solutions to the problem through products. It means that users no longer need a refrigerator, washing machine, and air conditioning, but fresh food, clean clothes and comfortable temperature."

Given changes in the market, Haier makes three changes. The first is to change from "company informational" to "informational company." Demands of customers are changing. Customers are no longer just concerned about the functional use of the product, but are also concerned

317

about whether the product is environmentally friendly and energy efficient. This change causes Haier to reverse the past conditions that companies manage transformation to using information as the mainstay for innovation. Now they should center on markets and customers, creating a process of creating value for customers through information technologies and supply products and services customers need as soon as possible.

Second, change from a manufacturing company to a service-oriented company. It will achieve the goal to sell products through services and to sell services through products, enrich and extend the product chain, and turn the end of one-time sales into the starting point of building a long term relationship with the customer.

Third, changes to win-win culture of combining people with orders. In order to transfer from manufacturing to services industry, Haier need to change its "triangle" linear functional structure to "inverted triangle" matrix structure and to set up a management body to face the customers. Front line managers and employees face customers, while managers supply resources and services to the front line managers and staff at the bottom, changing from those who give orders to resource providers. This requires breaking down barriers within the various departments, establishing an autonomous body to face customers, taking the initiative to create valuable solutions for the users, and to account the input and output independently and to maintain continuous innovation.

It has been 19 years since Haier refrigerators decided to "go out" into the world in 1990. Among Chinese companies adopting international strategy, Haier Group can be described as being the first. Creating a global company is the dream Haier is going to achieve.

Source: Hu Yang, Jing ling, *Chinese Companies*, November 19, 2009.

Review

Haier grows and develops into a transnational corporation with a good reputation at home and abroad from a small plant on the verge of bankrupt. From the question in the industry of Haier refrigerators when it determines to "go out" into the world in 1990, to the fact that "Haier" brand becomes the world famous home appliances brand, Haier Group has been accelerating the pace of overseas development and expanding overseas layout for these years. Haier builds its own "foreign kingdom" around the world, achieve to create Chinese own world famous brand and set a shining example for Chinese companies to adopt international strategy of "going out."

Questions

1. What are the basic steps of transnational companies' strategy formulation and management? What are the concepts of every step?
2. What are the concepts of the missions of transnational companies?
3. What are the characteristics of the strategic objectives of transnational companies?
4. Select a typical case and make analysis and discussion.

Notes

(1) (U.S.) Fred. R. David, *Strategic Management*, Li Kening trans., 1st edition, Economic Science Press, June 1998, p. 330.
(2) (U.S.) Fred. R. David, *Strategic Management*, Li Kening trans., 1st edition, Economic Science Press, June 1998, p. 330.
(3) Wang Chao, *Transnational Strategy - Transnational Business Management*, 1st edition, China Foreign Economic and Trade Press, January 1999, p. 38.

BIBLIOGRAPHY

〔U.S.〕 Michael Porter, *Competitive Strategy* 1st edition, Huaxia Publishing House, January 1997.

〔U.S.〕 Michael Porter, *Competitive Advantage*, Introduction, Huaxia Publishing House, January 1997.

〔U.S.〕 Jack Trout, *Trout on Strategy*, 1st edition, China Financial and Economic Publishing House, October 2004.

〔U.S.〕 Arthur Thompson, Stickrod, *Strategic Management: Concepts and Cases*, 10th ed, Duan Shenghua, Wang Zhihui trans., Xu Erming revision, Peking University Press, 2004.

〔U.S.〕 Fred. R. David, *Strategic Management*, Li Kening trans., 1st edition, Economic Science Press, June 1998.

〔CAN.〕 Henry Mintzberg, *Strategy Safari*, 2nd edition, Machinery Industry Press, June 2006.

Wang Chao, *Transnational Strategy - Transnational Business Management*, 1st edition, China Foreign Economic and Trade Press, January 1999.

Editing group of required MBA core courses, *Business Strategy*, 1st edition, China transnational Radio Press, September 1997.

Editing group of required MBA core courses, *Business Strategy*, 1st edition revision, China transnational Radio Press, 2000.

Liu Jisheng ed, *Company Operation Strategy*, 1st edition, Tsinghua University Press, April 1995.

Xu Erming ed, *Company Strategy Management*, 1st edition, China Economic Publishing House, May 1998.

Chiang Yuntong ed, *Company Operation Strategy Management*, 1st edition, company Management Press, April 1996.

CHAPTER 10
Strategic forms and operational principles

Abstract

This chapter starts with China's *Art of War* and American companies' art of war *Marketing Warfare,* revealing the consistency between laws of military forces using and laws of company strategic form choosing. Then, it takes four major car companies in the United States in early 20th century as examples, that is, General Motors, Ford Motor Company, Chrysler and American Motors, describing how to select a strategic form from defensive, offensive, flanking and guerrilla warfare. Subsequently, this chapter discusses operational principles of four of these strategic forms. Finally, it has appendix of four cases and their comments.

Learning Objectives

- To clear and grasp laws of company strategic form choosing.
- To understand and grasp operational principles of four strategic forms.
- Try to choose the strategic form that suits for your company according to theories in Art *of War* and *Marketing Warfare.*

Introduction

In *Art of War*, there are sentences of "Military tactics are like unto water; for water in its natural course runs away from high places and hastens downwards. So in war, the way is to avoid what is strong and to strike at what is weak. Water shapes its course according to the nature of the ground over which it flows; the soldier works out his victory in relation to the enemy whom he is facing. Therefore, just as water retains no constant shape, so in warfare there are no constant conditions. He, who can modify his tactics in relation to his opponent and thereby succeed in winning, may be called a heaven-born captain. The five elements (water, fire, wood, metal, earth) are not always equally predominant; the four seasons make way for each other in turn. There are short days and long; the moon has its periods of waning and waxing." (1) These laws of military forces using that Sun Tzu has said is be applicable for company to choose its strategic form.

321

Strategic advisory masters AL Ries and Jack Trout has said that there is not only one form of marketing war, but four, namely defensive warfare, offensive warfare, flanking warfare and guerrilla warfare. Your primary and most important decision is to know which strategic form should be chosen. It depends on your strategic location for victory. (2)

Lesson

I.   Strategic Forms Summarized from Four U.S. Car Companies

U.S. automobile industry provides the best example of what kind of strategic forms an enterprise should adopt. In the U.S. automobile history, there are four major car companies in the early 20th century, which are General Motors, Ford Motor Company, Chrysler and American Motors Corporation. In terms of market share, General Motors holds 59% of the market share. The combined market of the remaining three is less that of GM's. Ford's market share is 26%, Chrysler 13%, American Motors Corporation 2%, and the three combines total only 41%. It shows that the market share of these four major U.S. car companies is not balanced.

Victory has different meaning for these four car companies:
For Ford, to increase its market share represents a great victory;
For Chrysler, to survive and earn a profit can be called a victory;
For American Motors Corporation, to survive is enough to be considered as a victory.

Therefore, in certain market situations, each company has different resources, power and goals. For that reason, it is not surprising for each company to choose different strategic forms and marketing strategies.

So, which kinds of war should GM, Ford, Chrysler, and American Motors Corporation launch separately? Let's look at each company's situation first.

(I) Strategic form of the General Motors

First of all, who are GM's opponents? They are the U.S. Department of Justice, the U.S. Federal Trade Commission, the U.S. Security and Transportation Commission, and the United States Congress which includes the Senate and House.

General Motors Corporation is the leader in the industry. Any single enterprise alone feels in cannot compete with them. Therefore, to beat a single competitor is not its strategic goals. If it defeats one or more competitors, the courts or Congress will split it under the *Antitrust laws*. It can be known just by seeing the outcome of American Telephone and Telegraph Company, which is no match for U.S. Department of Justice.

Therefore, GM cannot win just because it is the leader; on the contrary, it should launch a defensive warfare strategy to protect its industry leader status. However, defense does not mean passive. Famous military strategist Clausewitz has once said that "Defense itself is a reverse action, because it is committed against the enemy's intentions, rather than being obsessed with his own intentions." (3)

Indeed, a good defensive warfare is aggressive in nature, and its goal is clear. It can protect the enterprise's dominant market under the *Antitrust Laws*.

(II) What should Ford do?

Ford ranks the second in U.S. automotive industry and has favorable conditions to attack. However, who should be its target? Willie Sutton has once said that "I rob banks because it is where the money is." Thus Ford should attack GM because it is who owns market share.

We calculate to make it easy to see why Ford should attack GM. If Ford can take 10% market share of GM, it will be able to make its market share increase 25%. If Ford can take 10% market share of American Car Company, it is too negligible to calculate its increased market share.

The pursuit of suppleness often induces people to plunder the weaker rather than the stronger. However, the fact is just the opposite. Because the smaller the size of the company, the more it will try to defend its own share. It will take measures, such as price reduction, discounts, and shelf life extension and other measures to resist its attacker desperately. Therefore, never fight with a wounded beast.

So, the best strategy Ford should take is to attack GM's weaknesses initiatively. And it may obtain valuable practical results only by attacking GM.

(III) What should Chrysler do?

There is an old African proverb that says that elephants fight while ants benefit. Chrysler should avoid direct involvement with the fight between GM and Ford and attack from the flank.

That's what Lee Iacocca has done. He launches classic flank attacks to the entire U.S. automobile industry, including the first convertible car, the first van, and the first front-wheel drive car which can hold 6 people.

Taking into account the starting point of Iacocca, his achievement is even more brilliant. Because he was replaced by Henry Ford II, he suddenly works for Chrysler after 8 years as general manager of Ford. It is expected that Iacocca will apply Ford's strategy to Chrysler. While he chooses a different strategy - flanking warfare in order to make it more applicable to the actual situation of Chrysler Corporation.

Generally, most people try to apply past successful strategies to battles today, resulting in failure. Iacocca takes the opposite approach, resulting in success and becoming a world-renowned entrepreneur.

(IV) What should American Motors do?

Being small in size, American Motors Corporation is too weak to attack GM. Even if it starts the attack well, it cannot afford continuous attacks due to lack of sufficient sales personnel, manufacturing capacities and marketing capabilities.

Nor can it launch a flanking attack on the entire automobile industry. It does not mean it is too small to attack, but it is unable to control the occupied shares after the attack.

Poor American Motors Corporation has no other choice but to form guerrilla forces.

For American Motors Corporation, the only undefeated victorious magic is with its jeeps. This is a typical guerrilla tactic. That is, to find a segment market in which large enough profits could be made and small enough to avoid other market leaders' interests.

In short, business is battle of the mind in the market. In the market of the
324

consumers' minds, there is a mountain whose pinnacle is occupied by the market leader GM. To deal with the mountain, there are four operational forms:

If you want to cross the mountain, you have to fight an offensive war. You'd better find a valley or curve as a breakthrough. Nonetheless, it will be a hard battle with high cost because leaders often have the ability to carry out violent counterattacks.

If you would like to stop the attack down the hill, you are playing defensive warfare. In fact, the best defense is an effective attack.

If you choose to thrust deep and outflank into the mountains, you are carrying out a flanking attack. It is usually the most effective and least costly marketing war. However, with the coming of a surplus economy, opportunities to launch an effective flanking attack method used in many industries are declining.

If you linger at the foot of the mountain, then your choice is guerrilla warfare. You need to find a quiet area, where is not only easy to defend safety, but also small enough to attract no interest of the market leaders.

II.   Principles of Defensive Warfare

There are three basic principles of defensive warfare, which are easier to learn than to do. If you want to fight a beautiful defensive warfare, you have to seriously study and practice them.

The first principle: only the market leader should consider a strategy of defense

Many companies believe that they are the leaders. However, most companies have established their position of leaders on the concepts created on their own rather than on the basis of the market facts. Companies cannot create a leader on its own, and only customers can do this. A leading firmly believes is the real leader.

Leaders in this article refer to the real leaders. There are many leaders in the computer industry, but only IBM is the true leader in the minds of computer users and customers.

An excellent entrepreneur must understand the real situation in order to make the right moves based on facts. You can fool the enemy instead of yourself.

The second principle: the best defensive strategy is to challenge oneself

Defenders occupy a leading position which dominates the minds of customers. The best way for defender to improve its status is to constantly impact the belief systems in the minds of customers. In other words, it is to constantly introduce new products and services to replace some of the old ones in order to consolidate its position.

IBM is an expert in this area. Seldom does much time pass before IBM launches a new series of mainframe computers, which has an absolute advantage compared with existing products in its price and performance category.

Gillette's products "Blue Gillette" razor and the subsequent "Super Blue Gillette" dominate the market.

To challenge oneself brings the cost of immediate self-interest, but is able to defend market share, which is the ultimate weapon to win the marketing warfare. Conversely, if a company is hesitating to challenge oneself, it will typically lose market share, and ultimately loss market leadership position.

Military expert Schlieffen has said that "Offence is the best defense. Relying on positional defense cannot get the victory, only offense can lead to victory. Even in the case of an absolute disadvantage, defense should be replaced by offence." (5)

The third principle: to be ready to stop onslaught of competitors

Most companies have only one chance to win, but there are two for market leaders. If the leaders lose their chance to challenge themselves, they can also copy other company's competitive methods. However, leaders must act quickly to stop attackers before they establish their positions.

Many leaders do not want to stop other companies, because they underestimate them. To make matters worse, it is already too late when they are about to defend.

For leaders, blocking is very effective, which is decided by the nature of battlefield, which is a mind of customers. For attackers, it takes time to leave an impression in the minds of customers. While under normal circumstances, this time is enough for leaders.

In short, defensive warfare's ultimate goal is to win the peace, forcing competitors into sporadic guerrilla warfare. Nonetheless, leaders should always remain vigilant. The first round losers will always provoke a second round, which requires leaders to be prepared to block at any time and not to take that lightly.

III.   Principles of Offensive Warfare

In fact, offensive strategy and defensive strategy is contrary in name but the same in nature. These two are closely linked, and difficult to separate. From the abstract sense, there is no absolute sense of good and bad. Good strategy is bad strategy, and vice versa. It all depends on who is going to use these strategies. A strategy is good for leaders, while bad for those left behind, and vice versa. Therefore, before using a certain strategy, a company should constantly check what position it occupies in the market.

Leaders should choose a defensive warfare but an offensive one also. Because offensive warfare fits for companies occupying the second or third position in the market, which should have sufficient forces to launch a sustained attack on leaders.

No one defines what sufficient forces are. The same in military combat, strategy and tactics is not an art, but a science. It is difficult to have a fixed quantitative criterion, which relies on judgments of entrepreneurs. Meanwhile, conditions vary between industries.

If a company has sufficient forces, it should be brave enough to launch an offensive warfare. But it should use the following three principles.

The first principle: the focus is strength of the leader in the market

It is identical with the first principle of defense. In comparison, it is relatively easier for leaders to concentrate on itself, while is more difficult for companies in the second or third position.

Thinking of most companies is contrary for their first reaction is to research themselves. They consider their own strengths, the quality, sales, prices and sales channels of their products. This is the reason why most companies all look like leaders finally.

Companies in the second or third position should concentrate on leaders and study their products, sales forces, product prices and sales channels. Regardless of how powerful a second company is in a certain category of products, if the leader is also quite strong in this regard, the former has absolutely no chance of winning.

Leaders occupy customers' minds. To win the battle in minds, one must first occupy the position of the leader, and then replace it. Besides, just winning is not enough, one has to defeat opponents, especially the leader.

Marketing plans of most companies require their market shares increasing. In a particular field, always half a dozen companies will develop similar schemes, not to mention new entrants. But the reality shows just the opposite, that most companies' sales plans are rarely achieved.

For companies that rank second in the market, the better strategy should be to firmly focus on leaders, and then ask them "How can I reduce their market shares?"

It does not mean to make enemies, which is an incorrect understanding of marketing warfare.

"Bear in mind that marketing warfare is a spiritual warfare. In this war, the human mind is the battlefield. All offensives should be conducted on this basis and your arms should be language, text, images and sound." (6)

The second principle: to find a weakness in the strengths of the leader and attack it

Sometimes leaders do have some weaknesses, which is not part of their inherent powers. They simply ignore the effect at some point, which is not important for their leadership. This kind of weaknesses should not be considered.

For example, the high price of IBM's product is not its inherent weakness. Because of its good product quality, high market share, high production scale, its production cost is relatively low in the computer industry. Therefore, an attempt to attack IBM in price is very dangerous, because it has sufficient financial resources to be profitable at lower prices.

However, attackers do not necessarily always avoid price war. If that is the inherent weaknesses of the leader's power, the use of a price war is very effective.

The third principle: to launch attacks in as narrow a positions as possible

A company can only focus on one product. A full range is a luxury that only leaders can afford. Offensive warfare should be fought in narrow positions, and focus on a single product as much as possible.

Business people should learn from the success and experiences of military wars. In World War II, attacks were usually launched in very small positions, sometimes only on a road. Only after blockade can the attacks start horizontal expansion, finally occupying all the positions.

To launch attacks in the narrow positions it needs to have a partial strength advantage. Military expert Clausewitz has said that if you cannot obtain an absolute advantage, you must be flexible and use your existing strengths to create a comparative advantage in a decisive location." (7)

If a marketing team invests a very wide variety of products in vast positions all of a sudden and launches a full attack in an attempt to get as many market shares as possible, then it will eventually lose all of them, and even more.

In short, leaders or the monopoly look very strong. However, it can be defeated, with the prerequisite of finding their inner weaknesses in strengths.

IV.   Principles of Flanking Warfare

Whether for marketing warfare or for military battle, flanking warfare is a bold action, which is like gambling, and a gamble. It needs to make careful plans weekly, daily, every time. Therefore, flanking warfare is the most innovative method in commercial warfare, which is used by small or new companies who should avoid the main battle.

Compared with other strategies, flanking attacks need to master operational principles. After the beginning of an attack, one should be able to foresee the development of warfare. This kind of ability is almost the same with the quality of an excellent player.

To fight a good flanking warfare, three principles below should be followed.

The first principle: a good flanking attack should be started in regions with an absence of competition

In military operations, commanders will not command paratroopers to parachute against enemy's guns. Similarly, in commercial warfare, entrepreneurs will not launch their products into the market where it has been possessed by someone else.

Launching flanking attacks does not need to produce any new product different from existing ones in the market. However, there must be innovative or unique parts in the product, which may allow customers to have new ideas.

Lenovo Group has launched a flanking attack on IBM by launching a personal micro-computer, named a home computer against IBM's business computer, and achieved great success. It allows computer get into hundreds of millions of families, and makes tremendous contributions to Lenovo's success today.

Traditional marketing theory calls this approach market segment, that is, to look for vacancies in the market, which is a very important capability. To launch a real flanking warfare, one must be the first to seize the segment market. Otherwise, it becomes simply an attack on the enemy with a stiff defense.

Effects of flanking warfare and offensive warfare are different. If there is no fortification on a mountain, or in a segment in the market, it takes a squad of troops or a little power to occupy it. However, if it has been fortified, then it takes the whole troops or the maximum of efforts to do the same.

The second principle: tactical surprise should be an important component of the plan

Flanking warfare is essentially a surprise, which is different with offensive warfare and defensive warfare. Directions of the latter two are predictable, while that of the former is hard to anticipate. Therefore, the most successful flanking attack is often completely not predictable. The stronger the degree of surprise, the longer it takes the leaders to respond and fortify.

Surprise also can undermine the morale of the opponent, making its sales staff be perplexed temporarily while their headquarters issue instructions.

The third principle: The pursuit is as critical as the attack itself.

This is an additional principle. Clausewtzian has said that if you do not chase, victory would not lead to very good results. There is also an ancient military maxim, "to consolidate the fruits of victory, and to eliminate the effects of failure."

Suppose a company has 5 products, including 3 leading and 2 laggards. Under normal circumstances, because of the emotional rather than economic reasons, many companies tend to focus on improving laggards not leading products, which is wrong. Right action is exactly the opposite, a company should give up laggard's products and use invested resources on leading products. It is same as the stock market where weak shares are given up to make way for strong stocks.

If the products used to start a flanking attack is successful, one must persist to do more. The goal should be victory, and is a great one. This kind of pursuit must not stop halfway, which will eventually lead to failure of the attack.

In short, the flanking attack strategy is not manageable for those timid or prudent people. A flanking attack is a gamble, resulting in possible a victory, or possible a heavy defeat. Moreover, launching flanking attack needs unique conventional vision, which cannot be replaced by normal market research. Potential consumers cannot know what they may purchase when there are huge changes of their interests and choices. Therefore, the success of a flanking attack demands to strongly affect interests and choices of consumers.

V.   Principles of Guerrilla Warfare

Histories of China, Cuba and Vietnam prove the power of guerrilla warfare.

Guerrilla warfare has many tactical advantages which even can make small companies stand among stronger ones.

Of course, the company size is a relative term. America's smallest automobile company, American Motors is much larger than the world's largest razor company, Gillette Company. However, American Motors should adopt guerrilla warfare, while Gillette should use defensive warfare.

Size of your competitors is more important than that of yours. "The key to success of commercial warfare is to formulate strategies and tactics aiming at your competitors and not yourself." (9)

To fight high-quality guerrilla warfare, one must follow the following three principles as well.

The first principle: to find a segment market, small enough to be defeated

There are several meanings of the word "small." It can be a small size in geographical meaning, and can also be small measure of capacity, and can also be small of other concepts. In short, it should be small enough that no larger company will take an interest in it and will have difficulty in attacking even if it is interested.

Guerrilla warfare does not change the military strength principle. It is still an example of small companies beating large companies. "Guerrilla warfare is intended to minimize the battle in order to win the strength advantage. In other words, it is like making you become a big fish in small pond." (10)

To achieve this goal, the traditional way is to rely on geographic location. Almost any well-known product or service can be under attack in an area. This is a classic guerrilla tactic.

The problem is a successful launch of guerrilla war needs to adopt the same idea to other situations. In these cases, regional boundaries are not obvious. There are other commonly used guerrilla tactics.

1. Population guerrilla warfare. Such guerrilla tactic is to attract certain populations, such as customers divided in age, income, occupation, or hobbies, etc.
2. Industry guerrilla warfare. This guerrilla tactic is to concentrate on a particular industry, such as food, clothing, health products,

computer, gaming industry, etc., which is also called vertical marketing. The key to success of industry guerrilla warfare is to be precise and deep in the industry. If the company adopting industry guerrilla warfare expands its systems to other industries, it is certain to be faced with many problems.

3. Product guerrilla warfare. This guerrilla tactic is to concentrate on a single product market from where profits are made. In this way, its sales will be so large that no larger company will take an interest in the same products.

4. High price guerrilla warfare. There are many companies adopting high price guerrilla warfare in modern society with rich products. In sales, high prices can create "visibility" and high quality and high prices will produce a corresponding effect, mystery, giving rise to the demand. However, you have to be the first and to create new features for products making it worth for money. To fight the high price of guerrilla warfare, there must be confidence and courage. You have to be confident in the future for innovative products, and have the courage to launch an unknown product.

5. Alliance development. In many industries, the development of alliances is a common strategy, particularly in the case when the main competitors are built up by many local guerrilla companies. The typical pattern is that a franchise holder sets up a joint nationwide sales network with a national name, and allows local ownership and control. This kind of strategy has the following two methods: top-down and bottom-up.

Top-down organization form is the development of an overall contract and operation of local businessmen. McDonald's, KFC, Coca Cola are typical examples. In other words, you have an idea, and then recruit a group of guerrillas to complete your plan.

Bottom-up is a more creative organization form. This method often achieves great success, as it requires few resources at the beginning.

All companies gain experience as isolated competitors. Principles of commercial warfare do not always turn individual companies into competitors but sometimes create more alliances, such as product alliances, regional alliances, consumer groups alliance, and so on. Principles of forces will encourage various guerrillas to get together to conduct self-protection consciously.

In some aspects, guerrilla warfare looks like flanking warfare. However, there are critical differences between them. "Flanking warfare is deliberately launched to the front-line close to leaders as the result of planning. Its goal is to win or weaken the market share of leaders." (11)

How small should the market be that guerrilla companies set their sights on? This is the basis for all judgments. It is necessary to try to find a segment market, which is small enough to make you become the market leader. While many people prefer the opposite approach, that is attempt to capture a market as large as possible and to pursue so-called product extension blindly. This is a trap leading to failure.

The basis for selecting a strategy depends on the resources owned by the company, which is the key for the company to choose its guerrilla strategy. "In essence, guerrilla company is limited in forces from the beginning. In order to survive, it must be tough enough to resist the temptation of distracting its forces elsewhere; otherwise, it can only lead to disaster." (12)

The second principle: No matter how successful you are, do not behave as a leader

Most successful companies adopting guerrilla warfare are very fortunate, because their leaders usually accept no formal business school education or training, nor study management experience of Fortune 500 like General Motors, General Electric and IBM. This is not to say that business schools in the world cannot train good leaders, on the contrary, they do develop a lot of good leaders for large companies, but the core of the cases they are teaching is management experience of large companies. However, "The nature of guerrilla strategy and tactics are opposite to those of 500 companies." (13)

Successful guerrilla warfare requires different organizations and different schedules.

First, organizations must be uncomplicated and streamlined. Large companies often have a huge organization system. Typically, the duty of more than half of all staff is providing services to other employees, and only a small number of people are assigned to the first line outside the company to face with the real enemy - competitors. Guerrilla companies should take advantage of this weakness of large companies, arranging more staff as much as possible into the front line, resisting the temptation of overcrowding the organization, formulating no organizational systems, job descriptions, job lifting systems or other forms which are mere formalities. All staff should be put into the front line as far as possible leaving no non-combatants. This simple and streamlined organization form is not only capable of putting more troops into the front-line, but can greatly improves the speed of guerrilla warfare, allowing companies to transform adapting to market changes.

Second, the decision-making should be fast and responsive. Being small, guerrilla companies can also make decisions quickly. This is a valuable asset when competing with large companies. Because large companies take 6 months to make a decision, while guerrilla companies often only spend 6 weeks, or even 6 days.

The third principle: find the signs of failure; be ready to retreat any time.

What should guerrilla companies do if the warfare gets tough? "If the situation of the warfare is unfavorable for you, you should give up your position or products without despair. Guerrillas do not have enough financial and human resources to spend on a losing warfare. They should give up the mess as soon as possible and move on." (14) As the saying goes, "Where there is life there is hope." As long as the company can survive, it can continue to compete with competitors.

Retreat is the opposite of advance. Guerrilla companies should take advantage of its flexibility to enter the market in a timely manner once a timeframe is chosen. It can make the company occupy positions that other brands abandon for various reasons. Guerrilla companies often act quickly and can fill vacancies in the market quickly.

In short, in commercial warfare, guerrilla warfare is almost everywhere. According to reports, among the 5 million companies in the United States, most have adopted guerrilla tactics. Large companies may occupy the news pages, while small companies have control of terrain. Experiences and lessons learned from commercial warfare have proved that: "Most companies should adopt guerrilla strategy. In general, in every 100 companies, only one company should choose defensive warfare, two of them should pursue offensive warfare, some of them should adopt flanking warfare and other 94 should fight guerrilla warfare. " (15)

Case Study

Gillette challenges itself

The best self-defense strategy is to challenge oneself. Gillette is a good example and its product "Blue Gillette" razor and the subsequent "Super Blue Gillette" razor occupy the razor market.

In the early 1960's, Gillette's competitor Wilkinson introduces the stainless steel blade and seizes the market first. Gillette is shocked. In 1970, Wilkinson launches the bonding blade, which is a kind of metal blade bonding on the plastic in the best shaving angle. At this time, Gillette begins to concentrate on preparing to fight a nice defense.

Soon, Gillette counterattacks by launching "Trac II" razor, which is the world's first double-edged razor. Success of "Trac II" razor has a great influence on later strategic guidance of Gillette Company. Just as Gillette says in the ad, double-edged is better than single-blade."

Gillette customers soon begin to purchase its new product, and believe that it is more useful than the one-chip "super blue Gillette." It is better to take the business away from oneself than be taken by others.

Six years later, Gillette launches "Atra" razor, which is the first adjustable double-edged razor. It means that the new product is even better than the double-edged "Trac II" razor which cannot be adjusted.

After that, Gillette does not hesitate to launch "Good News" razor, which is a cheap double-edged disposable razor. This is a hit to BIC who is also about to launch its own disposable razors.

"Good News" is not really good news for Gillette shareholders. Disposable razors cost much in production, while its sales are not as good as blades replaceable razor. Any purchase of "Good News" but not "Atra" or "Trac II" will actually bring losses of Gillette shareholders.

However, the launch of "Good News" is a very good marketing strategy. It prevents BIC from grabbing the disposable blade market. In addition, BIC pays a heavy price. Industry data shows that in the first three years, BIC loses 25 million U.S. dollars in disposable blade market.

Gillette adheres to the strategy of challenging itself tirelessly. Recently, it launches "Pivot" razor, which is the first disposable razor that can be adjusted. This time, Gillette's own product "Good News" becomes the attack target.

Gillette razor gradually expands its market share. Today, it already has 65% market share in razors.

Source: 〔U.S.〕 AL Ries, Jack Trout, *Marketing Warfare*, 1st Edition, China Financial and Economic Publishing House, October 2002, p. 58-60.
The best strategic choice for the leader is defensive warfare, and the form of defensive war is to challenge oneself.

Attack is the best defense. Relying on positional defense cannot get the victory, and only an attack can lead to success. Even in the case of an absolute disadvantage, defense should be replaced by attack.

To challenge oneself may bring the expense of immediate self-interest, but is able to defend market share, which is the ultimate weapon to win the marketing warfare.

Conversely, if the company is hesitating in self-attack, typically it will lose market share, and ultimately lose the position of market leader.

For defensive war, Gillette is a good example.

Haier breaks "iron triangle" of the microwave industry

The latest Sino statistics show that the Haier microwave oven enters the top three in the industry exceeding Midea with a market share of 12.7%. This indicates that the "iron triangle" consisting of Glanz, LG, and Midea that dominates the market over the years is broken. And the structure of the microwave industry changes for the first time. Well, how does Haier microwave oven breakthrough the "iron triangle"?

Ten years of one sword, to lead the industry by technology innovation Facing the price war its competitors launched over the years to gobble the market, Haier microwave oven always follows the business objectives of high-tech, high-quality, and environmentally soundness to occupy the market from high-end. It pioneers in launching microwave ovens with an electronic menu, IC card menu replaceable microwave oven, double roasted microwave oven, sun acoustic waveguide microwave oven, network-based microwave oven and a series of high-tech products. Leading technology innovation wins the industry's respect for Haier. Haier microwave oven becomes one of the industry's two "Chinese Famous Brand" in 2001 and wins the first "Product Exempted from Inspection" title given by General Administration of Quality Supervision, Inspection and Quarantine in 2002.

In 2003, supported by Haier Group's global R & D platform, Haier microwave ovens pioneers to launching a transfer wave oven at the international advanced level, bringing an unprecedented change to the microwave oven industry. Compared with domestic brands that bring down the market price of electronic ovens, Haier transfer wave ovens advances from the high-end market and triumphs to become the biggest bright spot in the microwave oven market.

In the international market, Haier transfer wave oven is first exported to the Japanese market, causing a sensation. According to related statistics, the introduction of transfer wave technology ends decline trend that continues for many years in the microwave oven market in Japan. Sales of transfer wave oven increase by 50% in Japanese market in 2003, bringing the whole Japan microwave oven market to grow by 50% and forming a powerful transfer wave height that affects the world.

The world workshop is named on the same day with the world's brand

On January 31, 2004, a piece of seemingly insignificant news alarms China's manufacturing industry. World Brand Lab announces the world's 100 most influential brands, in which Haier ranks 95th. Before that, never has a Chinese local brand entered the top 100 brands list.

It is well known that international brands can make the value of products multiply. The *Los Angeles Times* in the United States on November 24, 2003, writes according to statistics of the United Nations Industrial Programme, the world famous brands are less than 3% of brands in the world, while their products account for more than 40%   and sales account for more about 50% in the global market.

In China, we clearly feel the shortage of world-class brands. In recent years, although some Chinese brands gain more than 50% market share in very small industries in the world, such as lighter and microwave oven, there is still a wide gap between them and the world-class brands. Currently, only

Haier achieves the basic conditions for world-class enterprise and world-class brand, and thus is eligible to be listed in 100 most influential brands in the world.

For a long time, some brands are very good at creating an illusion in front of consumers, that is, its position in the market will be high as long as its yield are high. And many companies are also proud of tens of millions of production capacity. In fact, consumers naturally understand that brand is most critical in the measure of a product's position in the market. A company without a brand will still be a workshop no matter how big it is and will survive only on making processing fees but technological advances and new product development.

A good brand is also a guarantee of low-cost. Different companies have different means of reducing costs. Through advanced technology, improved logistics procurement systems, short marketing chains, world-class brands take method of quality to reduce costs.

As Haier has a strong world-class logistics procurement system, procurement of all parts of Haier household appliances are unified, which guarantees to minimize costs. Almost no domestic household appliance company has a purchasing scale as large as Haier, who procures all materials and parts of household appliances like microwave ovens, refrigerators, air conditioners, washing machines, etc. at the same time. It makes Haier microwave ovens have the ability to ensure low price products based on high-quality.

Haier microwave oven maintains steady growth in the fluctuations

In recent years, because the microwave oven market has ups and downs, market shares of many companies are very unstable. However, we can see from the market share chart of Haier microwave oven that its market share is increasing steadily. In particular, in early 2003 when the transfer wave oven is launched, market share of Haier microwave peaks, which allows Haier to get access to the top three in the industry with 12.7% of the market share and makes the microwave oven industry concerned about the momentum of Haier microwave ovens.

In fact, it is far enough along to rely on production or marketing to become market dominant, it is also not a wise choice to depend on playing numbers game on hearsay evidence to fight against competitors. A company can steadily expand its market share by relying on scientific and technological innovations, and providing more convenience and benefits for consumers like the Haier microwave oven proved. We can learn more from the scientific development path of Haier microwave ovens to triumph in the market.

Source: Tian Zhe, "Haier breaks 'iron triangle' of microwave industry" *Chinese enterprises,* June 2, 2004.

Haier microwave oven enters the top three in the industry exceeding Midea with a market share of 12.7%. This indicates that the "iron triangle" consisting of Glanz, LG, and Midea that dominate the market over the years is over, and the structure of the microwave industry has changes significantly for the first time. Well, how does Haier microwave oven breakthrough the "iron triangle?" It is done so by applying offensive warfare.

A principle of offensive warfare is to find the weaknesses of a strong leader's advantage and to launch an attack.

That is what Haier microwave oven does. It seizes the weaknesses of advantages of Glanz, LG, and Midea, that is, to occupy the market from the low end, and then launches an attack by acting in opposition to occupy the market from the high end. Finally it fights a nice offensive war.

Dell: the abolition of intermediaries

Over the past 20 years, the business model used by Dell Computer is one of the world's best business models. Michael Dell, as contemporary business entrepreneur, is at the forefront of commercial media. This young computer wizard makes a fortune by creating his own technology company as a college dropout. However, the really influential insight of Michael Dell does not lie in technical aspects, but in business. Early in 1980s, he begins to pay attention to the work mode of personal computer manufacturers and finds a better way. This approach eliminates unnecessary costs, allowing people to buy their own computers at lower prices.

This approach is direct selling to customers, by passing distributors, the intermediate links. Dell Computer receives orders directly from the consumer, and then buys their own parts to build computers. This means that the Dell Computer either needs plant and equipment or needs research and development investment. Consumers get the computer configuration they want, and Dell avoids the rise in prices by intermediate parts.

This is a wonderful business idea. Dell himself obtains a lot of wealth by eliminating intermediate links for consumers. He acquires the technology needed at a very low cost and obtains more profits than other personal computer manufacturers. Dell's direct selling business model is to use the existing value chain, and to remove any unnecessary and expensive parts which are called "disintermediation" or "disintermediation" in economics terminology. From the consumers' point of view, this new value chain is more efficient.

Dell does not expect so much opportunity when he drops out of college to start his own company. Manufacturing products in accordance with the customer's orders allows Dell to avoid costs and risks by not carrying large products inventories. No matter what happens to the business environment, this is a very good thing. Moreover, in the 1990s, along with the remarkable pace of innovation, Dell's business model becomes a profitable one.

A feature of the new economy is that the source of value transfers from specific things to creative things and from products to services. Dell's successful business model is further evidence that one can succeed with products as well as with services. What does this really mean? And why is that?

Inventory has been very important for the service industry. For example, if you work in an airline, for each flight you definitely have large fixed costs. These costs include the aircraft itself, fuel and crew, which will not change whether there are 300 or 30 passengers on board. In order to make money, you have to try to fill the aircraft. An airline is not able to save seats in the storehouse, so these seats are like a box of perishable strawberries which are cannot be saved. This is also the same problem faced by hospitals, which cannot put beds, equipment and highly trained medical staff in a storehouse. Also, each professional such as lawyers, doctors, consultants, etc., cannot save their time and use it later. Therefore, for the service industry with high fixed costs, to address the above issue is a major issue.

However, manufacturing companies in the past tended to act according to a different economic model. If the production amount is small enough, then you can place the product into the storehouse, until consumers are ready to buy. However, for companies whose products upgrade quickly, its product is can   quickly and easily to be out of date. Kevin Rollins, vice president of Dell Computer has once lamented that "We are now like a farmer selling vegetables, which are might go bad in our hands." He means that since the development of computer technology is very fast, if the company cannot quickly sell the computer, the product can easily become a bunch of obsolete machines, which are like already rotten fruits and vegetables. This awareness on the inventory and speed leads Dell in the past decade to perform well. So now no matter in what the industry, many CEOs consider speed as one of their priorities.

For ten years, the direct computer model allows Dell to maintain a pace that competitors are struggling to cope with, and allows Dell to establish direct contact with customers. This contact makes Dell grasp what kinds of products customers want and when they need such products. Then, Dell Computer impels cooperative suppliers' to timely produce and transports its parts to its assembly plants and uses this information. As Michael Dell has said, "We use the information instead of the stock." This is also benefit for Dell's suppliers because they can be more stable and be able to supply computer accessories to Dell.

Initially, other personal computer makers' disdain Dell's business practices. After 15 years of development, competitors slowly throw in the towel, and introduce Dell's direct computer model. Computer distribution agents who are dominant in the entire computer industry with total revenue over 75 billion dollars in 2000 can barely survives now. In 2000, al the three industry giants, including CHS Electronics, MicroAge Inc. and InaCom company cites "Enterprise Protection Act," Article 11 to seek U.S. government protection.

In a sense, the moral significance of this story is actually quite simple: when you can provide low-priced products and services, your company will grow by leaps and bounds. Affordable products and services are generated by a system or a business model, which is built on the vision of values. Only when a good business model is built, can a company provide customers affordable services.

Dell's own cost structure significantly reduces the variety of expenses, so it can provide more low-cost computers. What will Dell Computer do in future? With the slowdown in the PC market, Dell Computer Corporation will quickly expand its direct selling model to new areas, such as the server and so on. In fact, it is a very clear pattern, which is deeply understood by all managers of Dell Computer and helps them adapt to changes. There is no doubt that Dell Computer Corporation will continue to stick to its business model.

Source: (U.S.) Joan Magretta, Nan Stone, What *Management Is,* Electronic Industry Press, 2003.

When the 19-year-old Michael Dell starts his own small computer company, he knows that he could not compete with store channels with other large companies like IBM and HP, so he decides to break the routine. He launches a flanking warfare position in the industry by the abolition the use of intermediaries and adopts direct marketing. In 5 years, Dell creates a business worth 800 million dollars, and now it grows into one of the world's most successful companies in the computer industry.

Flanking warfare is suitable for small or new companies who should avoid the main battle. Selection of flanking warfare means to enter a field without competition and to create a strategic miracle. Flanking warfare usually attacks by force with a new concept, such as Dell's "PC Direct" is a successful model.

Hasee seizes initiative by the guerrilla warfare

In 2001, when Hasee decides to enter the computer market, it is competing in the same world as Lenovo, and DELL. Wu Haijun, chairman of Hasee believes that the dominant strategy of Hasee can only be won using guerrilla tactics.

In 2005, how can the little-known Hasee first sign popular star Li Yuchun? When the "Super Girl" contest comes to the stage of six to five, Hasee has been in contact with EE-Media Company in order to invite Super Girls to craft advertising. Because the contest of Super Girl at that time is still in progress, EE-Media Company rejects the request of Hasee. On August 26, 2005, Li Yuchun eventually wins the 2005 Super Girl title. Around 2 pm the next day, EE-Media Company takes the initiative to contact Hasee, indicating the product endorsement can be discussed.

Wu Haijun, chairman of Hasee, along with an associate immediately takes the 15:00 pm flight from Shenzhen to Changsha and arrives at 17:00 pm. Then Wu Haijun immediately invites senior leaders of EE-Media Company to eat dinner and they reach a verbal agreement. The next day at 2 o'clock in the morning, the two sides formally sign the cooperation agreement in writing. Early in the morning of the 28th, Wu Haijun returns to Shenzhen and about two in the afternoon, the creative advertising content and endorsement of Li Yuchun and Hasee is finalized. It takes only 24 hours for EE-Media Company to reply to Hasee. It can be described as a quick blitz.

Source: Xu Yinjie, Wu Wei, "Mao Zedong's military thought is a powerful weapon for the weak to defeat the strong," *China Business,* December 26, 2005.

Review

There is no one in world military history like Mao Zedong, one of modern Chinese strategists who always leads the weaker party to fight with stronger enemies (the Japanese army, the Kuomintang army and the U.S. military), and turns disadvantages into advantages, resulting in success.

For this reason, thought on strategy and tactics of Mao Zedong is a natural ideological weapon for a weaker company to compete. The essences of Mao Zedong's strategic thinking, guerrilla warfare, strategic retreat, and mobile warfare have practical significance for today's Chinese enterprises, especially SMEs and enterprises which are still not very strong.

Modern Chinese strategist Mao Zedong especially emphasizes the flexibility and speed of the guerrilla warfare. That Hasee signs Chinese the pop singer Li Yuchun within 24-hour shows the essence of guerrilla warfare.

Questions

1. What kind of commonly used strategic forms are there?
2. What are the principles of defensive warfare?
3. What are the principles of offensive warfare?
4. What are the principles of flanking warfare?
5. What are the principles of guerrilla warfare?
6. How do you choose the right strategy forms for an enterprise?
7. Try to choose the strategic form that suits your company according to the theories in *Art of War* and *Marketing Warfare.*

Notes

(1)Sun-Tzu(the original), Kung-sun Daoming ed, *Art of War and Thirty-Six Stratagems,* 1st edition, Guangxi Ethnic Publishing House, July 1995, p. 74-75.

(2) 〔U.S.〕 AL Ries, Jack Trout, *Marketing Warfare*, 1st Edition, China Financial and Economic Publishing House, October 2002, p. 49.

(3) 〔U.S.〕 AL Ries, Jack Trout, *Marketing Warfare*, 1st Edition, China Financial and Economic Publishing House, October 2002, p. 51.

(4) 〔U.S.〕 AL Ries, Jack Trout, *Marketing Warfare*, 1st Edition, China Financial and Economic Publishing House, October 2002, p. 51.

(5) 〔U.S.〕 AL Ries, Jack Trout, *Marketing Warfare*, 1st Edition, China Financial and Economic Publishing House, October 2002, p. 59.

(6) 〔U.S.〕 AL Ries, Jack Trout, *Marketing Warfare*, 1st Edition, China Financial and Economic Publishing House, October 2002, p. 74.

(7) 〔U.S.〕 AL Ries, Jack Trout, *Marketing Warfare*, 1st Edition, China Financial and Economic Publishing House, October 2002, p. 77.

(8) 〔U.S.〕 AL Ries, Jack Trout, *Marketing Warfare*, 1st Edition, China Financial and Economic Publishing House, October 2002, p. 91.

(9) 〔U.S.〕 AL Ries, Jack Trout, *Marketing Warfare*, 1st Edition, China Financial and Economic Publishing House, October 2002, p. 105.

(10) 〔U.S.〕 AL Ries, Jack Trout, *Marketing Warfare*, 1st Edition, China Financial and Economic Publishing House, October 2002, p. 106.

(11) 〔U.S.〕 AL Ries, Jack Trout, *Marketing Warfare*, 1st Edition, China Financial and Economic Publishing House, October 2002, p. 107.

(12) 〔U.S.〕 AL Ries, Jack Trout, *Marketing Warfare*, 1st Edition, China Financial and Economic Publishing House, October 2002, p. 109.

(13) 〔U.S.〕 AL Ries, Jack Trout, *Marketing Warfare*, 1st Edition, China Financial and Economic Publishing House, October 2002, p. 110.

(14) 〔U.S.〕 AL Ries, Jack Trout, *Marketing Warfare*, 1st Edition, China Financial and Economic Publishing House, October 2002, p. 112.

(15) 〔U.S.〕 AL Ries, Jack Trout, *Marketing Warfare*, 1st Edition, China Financial and Economic Publishing House, October 2002, p. 122.

BIBLIOGRAPHY

Mao Zedong, *"Elected Works of Mao Zedong,* four volumes, People's Publishing House, Beijing, 1966.

Art of War commentary group of War Theory Research Department of Academy of Military Sciences, CPLA, *New Commentary of Art of War*, 1st edition, Zhonghua Book Company, January 1977.

Sun-Tzu(the original), Kung-sun Daoming ed, *Art of War and Thirty-Six Stratagems* , 1st edition, Guangxi Ethnic Publishing House, July 1995.

Editorial board of *Art of War and Strategy for Business and Politics*, *Art of War and Strategy for Business and Politics*, 1st edition, Blue Sky Press, May 1997.

〔U.S.〕AL Ries, Jack Trout, *Marketing Warfare*, 1st Edition, China Financial and Economic Publishing House, October 2002.

〔U.S.〕AL Ries, Jack Trout, *Bottom-Up Marketing*, 1st Edition, China Financial and Economic Publishing House, October 2002.

〔U.S.〕Michael Porter, *Competitive Strategy*, 1st edition, Huaxia Publishing House, January 1997.
〔U.S.〕Michael Porter, *Competitive Advantage*, 1st edition, Huaxia Publishing House, January 1997.

〔U.S.〕Fred. R. David, *Strategic Management*, Li Kening trans., 1st edition, Economic Science Press, June 1998.

CHAPTER 11
Enterprise Strategy Implementation

Abstract

This chapter begins with brilliant expositions from Peter Drucker, Henry Mintzberg and Larry Bossidy to stress the vital importance of strategy implementation. Then it analyzes differences between strategy formulation and strategy implementation to indicate the contents of strategy implementation. Subsequently, it describes the specific requirements of strategy implementation. Finally, it has appendix of cases and comments in "Beijing International Bidding Co., Ltd."

Learning Objectives

- To profoundly understand the significance of strategy implementation.
- To clear differences between strategy formulation and strategy implementation.
- To clear and grasp contents of enterprise strategy implementation.
- To clear and grasp the content of company functional strategies.
- To clear and deal with management issues of strategy implementation.

Introduction

Peter Drucker stresses that even the best plans are only plans, or good intentions. Without responsibility and implementation, there are only promises and hopes but no plans. (1) Canada's strategic experts Henry Mintzberg has also said that "Most of the time, strategists should not be formulating strategy at all; they should be getting on with implementing strategies they already have." (2) Larry Bossidy, who has once served as senior leader of General Electric, AlliedSignal and Honeywell, also stresses in the introduction of his book *Execution: The discipline of getting things done* that "Many people regard execution as detail work that's beneath the dignity of a business leader. That's wrong. To the contrary, it's a leader's most important job. "(3)

347

Lesson

Successful strategy formulation does not guarantee successful strategy implementation. It is always more difficult to do something (strategy implementation) than to saying you are going to do it (strategy formulation). Although there are close links between strategy implementation and strategy formulation, there exist fundamental differences as well. Differences between the two are summarized in Table 11-1, and the contents of enterprise strategy implementation are reflected in Table 11-1.

Table 11-1 Differences between strategy formulation and strategy implementation

Categories \ Strategy formulation Items	Strategy formulation	Strategy implementation
Action time	Positioning forces before the action	Managing forces during the action
Primary process	Primarily an intellectual process	Primarily an operational process
Requirements	Good intuitive and analytical skills	Motivation and leadership skills
Objects	Requires coordination among a few individuals	Requires coordination among many persons
Focuses	Focus on effectiveness	Focuses on efficiency

I. Establishing Annual Objectives and Devising Policies

(I) Establishing annual objectives

Strategic objectives are long-term ones. Therefore the most important part of strategy implementation is to change long-term objectives into short-term objectives, i.e. the annual objectives.

Figure 11-1 Contents of Enterprise Strategy Implementation

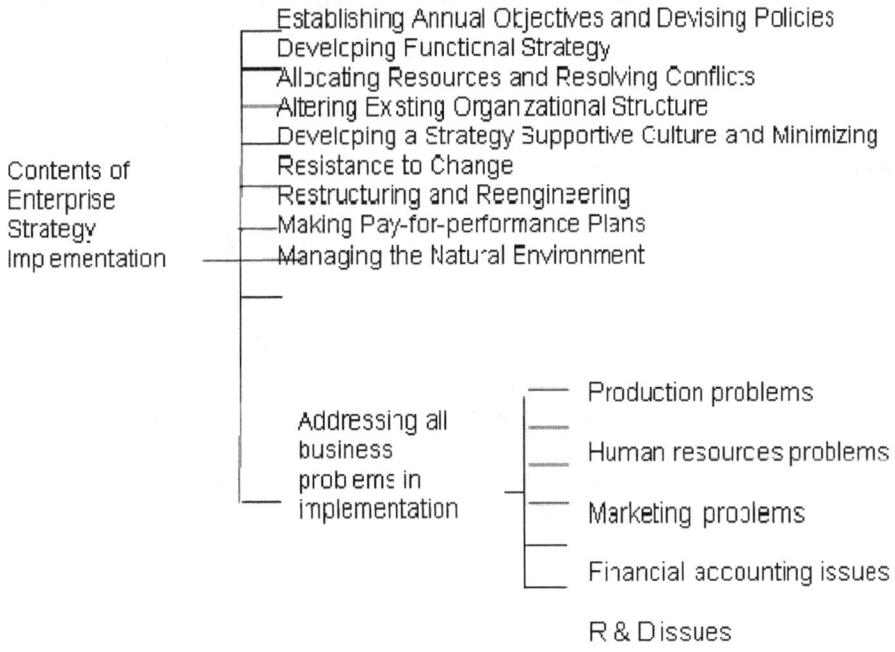

Contents of
Enterprise
Strategy
Implementation

- Establishing Annual Objectives and Devising Policies
- Developing Functional Strategy
- Allocating Resources and Resolving Conflicts
- Altering Existing Organizational Structure
- Developing a Strategy Supportive Culture and Minimizing Resistance to Change
- Restructuring and Reengineering
- Making Pay-for-performance Plans
- Managing the Natural Environment

Addressing all business problems in implementation

- Production problems
- Human resources problems
- Marketing problems
- Financial accounting issues

R & D issues

Annual objectives are decentralized activities in which all managers of the company are directly involved. Active involvement in establishing annual objectives can enhance a sense of identity and responsibility of managers. Annual objectives are important for strategy implementation because: first, it is the basis for allocating resources; second, it is the mechanism for evaluating managers; third, it is the tool to monitor progress toward long-term objectives; fourth, it establishes organizational, divisional, and divisional priorities. A company should invest time and effort to establish appropriate and reasonable annual objectives and to ensure they are consistent with the long-term objectives and supportive to enterprise strategy implementation.

Objectives that are clearly stated and disseminated are critical for companies of all types and sizes. Established annual objectives generally include profits, growth and market shares classified by business, region, user groups and product category, and so on.

(II) Devising Policies

Changes in directions of company strategies don't happen automatically. Strategy implementation needs specific policies to guide the company's daily work. Policies refer to generalized specific guidelines, methods, procedures, rules, forms and management activities which support and encourage hard work in order to achieve set objectives. Policies are the means by which annual objectives will be achieved. Policies set boundaries, constraints, and limits on administrative actions, and also define what a company can do and can't do in the pursuit of its objectives.

Policies set expectations for managers and employees, thereby increase the possibility of successful strategy implementation. Policies set a basis for management control and coordination, allow consistency and coordination within and between organizational divisions, and reduce time for decision-making of managers. Policies make it clear who should do the work and properly delegated decision-making authority to various different levels. Many companies have their own policies manual to guide employees' behaviors.

II.   Developing Functional Strategy

Company functional strategy, also known as functional division strategy or functional layer strategy, is developed by the middle managers under the guidance of the company's overall strategy. It is the specification of overall strategy in the aspect of specific functions and detail strategy of certain management fields to ensure the implement of the overall strategy and the business layer strategy. In other words, it is a short-term strategic plan of major functional divisions within the company, which can not only make managers of the division more clearly understand the responsibilities and requirements in the implementation of the overall strategy and the business unit strategy, but help them take effective use of management functions of the division to achieve strategic objectives. So company functional strategy is essentially the strategy and measures to achieve the overall strategy and the business layer strategy, serving as the bridge or ship to cross the river. As it is called "strategy" customarily in business and academic fields, so this book takes it as "functional strategy."

Functional strategy should cover all functional areas of the company, including the company's technology development, raw material supply, manufacturing, sales and all aspects of human and financial management.

Of which, five of them are the most important functional strategies, namely, marketing strategy, research and development strategy, human resource strategy, operations strategy and financial strategy. Elements of the company functional strategy are shown in Figure 11-2.

Figure 11-2 Company Functional Strategy

III. Allocating Resources and Resolving Conflicts

(I) Allocating Resources

Resources allocation is a central activity of strategic management. Strategic management sets allocation plan based on priorities identified by annual objectives. For strategic management, nothing is more harmful than not doing it like that.

All companies have at least four types of resources for the achievement of the desired objectives: financial, physical, human, and technological resources. The allocation of resources to specific divisions or divisions does not mean that strategies can be successfully implemented. There are some common factors that impede the efficient allocation of resources, including over-protection of resources, too much emphasis on short-term financial objectives, uncertainty of the company policy and strategic objectives, needless to take risks and lack of adequate knowledge.

The true value of any resources allocation scheme lies in the realization of company objectives. Sometimes effective allocation of resources does not guarantee successful strategy implementation because available resources can only call into play plans, personnel, controls and responsibilities. Strategic management is also sometimes called a "resource allocation process."

(II) Resolving Conflicts

Dependence and competition between the objectives often lead to conflicts. Conflict can be defined as differences between two or more parties on one or more issues. The establishment of annual objectives can lead to conflicts for reasons of different expectations and ideas of people, pressure brought by plans, personality clashes, and misunderstandings between divisions and personnel, and so on. For example, the objective for the chamberlain to reduce 50% bad debts will conflict with that for division to increase sales by 20%.

Conflicts may also occur during the process of overall plan establishment. It is because managers and strategists need to make trade-offs between contradictory elements as follows: short-term profit and long-term growth, profitability and market share, market penetration and market development, growth and stability, high-risk and low risk, social responsibility and profit maximization, and so on. Conflicts are inevitable in the production and management of the company. Therefore, it is important for management to resolve conflicts before the dysfunction impacts the business performance. Sometimes conflicts are not bad things, because the disappearance of conflicts is often a symbol of a lack of passion and indifference, while conflicts can motivate opposing groups to take actions to allow managers find the problem.

Solutions to conflicts can be divided into three categories: avoidance, mitigation, and confrontation. Avoidance methods mean to ignore the problem; hoping conflicts are resolved on their own and separate the conflicting individuals or groups. Mitigation methods refers to weaken the conflicts of both sides and to stress the common ground and common interests, to make a compromise with both sides regardless of the outcome, to adopt ideas of the majority, and to request the ruling of a higher authority, or to change the current position. Confrontation methods refer to exchange of personnel of opposing sides in order to facilitate mutual understanding, to focus on higher level objectives like the survival of the company, or to let the opposing sides express their views on a meeting in order to resolve their differences.

IV.   Altering Existing Organizational Structure

Structure follows strategy. Changes in strategy often require corresponding changes in organizational structure, for the following two main reasons: first, the organizational structure determines the company's objectives and policies to a great degree. For example, objectives and policies of a company with geographical organizational structure will be expressed in regional terms; while a company with product organizational structure is described with products to a large extent. Structure of organizations that set objectives and policies will have a considerable impact on all activities of strategy implementation.

Second, a company's organizational structure determines the configuration of its resources. If the organization is structured according to user groups, then the resources will also be configured according to that. Similarly, if the organization is formed on the basis of functional business structure, then the resources will also be allocated in accordance with that. Changing the focus of the organizational structure is usually part of strategy implementation activities, unless focus of the new or revised strategy is the same with the original one in the functional areas.

Redesign of organizational structure of the company should be able to promote its strategy implementation. Besides, organizational structure makes no sense at all without strategies or reasons for the company to exist (its task).

V.   Developing a Strategy Supportive Culture and Minimizing Resistance to Change

(I) Developing a strategy supportive culture

Strategists should pay attention to and preserve the existing company culture that supports the new strategy, and of course, confirm and change contradictions. Studies show that the new business strategy is often driven by the market, and dominated by the competitive forces. Therefore, developing a strategy supportive culture is much more effective than developing a culture supportive business strategy. There are a variety of ways to change strategy, for example, recruiting new employees, staff training, mobility and promotion, organizational structure changes, and model demonstration.

(II) Minimizing resistance to change

No company or individual can escape change. But change will raises anxiety or fear, and people concern the loss of economic benefits associated with it, inconvenience, uncertainty, and the destruction of the social model. Any change in organizational structure, technology, personnel or strategy is likely to disrupt the relationship that people have become accustomed to. Therefore, people tend to resist change. The implementation of the strategic management will lead to changes of individuals and business processes. Thus, it is not easy to change the company's management thinking, and make people think and act from the perspective of strategy.

Resistance to change can occur at any stage of the strategy implementation. Although there exists many ways to implement change, application of three strategies is more common, which are force change strategy, educative change strategy, and rational or self-interest change strategy. Force change strategy implements the change by forcing an issue and executing commands. Its superiority is its high speed, while its defect is low sense of responsibility and high resistance. Educative change strategy communicates to convince people the need for change. Its drawback is its low speed, but compared to force change strategy, it can stimulate a stronger sense of responsibility and reduce drags. Rational or self-interest change strategy makes people believe that change will benefit themselves. If it is successful, strategy implementation will be relatively easier. However, in reality, very few implementation of change will benefit all the people.

Strategists can take a variety of positive actions to reduce resistance of managers and employees to change. For example, they should let people who may be influenced by the change involved in the decision-making of determining change and implementing change; beside, they also should be able to anticipate change, and help managers and employees adapt to change through education and training; also, they should promote effectively to employees the need for change.

VI.   Restructuring and Reengineering

(I) Restructuring

Restructuring is also known as reducing the size of company, moderating the size of the company or decreasing hierarchical levels. It reduces the size of a company and aspects of employees, divisions or units, and hierarchical levels aiming at increasing organizational effectiveness and efficiency. Restructuring is mainly for the interests of shareholders rather than that of staff.

When the benchmarking against competitors in the industry shows that various indicators of the company fall behind, the company often has to be restructured. Benchmarking refers to a process in which a company compares its performance indicators with those of the most successful companies in its field. Ratios of benchmarking are widely used as the basis of restructuring, which includes per capita sales, ratio of workers and staff and standards of control range.

One of the main benefits of restructuring is cost reduction. For those highly bureaucratic companies, restructuring will actually prevent the company from being eliminated in global competition. Restructuring has side effects as well. The uncertainty of the future and fear of job cuts will damage the employees' sense of responsibility and enthusiasm for reform and innovation.

(II) Reengineering

Different than restructuring, reengineering pays more attention to the well-being of employees and customer but not shareholders. Reengineering, sometimes known as process management, process re-design or process innovation, refers to the redesign and re-structure of work, jobs and processes in order to reduce costs, improve product quality, raise service levels and speed up production. Reengineering usually will not affect the organizational structure, and means no job cuts or staff reductions. Restructuring is mainly related to the cancellation, reduction and adjustment of divisions or subsidiaries, while reengineering focuses on the change of how the actual work is conducted.

Reengineering is in relation to some major tactical (short-term and specific business functional) decision-making, while restructuring should be seen as a strategic (long-term and affecting all company functions) decision-making.

VII.   Making Pay-for-performance plans

Today, most companies have some form of performance awards for staff and all management personnel except for top leaders.

In the company, HR managers control the wage, which would prevent primary managers from using allowance as a strategic management tool. Flexibility in compensation systems is necessary when using short-term wage adjustment to inspire people to work for long-term objectives. Then how can one make a reward system more closely linked with performance of the strategy implementation? How to make the decision-making on pay raises, promotion and performance bonuses and support the achievement of a long-term strategic business objectives? There is no universal answer to these kinds of questions. Dual bonus systems concerning both annual objectives and long-term objectives are becoming increasingly common. Annul award ratio of managers based on short-term and long-term performances should vary according to different organization levels. Take aCEO as an example, 75% of his or her annul award should be based on short-term performance and 25% based on long-term performance. A very important point is that bonuses cannot be granted based on short-term performance alone, because this practice will make people ignore the company's long-term objectives.

In addition to a dual bonus system, there are a variety of other strategic incentives to encourage employees to work hard to promote the successful strategy implementation. These incentives include higher wages, stock options to employees, subsidies beyond wages, job promotion, recognition, performance recognition, criticism, pressure, increasing job autonomy and honors. In a particular company, there are almost limitless ways to impel individual employees, divisions and segments to actively support strategy implementation.

VIII.   Managing the Natural Environment

All companies bear the responsibility of protecting the ecological environment, which requires managers to be able to establish a business strategy capable of natural resources protection and pollution control. Natural environment issues include disappearance of the ozone layer, global warming, disappearance of tropical rain forests, destruction of habitats, protection of endangered species, development of biodegradable products and packaging, waste extraction, energy use, alternative fuels, environmental protection cost and waste recycling.

The impact of environmental disasters on the society is imposing. Those companies who cannot understand the importance and challenges of environmental issues will have to bear serious consequences. Environmental protection is no longer occasional or less important functions in the company's operations. Activities like product design, manufacturing, transportation, use and final disposal not merely reflect environmental factors, but also are driven by them. Companies who are good at management of environment affairs will benefit from the constructive relationship of users, government, environmental agencies, dealers and other market participants, which will greatly improve the company's business prospects.

Companies should protect the environment from an environmental perspective to formulate and implement their business strategies. Environmental strategies include the development or access to green business, cancellation or adjustment of operations that damage the environment, production costs reduction through reducing waste and energy consumption, and implementation of differentiation strategy depending on green features of products. In addition to the establishment of environmental protection strategies, companies should also do the following tasks: appoint a director in the board who is responsible for environmental protection, to conduct environmental analysis regularly, to reward achievements of environmental protection, to participate in environmental protection activities, to represent emphasis on environmental protection in statements on the company's mission, to establish operational objectives for environmental protection, to gain environmental protection skills, as well as to train employees and managers to protect the environment.

IX.   Addressing all business problems in implementation

The successful strategy implementation needs cooperation of managers within various functional divisions and segments of the company. They should work together to pay attention to functional management and to solve their business problems so as to achieve the strategic objectives. These problems include:

(1) Production problems

(2) Human resources

(3) Marketing problems

(4) Financial accounting issues

(5) Research and development issues

(6) Computer information system problems

In companies' strategy implementation process, the above six questions must be taken seriously and realistically because they will largely determine the success or failure of companies.

Case Study

Beijing International Bidding Co., Ltd.

Established in 1985, Beijing International Bidding Co., Ltd. is originally called Beijing Electric Equipment Bidding Company. It is the oldest Bidding Company in New China, and Comrade Ren Fuguang is its first general manager. Since 1999, Chan Naiming has been chairman and general manager. As the excellent representative of bidding companies, the path of birth, growth and development of Beijing International Bidding Co., Ltd. is a microcosm of the growth and development of Chinese bidding business.

Born at time of reforming and opening up

Bidding is a borrowed idea in our country. As an important means of public procurement, bidding has 200 years of history in foreign countries, while only 20 years in China from its start in 1980s. Bidding institutions is an important part of the intermediary, and it is begun and accompanied by the pace of reforming and opening up.

Before 1985, China has adopted a highly centralized planned economic

358

management system, which means that all the major investments and investment groups are directly determined by the government, so there is no bidding company in the country at that time. The highly centralized planned economic management system, in particular the major state and local government investment management system, makes decision-making power of significant investment of all levels of government and that power is concentrated into the hands of a few government officials. This management system not only excludes competition in the market, but lacks effective oversight mechanisms, resulting in a lot of corruption of trading power for money and major losses for the country.

After 1985, China begins economic reform, transferring from a planned economy to market economy. Comrade Zhu Rongji, leader of the State Economic Commission at that time, with knowledge of the World Bank and the Asian Development Bank, adopts a bidding system in the national investment management structure, and establishes the first bidding company in the country - Beijing International Bidding Co., Ltd., in 1985 to provide intermediary services in bidding processes. Then, another two bidding companies are set up in Shanghai and Guangzhou. Subsequently, the subsidiary bidding companies are established by various divisions and regions. According to incomplete statistics, there are about 6 000 bidding companies in the country.

Traditional mechanisms of institution

On March 14, 1985, Beijing Municipal Economic Commission issues [1985] Beijing No. 147 economic reform document deciding to set up a Beijing bidding company. On September 14 that year, [1985] No. 586 document is issued by the State Economic Council, approving the establishment of Beijing Electric Equipment Bidding Company.

On January 21, 1988, [1988] No. 3 secretariat document is issued by Beijing Municipal Government Office approving that Beijing Electric Equipment Bidding Company is Beijing municipal institution. On February 1 that year, [1988] No. 011 document of Beijing Code Office approves Beijing Electric Equipment Bidding Company as Beijing municipal institution.

Beijing Electric Equipment Bidding Company at that time only runs bidding business of import and export equipment. It is an actual institution so its operating mechanism is the traditional mechanism of state institutions, with neither strong pressure, nor a strong driving force. In addition, there is a serious egalitarianism with its relatively rigid employment system and similar income distribution.

At the early stages of the company, it has made some achievements due to the role of the national plan, combined with few bidding companies. But after 1994, along with the in-depth development of the country's economic system reform and the increase of bidding companies, the authority pushes companies into the market by requiring them to decouple their operations from institutions. This change had a tremendous impact on traditional old-fashioned concepts of cadres and workers of the company and the institutional operating mechanism of the company. As a result, the company's operating and management enter a period of difficult reforms and exploration.

Reforming the mechanism

In October 1999, the state requires that bidding institutions applying for eligibility must be restructured into companies. So according to the document, the company is restructured into joint-stock company. In this situation, comrade Chan Naiming is appointed chairman and general manager of the company.

Now Chan Naiming is under a lot of pressure. According to the actual operation, he does in-depth research, holds meetings at various levels and analyzes situations for workers, encouraging them to abandon the institutional complex, and establish confidence in the reform. With his high sense of responsibility, professionalism, extraordinary courage and perseverance, as well as his management experience accumulated over the years, he tailors a restructuring scheme after detailed research and careful consideration, which is to establish the Beijing International Bidding Co., Ltd.

Chan Naiming is aware of the enormity, complexity and risk of company restructuring. He has said that "Reform means Innovation and pain. Pain, in a sense, is struggle. There will be hope of success as long as there is struggle. Indecisive and timid people will never become reformers. Reform means breakthrough. "No breakthrough of pupae, there will be any colorful butterflies. The same with green mountains without breakthrough of bamboo shoots."

He often works all-night for sake of the operation and company restructuring. On one hand he analyses the complicated situation of the company, on the other hand he studies reform policies, trends and lessons learned from the industry. He first proposes the general reform principle of "to be responsible for history, for government, for the company for the staff and for investors" and insists its implementation. A restructuring scheme is soon approved by the supervisor units.

Beijing Electric Equipment Bidding Company is renamed to Beijing International Bidding Co., Ltd., with the aim to reform company systems, change its operational mechanism, expand its business scope and increase economic efficiency. In 2000, the Beijing International Bidding Co., Ltd. is set up successfully. Since then, the company changes from an affiliated institution into an agency with independent legal personality. It is self-reliant in bidding business and related professional technical advice. Its business also extends from international and domestic equipment bidding to project bidding, and government procurement bidding.

Reform of the mechanism develops a powerful driving force for the Beijing International Bidding Co., Ltd., and lays a solid foundation for the company's growth, and brings out a vigorous vitality. Thereafter, the company develops in a fast and efficient way, and achieves success.

The first brand of Chinese bidding industry

Beijing International Bidding Co., Ltd. is the first bidding company. In the past 20 years, the company has made outstanding achievements in bidding businesses like electrical and mechanical equipment, construction, government procurement at home and abroad. It has accumulated rich experiences and established a brand advantage and the leader position within the industry, worthy of the award "The first brand of Chinese bidding industry."

Since its inception, Beijing International Bidding Co., Ltd. sticks to the principle of high performance, and always puts improvement first and management system, service levels, and quality of employees very high. Its employees are the best in the areas of technology and research. Those technical, economic, foreign trade and legal expertise form professional team with business skills and experiences, of which nearly 70% of them have senior titles. With over 20 years of experience, they are able to complete all kinds of high quality project bidding and related consulting services. They have become the backbone of development of the company and ensure the steady development of the company.

To ensure a fair, scientific and high-quality bidding, Beijing International Bidding Co., Ltd. has also established a committee of experts on evaluating the process. It consists of the experts of central research institutes in Beijing, universities, key companies and authorities. The committee covers almost all industries and fields, and has become the solid backbone of business development.

In the bidding business, the company resolutely implements the provisions in *"Bidding Law of the People's Republic of China,"* always adheres to the principle of "open, fair, just and good faith," and considers customer satisfaction as the sole criterion for testing the quality of work. Whether it is an international bidding, or domestic bidding, the company always uses standard text in accordance with national regulations and international practice and operates seriously. It fully safeguards the legitimate interests of both parties in the bidding processes by adhering to the principles of fair competition and offering low-priced equipment of high quality to users. Special attention is paid to the selection of bidders, who must have a good reputation, first-rate service, prompt delivery and no poor record. It cannot only ensure the interests of bidding companies, but also clean up the bidding market. At the same time, it creates a fair competitive environment to ensure the legitimate interests of bidders with technological advantage, manufacturing strength and a good reputation.

In 20 years, the company has completed commissioned bidding of more than 20 divisions like the Ministry of Transport, Ministry of Railways and companies. The bidding covers international and domestic bidding of all kinds of mechanical and electrical equipment, construction, architectural design, government procurement, and so on. Bidding capital is made up of not only state funds and company's self-financing, but also loans of the international financial organizations and foreign government.

With its strength increasing, the company's business scope gradually changes from single equipment bidding to multiple biddings like project survey, design, construction, supervision and other areas. At the same time, the company provides import and export business agent services for domestic and foreign companies winning bids. It is particularly worth mentioning that after entering the field of project design bidding, the company wins eligibility for bidding against several bidding companies. It

362

has successfully operated the bidding of planning and design technical scheme of 135 hectares Beijing Olympic Park which has attracted worldwide attention and 500,000 m^2 Wu Ke Song Culture Sports Center. It also shows the world the strength of the company by doing well in bidding of 60,000 m^2 Beijing TV building design and 500,000 m^2 CCTV construction design. The company has achieved good economic and social efficiency, and has become a veritable "first brand of Chinese bidding industry."

"Three first class" concept

It is the business philosophy Chan Naiming has always advocated and the business objective he has preached for many years; to pursue "first-class service, first-class level, and first-class performance." In order to implement the "three first-class idea," Beijing International Bidding Co., Ltd always adheres to the "three best" principles in the bidding. That is "first-class design, first-class expert judges and first-class design results." The aim is to attract leading design companies and teams to be involved in the planning and architectural design of the bidding, to organize leading international expert judges to review, and to ultimately produce first-class design results approved by the construction unit, industry authorities and social aspects.

Work of first-class design companies and first-class design teams need the expertise of first-class planning and building design experts. For that reason, the company continues to augment the list of libraries and design units, and gradually establish and improve the list of planning and construction expert judges. Currently it has maintained cooperation with more than 200 foreign design units. As the bidding agency, Beijing International Bidding Co., Ltd. participates in the bidding of the overall planning and design of 135 hectares Beijing Olympic Park and 500,000 m^2 Wu Ke Song Culture Sports Center throughout the entire activity. Global advertising brings registrations to a total of 177 foreign design units. Proposals come from the United States, Australia, and Germany, France and other countries and regions.

In the assessment of these proposals, the company invites 13 international experts including Mr. Chris Johnson, chairman of Olympic Urban Design Review Committee, Mr. Arata Isozaki, Japanese modernist architect, and Mr. Wu Liangyong, academician of the Chinese Academy of Sciences and Chinese Academy of Engineering and Beijing municipal government advisory expert. Besides, Mr. Liu Thai Ker, director of Singapore National Arts Council is invited as chairman of the committee in this review.

Drawing support from unique and sharp visions and rich experiences of these experts, the company finally selects the overall planning and design scheme of the Olympic Park for Beijing 2008 Olympic Games among hundred schemes. Also, the scheme is embodied with Chinese characteristics. Similarly, the following designs are all with characteristics of the time: new unique "bench" shape design of the 500,000 m^2 Chinese TV station sites, conservative architectural design of 60,000 m2 Beijing TV Center, the overall recreation planning and design of Chaoyang Park, creative architectural design of second phase construction of Beijing Library Building and design of Beijing Bioengineering and Pharmaceutical Industry Base.

First-class experts in planning and architectural design help in choosing first-class designs for building units, and in providing practical and far-sighted revisions of designs deepening. Thus it can make a "first-class quality project" and reflect the "three-class" service commitment of the company.

Pioneer of electronic bidding

Electronic Bidding is an innovation bidding model that the bidding sector implements in the bidding procurement of goods, services, and engineering by use of electronic (network) technology and information technology. This model is a new thing that emerged in the process of bidding standardization, and is also a method that has spread rapidly in bidding procurement management and operating procedures. It indicates the future direction of the bidding process and has three advantages: first, it can improve the efficiency of bidding; second, it can increase transparency and reduce

corruption in bidding; third, it can promote the bidding system and management system to be scientific, electronic and informational.

In 2000, the e-bidding model is new in the bidding industry. Beijing International Bidding Co., Ltd. has acted as a pioneer in the industry in this innovation. In 2000, the government procurement in Beijing has just begun. In September that year, as a model for government procurement projects in Beijing, Beijing International Bidding Co., Ltd. is entrusted by the Beijing Municipal Health Bureau to organize bidding of medical equipment procurement of more than 30 capital medical organizations, including Anding Hospital, Anzhen Hospital, Beijing Children's Hospital, Beijing Maternity Hospital, Chaoyang Hospital in two financial years. In 2001, the procurement of equipment includes 109 categories, 1,698 sets, involving an amount of 41.5534 million Yuan. In 2002, the procurement of equipment includes 170 categories, 3,534 sets, involving an amount of 37.6897 million Yuan. The large amount, variety, complexity and intensity of procurement are all unprecedented. After being entrusted, the company divides bidding documents into 13 categories 65 packages through analysis of the bidding devices. There is expected to be at least 100 bidders and at least 180 copies of bidding documents. If adopting the traditional way, the opening alone will take as much as 9 hours, calculated with 3 minutes for each bidding copy reading. In that case, companies could only choose one or more bidding opening. But to open and reopen the bidding process over and over will permit hospitals to participate in but waste their time, and will affect the normal operations of the hospitals. To safeguard the interests of both parties in the bidding, the company decides to open the bidding once, which will pose serious challenges to the company.

According to a careful analysis of the development of Internet and computer trends, Beijing International Bidding Co., Ltd. is aware of the possibility to invite opening bidding on the computer. So it boldly uses a computer-aided system. First, it opens bidding with assistance of the computer, and only spends 4 hours on the whole process from acceptance of the bidding to the opening of the bidding and one week to evaluate. Compared with the traditional opening, it saves time, improves efficiency and also reduces costs. On the basis of this success in 2000, it begins a new effort. That is the use of computer-aided evaluation. In the bidding process, it developed a computer evaluation system, and applies it in the bidding in 2001. It takes a week or so to evaluate 65 subcontracted projects in the traditional way; while it only takes less than four days to complete using computer-aided evaluation. It cuts the time in half as compared to the electronic opening in 2000. The procurement of medical equipment not only lays a solid technical foundation for the implementation of e-bidding of Beijing International Bidding Co., Ltd., but also opens the way to carry out e-bidding in the industry.

Pursuit of Excellent Management

Under the leadership of Chan Naiming, Beijing International Bidding Co., Ltd. has done much, including company system reform, management mechanism change, making "The first brand of Chinese bidding industry," the implementation of the "three best" philosophy, the persistence of "three best" principle, technological innovation, and pioneering the electronic bidding. Simultaneously, it attaches importance to company management by pursuing excellent and efficient management.

Over the years, Chan Naiming innovates and improves the internal management constantly. He develops a set of bidding specifications, approaches of objectives, responsibility systems, employee manuals, and systems about administration, finance, management, project development, operations and management. In 2003, the company also gains the ISO9000 quality management system certification.

In recent years, Beijing International Bidding Co., Ltd focuses mainly on three points of innovation in the business management of intermediary companies:

First is the full implementation of the division economic contract responsibility system guiding by "Strategic Planning." In 2007, the company invites Zhang Xiuyu, Chinese consulting guru, founder of Success in China, chairman and general manager of Beijing Key to Success Consulting Limited Liability Company, to develop the "Overall Strategic Plan of Beijing International Bidding Co., Ltd. (2008-2010)." This is the company's first strategic plan. The plan makes it clear the company's strategic positioning and objectives at the first time and points out the company's development opportunities and potential risks based on a comprehensive, in-depth analysis of the company's strategic environment. It also determines the company's strategic thinking, strategy and strategic objectives of the company according to a comprehensive, in-depth analysis of strengths and weaknesses of the company and its competitors. In the plan, strategic priorities are identified, strategic phases are divided, implementation approaches are planned, and strategic measures are developed. The company adopts the division economic contract responsibility system after identifying its development planning. In accordance with the company's development objectives, divisions establish their own objectives, make sector implementation plans, and implement contract objectives. Contract responsibility systems with strategic planning objectives are more conducive to the sustainable development of the company.

Second is the implementation of modern service innovation based on updating service concept and improving the technological content, especially the innovation of network bidding. The company develops an effective computer management system which fits the bidding features.

Besides, LAN running helps to build a paperless office. Apart from that, the company also has a professional procurement bidding web portal and auction platform for the implementation, which laid a solid material and technical basis for electronic bidding.

Third is the implementation of the scientific, standardized and simplified management. Company hires well-known experts to do consultation and diagnosis for it and gets practical and feasible reform and management schemes based on its actual situation. Apart from the "Overall Strategic Planning," the company also develops "Modern Scientific Management Practices of Beijing International Bidding Co., Ltd." (including "Values of Beijing International Bidding Co., Ltd."), "Performance Appraisal Scheme of Beijing International Bidding Co., Ltd. " and "Wage Reform Scheme of Beijing International Bidding Co., Ltd.." These schemes are not only comprehensive and systematic summaries of the company's successful experiences of in-depth reform and scientific management in the past two decades, but also the distillation and development of that. In particular, it is the first to take the values of the company as an important part of performance assessment among bidding companies in the country. What's more, the company not only attaches importance to the development of strategic planning, reform and management schemes, but also perseveres and persists in assessment, rewards and punishments. These plans and schemes are not only scientific, innovative and effective, but also practical, simple and easy to operate, which are very consistent with the needs of the company.

Continuous significant achievements

No pain, no gain. For more than twenty years, Beijing International Bidding Co., Ltd. has completed more than 3000 biddings of various types accumulatively, of which commissioned amount of international bidding is estimated at more than 4 000 million U.S. dollars, and that of domestic bidding is more than 10 billion Yuan. It saves foreign exchange over 500 million U.S. Dollars for the country, with integrated festival information rate of 13.63%.

In the past five years, the company develops rapidly: the amount of bidding is up to 1 330 (235 international bidding and 1,095 domestic Bidding) with total commissioned number of 22.562 billion Yuan; the amount of winning bidding is 19.322 billion Yuan; international bidding 235, with total commissioned number of $ 1.84 billion, bidding amount of $1.54 billion, saving exchange $ 30 million, and saving rate of 16%; project bidding 523, with total commissioned number of 6.731 billion Yuan, bidding amount of 6.028 billion Yuan, saving capital 703 million Yuan, and saving rate of 10%; government procurement projects 441, with total commissioned number of 2.064 billion Yuan, bidding amount of 1.942 billion Yuan, and saving rate of 6%.

Along with the remarkable achievements, its revenue also increases from 9 million in 1999 to 31.40 million in 2008, an increase of 348%, and an average annual growth rate of 34.8%. Correspondingly, it also achieves a larger increase in taxes, wages, and bonuses.

In the past twenty years, the Beijing International Bidding Co., Ltd. has won many honors with its own strength and honest service. It is awarded the title of "National Outstanding Bidding Unit" by the former State Economic and Trade Commission, and the title of "Advanced Unit in International Bidding in 2001" by the former State Ministry of Foreign Trade. Besides, it has been granted successively the title of "International Bidding Unit with A Grade Qualification" by the Ministry of Commerce, the title of "Project Bidding Agency with A Grade Qualification" by the Ministry of Housing and Urban-Rural Development, the title of "Government Procurement Agency with A Grade Qualification" by the Ministry of Finance, and the title of "Central Government Investment Bidding Agency with A Grade Qualification" and "Engineering Consulting Unit with C Qualification" by the National Development and Reform

Commission. Chen Naiming, its chairman and general manager, also is awarded the "Award for Outstanding People of the eighth China's reform."

In the past two decades, the Beijing International Bidding Co., Ltd. strives to be better front even after receiving those outstanding achievements and honors. At present, the company continues to forge ahead under the leadership of Chan Naiming, the chairman and general manager, and in accordance with the "Overall Strategic Planning of Beijing International Bidding Co., Ltd." and related requirements of reform and management programs. It continues to innovate in order to help be "the first brand of Chinese bidding industry" to be better, stronger, bigger, and longer.

Source: Articles and reports published in "Economic Daily," "Economic Information Daily," "China Information News," "People's Political Consultative Conference News," "Hong Kong's Wen Wei Paper," "Xinhua

Daily Telegraph," "Outlook News Weekly" and information provided by Beijing International Bidding Co., Ltd.

Review

Peter Drucker stressed that even the best plans are only plans, or good intentions. Without responsibility and implementation, there are only promises and hopes but no plans. (4) Canada's strategy experts Henry Mintzberg has also said that "Most of the time, strategists should not be formulating strategy at all; they should be getting on with implementing strategies they already have." (5)

Vast majority of Chinese companies, especially SMEs, make no strategic planning. Among those few who have strategic planning, rarely can they ensure a real an effective strategy implementation. The most valuable point of Beijing International Bidding Co., Ltd. is that it not only develops a strategic plan, but also firmly implements that plan in order to achieve its objectives. The main learning objectives are:

① The full implementation of the division economic contract responsibility system guided by "Strategic Planning." The company will distribute the strategic objectives to divisions and individuals, to adhere to the quarterly assessment, extol and reprimand;

② The establish and shape of aims and values of the company, which can unify thoughts and behaviors of the staff;

③ The development of modern scientific management practices, which makes it possible to guide employees' behaviors with scientific, simple, and practical management practices;

④ The development of performance appraisal programs and the implementation which establishes and strengthens the company's restraint mechanism, truly identifies advantages and disadvantages, and sets the basis for commending and penalizing;

⑤ The development of wage reform scheme and implementation rules. It establishes and strengthens incentives for the company, effectively implement the principle "more work more gain, less work less gain and no work no gain," and creates the spontaneous thriving conditions.

Questions

1. What are the differences between strategy implementation and strategy formulation? Why is the former more important than the latter?
2. What are the main issues of strategy implementation?
3. What elements does company functional strategy include?
4. What management issues should be dealt with in strategy implementation? Why?
5. Try to make a strategy implementation plan for your company or unit referring to theories and methods of this chapter.

Notes

(1) 〔U.S.〕 Fred. R. David, *Strategic Management*, Li Kening trans., 1st edition, Economic Science Press, June 1998, p.276.

(2) 〔U.S.〕 Fred. R. David, *Strategic Management*, Li Kening trans., 1st edition, Economic Science Press, June 1998, p.276.

(3) 〔U.S.〕〔U.S.〕 Larry Bossidy & Ram Charan, *Execution: The Discipline of Getting Things Done, Introduction*, 1st edition, Machinery Industry Press, January 2003, p.1.

(4) 〔U.S.〕 Fred. R. David, *Strategic Management*, Li Kening trans., 1st edition, Economic Science Press, June 1998, p.276.

(5) 〔U.S.〕 Fred. R. David, *Strategic Management*, Li Kening trans., 1st edition, Economic Science Press, June 1998, p.276.

BIBLIOGRAPHY

〔U.S.〕 Peter Drucker, *Management: Tasks, Responsibilities, Practice*, 1st edition, China Social Sciences Press, June 1987.

〔U.S.〕 Arthur Thompson, Stickrod, *Strategic Management: Concepts and Cases*, 10th ed, Duan Shenghua, Wang Zhihui trans., Xu Erming revision, Peking University Press, 2004.

〔U.S.〕 Fred. R. David, *Strategic Management*, Li Kening trans., 1st edition, Economic Science Press, June 1998.

〔U.S.〕〔U.S.〕 Larry Bossidy & Ram Charan, *Execution: The Discipline of Getting Things Done, Introduction*, 1st edition, Machinery Industry Press, January 2003.

〔CAN.〕 Henry Mintzberg, *Strategy Safari*, 2nd edition, Machinery Industry Press, June 2006.

Editing group of required MBA core courses, *Operating Strategy*, 1st edition, China transnational Radio Press, September 1997.

Editing group of required MBA core courses, *Operating Strategy*, 1st edition revision, China transnational Radio Press, 2000.

Liu Jisheng ed, *Company Operation Strategy*, 1st edition, Tsinghua University Press, April 1995.

Xu Erming ed, *Enterprise Strategic Management*, 1st edition, China Economic Publishing House, May 1998.

Chiang Yuntong ed, *Company Operation Strategy Management*, 1st edition, company Management Press, April 1996.

CHAPTER 12
Enterprise Strategic Evaluation

Abstract

This chapter starts with brilliant expositions of Abraham Lincoln and Dale McConkey, emphasizing the significance of strategy evaluation. Then, it states main contents of strategy evaluation. That is, it analyses the effects, SWOT, prices and costs of the company's current strategy. Subsequently, it determines the strength of the company's competitive position, identifies the strategic issues faced by the company. Finally, it has an appendix of cases and comments of "learn duality before diversity."

Learning Objectives

- To define the importance of strategic assessment.
- To grasp the core issues that strategic assessment should address.
- To master methods for the company strategic effect evaluation.
- To grasp the main contents of the company's SWOT.
- To master the strategic cost analysis and value chain approach.
- To define issues and main signals that indicates strength of the company's competitive position.
- To grasp steps and methods of competitive strengths assessment.
- To clear aspects from which the company's strategic problem can be identified.

Introduction

Abraham Lincoln has said that "If we can know where we are and something about how we got there, we might see where we are trending—and if the outcomes which lie naturally in our course are unacceptable, it is time to make a change." (1) Strategic expert Dale McConkey also has said that "The strategic evaluation must allow managers to modify the plan easily and to reach a consensus on the changes quickly." (2) To assess the implementation of the company's strategy, you have to identify strategic issues that must be addressed. In order to make the company's strategy fit for the company's resources and competitiveness, as well as industry and competitive environment, you have to first conduct in-depth analysis of the situation.

Lesson

To assess the implementation of the company's strategy, you have to identify strategic issues that must be addressed. In order to make the company's strategy fit for the company's resources and competitiveness, as well as industry and competitive environment, you have to first conduct in-depth analysis of the situation.

I.   Effects of the company's current strategy

In the evaluation of company strategic effects, we must first find out what is the current business strategy.

Business strategy is concerned with the actions and the approaches crafted to produce successful performance in one specific line of business. Figure 12-1 is a core content of business strategy. In the case of a single-business company, corporate strategy and business strategy merge into one level. It only makes sense to distinguish them in a multiple-business company.

(I)Identify the main contents of company strategy

First; describe the current competitive strategy in detail.

(1) It is a struggle to become a low-cost leader, or to enable the company to provide diversity with a variety of approaches;

(2) The company's focus is a broad customer base, or a small concentrated market.

Second, consider the company's competitive scope within its industry.

How many fields should the company be engaging in throughout the production - distribution chain in the industry? Where are the company's geographic markets? Besides, what are the size and structure of the company's customers?

Figure 12 - 1 Corporate strategy of single-business company

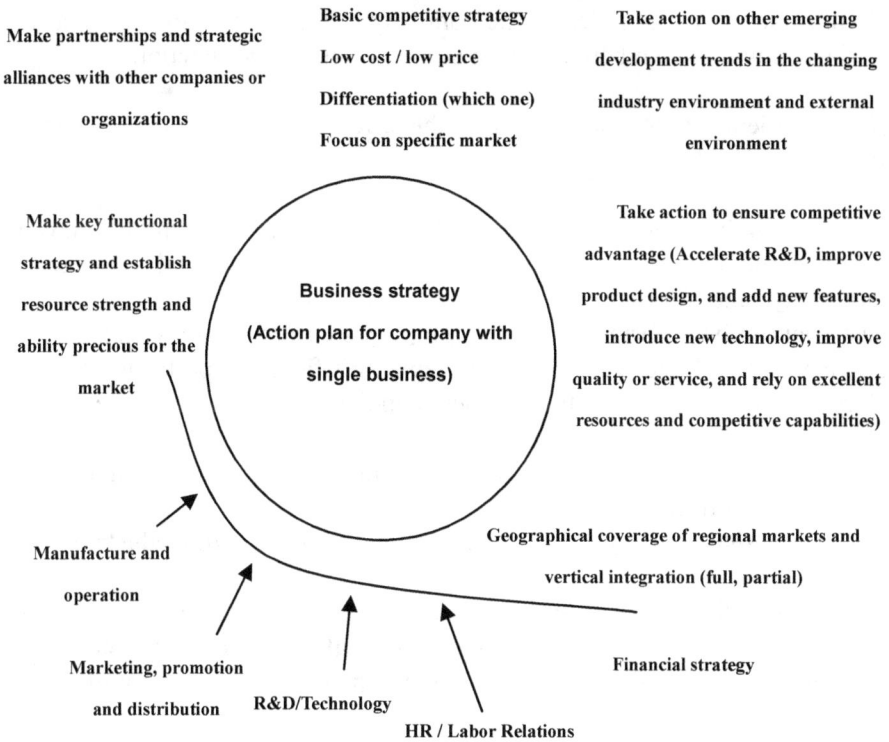

Make partnerships and strategic alliances with other companies or organizations

Basic competitive strategy

Low cost / low price

Differentiation (which one)

Focus on specific market

Take action on other emerging development trends in the changing industry environment and external environment

Make key functional strategy and establish resource strength and ability precious for the market

Business strategy
(Action plan for company with
single business)

Take action to ensure competitive advantage (Accelerate R&D, improve product design, and add new features, introduce new technology, improve quality or service, and rely on excellent resources and competitive capabilities)

Manufacture and operation

Geographical coverage of regional markets and vertical integration (full, partial)

Marketing, promotion and distribution

R&D/Technology

Financial strategy

HR / Labor Relations

Source: (U.S.) Arthur A. Thompson Jr. & A. J. Strickland, *Crafting and executing strategy the quest for competitive advantage concepts and cases,* 2004, Peking University Press, p.43.

Third, state the characteristics of the company's strategy.

The characteristics of corporate strategy are often reflected in strategies of the following functions: production, finance, human resources, information technology, new product innovation and so on.

Finally, fully consider the company's recent strategic actions.

Strategic actions that have been recently taken may also be an important part of corporate strategy, including introducing new-designed styles and models with price cut, increasing advertising inputs, entering new geographic markets, or merging with a rival. The purpose is to steadily improve the competitive position and competitive advantages under ideal circumstances. We can clearly the company's current strategy by exploring the basic logic hidden between each strategic action and function.

(II) Experience indicators to assess the effects of the company's current strategy

Although it has certain advantages from a qualitative point of view to evaluate the company's strategy, such as integrity, internal consistency, rationality, and appropriate, so does it from a quantitative approach. The best quantitative information of the company's current strategy can often be obtained through studying resent strategic and financial performance data. Here we introduce two useful experience indicators.

1. Is the company completing its planned strategic and financial objectives?
2. Is the company's performance above average in the industry?

If the company has been unable to complete the established performance objectives, and is far worse off than its rivals, then it shows either the establishment or implementation of the company's strategy is not effective, or both.

(III) Specific indicators to assess the effects of the company's current strategy

Sometimes, the company's objective is not clear enough, especially for people outside the company. Because of that, it is difficult to measure practical performance of the company. However, if we carefully study the following areas, we are often able to make a real evaluation of the company's strategy:

1. Is the company's market share position in the industry increasing, decreasing, or remaining stable?
2. Are the company's profits rising or falling? How big is the gap with its rivals?
3. Trends of the company's net profit margin, return on investment, economic value-added and comparison of these changes in the profitability with rivals within the industry.

4. Are the company's overall financial strength and credit ratings rising or falling?
5. What are the trends of the company's stock price? Does the company's strategy make it possible for the stock price to the rise?
6. Is the company's sales growth rate faster or slower compared with that of the overall market?
7. How are the company's image and reputation with customers?
8. Is the company seen as a leader for sake of some important customer factors such as technology, product innovation, product quality, customer services, and so on?

The stronger a company's current overall performance, the less likely the need for radical changes in strategy. The weaker a company's financial performance and market standing, the more its current strategy must be questioned. Similarly, a company's weak business performance always shows either the establishment and/or implementation of the company's strategy is not effective. Good performance and market position illustrate the well-established or implemented strategy.

II.   Resources SWOT of the company

SWOT analysis is an appraisal of a company's resource strengths and weaknesses as well as a listing of external opportunities and threats. SWOT analysis requires the company's strategy to size up its resource strengths and competitive deficiencies, its market opportunities, and the external threats to its future well-being. Thus, a clear understanding of the company's SWOT is important.

(I) Identifying the company's strengths and resources competencies

A company's resource strengths represent its competitive assets and determine its competitive power in the marketplace. Followings are several forms:

1. An important skill or expertise.
2. Valuable tangible assets.
3. Valuable human resources.
4. Valuable organizational assets.
5. Valuable intangible assets.
6. Competitiveness.
7. Achievements or attributes that can make the company

377

obtain a competitive advantage on the market.

8. Alliances or joint ventures with other companies.

A company that is well equipped with powerful resource and strengths has considerable competitive control to succeed.

(II) Identifying the company's weaknesses and resource deficiencies

A resource weakness or competitive liability is something a company lacks or does poorly or a condition that puts it at a disadvantage in the marketplace. A company's resource weaknesses can relate to:

1. Lack of competitive skills and expertise;
2. Deficiencies in competitively important tangible, human resources, organizational, or intangible assets;
3. Missing or competitively inferior capabilities in key areas.

A company's resource strengths represent competitive assets; its resource weaknesses represent competitive liabilities. Only the former can create competitive values.

For a company, its resources - whether they are specific capabilities, tangible assets, human resources, organizational, or intangible, achievement, or a competitive edge - they must get through the following four competitive value tests if it is to become a sustainable competitive advantage.

1. Is the resource easily replicated? The greater cost and difficulty of imitation, the greater potential competitive values it embodies.
2. How long can this resource be maintained? The longer duration of the resource, the greater value it embodies.
3. Is this resource really superior to the competition in value?
4. Can this resource be offset by other resources or capabilities of rivals?

(III) Confirm opportunities faced by the company

Market opportunity is a big factor in shaping a company's strategy. Indeed, managers can't properly tailor strategy to the company's situation without first identifying its market opportunities and appraising the growth and profit potential each one holds.

378

In evaluating the attractiveness of a company's market opportunities, managers have to guard against viewing every industry opportunity as a suitable opportunity. Not every company is equipped with the resources to successfully pursue each opportunity that exists in its industry. Some companies are more capable of going after particular opportunities than others. The market opportunities most relevant to a company are those that match up well with the company's financial and organizational resources and capabilities, offer the best growth and profitability, and present the most potential for competitive advantage.

(IV) Identifying threats to a company's future profitability

Often, certain factors in a company's external environment pose threats to its profitability and competitive well-being. Threats can stem from the emergence of cheaper or better technologies, rivals' introduction of new or improved products, the entry of lower-cost foreign rivals into a company's market stronghold, vulnerability to a rise in interest rates, the potential of a hostile takeover, unfavorable demographic shifts, and so on. External threats may pose no more than a moderate degree of adversity or they may be so imposing as to make a company's situation and outlook quite tenuous. It is management's job to identify the threats to the company's future prospects and to evaluate what strategic actions can be taken to neutralize or lessen their impact.

A successful strategist aims to seize the best opportunities for the company's growth, and to protect against external threats that endanger the company's competitive position and future performance.

It requires the following in order to match the company's strategy with its situation. First, pursue market opportunities that suit for the company's resources; second, establish relevant resources capabilities to protect against external threats that threaten the company's business.

Simply making lists of a company's strengths, weaknesses, opportunities, and threats is not enough; the payoff from SWOT analysis comes from the following conclusions about a company's situation and the implications for strategy improvement.

1. How should the company best take advantage of its resources in its current internal and external environment?

2. How to explore future resources in the company's future internal and external environment?

SWOT analysis comes to its end only after getting the answers to the following questions: what kinds of adjustments to resources should be taken in order to react better to newly emerging industry and competitive environment? Is there a gap of resources? In which aspects shall the company strengthen its resources? What are the actions to explore the company's future resources? Which opportunities shall have the highest priority in the allocation of the company's resources?

III. Costs and Prices of the company

(I) Costs is the most important signal of the company's competitiveness

It is necessary to evaluate the competitiveness of costs of the company compared with its direct rivals.

Company managers are often stunned when a rival cuts its prices to "unbelievably low" levels or when a new market entrant comes on strong with a very low price. The rival may not, however, be buying its way into the market with super-low prices that are below its costs—it may simply have substantially lower costs. One of the most telling signs of whether a company's business position is strong or precarious is whether its prices and costs are competitive with industry rivals. Price and quality comparisons are especially critical in industries where price competition is typically the ruling market force. But even in industries where products are differentiated, rival companies have to keep their costs in line with rivals offering a similar mix of differentiating features.

(II) General sources of cost differences

Rivals in the industry often bear different costs when they provide products to their end-users. Even a tiny small difference in costs may have an important significance. Cost differences may appear due to the following factors:

1. Price paid to purchase materials; spare parts, energy and other products from suppliers are not the same.
2. Basic technologies applied and life spans of plant and equipment are different. As investment in plant and critical equipment is often

carried out at different times, so technical efficiencies of operating facilities are to some extent differ, so as their fixed costs such as depreciation, maintenance, property taxes and insurance. Older equipment is often less efficient. However, if their construction costs are relatively low, or purchase price is cheap, they still may be cost competitive compared with modern equipment.

3. Differences in the efficiency of production plants, learning and experience curve effect, wage rate, productivity and also production cost of all rivals.
4. Differences in marketing costs, sales and promotional costs, advertising costs, storage and distribution costs, as well as management costs.
5. Different transportation costs of incoming and shipping.
6. Different distribution costs of forward channel, such as the cost and structure of distributors, wholesalers and retailers, which is related to the process to distribute products from producers to end-users.
7. Different impacts of changes on inflation, foreign exchange rate, and tax rate. It happens usually for the global industry because rivals often are located in different countries, where their economic conditions and government tax policies are often not the same.

The higher costs a company takes than its most direct rivals, the more vulnerable its competition is. If a company wants to succeed in the competition, then its costs must be in unity with that of its rivals. As long as there are differences between the company and its

most direct rivals, some cost differences are normal. On the other hand, the more a high-cost company's costs than that of its rivals, the more vulnerable its market position is.

(III) Strategic cost analysis and value chain

1. Strategic cost analysis

Strategic cost analysis compares the costs of business activities of the company and its key rivals one by one based on an industrial value chain. It is a comprehensive cost analysis to accurately identify the sources of cost advantage or disadvantage.

The company must watch out the degree of costs differences with its rivals. On the one hand, each company will conduct an internal cost analysis to provide a detailed understanding of their situation and possible changes or trends in cost; on the other hand, strategic cost analysis goes one step further, it examines the costs comparisons with its rivals. The core of strategic cost analysis is the relative cost position of the company and its rivals.

Each business of the company consists of a series of activities, including design, production, marketing; shipping, products and services support, and each of them will bring costs. The costs of all these activities form the company's internal cost structure. Moreover, each cost will affect the overall relative cost position of the company and its rivals. Strategic cost analysis aims to compare costs of activities one by one with its key rival, so as to understand which activities are source generating competitive advantages, and which ones are producing competitive disadvantages. As mentioned, the higher the costs a company takes as compared to its most direct rivals, the more vulnerable its competition is. A company's relative cost position is the function of the relative value of total costs of all activities compared to that of its rivals.

2. Value chain

Value chain is the main analytical tools used in determining whether a company's prices and costs are competitive. It consists of a collection of activities undertaken in the course of designing, producing, and marketing, delivering, and supporting its product or service. A company's value chain is embedded in a larger system of activities that includes the value chains of its suppliers and the value chains of whatever distribution channel allies it utilizes in getting its product or service to end users.

A company's value chain identifies the primary activities that create customer value and related support activities. As shown in Figure 12-2, a company's value chain discovers all of the various activities that a company performs internally. Value chain also includes margins because a structure is needed besides costs to perform value creation activities.

Figure 12-2 A Representative Company Value Chain

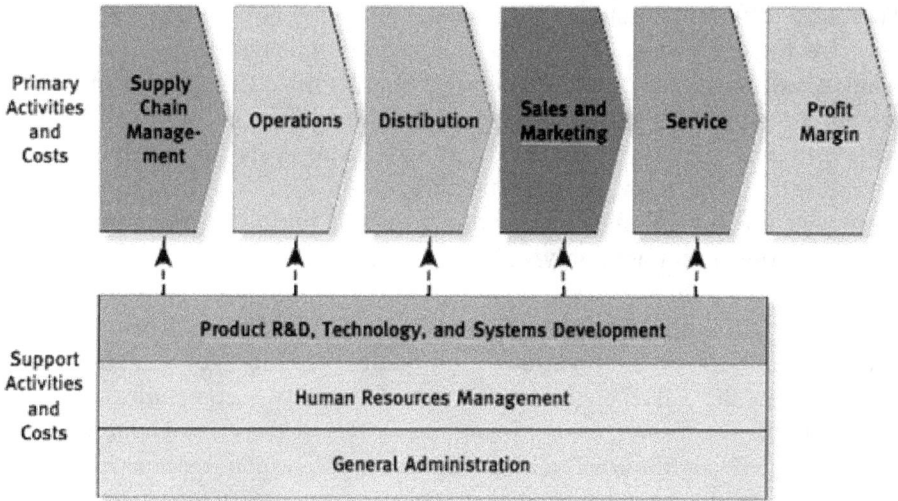

Source: (U.S.) Arthur A. Thompson Jr. & A. J. Strickland, *Crafting and executing strategy the quest for competitive advantage concepts and cases*, Peking University Press, 2004, p.101.

Generally, this component is part of the price the consumer ultimately pays, or the total costs. To create a total value overall the costs is the fundamental goal of the company's business. Breaking the business activities of the company down into processes is significant in strategy and can show each important element of the company's cost structure. Every activity in the value chain has certain costs, which will occupy parts of the company's assets. Allocating the company's operating costs and assets in each activity of the value chain can assess the cost of each activity. In general, there are links among activities. So the way to conduct an activity will impact the cost of another activity. For example, the Japanese VCR manufacturers decide to substantially reduce the number of parts after accurately determining the impact of the continued activity (product design) and subsequent activity (production) in the value chain. It cuts down cost from 1,300 dollars in 1977 to 300 dollars in 1984.

(IV) Reasons for the differences among the value chain of rivals

A company's value chain and the way it performs individual activities are a reflection of its history, its strategy, its approach to implementing its strategy, and the underlying economics of the activities themselves. Therefore, differences among rival value chains are normal and sometimes they are huge. Because of that, it is more complicated to evaluate their relative cost positions. For example, degrees of vertical integration of rivals are not the same, in that case, compared with the value chains of companies with different integration degrees and require corresponding adjustment. Obviously, internal total costs of manufacturers who produce all parts on their own are higher than those who purchase the necessary parts from external suppliers for assembly.

Similarly, if a company's strategy is low cost and low price, while another company aims to produce various high-quality products for a high-priced market, then the value chains and costs of these two companies will be different. For the former, costs of some activities of the value chain may be relatively lower; while for the latter, more costs are spent on activities that can increase added values and special features.

Differences between costs and prices among rivals may also come from activities carried out by its suppliers, or distribution of the product to end-users of its forward channel. Cost structures or profit margins of suppliers and forward channel allies may be too high or too large, so the company's cost competitiveness may be less even if its costs of internal activities are competitive. Therefore, in order to evaluate price and cost competitiveness of a company from the customer's point of view, activities and costs of its suppliers and forward channel allies should be considered in addition to costs of activities within the company. In short, cost competitiveness of a company depends on costs of both sides.

Accurate measurement of the company's competitiveness on the end market requires the company's managers to understand the value chain system distributing products or services to end-users, not merely the value chain of its own. This at least means they should consider the value chains of supplier and forward channel allies, if any, as shown in Figure 12-3. Value chains of suppliers are significant because suppliers carry out certain activities as well as incur costs when they create and offer what the company purchases. Costs and qualities of their production inputs in their value chains affect the company's costs or differentiation capacity.

Figure 12 -3 The Value Chain System

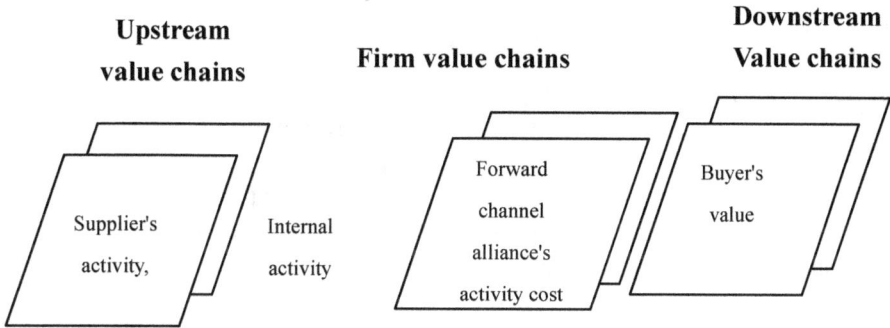

Upstream
value chains

Firm value chains

Downstream
Value chains

Supplier's
activity,

Internal
activity

Forward
channel
alliance's
activity cost

Buyer's
value

Source: Adapted from Michael Porter, *Competitive Advantage*, Huaxia Publishing House, January 1997.

In order to enhance its own competitiveness, the company takes steps to reduce or increase its suppliers' costs or improve its suppliers' effectiveness. That's also the reason why the company should work closely or make an alliance with suppliers.

Value chain of forward channel is important. That is because, costs and profits of suppliers are parts of the price paid by end-users and activities of the forward channel allies will affect satisfaction of end-users. This also indicates that the company should work closely with its forward channel allies, or modify and re-design their value chains to enhance their common competitiveness. For example, some aluminum producers put their production plants near sites of breweries and deliver their products directly to the breweries' bottling lines by top transport equipment. It will reduce costs of both like production arrangements, shipping and inventory. We can get from the example that the company's relative cost position and overall competitiveness is related with value chain system of the entire industry, as well as that of customers.

(V) Strategic options for getting a cost disadvantage

The value chain provides the basic tool for cost analysis. A basic finding of strategic cost strategy of a company's competitiveness depends on to what extent it manages its value chain compared with its rivals. To study the company's value chain and compare it with others can help identify how much competitive strengths and weaknesses it has, and what are the cost factors that lead to this situation. This plays an important role in formulating a strategy to remedy cost disadvantage and create cost advantages.

Strategic options for remedying cost disadvantage have to count on the value chain in order to find the source of cost difference.

Let us return to Figure 12-3. There are three main areas in a company's overall value chain where important differences in the costs of competing companies can occur: the suppliers' part of the industry value chain, a company's own internal activities, and the forward channel portion of the industry chain. If the difference comes from forward (upstream) or backward (downstream) part of the value chain, then the company should take measures beyond its internal operations in order to re-establish cost strength.

    1.   Supplier- related cost disadvantage

If a company's cost disadvantage comes from product costs of the supplier, or upper reaches of the industrial value chain, then the company's managers can take some of the following strategic actions:

    (1) Get more favorable prices from its suppliers through negotiations.
    (2) Reduce costs by cooperating with suppliers.
    (3) Gain control of costs of purchased products through backward integration.
    (4) Try to use lower-cost alternatives.
    (5) Manage links between value chains of suppliers and the company. For example, the company can work closely with its suppliers to get JIT delivery to identify win-win opportunities to reduce costs, including storage and internal logistics costs of the company, as well as storage shipping and production arrangements costs of its suppliers. It avoids the effect of "zero-sum" game, which makes the company earns what its suppliers lose.
    (6) Try to cut costs elsewhere to compensate.

    2.   Cost disadvantage associated with activities performed by forward channel allies

Strategic options to remedy cost disadvantage that comes from the forward part of the value chain system include the followings:

(1) Promote distributors and other forward channel allies to reduce profits.

(2) Work closely with its suppliers to identify win-win opportunities to reduce costs. For example, a chocolate manufacturer learned that by shipping its bulk chocolate in liquid form in tank cars instead of 10-pound molded bars, it could not only save its candy bar manufacturing customers the costs associated with unpacking and melting but also eliminate its own costs of molding bars and packing them.

(3) Turn to more economic distribution strategies, including forward integration.

(4) Try to cut down costs of several early stages of the cost chain to compensate.

3. Internal cost disadvantage

When the company's cost disadvantage stems from performing internal value chain activities, then managers can pursue any of the following nine strategic approaches to restore cost parity:

(1) Simplify management and operations of high-cost activities.

(2) Reengineer business processes and work practices to increase employee productivity, efficiency of key activities, utilization rate of company assets, or to improve management of costly elements.

(3) Try to eliminate some cost-producing activities altogether by revamping the value chain. For example, adoption of different technologies which may help the company directly sell products to end-users, going beyond the value chain of forward channel allies.

(4) Relocate high-cost activities to geographic areas where they can be performed more cheaply.

(5) See if certain internally performed activities can be outsourced from vendors or performed by contractors more cheaply than they can be done in-house.

(6) Invest in productivity enhancing, cost-saving technological improvements, such as automation, robotics, flexible manufacturing techniques, state-of-the-art electronic networking.

(7) Innovate around the tricky cost elements, such as investment increasing in plant and equipment.

(8) Simplify product design to make its production more economical.

(9) Try to make up the internal cost disadvantage by reducing costs in the forward and backward channel portions of the industry value chain.

IV. Strength of the company's competitive position

It is a key step in the analysis of the company's situation to systematically evaluate the strength of its competitive position as compared with its most direct rival.

(I) Problems that should be considered for evaluation.

It is necessary to identify a company's cost competitiveness by using tools like value chain and strategic cost analysis. While that is not enough because it should be measured from a broader perspective. Problems that should be considered include:

1. Does the company's market position improve or deteriorate if the current strategies, which can be adjusted slightly, keep on being implemented?
2. How would the company rank in measurement indicators with industrial critical success factors, such as competitive strengths and resource capabilities as compared with its key rivals?
3. Company lies in a relative favorable or unfavorable position?
4. How affective is the company at defending its market position after knowing the change motivations, competitive pressures and expected actions of rivals?

(II) Main signals of strength and weakness of the company's competitive position

Some indicators of changes in the company's position are listed in Table 12-1. However, the company's managers need to do more than just determine areas where the company's competitiveness is improving or declining. They also have to know their competitive advantage or disadvantage compared with key rivals, in addition, improvement or aggravation of the company's market position and performance.

Table 12—1 Signals of strength and weakness of the company's competitive position

---

Signals of competitive strength

- Important resource strengths, core competencies and distinctive capacities
- Distinctive capabilities of value chain activities with important competitive values
- Strong market share or biggest industrial market share
- Pioneering leader or distinctive strategy
- Increasing customer group and improved customer loyalty
- Market visibility that above average
- Choosing among favorable strategic groups
- Owning an excellent position in attractive market segments
- Products with strong differentiation
- Cost advantage
- Profit margins that above average
- Technology and innovation capacity above the average level
- Innovative and entrepreneurial management team
- Choosing the position where new-emerging market can be used

Signals of competitive disadvantage

- Facing the competitive disadvantage
- Rivals are seizing the company's position
- Revenue growth below the average level
- Lack of financial resources
- Declining reputation among the customers
- Lagging product development and innovation capacity
- Position of its strategic group is doomed to lose
- Weak in field where exists many market opportunities
- High cost
- Too small to be a major factor in the market
- Situation in which the threat cannot be well dealt with
- Poor product quality
- Lack of skills, resources and competitiveness in key areas
- Weaker distribution capabilities than rivals

Source: (U.S.) Arthur A. Thompson Jr. & A. J. Strickland, *Crafting and executing strategy the quest for competitive advantage concepts and cases*, 2004, Peking University Press, p.110.

A company's managers can start to evaluate the company's competitive strength by comparing the company with its rivals within the industry. They need to compare indicators like costs, product quality, customer service, customer satisfaction, financial strength, technical skills, and product cycle time, which means how fast a product goes from being an idea, to being designed and brought to the market, as well as resources and capabilities needed that make it significant for competition to become aware of.

(III) Steps to assess the competitive strength

The most effective way to determine a company's competitive position is to compare the company and its close rivals. That is, to assess every industrial success factors, every important competitive features and potential competitive advantage. There are four main steps:

1. List a number of industrial critical success factors and the most powerful decision variables of competitive advantages or disadvantages. Usually 6-18 variables are enough.
2. Give a score to each strength indicator of the company and its key rivals. Score assignment is preferably from 1 to 10. But if little information is required and data evaluation will bring errors or inaccuracies, then it can be expressed as strong (+), weak (-) and equal (=).
3. Add the total score of each variable, and you will obtain scores of the competitive strength of each rival.
4. Make conclusions about the company's net competitive advantage or disadvantage. At the same time, make more detailed analysis of strength indicators about the strongest or the weakest areas.

A High score of competitive strength indicates the company's strong competitive position and its competitive advantage; and low score means just the opposite.

(IV) Cases of competitive strength assessment

Table 12-2 shows two cases of competitive strength assessment. Unweighted competitive strength assessment is used in the first one. In this case, every indicator of critical success factors and competitive strength is treated equally, which is a questionable assumption. Any company that gets high scores of a given indicator is considered as having an advantage in this indicator. The size of its advantages is reflected in a score difference between it and the other companies.

Table 12-2 Weighted and Unweighted Competitive
Strength Assessment Models

A. Unweighted competitive strength assessment

Assignment: 1 = very weak; 10 = very strong

Critical success factors/ strong indicators	ABC company	Rival 1	Rival 2	Rival 3	Rival 4
Quality / product performance	8	5	10	1	6
Reputation / image	5	7	10	1	6
Manufacturing capacity	2	10	4	5	1
Technical capacity	10	1	7	3	6
Dealer network /distribution capabilities	9	4	10	5	1
Innovative capacity of new products	9	4	10	5	1
Financial resources	5	10	7	3	1
Relative cost position	5	10	3	1	4
Customer service	5	7	10	1	4
Sum of unweighted competitive strength scores	61	58	71	25	32

B. Weighted competitive strength assessment

Assignment: 1 = very weak; 10 = very strong

Critical success factors/ strong indicators	Weight	ABC company	Rival 1	Rival 2	Rival 3	Rival 4
Quality / product performance	0.10	8/0.80	5/0.50	10/1.00	0/.10	6/0/60
Reputation / image	0.10	8/0.80	7/0.70	10/1.00	1/0.10	6/0.60
Manufacturing capacity	0.10	2/0.20	10/1.00	4/0.40	5/0.50	1/0.10
Technical capacity	0.05	10/0.50	1/0.05	7/0.35	3/0.15	8/0.40
Dealer network /distribution capabilities	0.05	9/0.45	4/0.20	10/0.50	5/0.25	1/0.05
Innovative capacity of new products	0.05	9/0.45	4/0.20	10/0.50	5/0.25	11/0.05
Financial resources	0.10	5/0.50	10/1.00	7/0.70	3/0.30	1/0.10
Relative cost position	0.35	5/1.75	10/3.50	3/1.05	1/0.35	4/1.40
Customer service	0.15	5/0.75	7/1/05	10/0.50	1/0.15	4/1.60
Sum of weighted competitive strength scores	100	6.20	8.20	7.00	2.15	4.90

Source: (U.S.) Arthur A. Thompson Jr. & A. J. Strickland, *Crafting and executing strategy the quest for competitive advantage concepts and cases*, 2004, Peking University Press, p.111.

The difference between scores of other companies. A company's total competitive strength score comes from the sum of scores on all indicators. The higher it is, the stronger the company's position is. The larger the differences between the scores of the company and the lowest score of its rival, the greater its competitive advantage is. Total score of ABC company is 61, as seen in the top part of Table 12-3. Its net competitive advantage compared with rival 4, whose score is 32 is greater than that with rival 1, whose score is 58.

Weighted competitive strength assessment method is better than unweighted competitive strength assessment. Because the latter assumes all indicators are equally important with the same inherent flaws, which is obviously not realistic. So the former is better due to differences in the importance of all indicators.

By giving a score on each indicator, and then applying the 1-10 assignment criteria, and multiplying the weight of the assignment, will result in the weighted score. For example, you get a score of 4 on an indicator, and multiply its weight 0.20, then you obtain the weighted score 0.80. In this way, the company with highest scores on a certain indicator has a competitive advantage in terms of that indicator; The size of its advantage is reflected in differences of scores of itself and its rivals. The weight of the indicator shows the importance for getting a competitive advantage. The sum of all weighted scores makes up the total score of the company, the comparison of which can identify companies that lie in the highest and the lowest position, as well as sizes of all evaluated companies' net competitive advantages.

(V) Significance of competitive strength assessment

Competitive strength assessment can finally identify a company's competitive position. These results can show its relative position of the company compared to its rivals by each factor and each ability. Moreover, the total score of competitive strength indicates its net competitive advantage or disadvantage compared with each rival. Therefore, the company with the highest total score has a net competitive advantage over all its rivals.

Competitive strength and competitive advantage can consolidate and improve a company's long-term favorable competitive position.

It means a lot to understand the areas where a company has competitive strength or weakness, especially for the formulation of strategies in order to strengthen its long-term competitive position. Generally, a company should turn its competitive strength into sustainable competitive advantage, and take strategic actions to protect its competitive disadvantage. Meanwhile, scores of competitive strength also show which company gets hurt the most and also uncovers its weakest area. If there are weak companies in some certain fields, then a company with competitive strength can take offensive actions.

V. Strategic problems faced by the company

Above all, the company's managers must "lock" their strategic focus areas and they should be cautious to consider the overall situation faced by the company. If the problems are not determined preciously, then managers cannot make full preparation to formulate or adjust the strategy. That is because a good strategy must be able to solve all strategic issues that need to be addressed.

In order to accurately determine the problems on the company's strategic action agenda, the company's managers should seriously consider the following questions:

1. How well the current strategy defends five competitive forces, especially those who would intensify competition?
2. Whether the current strategy should be adjusted to respond better to important drivers of the industry?
3. Is there a good match of the company's current strategy with the future success factors of the industry?
4. Can the current strategy of the company take advantage of strengths of the company's resources?
5. What should be the priorities of market opportunities faced by the company? Which of them are suitable for the company's resource strengths and capabilities?
6. What measures should be taken to overcome weaknesses in resources and prevent external threats faced by the company?

7. How weak is the company after it suffers from the competitive actions taken by one or more rivals? What kind of measures can be taken to reduce this vulnerability?
8. Does the company have a competitive advantage? Should the company take action to offset the competitive disadvantage?
9. What are strengths and weaknesses of the company's existing strategies?
10. Does it need to take additional measures to consolidate the company's low-cost position, and to take advantage resources, capabilities and competitive position of new opportunities?

Answers to these questions indicate whether the company actually can carry on the current basic strategy through some small adjustments, or must it make a lot of changes.

In summary, if a company's current strategy matches well with the external environment and the company's resources strength and ability, then it needs less change. But if not, then the managers of the company should adjust and control it in time. Even sometimes when that won't work, they shall be decisive for strategic change.

Case Study

"To learn duality before diversity"- Lenovo advances along with understanding and adjustment

On April 20, 2001, Yang Yuanqing takes charge of Lenovo and officially announces the next three-year strategic plan ("new century, new strategy and new journey") on the same day. After three years of implementation, he finds that diversifying is beyond the scope of Lenovo due to its limited resources and capabilities, which influence the development of the core business. Then in February 2004, he makes adjustments in time by announcing the idea to "learn duality before diversity." This case is adapted from speeches of Liu Chuanzhi and Yang Qingyuan. (3)

After the Spring Festival in 2004, every employee of Lenovo has received a letter from President Yang Yuanqing. In this letter, Yang publicly indicates his concern of slow growth for the company and dissatisfaction with inefficient company operations. Some smart employees sense the change of atmosphere. Twenty days later, Yang releases his package of modification programs, including strategy, mechanisms, institutions, and even staff. This is the largest reform movement launched by Yang since he took charge on April 20, 2001. The task of this reform is to change the way in which Lenovo has gone with its diversification efforts.

Yang admits that the issues for the last three years primarily lie in the aggressive steps towards diversification. In 2000, business of Lenovo is relatively simple, mainly producing PC's. At that time, they think diversity is the way to be stronger, besides, investors require growth of the company, so Lenovo decides to be "international, service oriented, and high-tech."

As time passes by, it faces problems capacity shortfalls for diversity management. In addition, new business has been affected, which is because it cannot get enough support due to limited management and financial resources. Worse than that, the core business faces very severe development challenges which limit the increase of business size and profit growth of the company.

Another adjustment is to establish a more sound customer-oriented business model. Lenovo is used to channel distribution modes other than direct marketing. But with careful analysis, it understands what is important is a suitable service model for various types of customers with lower incomes. In fact, its model is very effective for customers like retailers, small and medium sized enterprises, government educational organizations and its channels can be extended to remote areas with high efficiency and low cost. However, there is one aspect that Dell does better, that is, the expansion and servicing of key large customers. For such a class of customers, plans to service them aggressively rather than just passively wait for orders. Therefore, Lenovo has to establish a model that can develop and maintain valuable large customers in the long run.

Strategy should be the premier issue in handling these challenges. Diversification strategy of Lenovo is not incorrect, but just like Yang has pointed out "Diversity is good, while a company cannot have too much on its plate." Besides, the success of a well formulated strategy depends on its implementation. In steps of 1 to 6 to implement the strategy, one should understand how a step can achieve success and then apply the experience to other steps. Then you will be cautious after knowing how to migrate the existing competitiveness to new business. Yang says since he chooses the current business, he will strive to improve competitiveness of it, and that is also the reason he promotes the idea of "learn duality before diversity."

However, he doesn't mean he wants to return back to the simple core PC business. That is only one of the options. Other key services such as mobile communications business should get adequate management and financial resources. The so-called financial resources means Lenovo allows this business to lose money over a period of time. It is impossible to raise a big business without failures.

"Duality" Yang says refers to the mobile communications business. He classifies other business they have run to the third category, such as IT services, network and software. He says "We still provide services; but our focus is to offer a better mechanism for their independent development over a short period of time. It will make management of resources more open. "

He says, "This time we take the initiative to adjust the diversification strategy. First, it does not mean that Lenovo will now be inclined to adopt a more defensive market strategy; on the contrary, it is a sign of precisely a proactive attack. Or it can also be said to be a change or reform in offensive strategy. Currently we focus on our core business in order to compete better with foreign rivals. We need to be more aggressive, like a group of hungry tigers that I have written to you in e-mails. Second, duality means never giving up. That requires that the business depend on their own creativity and entrepreneurial spirit rather than support from the headquarters only."

Now Lenovo turns back to the PC business. Although there are thin profits, it believes better less than nothing. Its business mode is a key point, especially for new customers like branches of multinational companies in China and private companies. China's economic structure is changing. State-owned large enterprises dominate the economy, while now more types of companies participate. Purchase methods of private enterprises and foreign-funded enterprises are very different from previous state-owned enterprises and new services are needed.

For the duality part, Lenovo has invested in the mobile communications business for two years. Yang says, "I began to run the PC business in 1994 and started to make profits in 1998. It takes four to five years to form a relatively good size. But I believe 2 years is long enough for mobile phones."

In the last two years, Lenovo has invested a lot of money and energy on the development and promotion of related products. These products and technologies can probably pay off in three to five years.

China's market has become so big after joining the WTO. Foreign enterprises attach great importance to the new open market and enter the market in droves. They bring with them highly integrated business models and efficient business processes which have been proven in market-oriented countries to the Chinese market. Lenovo faces a new round of competition with them.

Why should Lenovo focus on its core business? It is because it has ignored the past environment where it was most successful. Actually, there is still a long way to go compared with the best companies in the world.

Nowadays, Lenovo has certain strengths in the field of PC business. It is in one of top ten PC makers in the world, ranking 7 to 8. There are only a few companies that make profits. Dell is first, and then comes Lenovo, which has 5% of the net profits. Objectively speaking, there still exists room to refine management and processes for Lenovo compared with the world's best companies like IBM and HP, not to mention Dell. So at this time, Lenovo aims to gain more market share in the Chinese market using innovative ways including the further improvement of business model.

Of course, people at Lenovo are constantly learning and understanding. Understanding does not mean to turn to consulting companies. Though they are needed, decision-making depends mainly on one's own struggle. Only when you realize the problem, can you really take advantage of previous training and learning. Otherwise, they are all done in vain.

Lenovo will restructure and reform within two years. Motivation and the significance of change this time is much larger than before, especially in terms of its strategic management. Therefore, it should be a milestone on the road of Lenovo's diversification.

Yang Yuanqing particularly points out the attention paid by chairman Liu, who is very concerned about them and often makes demands. Besides, his opinion is still very important.

On June 2, 2004, Lenovo Group announces its performance in the 2003/04 fiscal year (April 1, 2003 to March 31, 2004) in Hong Kong. Its overall turnover is 23.18 billion Hong Kong dollars, rising 14.5% over last year and its net profit increase 3.5% of the last year. Yang Yuanqing, president & CEO of Lenovo Group points out that core business in the 03/04 fiscal year continues its healthy development and achieves satisfactory results. The development of new business has a certain impact on the overall performance of the company.

Yang says practice has initially proved the success of adjustment and change starting from February. Reform is compiling with market needs in China and is implemented quickly and resolutely among all systems, departments and areas of Lenovo Group. On the one hand, supportive policies about the company's objectives, assessments, and incentives have been introduced when the organizational restructuring is finished. One the other, every employee on the first line is well aware of his or her own goal and actively participates in change. Yang believes all managers have the determination and confidence to achieve substantive results in a short time. And it will ultimately help the company to develop better, giving investors a better return on investment.

Liu Chuanzhi, board chairman of Lenovo Group confirms the management performance on a news conference in Hong Kong. It is achieved in a more challenging and competitive environment. He says, "As a representative of substantial shareholder, I have confidence in adjustment at this stage. And I believe Lenovo can give full play to its strength, seize the opportunities to grow and achieve long-term and ground-breaking development after adjustment. "

Source: *China Business*, March 24, 2004; Sohu IT Channel, June 2, 2004.

Review

On April 20, 2001, Yang Yuanqing takes in charge of Lenovo and officially announces the next three-year strategic plan ("new century, new strategy and new journey") on the same day. After three years of implementation, he finds that diversity is beyond the tolerance of Lenovo due to limits of resources and capabilities, which influent the development of the core business. Then in February 2004, he makes adjustments in time by coming out the idea to "learn duality before diversity."

In particular, he points out that "Diversity is good, while a company cannot have too much on its plate." "This time we take the initiative to adjust the diversification strategy. It does not mean that Lenovo will now tend to adopt a more defensive market strategy; on the contrary, it is a sign of precisely active attack. Or it can also be said as change or reform in offensive strategy. Currently we focus on core business in order to compete better with foreign rivals. "

Strategic Master Dale McConkey also has said that "The strategic evaluation must allow managers to modify the plan easily and to reach a consensus on the changes quickly."(4)

The wisdom of Liu Chuanzhi and Yang Qingyuan is that they cannot only formulate strategy scientifically, but also can adhere to implement it firmly. The especially can evaluate the implementation of the strategy according to objectives and subjective circumstances, and can adjust it based on new circumstances and new problems in order to lead the company to advance in a correct, stable, high-speed and continuous manner. That's why Lenovo succeeded while others failed because of company's poor decision-makers.

Questions

1. What are the core issues that strategic assessment should address?
2. How to evaluate the effects of the company's current strategy?
3. What should be considered on evaluating the company's SWOT?
4. What is strategic cost analysis? What are options to gain cost competitiveness? What are steps of each option?
5. What are the steps to assess competitive strength? How about the methods? What are the importances of competitive strength assessment?
6. What should the company's managers seriously consider in order to accurately determine the company's strategic issue agenda?
7. Try to evaluate the current strategy of your company and make adjustments with theories and methods in this chapter.

Notes

(1) (U.S.) Arthur A. Thompson Jr. & A. J. Strickland, *Crafting and executing strategy: the quest for competitive advantage concepts and cases*, 10th ed, Duan Shenghua, Wang Zhihui trans., Xu Erming revision, Peking University Press, 2004, p.208.
(2) (U.S.) Fred. R. David, *Strategic Management*, Li Kening trans., 1st

edition, Economic Science Press, June 1998, p.302.

(3) On April 20, 2001, Yang Yuanqing takes in charge of Lenovo and officially announces the next three-year strategic plan ("New century, new strategy and new journey") on the same day. After three years of implementation, he finds that diversity is beyond the tolerance of Lenovo due to limits of resources and capabilities, which influent the development of the core business. Then in February 2004, he makes adjustments in time by coming out the idea to learn duality before diversity. This case is written based on speech of Liu Chuanzhi and Yang Yuanqing.

(4) 〔U.S.〕 Fred. R. David, *Strategic Management*, Li Kening trans., 1st edition, Economic Science Press, June 1998, p.302.

BIBLIOGRAPHY

〔 U.S. 〕 Peter Drucker, *Management: Tasks, Responsibilities, Practice,*1st edition, China Social Sciences Press, June 1987.

〔U.S.〕 Michael Porter, *Competitive Strategy*, 1st edition, Huaxia Publishing House, January 1997.

〔U.S.〕 Michael Porter, *Competitive Advantage*, 1st edition, Huaxia Publishing House, January 1997.

〔U.S.〕 Arthur A. Thompson Jr. & A. J. Strickland, *Crafting and executing strategy: the quest for competitive advantage concepts and cases*, 10th ed, Duan Shenghua, Wang Zhihui trans., Xu Erming revision, Peking University Press, 2004.

〔U.S.〕 Fred. R. David, *Strategic Management*, Li Kening trans., 1st edition, Economic Science Press, June 1998.

〔CAN.〕 Henry Mintzberg, *Strategy Safari*, 2nd edition, Machinery Industry Press, June 2006.

〔British〕 Gerry Johnson & Kevan Scholes, *Exploring Corporate Strategy*, 1st Edition, Jin Zhanming & Gu Xiumei tran, Huaxia Publishing House, April 1998.

Editing group of required MBA core courses, *Business Strategy*, 1st edition, China International Radio Press, September 1997.

Editing group of required MBA core courses, *Business Strategy*, 1st edition revision, China International Radio Press, 2000.

Liu Jisheng ed, *Company Operation Strategy*, 1st edition, Tsinghua University Press, April 1995.

Xu Erming ed, *Company Strategy Management*, 1st edition, China Economic Publishing House, May 1998.

Chiang Yuntong ed, *Company Operation Strategic Management*, 1st edition, Company Management Press, April 1996.

CHAPTER 13
Enterprise Strategic Control

Abstract

This chapter starts begins with statements from Henri Fayol, father of management theory, which indicates the extreme importance of strategic control for achieving strategic goals. Then, it briefly introduces concepts of strategic control. Later, it explains in detail the contents of strategic control. Finally, it has an appendix of cases and comments in "Qingqi Group defeats itself."

Learning Objectives

- To master concepts and Necessities of Strategic Control.
- To master meanings of strategy and contents of each.
- To understand and master composing factors of strategic control.
- To correctly understand and grasp characteristics of strategic control.
- To master procedures, systems, principles, methods and modes of strategic control.

Introduction

Henri Fayol, father of management theory, has once said that "In an undertaking, to control consists in verifying whether everything occurs in conformity with the plan adopted, the instructions issued and principles established." (1) He also stresses that like other elements of management, planning, organizing, coordinating and commanding, controlling always needs more long-lasting concentration spirits and skills." In the implementation of strategy, enterprises have to strengthen strategic control. Otherwise, it will not only be hard to achieve their set strategic goals, but also lead the company to failure.

Lesson

I. Concepts and Necessities of Strategic Control

Strategic control is the means to monitor the processes of strategy implementation, correct deviations timely, and assure the achievements of strategic plan. Strategic control is the guarantee for strategy implementation.

Strategic control is necessary because two inevitable situations will be expected in the process of strategy implementation. First, some actions may take place during the process that does not meet with the strategic plan. It is mainly because factors such as individuals' limitation in knowledge, abilities, and information under control, as well as discordance of individuals' goal with that of the corporate; Second, some parts or even the whole strategic plan may not fit into present internal and external situations. The reasons could be the fact that the original strategic plan is not properly designed, or the environmental development or changes are different from what the firm has predicted. Therefore, firms need to control the strategy implementation process, and adjust and modify the strategic plan in the proper time.

Figure 13-1 Enterprise Strategic Control Map

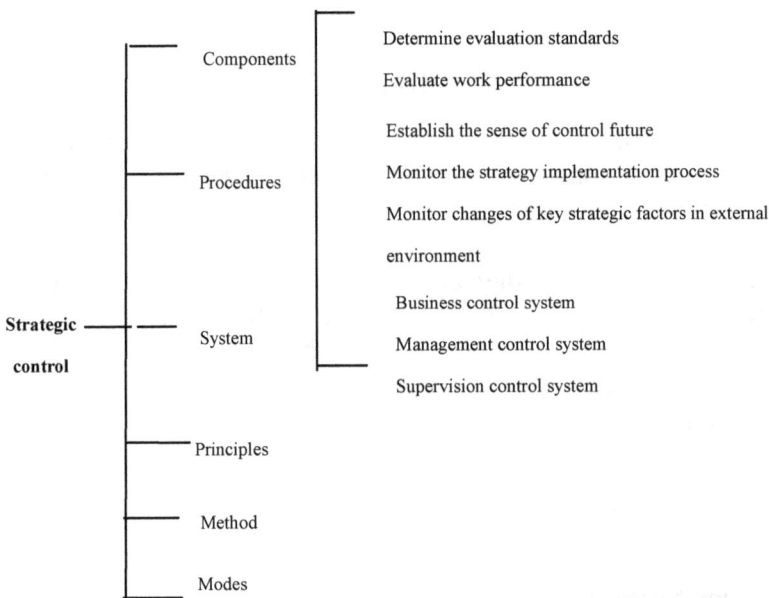

II. Components of strategic control

Strategic control is to measure the implementation of strategy according to the previously determined standards and to adjust the identified errors to assure the realization of strategic goals.

Strategic control is composed of following three basic factors:

(I) Determine evaluation standards

Evaluation standard are a series of indexes used to measure the outcomes of strategy implementation. They include the firm's strategic goal, organizational goals at all levels, individual goals or plan, requests, and so on. In addition, they should be quantified to make it easier to measure and to check up. However, some standards are hard to quantify. In that case, in order to get the relatively objective and general outcomes of the implementation of strategic plans, quantitative and qualitative standards can be combined used.

(II) Evaluate work performance

This is to compare the real strategy implementation outcomes with evaluation standards, give appraisals, find differences, and analyze the causations. Work performance should be evaluated from time to time in order to provide enough information. Of course, it cannot be overdone; otherwise the associated cost of the evaluation could be too high. The key issue for the measurement is to determine when, where and how often the evaluation should be conducted.

(III) Correct errors

It means to identify reasons of errors made in the process of strategy implementation and to take corresponding actions in order to assure the realization of strategic control.

III. Procedures of Strategic Control

Control of business strategy implementation is very important. But it follows no fixed shape. So a specific procedure is needed to do that. The basic procedure is illustrated in Figure 13-2.

Figure 13-2. The Procedures of Strategic Control

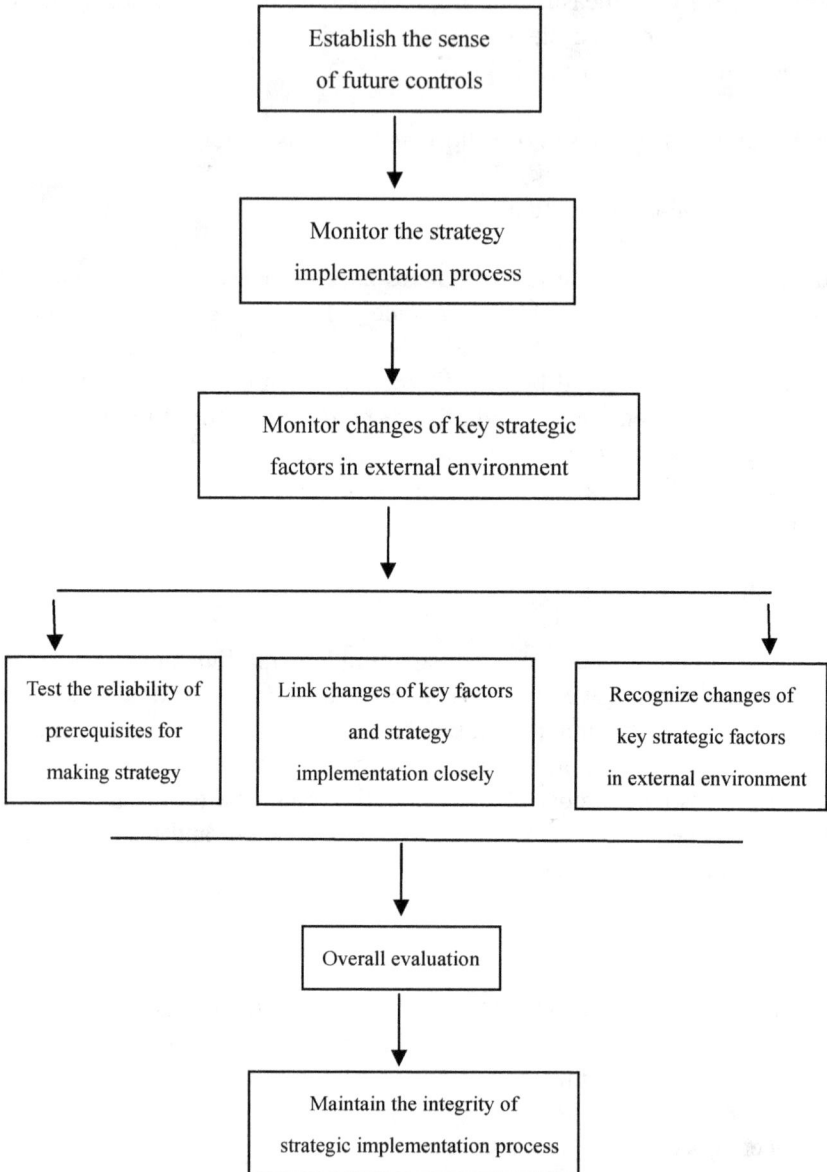

```
          ┌─────────────────────────┐
          │    Establish the sense   │
          │    of future controls    │
          └─────────────────────────┘
                       │
                       ▼
          ┌─────────────────────────┐
          │    Monitor the strategy  │
          │  implementation process  │
          └─────────────────────────┘
                       │
                       ▼
       ┌──────────────────────────────────┐
       │  Monitor changes of key strategic │
       │  factors in external environment  │
       └──────────────────────────────────┘
                       │
                       ▼
```

| Test the reliability of prerequisites for making strategy | Link changes of key factors and strategy implementation closely | Recognize changes of key strategic factors in external environment |

```
                       │
                       ▼
             ┌──────────────────────┐
             │   Overall evaluation  │
             └──────────────────────┘
                       │
                       ▼
       ┌──────────────────────────────────┐
       │    Maintain the integrity of      │
       │  strategic implementation process │
       └──────────────────────────────────┘
```

(I) Establish the sense of future controls

The general control subject is the present business; its method is to compare the real business outcomes, usually gotten after the work is finished, as defined by a standard. Stated differently, business strategy involves new business or the adjustment to the present business, the subject for strategy implementation control is facing the future, not knowing what that has not happened yet. Therefore, the traditional concept of administrative control and its methods must be renewed in strategy implementation process control; it must be established based on the concept of future.

(II) Monitor the strategy implementation process

The actions of strategy implementation process are distributed in a series of detailed plans and activities. Progress should be divided into a few steps; and detailed plans should be made for the earlier steps of the implementation. At the same time, it is necessary to fully and rationally allocate resources to fulfill the requirement of the earlier steps. In this case, strategic managers are able to convert the implementation of large and general strategy into individualized actions and results that are specified and planned. And the control can start from monitoring these specified earlier actions. Once partial plans are made and evaluated, strategic implementation controllers and strategic managers will be able to get the data of the development and related results. Then, they can inspect the progress in a specified period of time. Two aims can be realized in monitoring the progress of strategy implementation: one is to ensure every strategic action is in accordance with the general strategy goal; another is to discover earlier whether or not the strategy needs to be adjusted or modified.

(III) Monitor changes of key strategic factors in external environment

Generally speaking, strategies are made according hypotheses and predicted surroundings. Usually the strategic decision makers tend to make predictions with or without consciousness about demand, technology, price, government policy, market competition, as well as a series external change factors in the future. These predictions are presupposition for making strategy, while the external environment changes usually influence the effectiveness of predictions. Accordingly, it will become very necessary to monitor the external environment changes, especially that of key strategic factors. Generally the following works need to be done:

1. Test the reliability of prerequisites for making strategy

The prerequisite condition for making strategy is prediction of the key strategic factors. If the prediction for one key strategic factor is not reliable, then the strategy needs to be adjusted. The faster modified prerequisite is accepted, the better strategic change will be. Therefore it is necessary to mark out the key strategic factors in the external environment when a firm makes its strategy, and to systematically monitor them. For example, one company makes a strategy to occupy a leading position in the industry in the marketing area. It also makes a strategic plan that includes technology, price, promotion activities and a strategy for getting listed in the stock market after one year. Unfortunately, it doesn't monitor changes of key strategic factors in the financial market. So it doesn't reach its goal when changes take place in financial markets. Of course, we have no clue in advance to know monitoring the financial market changes will benefit the company for financing or not, but it will at least contributes to investment direction control of its internal capital.

2. Recognize changes of key strategic factors in external environment

Key strategic factors of external environment generally can be classified into two classes; they are non-human forces and major "roles." Non-human forces factors refer to environmental factors that are non-controllable by the firm and indirectly related with competitive activities among firms, such as science and technology, inflation degree, government's import protection, consumer preference, bank deposits and interest rates, etc. Every firm must judge and monitor their changes to determine their direct influences on its own differentiate advantages. The variables that often under monitoring are: the possible occurring changes, and degree of their influences when they occur. Major "roles" refer to environmental factors that directly related with the competitive activities among firms, such as its competitors, suppliers, industrial group, etc... Changes to them will generate great influences on the firm's strategic implementation.

3. Link changes of key factors and strategy implementation closely

Selected variables of monitoring key factors change in the external environment and mainly include: 1) collecting the newest and whole information about non-human forces or major roles; 2) predict their future behavior; 3) indicate the possible significant influences that predicted behaviors may have toward the firm's implementation of strategy. Then interactions should be systematically collected, analyzed, and studied. The company should link changes of key factors and strategy implementation closely and report unusual threats or opportunities to the next procedure for evaluation.

(IV) Overall evaluation

Overall evaluation is a kind of an inspection of the whole process of strategic implementation. Generally, it is conducted only when the next step of strategic implementation needs effective assurance. Usually there are three situations that need overall evaluation:

1. Milestone of the strategic implementation plan. Strategic implementation is divided into several stages; each of them symbolizes a milestone of the strategic implementation. It means that overall evaluation is necessary for every stage of the strategic implementation. Generally, it is listed in the plan the time to make overall evaluation, which allows to collect related information and data targeted.
2. Alarms for external environment changes monitored. In this case, overall evaluation is needed even if it is not the time because great changes of external environmental factors may bring significant influences on business strategy. Therefore overall evaluation is necessary to conduct according to contents of monitoring reports.
3. Strategic projects lasting a very long in implementation. For those projects, overall evaluation should be made even it doesn't reach the milestone and encounter great changes. It is because its implementation lasts so long, usually over one year, enough for changes take place in the internal and external environment. Therefore it is necessary so as to help strategic implementers' to consciously correct errors in made prior.

(V) Maintain the integrity of strategic implementation process

It is important to include the monitoring of the strategic implementation process, monitoring changes of key strategic factors in external environment and conducting overall evaluation during certain times all reach two goals of strategic implementation. Namely, on one hand they check the effectiveness of the present strategic implementation, on another they provide the internal mechanism for business strategy to fit in the changing environment. There still exists another important objective for strategic implementation control, which is to maintain a balanced progress. It requires balancing the ratio and time of all departments, which means works of all departments should go ahead simultaneously, and get balanced recourses and problem solving support. Problems here include long-term and short-term issues, routine business and strategic implementation, internal and external pressures, implementation and modification of strategic plans, and creative cooperation of various administrative methods, etc. Meanwhile, it requires balancing things outside the company and setting up a new balance of external relationships. For example, the company should handle relationships well with major "roles," and suppliers, as well as deal with various activities and opportunities that relate to strategy. This can assure the integrity of strategy implementation process, leading the implementation of strategy to move along the track that has been previously determined.

IV. Characteristics of Strategic Control

Except for basic characteristics of management control, enterprise strategic implementation control has the following characteristics compared with the routine business operation management control. They are:

(I) Inconsistence of overall and partial interest, as well as of long term and short term interest

The whole company is consisted of parts. So theoretically, interests of the whole and its parts should be consistent. But they might be inconsistent in a specific issue. For example, when a firm puts its profits to accumulate capital by expanding the scale of reproduction, which is the firm's strategic development goal, employees cannot get a large increase in wages. Another example is that the company may meet barriers set at operating levels when it plans to adopt a low cost strategy, which requires less input in materialized labor and living labor. In particular, low cost strategy increase difficulties in operations in using substitute materials, and decreases the employees' income by hours for the working hours are reduced. Business strategy implementation control aims to deal with and adjust those types of conflicts in terms of inconsistent issues. It is not the same with that of production technological process. For the latter, easier and more standard process brings higher productivity and income to employees, which increases the difficulties of strategy implementation control. While the former one requests coordinative works and communications with workers as well as proper adjustment measures in the strategy implementation process. It is impossible to gain the expected result of control if a manager simply considers the strategy implementation control as a pure technical work and routine business management.

(II) Diversity and uncertainty

American management scholar Robert Waterman believes that strategy is uncertain. He indicates, in his book *Innovative Management: How Do Outstanding Firms Win and Maintain Competitive Advantage,*" that to trace real strategic routes of a firm, is just like observing a butterfly's routes when it flies over the grass in the summer. It could be a straight line, or could be diverted. In his opinion, strategy is a direction with meandering and changeable routes, so is its control, or options to control. Moreover, generally strategy is clear, stable, and authoritative, but it needs to be adjusted and modified in time in practice according to changes in environmental conditions. Hence, control methods must be provided properly. It demonstrates that control has the characteristic of diversity and uncertainty. This characteristic of control requests the managers to set up a twofold way of thinking about accuracy and vagueness in strategy implementation process, and to adopt diversified control methods.

(III) Elasticity and flexibility

Due to over control and frequent involvement, a series of reactive responding will usually occur when a firm implements its business strategy. For example, the upper level managers may pass along high pressure to the lower level, which stimulates resistance to them. Besides, high-pressure policies of higher levels leads to short term actions of lower level staff. For instance, a manager may sell the idle equipment to increase the profits in his tenure. Therefore in strategy implementation process, flexibility is needed facing various conflicts and problems. It means sometimes they should be carefully dealt with and seriously controlled, sometimes they shouldn't. Moreover, the implementation of strategy is under normal control as long as it keeps in accordance with the strategic goals. Therefore, much room and flexibility of strategic control exists in the strategy implementation process. This characteristic of control requires little involvement of managers. In other words, managers should grant the power to lower lever staff as much as possible and allow them to handle small problems and low level issues within their capacity, which could be even more effective in problem solving.

V.   Strategic Control Systems

Generally speaking, a business organization can be divided into four levels: senior level (or business level), middle level (or management level), primary level (or supervision level), and operation level. In accordance with this division, the enterprise strategic control system could be divided into the following three subsystems, namely business control system, management control system, and supervision control system.

(I) Business control system

Senior managers of the firm, especially members of strategic leadership groups, are in charge of the whole strategic management process. They need not only to set up strategic goals for the whole business, but also to investigate, predict, and control performance of the whole business strategy implementation progress in a certain period of time. Only in this way can they assure the strategic plan be implemented entirely, and adjusted timely when great changes in the environment occur.

(II) Management control system

Departments at the middle level of the firm, such as production, technology, supply, marketing, human resources, and financial department, should establish divisional goals and control standards, as well as adopt proper ways and methods to control their own works according to their works' nature, contents, scopes requests and real conditions.

(III) Supervision control system

Supervisors at primary levels of a firm design operation plans and progress plans, as well as collect the activities information of subordinates so as to assure the daily business activities are successfully carried out according to plans that previously made.

In short, all the above stated subsystems realize the whole enterprise strategic control through the dual directions information exchanges from top to bottom and from bottom to top. In particular, communication from top to bottom delivers the goal and plans made by upper managers to direct organizational activities of lower levels; while communication from bottom to top can assist senior managers to inspect and supervise performance of departments and staff under control through report, printed result and other format of data. These two directional information channels organically link partial control and overall control, forming a complete strategic control system.

VI. Principles of Strategic Control

A firm should follow the principles listed below when conducts strategic control:

1. The principle of suitable leadership with the strategy. It means leaders of the firm must be responsible for strategy formulation and implementation.

2. The principle of suitable organization with strategy. It means business strategy is in need of suitable organizational structure.

3. The principle of suitable action plans with strategy. It means that action plans are needed to support the business strategy.

4. The principle of suitable resources allocation with strategy. It means the allocation of resources must support the realization of strategic objectives.

5. The principle of suitable corporate culture with strategy. It means corporate culture; especially psychology of leaders at all levels must fit for the implementation of strategy.

6. The principle of carrying out reward and punishment. It means a firm must reward and compensate those who are successful in implementation, and punish those who are not to assure the realization of strategy.

7. A good control and an earlier alarm system for correction of strategic deviation.

VII. Methods of Strategic Control

The methods of strategic control can be divided into behavior control and output control. Behavior control is based on direct observation of individuals. It is called behavior control when managers conduct closely individual observation of workers. Output control is based on measurement of quantitative data, such as sales, finance or production records, etc. These two methods are not substitutable. Output control can provide the evidence for working accomplishments. However, when working accomplishments become well-known and individual observation can increase the effectiveness, then the behavior control should be implemented.

Output control is the most used method in measurement of accomplishments of the large and complicated organizations and the major subordinate units of these organizations.
It can compare performance of an organization to that of others, and can make internally compare of the subordinate units. However, behavior control is still necessary at the lower level in order to increase the effectiveness and give the detailed direction to individual employees. A firm can combine output control and behavior control together in using for they meet various need of the organization.

VIII.   Modes of Strategic Adjustment and Control

The strategic adjustment can be divided into initiative adjustment and passive adjustments. Passive adjustment is usually reorganization afterwards, therefore it can let the strategy lose its directive function and create big losses. Initiative adjustment will loss less and even sometimes brings benefits. So a firm should make efforts to initiate and plan to make strategic adjustments.
The planned initiative adjustment includes the following two methods:

(I) Critical point method. Critical point refers to critical levels of changes of the key factors for success. The key success factors of the firm are determined when it makes its strategic plan. They could be representatives of unusual opportunities, or serious threats. Take a firm adopting low cost strategy as an example. If cost of one business item is more than the expected level, the firm needs to immediately consider adjusting its strategic plan as long as it reaches the critical point.

(II) Contingent plan method. This method is a further development of the critical point method. It implies that a firm will prepare several strategic options when it makes strategic plans, and will outline the various conditions and scopes for different strategies beforehand. Once the objective condition changes beyond the suitable scope of the original strategy, the firm can stop the original strategy immediately and start to use the new strategic plan. In this case, the firm can adapt to changes at a high speed and avoid losing its internal effectiveness and stability caused by rushed changes because of the sufficient preparations before.

Case study

Qingqi Group defeats itself

A former leader in the industry with potential market values falls into troubles. Qingqi Group gets through a lot of ups and downs. In the beginning, its decision makers emphasize the development of company strategies; they make scientific and feasible strategic plans and take effective measures. That leads Qingqi to a bright future with many outstanding achievements, especially in the early and middle periods. However, after that, they start to lose control of the company because of its excessive expansion in the implementation of the strategy. Moreover, they don't evaluate and adjust the strategy in a timely manner in accordance with the problems it encounters during its implementation. Together with the fact that joint-stock company transformation is not yet completed, these factors all result in Jinan Qingqi huge losses. Therefore, good strategic management includes not only the formulation of strategy, but also its implementation, especially its evaluation and adjustment. Otherwise, the company will likely face the challenge of failure.

Huge losses of Qingqi Group

In 2000, three listed companies that Qingqi Group was once so proud of are all running poorly. Jinan Qingqi made a net profit of 272 million RMB Yuan in 2000; a 1400% decrease compared to 1999. And its earnings per share are 0.28 RMB Yuan. Qingqi Group has a substantial shareholder, with 2.58 billion RMB Yuan of receivables outstanding. Jinan has a rare heavy snow on New Year's Day in 2003. The story begins in the cloudy and snowy eastern suburbs of Jinan City, an ordinary six-story office building. Senior leaders of Jinan Qingqi keep silent and are disturbed as they sit in a dim room. Since it has the huge loss of 272 million RMB Yuan in 2000, Jinan Qingqi, whose stock is added ST ahead encounters the winter incessantly. Even in 2002 when everyone believes things will change, it still faces an unproductive outcome. It seems for Jinan Qingqi that another dreadful winter in business is still waiting for them even as spring is coming outside the windows.

The 2002 annual report of Jinan Qingqi comes out late on April 25, 2003. The company continues to lose as much as 3.4 billion RMB Yuan. Besides, because of 3 consecutive years of losses, its stocks trade in the SSE is suspended on April 28. This news shocks its investors as soon as it is released.

Successful companies are well-known, while ill-fated companies are poles apart. The distance between success and failure is just a step for Jinan Qingqi, which was once as famous as Haier and Changhong. It takes the first step toward failure at the same time when it adheres to its successful experience.

Its past glories that make it outstanding

In mid-1960s, Jinan Qingqi has made the first motorcycle when Chinese people don't even know what it is. At that time, a large number of experts and scholars gather in Jinan and the staff is full of passion for Jinan Qingqi Motorcycle Factory; it has become the absolute authority on motorcycles. By the mid-80s, Qingqi already has an annual output of 30,000 motorcycles, with total assets of tens of millions. It really stands out in the industry.

Its success can be attributed in part to of a brilliant man, Zhang Jialing. He is aggressive and middle age. In 1984, Zhang Jialing takes charge of the company. At that time, there is seldom a competitor in the market and Qingqi ranks the first in domestic motorcycle market. He can choose to do little but to remain the past in a seller's market. But Zhang Jialing has keen insight into the market in the future. He believes that since the motorcycle technology is simple, the competition must be fierce as long as there are enough rivals. So he decides to take advantage of its advantages as a state-owned company with open policies to launch the "Qingqi Mulan" series of products. It produces all kinds of products from high end, middle to low level; for both males and females. "Qingqi Mulan" soon broadens the horizon of consumers depending on its color, quality and design and receives huge demand that exceeds supply.

By the early 90s, its motorcycle factory in Jinan already has an annual production capacity of 500 thousand units. The company also changes its name to China Qingqi Group. At that time, the popular motorcycle brands like Lifan, Zongshen, Loncin are just family workshops with a few people and production lines.

In 1992, Qingqi Group restructures its 3 core units, including engine plant, the first assembly plant and the second assembly plant and forms the Jinan Qingqi AG, which comes at the right time and gets the approval to be listed in the stock market as the first company in Shandong province.

Its share price increase rapidly, which is interpreted as "Qingqi myth." With the aid of the capital market, motorcycles of "Qingqi" and "Mulan" series sell well, earning up 1.9 billion RMB Yuan of main business revenue that year. It becomes fashionable to ride its motorcycles.

In addition, Jinan Qingqi also catches the chance to enter the B share market. It is listed among first batch of 33 companies selected to enter the B share market in 1996. In 1997, it becomes the first listed company who enters both the A and B share markets in the industry and in Shandong Province. There is a saying that if you don't know which stock to purchase, then tries Jinan Qingqi.

Its development strategy

China's motorcycle industry starts in the 1950's and develops slowly before the 80s. It gains rapid development after reform and opening up its borders. Its average annual increases are about 34.7% between 1980 and 1990, about 52.3% between 1990 and 1994. In 1993, China's motorcycle output for the first time surpasses that of Japan, reaching the entire world. Its production increases from 49 thousand units in 80s to 8.91 million in 1996. Chinese companies already have production capacity of ten million units per year. At that time, more and more companies join the motorcycle production industry all over the country. According to some statistics, in addition to 118 manufacturing plants on record, there are more than 300 production plants off the record. Many manufacturers of them lack necessary infrastructures and produce poor quality goods. It encounters many problems and has a dreadful impact on the normal motorcycle production coupled with local protectionism. In particular, famous motorcycle producers and consumers bear great losses. In that case, in order to keep the market shares, manufacturers have to decrease the sales price of their products. Then a price war occurs in the Chinese motorcycle industry with a significant feature of "lower price for maintaining market share." And the average price cut is up to 15% at that time.

Cut-throat competition makes a large number of motorcycle manufacturers face problems like declining profits, cash flow difficulties, passive

417

production and poor management. However, even in such a grim situation, Qingqi Group maintains good momentum of both production and sales, and leads the industry all the way. In 1996, it ranks first in the industry, which attracts the attention of people inside and outside the industry. There are many successful experiences of Qingqi, of which the most important one is being proactive. It can make the right forecast of the situation, formulate the corresponding strategy and take effective measures, which makes full preparation for the coming motorcycle competition.

In order to win the final victory, people of Qingqi conduct a deep study of competition in the motorcycle industry and put up the slogan of "put full into the battle for Qingqi's glory" on the conference in Guangzhou in 1993. On June 30, 1994, they hold conferences in Zhengzhou and Luoyang to analyze current situation and development trends of the motorcycle industry. They divide the battle into three phases from a strategic perspective and formulate development strategies for each one.

The first strategic phase (1994-1996) is preparation phase, at which time the business objective is to strive to be the first in the industry.

The second strategic phase (1997-2000) is competition phase, at which time the business objective is to continuously enhance the Group's strength and solidify its position as industrial leader.

The third strategic phase (2001-2005) is stable development phase, at which time the business objective is to gradually enter the international market and build a great big company."

Qingqi Group is also prominent as Jinan Qingqi reaps the glory. Its decision-maker Zhang Jialing begins to merge companies. By 1997, he puts more than 30 companies under the charge of Qingqi Group. Media report its expansion with low cost, claiming it control 11 billion RMB Yuan of total assets with only 800 million RMB Yuan of state assets. Many companies come to learn from its operation.

Qingqi Group is then titled "motorcycle kingdom." It mainly manufactures motorcycles, and engages in industry, commerce, trade, science and agriculture. It becomes a large company that runs its business cross regions, industry, border and ownership. It has 30 thousand employees and total assets of 11.5 billion RMB Yuan. It owns 3 listed companies, 27 wholly state-owned companies, 6 wholly-owned group company, 17 joint venture companies, 16 domestic joint ventures, and 12 overseas companies. It also sets up a state-level company technology center, a staff training center, 80 sales business department all over the country with 3,000 sales outlets, and 1500 service stations, as well as 300 affiliates companies. Its leading products develop into 10 main series with more than 200 varieties of motorcycles and bicycles and 6 main series with more than 20 varieties of light trucks and agricultural vehicles. Qingqi Mulan motorcycles win the "Golden Bridge Prize" for best-selling domestic brand goods for four times in a row and products are exported to more than 50 countries and regions such as Europe, America and Asia.

Uncontrollable management due to blind acquisition

In 1997-1998, Qingqi group launches a vigorous large acquisition. It buys a total of nearly one hundred companies within just two years.

But it is obvious that Qingqi decision-making efforts of acquisitions are problematic. On February 18, 1997, Jinan Qingqi Group mergers Jinan Gangsi Motor Co., Ltd.; on March 28, Pingyin Standard Pats Factory; on May 13, Shanghe Auto Back Shop and Shanghe Daling Farm; in October, Hefei Qingqi, Guiyang Qingqi, Hubei Qingqi respectively. At the beginning of 1998, it purchases Qionghai Drug Group at a high cost, and on 18 May, it mergers Muping Engine Group. We can see that Qingqi Group buys all kinds of companies both big and small.

The previous acquisitions of Qingqi Group make it expand 10 times in assets just within a few years. Qingqi Group gets rave reviews outside, and reaches great achievements inside, which makes some leaders so optimistic that someone even claims that the core of Qingqi Group's success is the mergers and acquisitions and makes the company expand with low cost, useful state-owned assets and better structure.

Once the successful experience of a period is finalized as a programmatic document, it will play its role doggedly. However, sometimes this kind of role is a double-edged sword that can hurt others as well as itself.

Actually, mergers and acquisitions do restrict the development of Qingqi Group but lead it to be a "super carrier." Qionghai Drug Group is the 28th company it mergers with. At first, Qingqi Group holds the opinion that Qionhai Drug Group is the largest pharmaceutical companies in Hainan Province and some of its drugs are expected to become profitable since they have been listed in key national pharmaceutical projects. However, Qionghai Drug Group invests large amount of money in real estate though its main business is pharmaceutical drugs. It has already carried a huge debt due to the real estate bubble burst in Hainan. It doesn't grow. Even Qingqi Group puts in 300 million RMB Yuan and sends representatives who know little about the pharmaceutical industry because they are managers in the motorcycle industry. This acquisition becomes a hot potato that makes Qingqi Group feel disheartened.

It is more dramatic of its merger with Muping Engine Group. Qingqi Group has long been planning the development in the automotive industry. So it hopes to achieve this goal by cooperating with Muping Engine Group. Unexpectedly, it finds out that that company is bankrupt after it invests 70 million RMB Yuan. Even the official seal on the agreement contacts is made up of former officers of Muping Engine Group. Temporary loss of vision leads Qingqi to loss 70 million RMB Yuan and has to repay the debt left over by the original Muping Engine Group. Later, Qingqi sues the company in court.

Qingqi invests70 million RMB Yuan into Guiyang Qingqi. Former workers of that company file a petition for their unsatisfactory treatment and sue for a settlement. So senior leaders of Qingqi have to travel between Jinan and Guiyang and are exhausted. Moreover, former workers of other companies with which it mergers also do the same. Still there is something that comforts its senior leaders that among them, there is no former worker of Qingqi, including the original two assembly plants and one engine plant. Maybe it is the most precious cultural heritage of Qingqi.
Other dozens of companies are not profitable at all. Qingqi loses several hundred million in the real estate projects in Shanghai and has to solve the petition problems cased continuously by employees of Guiyang Power Machinery Factory. Most of the companies Qingqi Group invests are near the edge of bankruptcy after receiving the capital sources.

Meanwhile, internal management problems appear. Previously, Qingqi Group allows all its subsidiaries to use its trademark in order to accelerate their developments. While dozens of companies begin to lower their prices to meet the competition and results in inconsistent qualities of Qingqi motorcycles and hurts the brand. Sometimes, there are even fierce competitions among its own subsidiaries.

Disaster spreads to Jinan Qingqi as the fish in the pond.

Although Jinan Qingqi is a public company, yet its reorganization is not complete. It seems more like a large assembly plant made up of the former engine plant and assembly plant of Qingqi Group. It is only responsible for production while Qingqi Group ia charge of raw materials procurement and product sales. Besides, all leaders at various levels of Jinan Qingqi are replaced by leaders of Qingqi Group. Over the years, the group and the public company share the same leaders and staff.

This system ties the two companies together. Once bad things happen to Qingqi Group, disasters will spreads to Jinan Qingqi, which is like the fish in the pond.

Some reports say that Jinan Qingqi's debt of 2.58 billion RMB Yuan owes to its parent company is mainly genetically determined by their related party transactions. Its listing and reforms are all manipulated by Qingqi Group, and its role is restricted to an assembly plant with no responsibility to purchase raw materials and sell products. Payments cannot be withdrawn in time due to its product sales that takes large shareholders as channel. So accounts receivable piles up year after year.

How to solve the financial problems? Jinan Qingqi became the last resort. Moreover, there is no definite line between Qingqi Group and Jinan Qingqi, so Qingqi Group continuously occupies the payment of Jinan Qingqi's products to fix its own problems appearing in its mergers.

Qingqi Group takes 1.07 billion RMB Yuan from Jinan Qingqi in 1997. By 1998, that number increase to 16.7 billion, 1999 to 23.4 billion and 2000 to 2.58 billion.

With lots of payment to make, Jinan Qingqi has no money to put into production. Thus its core business declines rapidly to 1.9 billion RMB Yuan in 1998. In 2000, its profit falls lower because its income is 540 million and profit of 19.75 million, which is less than 5% of its peak. Price of its stock also drops like a stone.

A fatal blow of being fined for illegal operation

In only two years, radical heroism and greed of Qingqi Group puts both the group and its subsidiaries into trouble. A group with great prospect moves in to a dead end, so do all the large and small companies it acquires.

In order to save all these companies, Zhang Jialing takes risky steps. Since 1997, Qingqi Group security department has spent hundreds of millions of dollars to hold its own three stocks of Jinan Qingqi, SUNDIRO, and Qingqi Haiyao in name of its staff. Of course, prices

of these three stocks rise to a large extent. Leaders of Qingqi Group cannot help but exclaim that its several companies can be out of business shortly.

They don't notice that relevant authorities have watched the strange development of Jinan Qingqi. In November 1999, the illegal stocks operation of Qingqi Group is verified by the relevant authorities. Then they take over all earnings of 100 million RMB Yuan in the stock market and impose a fine of 5 million. In addition, its chairman Zhang Jialing cannot enter the security market within 3 years and the secretary of the Board is banned from the stock market forever. What's worse, tax department also fine Jinan Qingqi of more than 80 million in back taxes.

It makes running Jinan Qingqi more difficult as it has already suffered a lot. As a big company, neither Qingqi Group nor Jinan Qingqi is able to offer these life-saving funds. The only valuable product is the inventory of motorcycles for sales in peak season. Zhang Jialing decides to sell them with tears. The tragic scene witnesses how workers unwillingly move motorcycles to the cart and sell them at a low price bursting into tears.

Nevertheless, its entire marketing system suffers a heavy blow as large numbers of low-cost motorcycle flows to the market. Some dealers come to ask whether the company will compensate them for the loss caused by the low price products sold by Jinan Qingqi directly. Parts of them desert the deal with it after getting no satisfactory answer. Its credibility has been seriously affected for its disregard of its dealers.

Bad things never come alone. When vendors perceive the status of Jinan Qingqi, its raw material suppliers and banks request it pay the debt. At that time, cash on the account will immediately be taken away, resulting in no capital left for its operation. What's more, many creditors who cannot get the money even sue in court.

Yang Renfa, vice president who is responsible for litigation finds joy amid hardship by saying jokingly that he has become the "president of the High Court."

Almost at the same time, several major domestic motorcycle giants like Lifan, Loncin, and Zongshen has completed their initial accumulation and begin to rise up in the high-profile national market. Ads of Lifan even appear near the location of Qingqi Group.

Shrink to concentrate on only a few fields

Qingqi renovates and expends large numbers of professional support base for production. But this kind of achievement is negligible compared with the huge losses in all kinds of its businesses.

Qingqi Group is big but not strong. Therefore, it starts to shrink intentionally through cutting off or withdrawing shares or even announcing bankruptcy of its subsidiaries. Qingqi has to invite strategic investors in order to grow stronger.

Qingqi Group also assists Jinan Qingqi deal with legacy issues. It breaks up their related transactions as soon as possible, and further transfers good assets to Jinan Qingqi. Its strategic restructure also gains support from local governments of Shandong Province and Jinan City. Its position of president is also eliminated so as to achieve the goals. We can see from above descriptions that Qingqi Group gives up much to protect and count on its loyal company Jinan Qingqi.

Qingqi Group takes actions to shrink its businesses. Its original sales network has been successfully transferred to Jinan Qingqi for direct marketing. At the same time, its trademark "Qingqi Mulan" is not available for its subsidiaries because Zhang Jialing realizes the significance of brand management for product quality and brand values. In this way, Qingqi Group gives sales companies to Jinan Qingqi as well as good assets. The measures taken in crisis have been already implemented.

It is learnt that Jinan Qingqi has already received assets transferred by the group for. Specifically, it includes the 4140 equity shares (5.89% of its total share capital) of Shandong Securities Co. Ltd., which values 99.36 million RMB Yuan. In addition, 3,000 shares of equity (7.5%of its total equity) of Shandong Silver Plaza Co., Ltd., this is worth 45 million RMB Yuan. Besides, it also includes the offset of debts receivables of the group, which is up to 14. 436 million RMB Yuan. Recently Jinan Qingqi intends to take Qingqi Group's real estate sales company all over the country, which accounts to about 70 million. Moreover, it also will get equity of Shandong Yuquan Group Co., Ltd., which values 14.2285 million RMB Yuan (20% of the total share capital) and that of Zibo Automobile Factory that is worth 38.56 million RMB Yuan (80% of the total share capital) and 35.7% of the shares of Shandong Information Industry Group Corporation. Furthermore, real estate located in Heping Road will also be transferred to Jinan Qingqi, which is equal to 12.42 million RMB Yuan (nominal value).

The reason why Qingqi prefers Jinan Qingqi lies in its personality. That is, Jinan Qingqi is a company set through shareholding reform of the old state-owned China Qingqi Group Company in 1992. It combines the former three core branches together, including engine plant, the first assembly plant and the second assembly plant. Moreover, it is solely owned by Qingqi Group. On October 20, 1993, the company issues 55 million A shares, raising funds of 438 million RMB Yuan. On December 6 of the same year, it is listed in the SSE. In 1996, it issues 10:3 rationed shares, raising funds of 298 million. It is also the first listed company in both China's motorcycle industry and Shandong Province.

It is said that Guiyang Qingqi is completely a local company's trusteeship and Liaocheng Watch Factory is applying for bankruptcy.

Seeking to survive through restructuring

Jinan Qingqi has to exit the stock market if it is not profitable within 3 years after "ST" mark is added. Unfortunately, its parent company Qingqi Group has too many of its own problems and cannot help it out. So Qingqi Group begins to seek companies that are intended to restructure Jinan Qingqi since 2001 so that Jinan Qingqi can get out of the woods.

It is difficult for Qingqi to resolve problems of its own currently. That is because it is incapable of financing in troubles. However, it has complete inner structure through lack of funds. What Qingqi depends on to attract investors are the size of the entire group, brand that once has reached 3.2 billion RMB Yuan, sales network as well as development and production technology of motorcycles.

Its first partner of restructure is Han Group. It is a rich multinational corporation registered in Indonesia, which is involved in a number of industrial investments such as real estate, building materials, port development, international trade and finance. Ancestral home of its boss Han Jinfu is said to lie in Fujian Province and his family has net assets of 5 billion US dollars. Han Group attaches great importance on the good relationship between Jinan Qingqi and local government, as well as brand market value of "Qingqi" trademark which has reached 3.3 billion RMB Yuan. What's more, it can ask local government for more help as long as it plays the "savior" role to help Jinan Qingqi out. For Qingqi Group, what is more important is that there is a company which is willing to take over the restructuring.

Agreement is reached quickly as their wishes are reached. On November 11, 2001, Han Jinfu is immediately selected as vice chairman and president of Qingqi Group. All parties are very happy about the results. Han Jinfu indicates on the spot that he can bring Jinan Qingqi back to normal within one year. Han Group will deal with management, relationships of the company and will invest funds to it.

Price of ST Jinan Qingqi stocks raises on the day when the news comes out. At the same time, that of stocks in foreign capital merging stock block goes upward. However, people soon discover that within nearly a year of their cooperation, Han Group inputs neither funds nor advanced management to Jinan Qingqi. Furthermore, as general manager of Jinan Qingqi, Han Jinfu even rarely appears in the company.

According to insiders, what really attracts Han group is that local government has promised to indirectly give high-quality assets to Jinan Qingqi. It means a piece of land locating about 30 km southeast to Jinan City, which is named Dragon Cave. It covers about 8.8 square kilometers or 10,000 acres and is considered an ideal tourism development area because the natural distribution of a large number of karst caves. However, due to the fairly complex approval process of the land, Han Group decides to give up after it waits for a year in vain.

Jinan Qingqi's reorganization ends in failure. It is again put to the edge of bankruptcy. Its original peak production of 800 thousand motorcycles has been reduced to less than 200 thousand.

On April 25, 2003, ST Qingqi announces its 2002 annual report. It claims that the company has a huge loss of 3.4 billion RMB Yuan. It is the third consecutive year of losses. Afterwards, stock of ST Qingqi is suspended trading in the SSE on April 28. It faces the risk of exiting the stock market.

In order to help oneself out, in 2002, Jinan Qingqi discharges a large number of non-performing loans accumulated over the years. It also looks forward to a second reorganization.

Zhang Jialing announces to make a decision that the entire group stops all businesses for modification and half of its staff will be laid off. Then a large team of 15 thousand laid off workers appeals to the higher authorities for help. That period of time sees Zhang Jialiang getting older, even his straight back turns into somewhat humpback.

Zhang Jialing, at his age of 61, often feels he hasn't fulfilled his dreams. Then he determines to retire after he has dug Qingqi Group out of the trouble. A senior social scholar gives an emotional appraisal of Qingqi that "it is just a giant in shock now, and it will definitely wake up one day."

In the first quarter of 2003,the main business income of Jinan Qingqi is 188 million RMB Yuan, operating profit is 24.2 million, and net profit just slightly losses 1.68 million.

All expectations and concerned are waiting to see its future...

On September 23, 2003, Intermediate People's Court of Jinan accepts the application case proposed by Jinan Guanghua Packaging Plant who requires Jinan Qingqi's bankruptcy for its debts. On December 29, 2003, the two sides reaches a settlement agreement, which states that Jinan Qingqi has to pay off its debt of about 832 million RMB Yuan within three months after the debt settlement agreement comes into effect.

As the huge debt of more than 800 million RMB Yuan has been fully cleared up, Jinan Qingqi receives the civil written verdict of the bankruptcy issue from Intermediate People's Court of Jinan. Thenceforward, Jinan Qingqi is totally free from the troubled six-month bankruptcy disputes.

ST Qingqi, which attracts attention of many domestic and foreign investors, finally comes back from bankruptcy. The Court announces to close the case of Qingqi's bankruptcy since the debt settlement agreement made by Qingqi and its creditors has been carried out completely. That means Qingqi finally gets rid of its critical situation and that also wipes away major obstacles on Qingqi's way to go back to the stock market and to restructure its assets.

Soon after Jinan Qingqi steps out of the risk of bankruptcy, production of ST Qingqi increases 45.56% in the first quarter; sales revenue increases 38.58% compared with that in last year; its profits also grow significantly.

Meanwhile, exciting news comes along with its reorganization. In the morning of May 27, 2004, Qingqi co-signs a "Joint Venture Memorandum of Cooperation" with Brazil CBB in Beijing. According to the memorandum, the two sides will cooperate to establish motorcycle production bases in Brazil. It will help Jinan Qingqi take more initiative in its restructuring.

According to study, CBB is Brazil's largest production base of motorcycle, whose current production is only behind Brazil Honda and Yamaha. Memorandum that is signed today is one of the 9 memorandums of joint venture cooperation of China and Pakistan, and also one of important projects for which President Lula of Brazil comes to China.

Qingqi, said Wang Limin, Chairman of shares, if shares of bankrupt Qingqi back from the dead end to solve the problem, then the strategic investment partners in the injection of quality assets, you can make with scooters shares continued profitability and sustainable development.

Let us eagerly look forward to the rebirth of the Qingqi Kingdom.

Source: This case is edited according to information reported on "Chinese companies," *China Business* in 2004

Review

Qingqi Group's decision makers emphasis on the development of company strategies; they make scientific and feasible strategic plans and take effective measures. That leads Qingqi go to a bright future with lots of outstanding achievements, especially in the early and middle periods. Policy makers develop more emphasis on company development strategy, action ahead, and effective measures, strategic planning is also more scientific and feasible. Therefore, the early and mid-term planning made outstanding achievements resulting in a bright future.

However, after that, they start to lose control of the company because of its excessive expansion in the implementation of the strategy. Moreover, they don't evaluate and adjust the strategy timely in accordance with problems that appear in its implementation. Together with

the fact that joint-stock company transformation is not yet completed. These factors all cause Jinan Qingqi to experience huge losses.

Therefore, a good strategic management includes not only the formulation of strategy, but also its implementation, especially its evaluation and adjustment. Otherwise, the company will face the challenge of failure. Qingqi Group is a painful lesson.

Questions

1. What are the necessities of strategic control?
2. What are the components of strategic control?
3. How to understand and master the characteristics of strategic control?
4. What are the procedures of strategic control?
5. What are enterprise strategic control systems?
6. What are the principles of strategic control?
7. What are the methods of strategic control?
8. What are the means of strategic adjustment and control?

Notes

(1) [France] Henri Fayol, *General and Industrial Management*, 1st edition, China Social Science Publishing House, November, 1982, p.119.
(2) [France] Henri Fayol, *General and Industrial Management*, 1st edition, China Social Science Publishing House, November, 1982, p.122.

BIBLIOGRAPHY

[France] Henri Fayol, *General and Industrial Management*, 1st edition, China Social Science Publishing House, November, 1982

〔U.S.〕 Peter Drucker, *The Effective Executive*, 1st edition, Qing-Wen Printing Co.Ltd., March, 1978.

〔 U.S. 〕 Peter Drucker, *Management: Tasks, Responsibilities, Practice*,1st edition, China Social Sciences Press, June 1987.

〔U.S.〕 Arthur A. Thompson Jr. & A. J. Strickland, *Crafting and executing strategy: the quest for competitive advantage concepts and cases*, 10th ed, Duan Shenghua, Wang Zhihui trans., Xu Erming revision, Peking University Press, 2004.

〔U.S.〕 Fred. R. David, *Strategic Management*, Li Kening trans., 1st edition, Economic Science Press, June 1998.

Editing group of required MBA core courses, *Business Strategy*, 1st edition, China International Radio Press, September 1997.

Editing group of required MBA core courses, *Business Strategy*, 1st edition revision, China International Radio Press, 2000.

Liu Jisheng ed, *Company Operation Strategy*, 1st edition, Tsinghua University Press, April 1995.

Xu Erming ed, *Company Strategy Management*, 1st edition, China Economic Publishing House, May 1998.

Chiang Yuntong ed, *Company Operation Strategic Management*, 1st edition, Company Management Press, April 1996.

CHAPTER 14
Enterprise Strategic Change

Abstract

This chapter begins with brilliant words on company change from former GE chairman Jack Welch to reveal the significance of a strategic change for sustainable and everlasting development of the company. Then, it takes the extinction of dinosaurs as an example to talk about the significance of change, and to introduce the rule prevalent in both biosphere and business "survival of the fittest in natural selection." Subsequently, it describes in detail the motivation, type and model of company strategic change and points out changes in business strategy, and points out basic steps, guarantees measures and the key to success of company strategic change. Finally, it has appendix of cases and comments in "Strategic Shift of Double Star."

Learning Objectives

- To profoundly understand the significance of company strategic change
- To understand and grasp the motivation, type and model of company strategic change
- To understand and grasp basic steps, guarantee measures and the key to success of company strategic change
- To improve your company's strategic change using company strategic change theory

Introduction

Jack Welch, former GE Chairman has always believed that "when the rate of change inside an institution becomes slower than the rate of change outside, the end is insight. The only question is when." (1) At the last meeting of GE's 550 top leaders in early January, 2001, which is also his farewell to GE, he says emotionally that "I got this job 20 years ago, and together we changed a lot. It has been a fun, wonderful journey filled with great memories and lasting friendships. For much of what we've done, forget it." He also makes the message clear that "This will be a whole new ball game: Change, as you have never seen it, at speeds you've never seen. What fun for those who relish it? What fear for those who don't grasp it?" He ends by telling everyone to turn the organization upside down, shake it up, and go blow the roof off. (2) What Welch requests "to turn the organization upside down, shake it up, and go blow the roof off." is to keep strategic change.

Lesson

I. Significances of change learning from the extinction of dinosaurs

Dinosaurs were the dominant terrestrial vertebrates of the Jurassic from its appearance and development in the Triassic. All kinds of dinosaurs gather together, constituting a mix of the dragon world. In addition to huge dinosaurs on land like brontosaurus and diplodocus, etc., there are also a large number of dinosaurs in the water and pterosaurs.

Cretaceous is the last century for dinosaurs; it is also the period when there are great changes of landscape on the earth. The shape of continents is very similar with that of today after the sea reaches a record height. Flowering plants appear, and many insects - from bees to ants - also appear. Giant lizards and giant sea turtles swim in the ocean together. In the air, the wings of pterosaurs are expanded up to 12 meters. Dinosaurs dominate the land, and their sizes and shapes are beyond all previous types. Weighs of herbivorous dinosaurs are up to 100 tons and body lengths of carnivorous dinosaurs are up to 12 meters.

Mammals are present throughout the age of dinosaurs. For millions of years, they are small. Some of them may lay eggs. Mammals begin to change during Cretaceous.

Nearly 70 million years ago, mammals develop into two main groups. One group is placental mammal with their well-developed newborn pups. Another is the marsupial, who gives birth to tiny cubs that climb into the mother's pouch for feeding. The two groups still exist today, but their early species have become extinct long ago.

People have believed for a long time that mammals have had the opportunity to develop into many different types since dinosaurs disappeared during Cretaceous. But new evidence indicates that the evolution of mammals has begun millions of years before the extinction of dinosaurs. So what is the reason that makes mammals flourish? Now scientists believe that the new lands created by continental drift and sea-level provide possibilities for the emergence of new types of mammals.

Dinosaurs disappear from the land 65 million years ago, so do many other types of animals in the ocean or in the air. Giant marine reptiles and flying reptiles are examples of them. Scientists have explored many kinds of theories to explain the death of the dinosaurs - from the very cold weather to the stomach flatulence. In the past decade, increasing evidence has made a new theory. It is possible the last and worst change in the environment, which is at last more severe than anyone ever discovered that leads to the extinction of dinosaurs. Specifically, a giant asteroid strikes the Gulf of Mexico. The bump generates a huge tsunami that sweeps across the earth, and cause many fires. Blotting out the sun, smoke cools the earth; resulting in volcanic eruptions. Huge dinosaurs as well as many animals are unable to adapt to dramatic changes in weather and hence become extinct. However, birds, mammals, crocodiles and many other animals survive inexplicably.

Why are huge dinosaurs' extinct while small birds, mammals, crocodiles and many other animals are able to survive enigmatically?

Darwin gives a clear answer in *Origin of Species* that "Species existed in the lone term are neither the most powerful, nor the most intelligent, but the most able to adapt to environmental changes!"

The law revealed by evolutionist Charles Darwin is that "survival of the fittest in natural selection" applies not only to the biosphere, but to business. It is the rules for companies to become stronger or be eliminated by competition. As a cell of society, companies get all the resources it needs from the large social environment whether the natural and ecological environment, or the social environment, and is subject to the constraints of the environment. Therefore, a company must take the initiative to adapt to environmental change. For instance, a company shall change its strategy or form according to environmental changes. Especially in the situation of earth's climate warming, environmental degradation, economic competition, and accelerating social change, a company must make changes. Otherwise, even a large company or group will be eliminated as the dinosaurs were.

The rare world financial crisis that breaks out in 2008 imposes a company to understand profoundly the necessary and urgency to upgrade and change. In that crisis, survivors are the most flexible companies that adapt to the changes and losers are wandering companies that remain unchanged in crisis.

It is just as the words of "transition" master Larry Bossidy & Ram Charan "Now, it's high time for us to completely change the mentality of companies, either change or head to bankruptcy."

Peter Drucker, the father of modern management has said that "The manager always has to administer. He has to manage and improve what already exists and is already to adapt. But he also has to be an entrepreneur. He has to redirect resources from areas of low or diminishing results to areas of high or increasing results. He has to slough off yesterday and to render obsolete what already exists and is already known. He has to create tomorrow. " (3)

II. Motivations of strategic change

There are usually two motivations of strategic change, one is external force, and another is internal drive. These motivations often represent two forces and forms, one is passive change under strong external pressures - "no alternative policy helpless policy"; another is active change driven by strong internal dynamics - "wise move"

(I) Passive change under strong external pressures - "No alternative policy"

Such as:
A major crisis of the macroeconomic environment, like the rare global financial crisis that breaks out in 2008;
Rapidly depressed market conditions;
Selection policies formulated by the government;
Vicious competition of competitors;
The end of the industry life cycle, like the forced withdraw of VCD, pager, and PHS from the market.

A reporter has asked Wang Hai, president of the Double Star Group that "Why should Double Star develop by taking new roads across industries? In answering this question, Wang Hai admits that "The adjustment of Double Star, including going outside of the parent companies, forming strategic models named "big Double Star" and transferring from industrial production to service provision is actually forced by the situation at that time. Despite the fact that some people call it a great decision-making and strategic shift."

(II) Active transition driven by strong internal dynamics - "Wise move"

Such as:

    Rapid warming of market demand;
    Preferential policies formulated by the government;
    Less and weaker competitors;
    Companies' own new inventions, new creations and new patents.
    For example Shandong Himin Solar owns patents of solar technology; Beijing Rechsand Science and Technology Group can change "sand into gold" and so on.

III. Types of strategic change

(I) Divided by the nature of company change

    1. Change of strategic direction - Industrial transfer

Companies of this type refer to those who enter new industries or industries with little association with their current industries. Typical examples are Glanz, the king of microwave ovens who transfers from reproducing down coats to microwave ovens, and Geliahao Group who changes from quarrying to the fine chemical industry.

    2. Change of business model - Business model innovation

The so-called business model refers to the way a company creates value and makes profits. There are many examples of this type. A company can shift its market from foreign to domestic, can produce from OEM production to own brand creating, can change from manufacturing to service, can update from low-end to high-end, and can improve management from extensive to elaborate. Besides, it can adjust product structure, develop new technologies, apply for new patents, and launch new products. Moreover, change of business model includes business expansion and contraction, whole industry chain integrating from a single business, group forming of the company and changes of the operating regions.

(II) Divided by the trend of company change

1. Expansion type: such as enlarging the scale, merger, restructuring, increasing diversification, forming groups within the company, and going from localization to globalization.

2. Shrink type: such as downscoping, streamlining, selling, and changing from diversification to specialization and from globalization to localization.

IV.   Modes of strategic change

(I) Industrial strategic change: To enter new industries

In this regard, "number 1 or number 2" strategy proposed and implemented by Jack Welch, former chairman and CEO of GE is an excellent example.

At Jack Welch's first briefing meeting as CEO with Wall Street analysts on December 8, 1981, he introduced his vision that GE's operating divisions would either be number 1 or number 2 in their field or be sold off.

He has asked that "Where are we going? What will General Electric be? What is the strategy?

The challenge for General Electric when we participate in these real growth industries, when we are number one or number two, is to ask ourselves – how big, how fast? Yes, how many resources – people and money – can we put behind the opportunity to ensure that we capitalize on this leadership position.

In this slower growth environment of the '80s, as companies and countries fight for that reduced volume, fight their own unemployment problems, there will be no room for the mediocre supplier of products and services-the company in the middle of the pack. The winner in this slow-growth environment will be those who search out and participate in the real growth industries and insist upon being number one or number two in every business they are in – the number one or number two leanest, lowest-cost, worldwide producers of quality goods and services or those who have a clear technological edge, a clear advantage in a market niche.

We believe this central idea – being number one or number two - more than an objective – a requirement will give us a set of businesses which will be unique in the world business equation at the end of this decade. "(4)

Practice has proved that market value of the GE that Jack Welch inherited in 1981 has reached 450 billion increasing 30 times in the short span of 20 years. GE's rank in the world is upgraded from tenth to second place.

In China, there are similar companies. Such as Gram, it shifts from down coats production to microwave ovens production, and becomes the world-famous "microwave king."

(II) Industrial strategic upgrade: To improve the industrial level

Zhejiang Tiansheng Holding Group Co., Ltd is a good example of taking precautions before it is too late to upgrade industrial level. It is a large comprehensive enterprise group which is engaged in textile, printing and dyeing. As early as two or three years ago, the company begins to manage innovation and invest RMB Yuan 1.2 billion last year to upgrade its subordinate companies. Now, the group has more than 3800 workers, decreasing from 6,000 workers, while its sales increase more than 3 times. The effectiveness of the company is still flourishing in the crisis. Sun Yonggen, the chairman of the company says that "Forewarned is forearmed. It is wise to sew a coat early than to wait to find there is no coat for the heavy snow."

Another example is the Jiangsu shipbuilding industry that changes from general manufacturing to high-end invention. In the late 20th century, most of the thousands of Jiangsu shipyards engage in low-end process and assembly relying on cheap labor and raw materials according to foreign ship drawings. From the beginning of 21 century, a number of shipyards work hard to make benefits depending on design and R&D. They design by themselves in accordance with requirements of foreign ship-owners, and invest to develop core components like the engine.

It only takes a few years for eight to nine giant shipyards whose outputs occupy 90% of the total industry to spring up along the north of the Yangtze River in the province for hundreds of miles. Other shipyards also do their best to upgrade their technologies for supporting and to constitute the industrial chain. In that case, competition of differences takes shape, eliminating the previous homogeneous low-end competition. The entire shipbuilding industry shows the characteristic of high cost with higher profits and the trend of pressing forward vigorously.

Exports of ships and profit margins soar 80% and 66% of during the first half of 2009. The total orders held take up 35% of the country, accounting for 11.5% of the world. The secret lies in the change of the shipbuilding industry from general manufacturing to high-end innovation, or from OEM (original equipment manufacturer) to ODM (original design manufacturer).

(III) Product strategic change: to adjust the products structure

The success of high-end development strategy of Double Star Group is a great example. In domestic footwear and machinery manufacturing industry, there are too many homogeneous products, serious "low-end melees" and companies at the edge of bankruptcy under these circumstances, Wang Hai, president of the Double Star Group, makes a decision early to engage in high-end products, build up his own brands and make a good impression at a strategic height.

It is the implementation of this strategy that makes Double Star footwear and machinery to be raised to a higher product level and successfully seize the high-end market in pressing forward. It can be proven that footwear and machinery of the Double Star have not been significantly affected, or even achieved a better development than before in the crisis. In 2008, the sales proportions of high-end products like the molding machine, dual curing machine, and large rubber mixing mill to sales of the Double Star Rubber Machinery Company are respectively 17%, 54% and 12%, while other generic products account for only 12.8%. The high-end market is opened quickly by Double Star Rubber Machinery Company, whose main economic indicators rank fist in the country. Besides, Double Star Foundry Machinery has successfully won the national "High-tech Enterprise" certification, which is one of the first national approved high-tech companies since the identification approach of national high-tech companies is implemented in 2008. It also earns foreign currency of $35 million in footwear exports in adverse economic conditions. Numerous international clients represented by U.S. customers give bulk orders, which make the Double Star go popular during the crisis. Its export orders for shoes have been extended to June 2009.

438

(IV) Technology strategic change: To develop new technologies and patents

The growth of Hisense Group in adverse economic condition relying on technological innovation is the result of core technological breakthroughs that Hisense has always stressed. Some of the world's leading home appliance giants suffer major blows in the current spreading financial crisis. While Hisense's new products not only stand out in the Canton Fair, but also contribute to the growth of Hisense against the crisis. The overall efficiency (profit) growth of Hisense in the first quarter of this year is estimated at 40% conservatively. In the domestic market, compared to prior sales, that of LCD TVs in January 2009 occupies up to 262.60%. Market share of Hisense flat-panel TV in February reaches 15.84%, ranking first. The same thing happens to Hisense TV among household appliances for the countryside that ranks first with market share of 22.4%. In international markets, compared to prior sales, that of Hisense products in Australia in 2008 rises as high as 114%. The proportion of products with independent brands makes up to 70% of the overall businesses in January 2009.

Another example of technological innovation is the reversal of Baofang printing & dyeing Co., Ltd.company. A project named "Batik" aiming at changing the production line makes Zhejiang Baofang printing & dyeing Co., Ltd.(hereinafter is called "Baofang printing and dyeing" for short) become one of unbroken "eggs" when the "nest" is overturned - the global financial crisis. According to statistics of Shaoxing customs on the textile and garment export, there are more and more companies with negative earnings in January and February of 2009; the number of these companies increases by 13% as compared with the prior year. However, the growth rate of "Baofang printing & dyeing" in textile exports reaches upwards of 20%.

Operators led by Gao Jianzhang, the general manager of "Baofang printing & dyeing" find an opportunity in times of crisis. A wax print cloth production line is modified in mid-2007 and the products are exported to countries in West Africa, allowing the company to alleviate losses that year. Then, another 5 production lines are altered or introduced. Export orders from West Africa come in a steady flow, which help the company successfully change during the crisis.

(V) Business strategic changes: To expand or contract operations

Haier Group develops from branding or specialization to diversification, while Lenovo returns from diversification to specialization.

(VI) Regional strategic change: to broaden or change operating areas

Along with the implementation of international strategy - go out, walk in and walk up, Haier has now become a "global company."

Another example is foreign trade company who changes from a foreign trade based strategy to domestic demand oriented strategy. Take Chongqing Minmetal and Machinery Import and Export Co., Ltd. (hereinafter refers to CMMC) as an example, it develops resourcefully in adverse economic situations. Under the influence of the financial turmoil, many companies that engaged in import and export trades complain incessantly, while CMMC moves forward promptly relying on the implementation of these "three changes." First, it changes the export markets. Namely it chooses new emerging markets like Southeast Asia and the Middle East in place of former markets like Europe. Second, it adjusts the export structures. Specifically, it exports mainly complete sets of equipment instead of common foreign trade products (metal, machinery and electronic products). Third, it broadens the form of foreign economics. That is, it exports "software" products like process, technology and service as well as "hardware" products to avoid the impacts of the turmoil.

(VII) Organizational strategic change: To implement group strategy

Generally, the steps of organizational strategic change are factory - company - group. NARI Technology Development Co., Ltd. (abbreviated as NARI-TECH), which is set up by National Grid Electric Power Research Institute is a great example. National Grid Electric Power Research Institute seizes the opportunity to transform applied scientific research institutions into companies. So the 12 industries under its control are 12 companies that combine scientific research with production. The innovation path adopted is "starting a research project - testing in the middle - validation inspection - on-site operation - mass production," along which there emerge continuously new industrial groups.

Over the years, NARI-TECH continues to invest more than 5%, sometimes even up to 8% of sales into R & D per year, approximating RMB Yuan 300 million net investments a year. As a result, it has been ranked in the world in areas like power dispatch automation, and stability control system. What's more, high-end products account for more than 50% of the domestic market and has been put on the Southeast Asian market.

Another example is the risk reduction of Giant Eagle Group through integration. Giant Eagle Group is the largest knitting exporter in Xiangshan. In recent years, Giant Eagle Group builds a complete industrial chain within the company through the implementation of horizontal integration and vertical integration strategy. It integrates the original Xinjiang Tuofeng Cotton Textile Co., Ltd. and other companies and builds cotton yarn, combed, textile production bases in Xinjiang. A complete industrial chain allows Giant Eagle Group to reduce risks greatly in fluctuations of raw material market and benefits a lot in competing in the global markets.

Fu Jinguo, general manager of the group states that "Since last year, production costs of knitting are difficult to control due to the volatile prices of cotton. Now, with our own raw materials base, we will not be affected by fluctuations in the price of cotton. Moreover, the vertical chain also allows the company to control the product quality from all aspects, thereby enhancing the quality of the final deliverables. "

(VIII) Expansion strategic change: Mergers and acquisitions strategy

A well-known case is the merger and acquisition of IBM PC division by Lenovo, which creates a miracle of a "snake" swallowing an "elephant" and assists Lenovo to leap forward into the world's top three in the PC industry as well.

Another example is Meibang textile who leaps ahead to become the global champion through mergers and reorganization. Zhejiang Meibang Textile Co., Ltd. ("Meibang Textile" for short) merges two U.S. Companies in the industrial changes due to the global economic crisis. In October 2008, "Meibang textile" and two U.S. companies sign letters of intent for their OEM. However in November, these two U.S. Companies suddenly announces the cancelation the procurement plan. At that time, along with the spread of the financial crisis, the lending banks of these two U.S. companies draw back loans, causing the liquidity predicament. In this case, "Meibang textile" buys the entire equity interest of the two U.S. companies with cash, resulting in the successful acquisition of two U.S. companies and the global industry champion position.

V. Basic steps of strategic change

1. Given the actual business, a company should self-diagnose or be diagnosed by outside brains;
2. Focusing on its own issues, a company should re-shape its philosophy and values;
3. A company should determine its new development vision;
4. A company should make strategic change planning;
5. A company should formulate workable implementation schemes;
6. A company should form project working groups to promote strategic change solely.
7. Guarantee measures of strategic change
8. Senior leaders are expected to unify understandings to commit strategic change;
9. Communication between workers and staff shall be done well to eliminate resistances to change;
10. A good horizontal coordination should be ensured in order to strengthen cooperation between departments;
11. Funds and resources needed for change fulfillment shall be prepared to meet the requirements of changing objectives;
12. A system for change progress and objectives evaluation shall be established;
13. The company shall sum up and adjust the strategy in time.

VI. Key to the success of strategic change

(I) To improve the strategic positioning

The core of strategic positioning requires a company to be clear about what it will do and to what extent. In short, the direction and objectives of the company have to be determined. This is a prerequisite for the success of strategic change. Success guru Napoleon Hill has said that "You have to know what you want to pursue in your life and determine to get it. Focus on your goals, and you will succeed. To think and plan your goals, and completely ignore other interference; this is the formula followed by all successful people. "(5) Although what he is talking is about how "people" can be successful, yet "companies are people"(by Jack Welch)" and "to run a businesses is to organize people"(Liu Chuanzhi, and Chinese entrepreneur), so his words are fully applicable to managing companies.

(II) To develop change plans

There is an old saying "Those who do not plan for the future will find trouble at their doorstep."(6) Therefore, a strategic change plan ensures the success of strategic change. The plan can be made on your own, or by the hired foreign "brains" - expert consultants, or by two parties. The last option is more conducive to benefit from each other and to make scientific, innovative, practical and operable plans.

(III) To seize the opportunities for change

Successful strategic changes cannot do without both good opportunities and people's efforts. A company is only half way there when it is able to seize a good opportunity. But the opportunity only supports the prepared mind. So whether or not a company can seize the opportunity does not depend on knowledge and experience, but depends on the courage and determination.

(IV) To strengthen the confidence of victory

A company will inevitably encounter many difficulties and obstacles at the time when it plans to make strategic changes, especially major strategic changes.
Therefore, it can succeed in change only when it strengthens the confidence of victory.

Chinese premier Wen Jiabao has said that "Confidence is more important than gold! Only confidence can lead to courage and strength, which can overcome the difficulties. With confidence, we have hope!" Confidence is a state of mind, a positive attitude, the source of the soul, and a great cornerstone. In all aspects that people have influence on, confidence can create miracles.

Napoleon Hill points out that "With confidence, you can move a mountain. As long as you believe you can succeed, you will." (7)The power of confidence is inexhaustible; it is a resource that can be reused indefinitely. Confidence is life itself, is power and miracle. Besides, it is the basis of business, as well as the success of strategic change.

(V) To remain dedicated

"To remain dedicated" requires the company adhering to the positioning of strategic change and implementing the changes in accordance with the requirements until the changes are successful. Alter the strategic positioning rashly is a taboo of reform and is also the root causing failure of strategic change.

Napoleon Hill cautions that "One should only concentrate on one thing, and throw himself into that and actively want it to succeed. Never let your mind slide into something else, other needs or other ideas. Concentrate on the important project that you have decided to do and give up all other things. Successful people focus on one thing at a time instead of distracting attentions resulting in knowing everything but mastering none."(8)

Therefore, "to remain dedicated" is a magic key to success. It can constitute an irresistible force to ensure the success of strategic change."

(VI) To carry forward the indomitable spirits of not being afraid of setbacks

Strategic change can never be smooth; it will certainly encounter many setbacks and temporary failures. In face of that, to carry forward the indomitable spirits is the key to the success of change.

Napoleon Hill warns us that "when you run into trouble, do not waste time calculating how much you suffer a loss; instead, you should calculate how much you harvest and get from the frustrations. You will find you get much more than you lose. Failure can be a stepping stone or a stumbling block depending on if your attitude is positive or negative. For those people who have a positive attitude, each adversity contains seeds with equal or greater interests. Sometimes, it is a good opportunity to masquerade in the face of adversity." (9)

Case Study

Strategic Shift of Double Star

The footwear industry is an internationally recognized industry with too little profit. Qingdao Double Star Group rises in this small profit industry after 12 years of difficult times. Its economic indicators jump to grow with an abnormal increase at rate of 30% in the nearly 3 years, and its state-owned assets appreciation also grows rapidly. By the end of 1996, its sales are expected to be RMB Yuan 2 billion, its profits and taxes are RMB Yuan 160 million, and state-owned asset appreciation will rise to RMB Yuan 1.68 billion. With the absence of a penny from the state, accumulated profits and taxes that the company has paid it can build 33 "Double Star" companies as large in 1984. It helps millions of its employee's live well-off and leads more than a hundred thousand people in rural areas out of poverty. It is the first well-known Chinese trademarked company in the footwear industry on record; the first one on the stock market, and the first one running a transnational business, and participating in international competition with overwhelming success.

To adopt brand strategy: engaging in new products

There stands a beautiful rock formation a dozen meters high in the same town as Qingdao Double Star. It is built by the Double Star employees with pebbles. Wang Hai, president of the Double Star explains the purpose of building it is to remind employees not to forget the mountainous unsalable yellow shoes.

In the early 80s of 20th century, the Double Star faces the problem of few product sales and no profits to pay wages. Wang Hai proposes a decisive plan to replace products completely.

In the difficult initial stage, Double Star invests heavily to develop the market, including introducing new production lines, adopting new technologies, new processes, new materials, and even three-dimensional computer design, and founding the first shoe research center in the country, and organizing a professional development and design team. Product design of Double Star achieves the method of "produce a generation, reserve a generation, and develop a generation." 10 years later, the Double Star finally owns a full set of professional production technology of heat curing, cold viscosity, injection, leather, cloth and sports shoes in the world. It produces shoes in six categories, with 45 series, 600 varieties, and 3000 multiple designs. It becomes the king with the feature of "new, excellent, unique and famous." Facing the challenge of foreign high-end shoes that have made inroads into the Chinese market, it strives to be the "ideal brand," "preferred shopping brand," "actual purchased brand" in people's mind. In addition, it has entered the markets of developed countries to join the global commercial war.

To establish the western strategy: to transfer to the interior

On September 9, 1996, Meng Fanwen, a 70-year-old revolutionary veteran cut the ribbon with local city and county leaders in his hometown Yishui County for the Double Star Hanhai Co., Ltd.. At that time, the second strategic shift of the Double Star, the western development strategy begins to be carried forward.

The people of Double Star in the eastern coastal areas have understood the development trend of the international footwear industry, and thus propose to allocate shoe production to the interior after preparations. This strategic shift is put forward at the time when the company is prosperous and going upward.

In 1987, the Double Star sets up its first shoe town across the Jiaozhou Bay. It is built up in the Qingdao Economic and Technological Development Zone that is under construction at that time and has always been one of the pillars of its industrial economy.

In 1989, the second shoes town - Double Star Industrial Park, is completed in Jimo City. With abundant local cheap labor, the company grows rapidly in its scale, level and quality.

In 1993, the Double Star anticipates opening up facility in the poor mountainous areas. It moves to the hinterland of Shandong Yimeng Mountain and sets up its third shoe town, Luzhong Company in Yiyuan County. For 3 years, sales revenue of Luzhong Company of Double Star has been RMB Yuan 287 million, contributing to RMB Yuan 17 million profits after taxes.

In 1996, as the fourth Double Star shoes town, the newly opened Hanhai Co., Ltd. is estimated to achieve 150 million annual output value and ten million profits after taxes. The former "women of literacy" (local title for unmarried woman) have become skilled workers in the production-line of the company.

Strategy of shifting to the interior makes the future of Double Star suddenly brighter. It not only solves development problems, but also revitalizes the local economy, driving more than hundred thousand people out of poverty. Currently, Wang Hai, the president of the Double Star Group, along with his unique contribution to poverty relief, is elected as one of the top ten "the very best in supporting the poor" this year.

To transfer to a multi-industry, establishing multifaceted strategy

The footwear industry is a processing industry with low value added and high risks due to its single business. In 90s, the Double Star starts its industrial expansion. It not only changes to focus on multi-industries giving priority to footwear, but also engages in the integration of industrial capital and financial capital in. Its industrial expansion begins with what the Double Star is familiar with. Based on the sports shoes, it produces the sportswear, sports bags and sports socks; and then it develops and produces sports drinks, healthy food and fitness exercise equipment. Double Star has currently become the most typical domestic company who produces sports products in series and in varied forms.

The third industry of the Double Star has opened for operations. The main plant has a great location within Qingdao. Along with its relocation, Double Star products town and Commercial Street rise in the old factory site with weaving visitors. Besides, Double Star resort village with a set of tourism, resort and entertainment businesses is booming. Now the Double Star Town with its unique style is becoming a new scene of Qingdao city.

Double Star is marching forward into a higher industrial level, involved in real estate, securities, and tourism, advertising, film and television transmissions. In 1995, production value of the three main industry groups of Double Star is nearly RMB Yuan 200 million, accounting for more than 13% of the gross production value. It creates new growth points for the company.

To make shoes for cars

The so-called "to make shoes for car" refers to engaging in the tire industry which belongs to rubber industry as well as the footwear industry. In 1996, Double Star puts its quality assets - cold sticky shoes business into the market successfully and is able to raises funds because of how well the firm has performed and operated. The strength of the company is expanded. However, the footwear industry has undergone new changes. Competition has become more vicious in the footwear market for reasons such as: foreign investments inroads into the Chinese market; second, individual and private companies achieving rapid development with certain growth; and third, the industry itself sets low entry barriers and pays off quickly. Meanwhile, the Double Star Group considers the traditional manufacturing and processing industry as Chinese main industry, which can solve the feeding, clothing and poverty relief problems and shoulder the important national task to remain stability and unity. So when the companies in the whole country start projects in the high-tech industry, Double Star does exactly the opposite to put the funds raised into the traditional tire industry. That acts as a new growth point for the development of the company, which begins to make shoes for cars in addition to people.

In a few short years, the Double Star enters into the tire industry as "small eats big" (merged with the original Hua Qing tire company). Then its acquisition of the former Dong Feng Tire forms a special case of "fast eat slow" and "state-owned companies eat each other" and helps Double Star, the rising star in the tire industry become bigger and stronger.

At present, the Double Star Group has set up three major tire production bases in Qingdao, Zhongyuan and Shiyan, Hubei Province. Its products involves seven major series of steel radial tires, semi-steel passenger car tire, bias truck tires, agricultural light truck tires, military tires, construction tires, and specialty tires. With more than 600 varieties, annual production capacity of 10 million sets of various tires; it ranks among the top six and receives the title of China Famous Brand. Development of the tire industry spurs the development of the foundry machinery and rubber machinery for supporting. So Double Star ranks among the best in the country in these two industries. Visibility and market share also grow rapidly.

Currently, tire manufacturing has accounted for 90% of the company revenue, while footwear production only contributes 10% of income. Tire manufacture has become the absolute main business of Double Star. Double Star has five pillar industries, eight sectors across 17 areas, and 60,000 employees. It feeds hundreds of thousands people directly or indirectly, creating huge economic and social benefits. Its total assets grew from less than 10 million in the early 80s to 6 billion and export volume increases from $ 1.75 million to $ 200 million. Besides, its pays more than RMB Yuan 3 billion of total profits and taxes in the past two decades, which is equivalent to hand in more than 300 ninth rubber plants without asking the state for financial aid. And its sales revenue increases from 30 million to 10 billion.

Source: Wang Zhaodong, Hu Kaoxu, *Economic Times*, November 2, 1996; articles reported by other media and information provided by Double Star Group.

Review

Strategic scholar Robert Waterman has said, "Most of us are afraid of change. Although we know that changes are normal, we still shake in our hearts for the changes coming. But for today's strategists and managers, you have no choice but change." (10)

So, Peter Drucker reminds us that "Tomorrow will come, and is always different from today. If you do not proceed in the future, the most powerful company will have troubles. It is dangerous to be surprised at what is happening. Even the largest and richest companies have to bear the risk; and even the smallest company should also be alert to this danger. " (11)

World renowned company strategy expert John W. Dizi has said that "The task of a strategist is not to see what a company is like today, but rather to see what kind of company it will be in the future." (12)

These experts tell us that we must first become a strategist and innovator before being a successful entrepreneur. So we must strive to focus on the future, have global visions, look forward, design good strategy, dare to change and be good at innovation.

Wang Hai has "general complex" since his childhood. He determines to grow up to be a general to serve the motherland. But fate gives him no choice but to abandon his main dream. Strange combinations of circumstances transfer him to be civilian and make him create the famous double star. His dream comes true. Military career makes him know well of art of war, and apply strategic and tactical skills of "military warfare" to "commercial war" with impressive results.

Wang Hai often warns his team to think of how the company should develop in the next 10 years. So he often makes sets new strategic decisions at critical moments when the business is growing and people are confused. For example, brand strategy, out of the city strategy, countryside strategy, uphill strategy, going west strategy, diversification strategy, car "shoes" strategy, and so on. It is under the guidance of these strategies that Double Star grows into a large company with a "big double star" strategy pattern.

In short, change is innovation. Just as management guru Thomas Peters has said, "Innovate or perish!" (13)

Questions

1. What are the significances of strategic change?
2. What are the motivations of strategic change?
3. What are the types of strategic change?
4. What are the models of strategic change?
5. What are the basic steps of strategic change?
6. What are the guarantee measures of strategic change?
7. What are the key to success of strategic change?
8. Try to guide strategic change of your company referring to strategic change theories and methods.

Notes

⑴ 〔U.S.〕 Jack Welch & John Byrne, *JACK: STRAIGHT FROM THE GUT The Autobiography*, 1st edition, CITIC Press, 2001, p. 389.
⑵ 〔U.S.〕 Jack Welch & John Byrne, *JACK: STRAIGHT FROM THE GUT The Autobiography*, 1st edition, CITIC Press, 2001, p. 393.
⑶ Zhang Xiuyu, Facing Challenge : *How Enterprises Enhance Inner Strength*, 1st edition, China City Press, June,1996. P.166.
⑷ 〔U.S.〕 Jack Welch & John Byrne, *JACK: STRAIGHT FROM THE GUT The Autobiography*, 1st edition, CITIC Press, 2001, p. 401-403.
⑸ Zhang Xiuyu, *How to be successful*, 1st edition, Enterprise Management Press, January 2005, p. 22.
⑹ Confucius & Mercies, *The Analects Of Confucius and The Mercies*, 1st edition, Beijing: People's Literature Publishing House, February, 2008, p.189.
⑺ Zhang Xiuyu, *How to be successful*, 1st edition, Enterprise Management Press, January 2005, p. 76.
⑻ Zhang Xiuyu, *How to be successful*, 1st edition, Enterprise Management Press, January 2005, p. 150.
⑼ Zhang Xiuyu, *How to be successful*, 1st edition, Enterprise Management Press, January 2005, p. 288.
⑽ 〔U.S.〕 Fred. R. David, *Strategic Management*, Li Kening trans., 1st

edition, Economic Science Press, June 1998, p.16.

⑾ 〔U.S.〕 Fred. R. David, *Strategic Management*, Li Kening trans., 1st edition, Economic Science Press, June 1998, p.63.

⑿ 〔U.S.〕 Fred. R. David, *Strategic Management*, Li Kening trans., 1st edition, Economic Science Press, June 1998, p.98.

⒀ Zhang Xiuyu, Facing Challenge : *How Enterprises Enhance Inner Strength*, 1st edition, China City Press, June, 1996, p.145.

BIBLIOGRAPHY

〔U.S.〕 Jack Welch & John Byrne, *JACK: STRAIGHT FROM THE GUT The Autobiography*, 1st edition, CITIC Press, 2001.

〔U.S.〕 Napoleon Hill, *Everyone Can Be Successful*, 2nd edition, Hubei People's Publishing House in February 2001.

Zhang Xiuyu, *How to be successful*, 1st edition, Enterprise Management Press, January 2005

〔 U.S. 〕 Peter Drucker, *Management: Tasks, Responsibilities, Practice*,1st edition, China Social Sciences Press, June 1987.

〔U.S.〕 Michael Porter & Gary Hamel, *The Future of Strategy Management*, 1st Edition, Sichuan People's Publishing House, April 2000.

〔U.S.〕 Arthur Thompson, Stickrod, *Strategic Management: Concepts and Cases*, 10th ed, Duan Shenghua, Wang Zhihui trans., Xu Erming revision, Peking University Press, 2004.

〔U.S.〕 Fred. R. David, *Strategic Management*, Li Kening trans., 1st edition, Economic Science Press, June 1998.

〔CAN.〕 Henry Mintzberg, *Strategy Safari*, 2nd edition, Machinery Industry Press, June 2006.

Editing group of required MBA core courses, *Business Strategy*, 1st edition, China International Radio Press, September 1997.

Editing group of required MBA core courses, *Business Strategy*, 1st edition revision, China International Radio Press, 2000.

Chiang Yuntong ed, *Company Operation Strategic Management*, 1st edition, Company Management Press, April 1996.

Confucius & Mercies, *The Analects Of Confucius and The Mercies*, 1st edition, Beijing: People's Literature Publishing House, February, 2008.

Zhang Xiuyu, Facing Challenge: *How Enterprises Enhance Inner Strength*, 1st edition, China City Press, June, 1996.

CHAPTER 15

Red Ocean Strategy and Blue Ocean Strategy

Abstract

This chapter begins with the famous saying "The fool make profits today, while the wise do it tomorrow", to confirm the necessity of adopting a blue ocean strategy instead of red ocean strategy. Then, it defines the red ocean strategy and blue ocean strategy and explains the differences between them. Afterwards, it details the cornerstone of the blue ocean strategy; six principles of formulating and executing the strategy, four action frameworks, the right strategic sequence and three characteristics of a good strategy. Finally, it has appendix of cases and comments of "Father of China's silica sand industry - Qin Shengyi."

Learning Objectives

- To define the concepts and differences of red ocean strategy and blue ocean strategy
- To correctly understand the cornerstone of blue ocean strategy
- To understand and grasp six principles of formulating and executing blue ocean strategy
- To understand and grasp four action frameworks and the right strategic sequence
- To understand and grasp three characteristics of a good strategy
- Try to guide the company's strategic innovation referring to blue ocean strategy

Introduction

There is a famous business saying "The fool make profits today, while the wise do it tomorrow." which does make sense. In a rapidly changing market, the one who plans to win in the future can get the initiative to allocate market resources. A market economy is like a wild horse. Companies that can tame it will lead the competition, while companies that can't, fail and collapse. Therefore, companies cannot merely adopt a red ocean strategy to fight for cost leadership, price and differentiation. Instead, they shall have a sense of awareness and crisis, make long term planning, and take measures in advance to deal with predicaments that may appear in the future. In short, they shall create a blue ocean breaking out of the red ocean.

Lesson

There is a famous business saying "The fool make profits today, while the wise do it tomorrow." which does make sense. In a rapidly changing market, the one who plans to win in the future can get the initiative to allocate market resources. A market economy is like a wild horse. Companies that can tame it will lead the competition, while companies that can't, fail and collapse. Therefore, companies cannot merely adopt a red ocean strategy to fight for cost leadership, price and differentiation. Instead, they shall have a sense of awareness and crisis, make long term planning, and take measures in advance to deal with predicaments that may appear in the future. In short, they shall create a blue ocean breaking out of the red ocean.

I.   Concepts of Red Ocean Strategy and Blue Ocean Strategy

In order to achieve lasting profitable growth, companies tend to be diametrically opposed to their rivals. Therefore, they try to fight for competitive advantages, for market shares and for diversity. However, in the current overcrowding industrial market, head-to-head competition can only lead companies to the bloody red ocean, where companies try to grab a greater share of the already shrinking demand in a highly competitive market space. This kind of strategy is called "red ocean strategy." Blue ocean strategy, in contrast, is a strategy to innovate values. That is, in order to win in the future, companies need to go beyond intensely competing and to create "Blue Oceans," a new market space to seize new profit and growth opportunities. It can enable the company to create a leap in value and thereby opening up new and uncontested market space.

To put it simply, the market universe is composed of two sorts of oceans: red oceans and blue oceans. Red oceans represent all the industries in existence today. This is the known market space. Blue oceans denote all the industries not in existence today. This is the unknown market space.

As the existing market space gets crowded due to new rivals, prospects for profits and growth are reduced. In that case cutthroat competition between companies turns the red ocean bloody. So this kind of strategy is called "red ocean strategy."

In the unknown market, due to none or few rivals, there is little competition for market share. In that case, the market is just like a vast boundless blue ocean. So this strategy is called "blue ocean strategy."

II. Value Innovation: The Cornerstone of Blue Ocean Strategy

Although the term blue ocean is new, their existence is not. They are a feature of business life, past and present. Many industries as basic as automobiles, music recording, aviation, petrochemicals, health care, and management consulting are unheard of or have just been around for a hundred years or more. Now turn the clock back thirty years. Again, a plethora of multibillion-dollar industries jumps out—mutual funds, cell phones, gas-fired electricity plants, biotechnology, discount retail, express package delivery, minivans, snowboards, coffee bars, and home videos, to name a few. Just three decades ago, none of these industries existed in a meaningful way. Now move the clock forward twenty years—or perhaps fifty years—and how many now unknown industries will likely exist then. If history is any predictor of the future, again the answer is many of them.

The reality is that industries never stand still. They continuously evolve. Operations improve, markets expand, and players come and go. History teaches us that we have a hugely underestimated capacity to create new industries and re-create existing ones. Just like W. Chan Kim and Renée Mauborgne have said in the preface of Blue Ocean Strategy, "Our research confirms that there are no permanently excellent companies, just as there are no permanently excellent industries. As we have found on our own tumbling road, we, like corporations, do smart things and less-than-smart things. To improve the quality of our success we need to study what we did that made a positive difference and understand how to replicate it systematically. That is what we call making smart strategic moves, and we have found that the strategic move that matters centrally is to create blue oceans. Blue ocean opportunities have been out there. As they have been explored, the market universe has been expanding. This expansion, we believe, is the root of growth. " (Korea) W. Chan Kim, (U.S.) Renée Mauborgne, Blue Ocean Strategy, 1st edition, Commercial Press, 2005, p. vi-vii.

Yet the overriding focus of strategic thinking has been on competition-based red ocean strategies. Part of the explanation for this is that corporate strategy is heavily influenced by its roots in military strategy. Described that way, strategy is about confronting an opponent and fighting over a given piece of land that is both limited and constant. Unlike war, however, the history of industry shows us that the market universe has never been constant; rather, blue oceans have continuously been created over time. To focus on the red ocean is therefore to accept the key constraining factors of war—limited terrain and the need to beat an enemy to succeed—and to deny the distinctive strength of the business world: the capacity to create new market space that is uncontested.

What consistently separated winners from losers in creating blue oceans is their approach to strategy. The companies caught in the red ocean follow a conventional approach, racing to beat the competition by building a defensible position within the existing industry order. The creators of blue oceans, on the contrary, don't use the competition as their benchmark. Instead, they follow a different strategic logic that we call value innovation. Value innovation is the cornerstone of blue ocean strategy. We call it value innovation because instead of focusing on beating the competition, you focus on making the competition irrelevant by creating a leap in value for buyers and your company, thereby opening up new and uncontested market space.

Value innovation places equal emphasis on value and innovation. Value without innovation tends to focus on value creation on an incremental scale, something that improves value but is not sufficient to make you stand out in the marketplace. Innovation without value tends to be technology-driven, market pioneering, or futuristic, often shooting beyond what buyers are ready to accept and pay for. In this sense, it is important to distinguish between value innovation as opposed to technology innovation and market pioneering. Our study shows that what separates winners from losers in creating blue oceans is neither bleeding-edge technology nor "timing for market entry." Sometimes these exist; more often, however, they do not. Value innovation occurs only when companies align innovation with utility, price, and cost positions. If they fail to anchor innovation with value in this way, technology innovators and market pioneers often lay the eggs that other companies hatch.

Value innovation is a new way of thinking about and executing strategy that results in the creation of a blue ocean and a break from the competition.

Importantly, value innovation defies one of the most commonly accepted dogmas of competition-based strategy: the value-cost trade-off. It is conventionally believed that companies can either create greater value to customers at a higher cost or create reasonable value at a lower cost. Here strategy is seen as making a choice between differentiation and low cost. In contrast, those that seek to create blue oceans pursue differentiation and low cost simultaneously.

Figure 15-1 depicts the differentiation–low cost dynamics underpinning value innovation.

Figure 15-1 Value Innovation: The Cornerstone of Blue Ocean Strategy

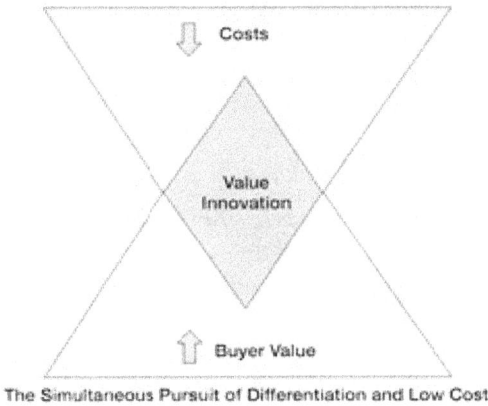

Costs

Value Innovation

Buyer Value

The Simultaneous Pursuit of Differentiation and Low Cost

Source: (Korea) W. Chan Kim, (U.S.) Renée Mauborgne, *Blue Ocean Strategy*, 1st edition, Commercial Press, 2005, p. 19.

As shown in Figure 15-1, the creation of blue oceans is about driving costs down while simultaneously driving value up for buyers. This is how a leap in value for both the company and its buyers is achieved. Because buyer value comes from the utility and price that the company offers to buyers and because the value to the company is generated from price and its cost structure, value innovation is achieved only when the whole system of the company's utility, price, and cost activities is properly aligned. It is this whole-system approach that makes the creation of blue oceans a sustainable strategy. Blue ocean strategy integrates the range of a firm's functional and operational activities.

457

III.   Red Ocean versus Blue Ocean Strategy

There are many differences between red and blue ocean strategies. Table 15-1 outlines the key defining features of them.

Table 15-1 Red Ocean versus Blue Ocean Strategy

Red Ocean Strategy	Blue Ocean Strategy
Compete in existing market space	Create uncontested market space
Beat the competition	Make the competition irrelevant
Exploit existing demand	Create and capture new demand
Make the value-cost trade-off	Break the value-cost trade-off
Align the whole system of a firm's activities with its strategic choice of differentiation or low cost.	Align the whole system of a firm's activities in pursuit of differentiation and low cost.

Source: (Korea) W. Chan Kim,   (U.S.) Renée Mauborgne, *Blue Ocean Strategy*, 1st edition, Commercial Press, 2005, p. 20.

IV.   The Six Principles of Formulating and Executing Blue Ocean Strategy

Although imperatives of blue oceans are rising, there is a general belief that the odds of success are lower when companies venture beyond existing industry space. The issue is how to succeed in blue oceans. How can companies systematically maximize the opportunities while simultaneously minimizing the risks of formulating and executing blue ocean strategy? If you lack an understanding of the opportunity-maximizing and risk-minimizing principles driving the creation and capture of blue oceans, the odds will be increased against your blue ocean initiative.

Of course, there is no such thing as a riskless strategy. Strategy will always involve both opportunity and risk, be it a red ocean or a blue ocean initiative. But at present the playing field is dramatically unbalanced in favor of tools and analytical frameworks to succeed in red oceans. As long as this remains true, red oceans will continue to dominate companies' strategic agenda even as the business imperative for creating blue oceans takes on new urgency. Perhaps this explains why, despite prior calls for companies to go beyond existing industry space, companies have yet to act seriously on these recommendations.

In order to address this imbalance, Professor W. Chan Kim and Professor Renée Mauborgne from the European Institute of Business Administration present the six principles and analytical frameworks to succeed in blue oceans in their book Blue Ocean Strategy after 20 years of research. Table 15-2 highlights the six principles driving the successful formulation and execution of blue ocean strategy and the risks that these principles attenuate. This book merely makes a brief introduction to main contents of a Blue Ocean Strategy, and readers interested can read the original. As the two professors hope to accomplishment in the preface of that book, "if you want to make a difference, to create a company that builds a future where customers, employees, shareholders, and society win, read on. We are not saying it is easy, but it is worthwhile. " [Korea] W. Chan Kim, [U.S.] Renée Mauborgne, *Blue Ocean Strategy*, 1st edition, Commercial Press, 2005, p. v—vi.

Table 15-2 Six Principles of Blue Ocean Strategy

Formulation principles	Risk factor each principle attenuates
Reconstruct market boundaries	↓ Search risk
Focus on the big picture, not the numbers	↓ Planning risk
Reach beyond existing demand	↓ Scale risk
Get the strategic sequence right	↓ Business model risk
Execution principles	Risk factor each principle attenuates
Overcome key organizational hurdles	↓ Organizational risk
Build execution into strategy	↓ Management risk

Source: [Korea] W. Chan Kim, [U.S.] Renée Mauborgne, *Blue Ocean Strategy*, 1st edition, Commercial Press, 2005, p. 25.

V.　Four Action Framework of Blue Ocean Strategy

To fundamentally shift the strategy canvas of an industry, companies must begin by reorienting their strategic focus from competitors to alternatives, and from customers to noncustomers of the industry. Alternatives are broader than substitutes. Consider cinemas versus restaurants. Restaurants serve as alternatives of cinemas. Although restaurants are not direct competitors and not substitutes serving a distinct function, yet they can take away people who want to enjoy a night out, and these people are potential buyers of cinemas tickets. There are three tiers of noncustomers that can be transformed into customers. First Tier: "Soon-to-be" noncustomers who are on the edge of your market, waiting to jump ship. Second Tier: "Refusing" noncustomers who consciously choose against your market. Third Tier: "Unexplored" noncustomers who are in markets distant from yours.

To pursue both value and cost, you should resist the old logic of benchmarking competitors in the existing field and choosing between differentiation and cost leadership. As you shift your strategic focus from current competition to alternatives and noncustomers, you gain insight into how to redefine the problem the industry focuses on and thereby reconstruct buyer value elements that reside across industry boundaries. Conventional strategic logic, by contrast, drives you to offer better solutions than your rivals to existing problems defined by your industry.

To reconstruct buyer value elements in crafting a new value curve, Professor W. Chan Kim and Professor Renée Mauborgne have developed the four actions framework. As shown in Figure 15-2 Four Actions Framework.

Figure 15-2 The Four Actions Framework.

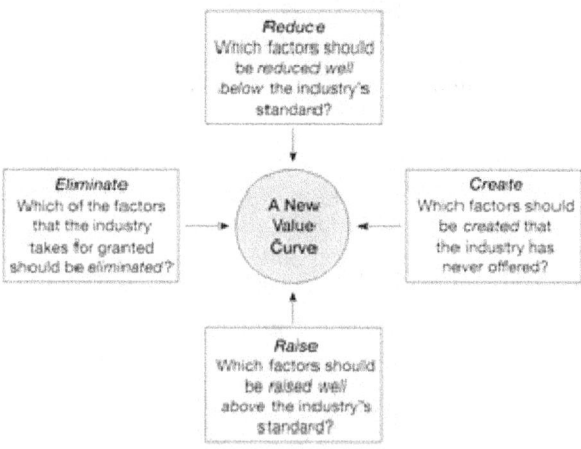

Reduce
Which factors should be reduced well below the industry's standard?

Eliminate
Which of the factors that the industry takes for granted should be eliminated?

A New Value Curve

Create
Which factors should be created that the industry has never offered?

Raise
Which factors should be raised well above the industry's standard?

Source: 〔Korea〕 W. Chan Kim, 〔U.S.〕 Renée Mauborgne, *Blue Ocean Strategy*, 1st edition, Commercial Press, 2005, p. 34.

As shown in Figure 15-2, to break the trade-off between differentiation and low cost and to create a new value curve, there are four key questions to challenge an industry's strategic logic and business model:

Which of the factors that the industry takes for granted should be eliminated?

Which factors should be reduced well below the industry's standard?

Which factors should be raised well above the industry's standard?

Which factors should be created that the industry has never offered?

The first question forces you to consider eliminating factors that companies in your industry have long competed on. Often those factors are taken for granted even though they no longer have value. Sometimes there is a fundamental change in what buyers' value, but companies that are focused on benchmarking one another do not act on, or even perceive, the change.

The second question forces you to determine whether products or services have been overdesigned in the race to match and beat the competition. Here, companies over serve customers, increasing their cost structure for no gain.

The third question pushes you to uncover and eliminate the compromises your industry forces customers to make.

The fourth question helps you to discover entirely new sources of value for buyers and to create new demand and shift the strategic pricing of the industry.

It is by pursuing the first two questions (of eliminating and reducing) that you gain insight into how to drop your cost structure vis-à-vis competitors. The second two factors, by contrast, provide you with insight into how to lift buyer value and create new demand. Collectively, they allow you to systematically explore how you can reconstruct buyer value elements across alternative industries to offer buyers an entirely new experience, while simultaneously keeping your cost structure low. Of particular importance are the actions of eliminating and creating, which push companies to go beyond value maximization exercises with existing factors of competition. Eliminating and creating prompt companies to change the factors themselves, hence making the existing rules of competition irrelevant.

VI.   Three Characteristics of a Good Strategy

Among companies that have successfully formulated and implemented blue ocean strategy, Southwest Airlines is a model who creates a unique and exceptional value curve to unlock a blue ocean. A look at Southwest Airlines' strategic profile illustrates three complementary qualities: focus, divergence, and a compelling tagline. Southwest Airlines created a blue ocean by breaking the trade-offs customers had to make between the speed of airplanes and the economy and flexibility of car transport. Here Southwest Airlines' strategy is taken as an example to explain three characteristics of a good strategy.

(I) Focus

Every great strategy has focus, and a company's strategic profile, or value curve, should clearly show it. Southwest emphasizes only three factors: friendly service, speed, and frequent point-to-point departures. By focusing in this way, Southwest has been able to price against car transportation; it doesn't make extra investments in meals, lounges, and seating choices. By contrast, Southwest's traditional competitors invest in all the airline industry's competitive factors, making it much more difficult for them to match Southwest's prices. Investing across the board, these companies let their competitors' moves set their own agendas. Costly business models result.

(II) Divergence

When a company's strategy is formed reactively as it tries to keep up with the competition, it loses its uniqueness. There are similarities in most airlines' meals and business-class lounges. On the strategy canvas, therefore, reactive strategists tend to share the same strategic profile. In contrast, the value curves of blue ocean strategists always stand apart. By applying the four actions of eliminating, reducing, raising, and creating, they differentiate their profiles from the industry's average profile. Southwest, for example, pioneered point-to-point travel between midsize cities; previously, the industry operated through hub-and-spoke systems.

(III) Compelling Tagline

A good strategy has a clear-cut and compelling tagline. "The speed of a plane at the price of a car—whenever you need it." That's the tagline of

Southwest Airlines. What could Southwest's competitors say? Even the most proficient ad agency would have difficulty reducing the conventional offering of lunches, seat choices, lounges, and hub links, with standard service, slower speeds, and higher prices into a memorable tagline. A good tagline must not only deliver a clear message but also advertise an offering truthfully, or else customers will lose trust and interest. In fact, a good way to test the effectiveness and strength of a strategy is to look at whether it contains a strong and authentic tagline.

With these qualities, a company's strategy tends to succeed easier; otherwise, it will likely be muddled, undifferentiated, and hard to communicate with a high cost structure. The four actions of creating a new value curve should be well guided toward building a company's strategic profile with these characteristics. These three characteristics serve as an initial litmus test of the commercial viability of blue ocean ideas.

VII.   Get the Strategic Sequence Right

You've discovered possible blue oceans. You've constructed a strategy canvas that clearly articulates your future blue ocean strategy. And you have explored how to aggregate the largest possible mass of buyers for your idea. The next challenge is to build a robust business model to ensure that you make a healthy profit on your blue ocean idea. This brings us to the fourth principle of blue ocean strategy: Get the strategic sequence right. It can ensure the strategy's commercial viability and dramatically reduce business model risk.

As shown in Figure 15-3, companies need to build their blue ocean strategy in the sequence of buyer utility, price, cost, and adoption.

The starting point is buyer utility. Does your offering unlock exceptional utility? Is there a compelling reason for the mass of people to buy it? Absent this, there is no blue ocean potential to begin with. Here there are only two options. Park the idea, or rethink it until you reach an affirmative answer.

Figure 15-3 The Sequence of Blue Ocean Strategy

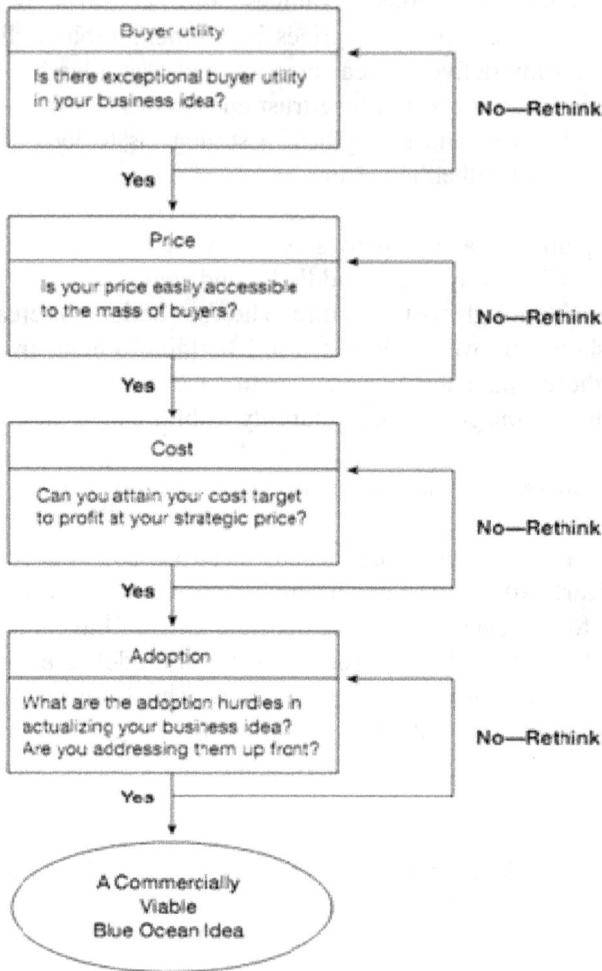

```
┌─────────────────────────────────┐
│          Buyer utility          │
├─────────────────────────────────┤
│ Is there exceptional buyer utility │ ◄──────────┐
│ in your business idea?          │              │   No—Rethink
└─────────────────────────────────┘              │
                │                                 │
              Yes ├───────────────────────────────┘
                ▼
┌─────────────────────────────────┐
│              Price              │
├─────────────────────────────────┤
│ Is your price easily accessible │ ◄──────────┐
│ to the mass of buyers?          │              │   No—Rethink
└─────────────────────────────────┘              │
                │                                 │
              Yes ├───────────────────────────────┘
                ▼
┌─────────────────────────────────┐
│              Cost               │
├─────────────────────────────────┤
│ Can you attain your cost target │ ◄──────────┐
│ to profit at your strategic price? │           │   No—Rethink
└─────────────────────────────────┘              │
                │                                 │
              Yes ├───────────────────────────────┘
                ▼
┌─────────────────────────────────┐
│            Adoption             │
├─────────────────────────────────┤
│ What are the adoption hurdles in │ ◄──────────┐
│ actualizing your business idea?  │             │   No—Rethink
│ Are you addressing them up front? │            │
└─────────────────────────────────┘              │
                │                                 │
              Yes ├───────────────────────────────┘
                ▼
          ╭───────────────╮
          │ A Commercially │
          │    Viable     │
          │ Blue Ocean Idea │
          ╰───────────────╯
```

Source: 〔Korea〕 W. Chan Kim, 〔U.S.〕 Renée Mauborgne, *Blue Ocean Strategy*, 1st edition, Commercial Press, 2005, p. 132.

When you clear the exceptional utility bar, you advance to the second step: setting the right strategic price. Remember, a company does not want to rely solely on price to create demand. The key question here is this: Is your offering priced to attract the mass of target buyers so that they have a compelling ability to pay for your offering? If it is not, they cannot buy it. Nor will the offering create irresistible market buzz.

These first two steps address the revenue side of a company's business model. They ensure that you create a leap in net buyer value, where net buyer value equals the utility buyers receive minus the price they pay for it.

Securing the profit side brings us to the third element: cost. Can you produce your offering at the target cost and still earn a healthy profit margin? Can you profit at the strategic price—the price easily accessible to the mass of target buyers? You should not let costs drive prices. Nor should you scale down utility because high costs block your ability to profit at the strategic price. When the target cost cannot be met, you must either forgo the idea because the blue ocean won't be profitable, or you must create your business model to hit the target cost. The cost side of a company's business model ensures that it creates a leap in value for itself in the form of profit—that is, the price of the offering minus the cost of production. It is the combination of exceptional utility, strategic pricing, and target costing that allows companies to achieve value innovation—a leap in value for both buyers and companies.

The last step is to address adoption hurdles. What are the adoption hurdles in rolling out your idea? Have you addressed these up front? The formulation of blue ocean strategy is complete only when you can address adoption hurdles in the beginning to ensure the successful actualization of your idea. Adoption hurdles include, for example, potential resistance to the idea by retailers or partners. Because blue ocean strategies represent a significant departure from red oceans, it is key to addressing adoption hurdles up front.

Case Study

Father of silica sand industry in China - Qin Shengyi

As early as 1984, the dean of China's scientific community Qian Xuesen has proposed the concept "sand industry." He believes that "barren land" in China like desert can be transformed into oasis by the development of knowledge-intensive agriculture-based industries with the assistance of modern technology and photosynthesis to converse solar energy directly. At present, this theory is becoming a reality. Rechsand Technology Group, led by Qin Shengyi, also comes up with the idea of "silica sand industry," which is remarked by Cheng Jinpei, Vice Minister of Science and Technology Department as industrial-type "silica sand industry." That is, sand is processed into a variety of technologies and products beneficial to humans through technological innovation. In this way, technology is applied in sand control, turning waste into wealth.

I.   Overview and Values of Rechsand Silica Sand Industry

Rechsand Technology Group comes from Beijing Great Wall New Technology Development Company, which was founded in 1993. It now is a high-tech company engaging in technology, industry and trade in Zhongguancun National Innovation Model Park. It is also in the first batch of national innovative companies and building unit of "State Key Laboratory of Silica Sand Resources Utilization." Through 20 years of aeolian sand comprehensive utilization innovation, the company has succeeded in solving technical problems in the desert. It explores new ways to control desertification represented by using silica sand to control flood, to increase petroleum and to do investment casting. Thus a green and recyclable industrial-type silica sand industry is formed. The company makes an outstanding contribution to help ease the three major global problems: desertification, water shortages, and energy depletion that have long plagued the society. After 20 years of struggle, Rechsand silica sand industry grows out of nothing and becomes mature step by step. Efforts have been made to lead it to be a movie today. It develops new technology, applies it to make new products, and then changes its strategy from producing to industrialization, marketization, and efficacy. Due to that, it can show remarkable new looks and new features nowadays.

(I) Notable results of independent innovation

Persevering independent innovation in aeolian sand comprehensive utilization, Rechsand Technology Group has developed more than 100 original scientific research results, 83 pending patents, 33 granted patents, and more than 40 proprietary technologies. Besides that, three of these receive national awards such as State Invention Award and China Patent Golden Award; four of these win provincial and ministerial prizes like the

First-grade Ministerial Scientific and Technological Prize. It also draws up 4 industrial standards and participates in a national public law making.

(II) International leading technologies

466

Rechsand Technology Group works out a number of worldwide technical problems in aeolian sand utilization and develops new technologies and products. Even advanced industrial countries like the United States and Russia haven't resolved those problems. It is the first to replace zircon sand with silica sand and use it in processing precise casting coated sand technologies and products which is resistant to elevated temperatures. It is the first to develop selective and supportive technologies and products which can bring substantial increases in petroleum production and reduction of water content. Besides, it is the first to apply technologies through which aeolian sand is used as raw material to produce permeable sand brick. Moreover, it is also the first to create a rainwater utilization system which contains a whole set of rainwater collection, filtering, storage, preservation, and recycling.

(III) Continuously improved innovation system

Combining traditional culture with modern technology, Rechsand Technology Group sets a unique system of independent innovation after exploring innovative laws and building new models. A "Rechsand pipeline pattern innovation mode" is formed as well. First, its innovation process is divided into five parts: "Create - Test - Pilot - Industrialize - Marketing"; and appropriate organizational structures are established. Next, integration innovation system covering technology, industry and trade and internal marketization operation mechanism are founded. Then, a complete management system is set up.

(IV) Accelerate development of independent industrialization

Currently, Rechsand Technology Group has owned three progressions of silica sand product: Coasted Sand, Fu Sheng Sand and Sheng Tai Sand.

First, coated sand is a new precise casting material made of aeolian sand through "silica sand casting." There are 10 types of 36 series products of this kind. A series of scientific research is made, upgrading the traditional casting materials. More than 97% of key castings of local-produced automotive engine are made by Rechsand coated sand.
Second, Fu Sheng selective sand is a new fracture propane made of aeolian sand. With characteristics of petroleum transparent and water impermeable, it aims to increase petroleum production. This technology, as well as the products, is entitled "a revolution in petroleum propane field." by experts of

petroleum industry. According to the application in oilfields like Daqing Oilfield, Shengli Oilfield and East China Branch Company of Sinopec, an average increase of petroleum production is more than 15% of the original.

Third, Shengtai sand is a new type of permeable material made of aeolian sand. Typical products are: sand-based permeable bricks, sand-based rainwater harvesting systems, and sand-based filtration membrane. It initially realizes to "control flood through silica sand." Science and Technology Department of the Ministry of Construction P.R.China assesses that "water penetration theory and molding methods of Sheng Tai permeable sand brick are the national initiative." It solves the worldwide problem of permeability, filtration, purification and storage of fresh water. Besides, it also provides systemic technical solutions for agricultural irrigation. It also has been successfully applied to the Olympic project, Zhongnanhai office zone, and Chang'an Avenue reconstruction projects for the sixtieth anniversary of National Day.

Recently, it succeeds in turning aeolian sand in the desert into breathable impermeable sand, an ecological waterproof and breathable material. It makes it possible to address the knotty global problem that desert plan is difficult to survive. If it is solved, then the desert can become an oasis.

Next, the company will take a couple of planned steps to put more than 100 inventions into production. It will process aeolian sand into furniture, eco-housing, high-speed roads and other silica sand products.

(V) Significant economic and social benefits

Successful development and application of products like coated sand, Fu Sheng sand, Sheng Tai sand and other products contribute a lot. For example, it makes use of aeolian sand, not only enhances petroleum recovery and reduces the water content, but also uses rainwater and improves the urban ecological environment. It plays a positive role in energy-saving, emission-reduction and regional economy promoting. In addition, it pushes forward the structure adjustment and upgrading of relevant industries, creating huge economic benefits. In the last 3 years, it achieves more than 100% of the annual sales growth and owns 95% of the market share. Currently, a new industrial chain has been formed, which consists of aeolian sand mining, transportation, processing, and application. Thus a new economic growth point of silica sand industry is created, followed by the related regional economic developments and significant economic, social and environmental benefits.

In short, emerging Rechsand silica sands industry takes sand in the desert as raw material, and transforms it into useful technology and products through innovation. It has the characteristics of "low input, high output, low consumption, less emissions, recyclable and sustainable," which not only meet the requirements of low-carbon economic development, but also meet that of ecological civilization. It has a long chain, and products in the chain are highly associated; besides, it offers wide range of employment, and brings more benefits with investment. Due to that, a new industry whose expected output value can reach one trillion RMB Yuan, that is, China's industrial sand industry can be cultivated. From the foregoing, the creation and development course of Rechsand silica sand industry is the miniature of that of China's silica sand industry.

II.   Qin Shengyi and silica sand industry in China

In 1984, Qin Shengyi graduates from Nanjing Institute of Mechanical Engineering As a secondary school student, major in casting. Later he studies philosophy in college on the job, studies law and business administration at the university, getting a master's degree. In 2002, he graduates from School of Management, Beijing University, major in Master of Business Administration (EMBA). Currently, he is the chairman and president of Beijing Rechsand Technology Group Co., Ltd., and the president of Beijing Rechsand Technology Research Institute. Besides, he has been awarded many honorary titles such as "Professorial Senior Engineer," "Casting Expert," "National Outstanding Professional and Technical Personnel," "Builder of Socialism in China," "Expert with Special Government Allowances," and "Invited Entrepreneurs of 60th Anniversary National Day Ceremony." He has served as a member of the standing committee of the eighth CPPCC, council member of committee of departments under the national association of industry and commerce, vice-president of Haidian District association of industry and commerce and part-time professor of Beijing University of Technology.

In 1984, Qin Shengyi begins to concentrate on sand study and develops covered sand technology in 1986, which wins the "Third-grade Technology Progress Award of Ministry of Machinery." In 1990, he develops products adopting "high-temperature coated sand technology" independently, which fills the gaps in the international foundry industry and wins "First-grade Science and Technology Prize of Ministry of Machinery and Electronic." In

1991, his "shell-shape casting high-temperature coated sand technology" wins the "National Invention Award." In 2003, his special technology of "coated sand configuration process" wins the "Gold Prize of National Invention Patent." In addition, he creatively comes up with "eggshell breakage-proof principle," and successfully produces new petroleum compression fracture propane - FSS, which has been identified by the Beijing Science and Technology Commission as technology reaching the international advanced level. In 2005, leading the Rechsand Group R & D team, he finds a new permeable method after 7 years of study. Permeability cannot just depend on the gap; instead, it can be realized by destroying the surface tension of water. Based on that, he develops excellent permeable snow-thawing and anti-skid Sheng Tai permeable sand brick or rock which uses the desert sand as raw material. It fills the gaps at home and abroad and provides a solution for urban storm floods and water shortages. Moreover, he also produces these kinds of products and has applied the technology and products into the construction of some Olympic venues like the Water Cube, Bird's Nest, National Stadium and Fengtai Softball Field.

Qin Shengyi is the founder of silica sand industry in China, and of Beijing Rechsand Technology Group. Starting from three small cottages and one big iron pot, he has developed the company into a high-tech group after 14 years. Now the company owns six subsidiaries and a research institute, engaging in technology, industry and trade. It is also in the first batch of national innovative companies. Under his leadership; people of Rechsand take obscure and harmful sand as their object of study. Through technical innovation, they have developed more than 60 research results that wholly own independent intellectual property rights, including more than 30 patents. These technologies have won many honors like the National Invention Award, Gold Prize of National Invention Patent, First-grade Ministerial Scientific and Technological Prize. They are also been used in production and form three major series of industrial silica sand products: coated sand for machinery manufacturing, Fu Sheng sand for petroleum mining and Sheng Tai sand as ecological building material. Desertification prevention in the past turns into scientific utilization of sand; it improves the relationship between human and nature. The new emerging silica sand industry shows broad prospects for development. It also realizes the dream or turning waste into treasure in order to make a more beautiful life. The establishment of silica sand industry in China has achieved enormous economic and social benefits, and been fully affirmed and highly praised by the community and official leaders such as president Hu Jintao, premier Wen Jiabao, Wu Bangguo, the chairman of the Standing Committee of the

National People's Congress, and Jia Qinglin, the chairman of the Chinese People's Political Consultative Conference. Qin Shengyi is well deserved the title of "the father of China's sand industry."

III.   Turning waste into treasure

So far, Qin Shengyi, as well as people of Rechsand Technology Group, have committed to research of the natural silica sand for more than 20 years. Relying on independent innovation and integration of technology, industry and trade, they develop relevant diversity of silica sand industry and produce three major silica sand products.

(I) Coated sand technology - technological achievements in machinery manufacturing

Coated sand technology for precise casting is one that wholly owns independent intellectual property rights in the machinery manufacturing field. Qin Shengyi, the inventor, boldly uses silica sand in the desert which is worth 10 RMB Yuan a ton to replace imported zircon sand which worth 7 000 RMB Yuan. He invents special performance additives, and then creates a new coasted sand configuration process. Depending on these bases, he develops a high-temperature coated sand with excellent overall performance. This research result applies for 16 patents on process, materials and equipment, including 8 innovation patents and 8 practical model patents, of which 15 have been authorized and have won a number of technology awards and invention awards at national, provincial and local levels. Its products have been widely used in major domestic car manufacturers. Besides, the company cooperates with Changchun FAW, and Dongfeng Motor Company, setting up a coated sand production base. This successfully resolves the domestic production problems of automotive engine castings.

(II) Fu Sheng sand technology - technological achievements in petroleum compression fracture propane

Fu Sheng sand technology is also a new fracturing technology that wholly owns independent intellectual property right in petroleum compression fracture propane field. Its main inventor Qin Shengyi creatively puts forward the "shell theory," and developed resin coating propane technology which uses silica sand as aggregate. It now has become a primary method to increase production and improve rate of recovery. While in the past, natural propane which mainly uses quartz sand can only fit small petroleum and gas wells with closure pressure, and ceramic propane has relatively high density. Especially, there is a kind of low temperature coated quartz sand propane which can be cured and be adapted to the alkaline environment. It has many special functions and its technical level reached international advanced level. Compared with it, there are a good deal of outcomes of pre-cured resin coated sand propane produced by the American Santrol Company and Boren Company. For example, high curing temperature is needed, its speed of curing is slow, intensity of consolidation is low and it cannot adapt to alkali.

This research result applies for 4 related patents, including 2 innovation patents and 1 practical model patents. It has been identified by the Beijing Science and Technology Commission as technology reaching the international advanced level and is competing for first-grade Beijing science and technology award. Through the actual fracturing applications of 11 petroleum fields like Daqing, ZhongYuan in over 700 wells, it is proved to increase an average of more than 30% petroleum yield. It is an initiative in the propane industry and a method to increase petroleum production. For that reason, it is entitled "a revolution in petroleum propane field." by experts of petroleum industry.

(III) Sheng Tai sand technology - technological achievements in rainwater utilization and ecological building materials

Sheng Tai sand technology in rainwater utilization and ecological building materials field is the achievement of Rechsand Technology Group after 7 years of research. Its development finds clues in more than 50 technological results which have won the National Invention Award and First-grade Ministerial Scientific and Technological Prize. The main inventor Qin Shengyi works out it combined with his 20 years of silica sand research. He is the first to use aeolian sand in the desert as raw material, skip sintering and process new eco-friendly materials after special process. It wholly owns independent intellectual property rights and is an international initiative. Currently, Sheng Tai sand technology applies for 23 related patents of which 12 have been authorized by the State Intellectual Property Office. Experts agree that Sheng Tai permeable sand-based technology can improve the utilization of urban rainwater and is an effective means of urban water use. Besides, it is in line with three concepts of "Hi-tech Olympics, Green Olympics and People's Olympics," in line with requirements of building "a resource-saving and environment-friendly" society. As a new technology for environmental protection, it can be used for application considering that its technology, products, processes, and constructions are all becoming mature.

Sheng Tai sand can be processed into permeable bricks, permeable rock, permeable ditches, permeable wells, cleansing wells, permeable tree ponds, Sheng Tai sand ceramic and other products. The product attracts attentions of leaders of the party and state, all levels of government and the community. It is first applied by the State Offices in Zhongnanhai, Ministry of Science and Technology and the Olympic projects. The application of it is listed as the highlight of the Green Olympics and Hi-tech Olympics project in 2008. From the winter of 2005 to the spring of 2007, over 150 thousand square meters of Sheng Tai permeable sand brick or rock have been laid. Furthermore, it is put on the "recommended list of energy-saving and land-saving building materials" of 50 companies and "energy-saving products industrialization demonstration base" by the national Ministry of Construction. It also is repeatedly reported by mainstream media like CCTV, BTV, Science and Technology Daily and Economic Daily, arousing wide attention at home and abroad. It is well accepted and people call it "a good product which benefits both state and civil" as well as confirming it as "amazing."

Industrialization Rechsand's coated sand has cultivated a silica sand industry with annual turnover of 700 million RMB Yuan after ten years of development. That of petroleum compression fracture propane is expected to cultivate an industry with annual output value up to 5 billion RMB Yuan. And that of technologies concerning environmentally friendly building materials is expected to nurture a gigantic industry with hundreds of billions of annual output value.

IV.   Blueprint for the future development of silica sand industry

(I) Guidelines

Under the guidance of scientific outlook on development, the people of Rechsand shall innovate adhering to the idea of "I will create what you need" to develop and utilize the desert comprehensively. We can turn the waste sand to valuable resources and then further turn desertification prevention in the past into scientific utilization of sand. In that case, a resource-saving and environment-friendly society can be easier built.

(II) Objectives and tasks

To further promote the development of silica sand industry, Rechsand Technology Group, acting as the sponsor, allies with related domestic units of silica sand production, academia, research and application to actively set up "China's Industrial Silica Sand Technology Innovation Alliance." The organization intends to process silica sand into a variety of beneficial products through united innovation and create a new industrial silica sand industry.

Currently, the company has made it clear its technology innovation objective and 8 focus areas in silica sand industry, including research of common technologies and basic theories, products development and demonstration, study of relevant policies, personnel training, etc.

1. To control flood using silica sand: technology development and application of systems such as rainwater harvesting, sewage treatment and desalination.
2. To increase petroleum production using silica sand: development of impermeable selective propane with petroleum permeability and research on supporting fracture fluid and construction technology.
3. To prevent desertification using silica sand: development of desert cultivation technology and product and demonstration of agricultural facilities application.
4. To neutralize alkaline using silica sand: development of cultivation technology and product and planting demonstrations on alkaline saline lands.
5. To cast using silica sand: development of low-temperature fast-curing coated sand and ultra-high temperature coated sand, and application of green accurate casting technology.
6. To make appliances using silica sand: take the sand as raw material to make furniture and so on.
7. To resist corrosion using silica sand: development of sand-based improved impermeable concrete.
8. To construct using silica sand: development of sand-based eco-residential materials and construction.

V.   Success secret of Qin Shengyi

Qin Shengyi is not only a successful inventor, but also a successful entrepreneur. It is his greatest advantage, as well as the most important difference between him and other successful inventors and entrepreneurs. So, what is the secret of his success?

Is it funding? No, because as a poor farmer's son, he doesn't have money in his hand. He "cannot afford food of two cents." in high school, and "can only borrow two Yuan as the registration fee to take the entrance examination for college."

Is it good research and development conditions? No. Because his R & D "starts from three small cottages and one big iron pot," and he "design his own instrument from nothing, or modify other instruments for use."

Is it education? Yet, because he is a secondary school student major in cast, who is looked down upon and dealing with sand all day long. In others' eyes, he only deserves to do "heavy lifting."

Is it relationships? Not at all, because lying in the bottom of society, he has no reliable relationships in politics, business, education, academia or other fields.

However, he has successfully created a miracle. And there are few successful inventors and entrepreneurs like him in China. There are many reasons why he is able to create a silica sand industry in China with nothing but determination and innovation, and so becomes the father of China's silica sand industry. Here the article mainly introduces several key aspects of that.

(I) "Innovation first means change of the concept." - Positive attitude, strong initiative and precise thought

The so-called "concept" is "thought," whose core content is attitude, initiative and way of thinking. Qin Shengyi often says that "any results come from the acts. Practice is dominated by thought, while thoughts come from continuous learning and practice. It needs self-cultivation." He concludes his innovative experience causes him alter the concept first. It shall consist of positive attitude, strong initiative, no superstition and correct way of thinking.

Napoleon Hill, world-famous guru of success defines "attitude" as "mental attitude" toward problems. "Positive mental attitude (PMA)" is essential to success and the most important principle of success which can be applied in life, study and any work. Personal initiative is you do what needs without other people reminding you. People who take initiative to do things that are needed and persist will succeed. The power of thinking has great strength; it can build a great kingdom, and can also ruin one. All concepts, plans, purposes and desires come from thoughts. Thought is the master of all energies; it can solve all the problems. Not learning how to think in a correct way, you can make no outstanding achievement.

The reason why Qin Shengyi is able to continue to innovate and succeed is, first of all, he has a positive attitude, strong personal initiative, and accurate thought.

(II) "My greatest wish is to make China's silica sand industry stronger and bigger." -   Clear positioning and lofty goal

Positive attitude is the first step to success, with which one can begin construction. While a clear goal is the groundwork for the success in construction.

Qin Shengyi not only has a positive attitude, but also has a clear vision for the future. He often says that, "China is where I initiate my business, so my greatest wish is to make China's silica sand industry stronger and bigger. I want to create a real silica sand industry kingdom and contribute more to build a resource-saving and environmental-friendly society. I have learned to cast, so I want to not only cast products, but also cast life, and cast a happy life for mankind. "Qin Shengyi is a youth full of dreams and sense of mission, whose motion and pursuit comes from his lofty goal.

He says "It makes me honored that Sheng Tai permeable sand brick becomes the highlight of the public and media on the exhibition for construction of a conservation society in December 2005. Especially it is noticed by party and state leaders as Hu Jintao, Wu Bangguo, Wen Jiabao, Jia Qinglin, Li Changchun and so on. They watch the exhibits of Sheng Tai permeable sand brick and permeability demonstration model, giving a high evaluation. President Hu is so excited to hold my hand twice and keeps praising it as an amazing product. He says we must put this brick to the international market in order to make more contributions for the benefit of

all mankind. That really encourages me and makes me more determined that my choice is correct and silica sand industry can benefit mankind."

Napoleon Hill says that "You have to know what you want to pursue in life and determine to get it. Only focus single-mindedly on your goals can ensure success. Think and plan the goal you pursue and ignore other interferences, that is the formula followed by all. "Qin Shengyi is an outstanding example of those successful people.

(III) "I will create what you need."- starting from market demands and operating from one's own strengths

Qin Shengyi has always stressed "the purpose of innovation is to meet the social demand." He introduces in many occasions that although I have been holding the concept I will create what you need for seven to eight years, and I have turn the normal aeolian sand into materials like coated sand for car making and Fu Sheng sand as propane in petroleum industry, while the most critical human needs is not energy. We can walk without car, we can burn straw without gas, yet we can't survive without water. Then I begin to wonder whether there is a way that I can use the sand that I familiar to develop a material to solve that problem."

"China is a dry country, and there exists no more than three ways to solve the water problem, that is to save water, to transport water in the south to the north and to collect rainwater. In my opinion, only one way in these there can really solve the problem, to collect rainwater and to protect groundwater resources. Then I explore the way to use sand to make permeable bricks that can be used in all kinds of ground to collect rainwater or to replenish groundwater. In this way, problems like urban water shortage, low groundwater level and rain flooding can be worked out. After realizing that, I start to study Sheng Tai sand. The research lasts for seven years and its final product Sheng Tai permeable sand brick comes out successfully."

Rechsand's business philosophy is "I will create what you need." which is entirely based on the needs of customers. By developing innovative products, it tries to meet the needs. Innovation of Rechsand is to meet needs, guide consumption and create the market. Rechsand is not trying to carve shares of the current market pie; instead, it identifies potential needs and turns them into products. That helps users solve the problem and creates a new market.

Founded in 1993, Rechsand experiences 14 years of development keeping innovate to meet the social needs. There are now three major series of silica sand products in Rechsand. This may seem irrelevant for they cover a large span, from casting to petroleum and to building materials. "But after analyzing their inner logic, you will find they are all about silica sand and it all depends on my strength of sand study."

There is an important principle of success, to run your own strengths! As long as you take advantage your strengths in the most critical place, you are more likely to succeed. And Qin Shengyi understands this well. On one hand, he can clear see and meet the social needs; on the other, he is well aware of his strengths, including he is most familiar with sand, expert in studying sand, and dedicated himself to operate his strength. In this sense, his success comes with reasons.

(IV) "Innovation needs bold imagination and courage to practice" - imagination and creativity, systemic innovation and continuous innovation.

Qin Shengyi always encourages staff to "innovate with bold imagination, brave practice, especially fearless challenge to authorities and traditions." And so he does.

He explains that "Many of my achievements and inventions are unconventional. For example, when I started to apply for support for my research, many experts believed there would be no positive results and would not help. But afterwards when I sat down to think about my technical programs and methods, I believed it was feasible, so I did not give up. So, I still did experiments in accordance with my own ideas step by step, and finally I worked it all out after 3 years of testing."

Not only does he encourage technical innovation, and take the lead in innovation but, Qin Shengyi also advocates systemic innovation and continuous improvement. He says that "Innovation should be systemized. There shall be innovations of systems, business, management and culture as well as technology." He summarizes a set of innovation systems by Renchsand on the basis of his own technology innovation and management innovations.

Qin Shengyi believes "Innovation should take sustainable development as the goal. The highest level of innovation is to fully exploit the human brain potential. That is to create material and spiritual wealth with usage of minimal natural resources and reuse of resources through technical innovation." he says, that brains of a great scientists like Albert Einstein have used only 3% of their brain capacity, demonstrating the great potential for brain development. Natural resources are limited, but the development of human brain potential and its usage to conduct technical innovation is very visionary.

The history of human nature shows that whatever your mind can conceive and believe it can achieve with a positive attitude!

According to success principles, imagination is the prototype of all junior achievements, is the station of the soul, and also the source of motivation to reach personal achievements. If you have this kind of ability, then you can pick and choose the best time of life and thereby create a great miracle. Qin Shengyi not only knows the true meanings of these words, but also hands-on, so he created a great miracle.

(V) "Sense of national self-confidence and dedication is the premise of innovation" - noble national spirit, dedication and confidence

Qin Shengyi often says "Sense of national self-confidence and dedication is the premise of innovation. A nation is supported by its confidence, so is a company. And confidence is the spiritual pillar of innovation." He explains further that "Innovation is not far away, it lies around each of us, around the enterprise. It doesn't necessarily need more favorable conditions, large amount of funds, and high academic qualifications. When the application for 'high temperature coated sand' is not approved, I use my own salary savings to buy materials for experiments and spend all my spare time to do it. I design my own instruments from nothing, or modify other instruments for use. Now I have invented the permeable brick, which enhances my confidence because it is an original invention. Permeable bricks worldwide all depend on gaps, well, why shall I just go along with that? So not only authority or experts in developed industrial countries can innovate, we also can as long as we have confidence."

He adds "Innovation requires support of a spiritual force, that is, dedication and sacrifice. As comrade Mao Zedong has said, ' a large price will be paid to achieve the aspirations of a changing the world, even lives.' Lack of spirit of sacrifice and sacrifice, we will be defeated in innovation. Soldiers of innovation have experienced tests of blood and fire, so do I?"

He tells a story, "In one test, an unexpected accident suddenly happened. A Burning hot door explodes and strikes my left arm; unbearable pain runs through my burned bloody arm. I have two options at that time: stop the research which has only 15 more minutes to complete and go to the hospital for medical attention or complete research test in progress ignore my injured arm and keep on testing for its continuity and data's accuracy and reliability. My firm belief forces me to continue the research despite the pain. According to indigenous method in my hometown, I cover the wound with a handful of straw ash. Blood never stops bleeding during the entire test, but the data I get plays a key role in the whole research. It also becomes one of my unforgettable memories. I am a man from Da Bie Shan, an old revolutionary base area, and a son of farmers, so I always feel the spirits of revolutionary martyrs and get inspired. I think that today's innovation also needs our courage and sacrifice. Reminding the elder generation will also become a kind of spiritual comfort and power."

Qin Shengyi is the head of the company's innovation, and only has a secondary education. There are more than one thousand people who excel in casting in China, while Qin is the first to win the State Science and Technology Invention Award. Without enough self-confidence, it is impossible to get there by just listening to traditional elders.

The most fundamental beliefs of success are: have faith, and you can move a mountain. As long as you believe you can succeed, you will!

(VI) "I am born in the year of the ox as its zodiac sign of, so I have a typical ox personality, one who will never give up easily once I consider it the right thing to do." - To maintain focus, be perseverance and do a little bit more.

Qin Shengyi recalls that "After graduation, in order to make a difference, I choose to be a common mechanical technician in the Foundry and Forging Factory in Ji'nan, where is the farthest one from my home. My education background brings me people's disdainful comments. I can only do some 'heavy lifting ', but I still strive and dream of a better future. I always wonder what my career path is going to be. I study casting, and thus I deal with sand naturally and frequently. For this reason, I decide to start with silica sand, which is seemingly harmful and inexhaustible. And my dream is realizing I want to serve my country in of silica and sand industry".

"So far, the people of Rechsand and I have been committed to research of the natural silica sand for more than 20 years. Relying on independent innovation and integration of technology, industry and trade, we develop relevant diversity of silica sand industry and produce three major silica sand products:

1. Coated sand technology - technological achievements in machinery manufacturing;
2. Fu Sheng sand technology - technological achievements in petroleum compression fracture propane;
3. Sheng Tai sand technology - technological achievements in rainwater utilization and ecological building materials.

Currently, I am leading my group to solve three major problems of l 'desertification, water shortages and energy depletion '. Through technical innovation, sand can be used as resources and waste turns into treasure. This is what the silica sand industry does."

Napoleon Hill has told people "To concentrate on the things which you can get a maximum return from; Do not waste time on useless things for success. Concentrate on one thing at one time and throw yourself into it, actively waiting for success. Do not let your mind slide into something else, other needs or other ideas. Concentrate on the important items that you have decided to do and give up all other things. Successful people all do that." Qin Shengyi is an example "a successful person "who "concentrates on one thing."

Qin Shengyi often says "The process of innovation is like the journey to the west. Numerous hardships and dangers test a person's will and endurance. Innovation is proportional to perseverance. Without the latter, innovation can only go half-way, especially at the early stage when there is greater resistance. But I have the courage to face all frustrations and challenges in the process of innovation."

In 1985, he boldly uses aeolian silica sand in the desert of Inner Mongolia to replace zircon sand imported from Australia as precise casting material. Only irony welcomes this idea. Most people consider it a dream because expansion of silica sand is 3 times that of zircon sand, which means silica sand is easier to distort when heated. There are also some statements that even a developed country with high science and technology like America needs to import zircon sand from Australia, not to mention China. However, Qin believes that the intelligence of the Chinese people cannot be underestimated. Chinese people may be able to do what Americans cannot do through hard work. So these disturbances and resistance don't stop his stride.

From an economic point of view, he roughly calculates that imported zircon sand is worth 7 thousand RMB Yuan per ton, while silica sand in Inner Mongolia is only worth 10 RMB Yuan per ton. If the research makes it, it will save the country a large amount of money. "I am born in a year of the ox as its zodiac sign, so I have a typical ox personality, who will never give up easily when I consider it right. After careful analysis and comparison of different views, I make my own decision. There is nothing in the world unchanging, including expansion of sand. With low wages, I live frugally to buy materials. 1.5 kg of sand is used per test and total over 9 thousand kg is used during 3 years. Over 900 days, more than 6000 tests, countless failures and great pressures finally bring the 'high temperature coated sand'. "

Setbacks always go along with innovation. So you will encounter many difficulties and obstacles that you cannot imagine on your way to innovation. It is impossible to succeed without a strong spirit of perseverance and sacrifices. Experiences of many successful people have proved that there is only a thin line between success and failure, walk the extra miles, and you can succeed, otherwise you will fail.

Edison, the so-called "King of the invention," conducts 10 000 experiments in order to invent the electric light. He turns the "unknown thing" into a "known one." Coincidentally, Qin Shengyi does that 6 thousand times to develop the coated sand. If he quits after his 5999 trials, maybe he will never succeed. On the country, he adheres to research and walk extra miles to make his achievement.

Napoleon Hill warns us that "when you run into trouble, do not waste time calculating how much you suffer a loss; instead, you should calculate how much you harvest and get from the frustrations. You will find you get much more than you lose. Failure can be a stepping stone or a stumbling block depending on whether your attitude is positive or negative. For those people who have a positive attitude, each adversity contains seeds with equal or greater interests. Sometimes, it is a good opportunity to disguise in the face of adversity."

He stresses that "doing more can confirm you that you are doing right and useful things, it makes you more responsible for your own conscience and

gives you confidence. People who take initiative to do things needed and persist will succeed. "

In short, success is a series of efforts! The reason why does Qin Shengyi succeeds is because of his dedicated spirit, tenacity and "doing more."

(VII) "I do not know how to manage, but I can learn it! It just replaces silica sand with people as the study object." - An entrepreneur as well as an inventor

Technological invention and innovation can only meet society's needs through application, which is the true value of inventions. Therefore, it is essential to go from producing to industrialization, marketization, and efficacy depending on operation and management. Then a good company is needed. Moreover, a good manager that excels at business is required.

It has long been the fact that entrepreneurs starting from an inventor are often not quiet skilled at business and management. But this has not convinced Qin Shengyi. He says "I do not know how to manage, but I can learn it! It just replaces silica sand with people as the study object. In philosophy, there are still commons although there are specials, which are to face, analyze and solve problems step by step."

Like many entrepreneurs, Qin Sheng studies further in order to improve his management skills and then accelerates the industrialization, marketization, and efficacy of the inventions. He studies casting in a secondary school, philosophy in college, law, and participates in an EMBA in School of Management, Beijing University for two years. But unlike many entrepreneurs, he learns with a serious attitude. Just like his invention, he is fond of self-exploration in management. There is an idea in the western management theories that compares people as screws, with which he quite disagrees.

He says that "Since the final purpose of people managing is to ensure things are done well, why not just directly administer people to manage things? Administer here not only means to put people in order, but to let them be polite. Under guidance, people can treat each other politely as well as identify their direction. I can teach if you don't know how to operate. That is what a leader should first be, coach and teacher."

Qin Shengyi forms a complete set of management models for administering people to manage things after study, practice, summary and improvement for more than ten years. It is used to coordinate the entire company's steps in order to achieve its business objectives.

Rechsand management philosophy: kindness oriented and advocating innovation; is realistic and sensible in managing both personnel and matter; everyone does the best for the company; and is results-oriented with positive mental attitude.

Qin Shengyi's management model is the result of his continuous learning, practice, thinking and improvement and it is proven in practice. Its implementation contributes to the remarkable achievements in business innovation of Rechsand Technology Group for the last three years.

For his outstanding performance in business and management, Qin Shengyi is named outstanding private technology entrepreneur in China in 2002, as well as Liu Chuanzhi, president of Lenovo Group, Duan Yongji, president of Stone, and chairman of UF software company. It is recognition of his innovative management accomplishments. He also receives many honors, such as the name of Capital Young Technology Entrepreneurs Star and Award for Outstanding Young Technological Business. He also is the member of the standing committee of the Beijing Youth Union and members of Beijing Science Association.

(VIII) "To create an innovative corporate culture is the key to innovation" - emphasis on corporate culture

Qin Shengyi often says "to create an innovative corporate culture is key to innovation." He believes that any outcome is the result of behavior, and any behavior is under the dominant of thought, which is affected by culture. So he attaches great importance to corporate culture. The success of Rechsand Group innovation is also that of corporate culture.

Extensive reading enables him to extract the essence of "Rechsand inscribed motto" (see in the Appendix). He comprehends the corporate culture of his company from Book of Changes, that is benevolence (Ren in Chinese), and creation (Chuang in Chinese). Statement in Book of Changes "The movement of heaven is full of power. Thus the superior man makes himself strong and tireless. The earth's condition is receptive devotion. Thus the superior man who has
breadth of character clutches the outer world and expresses both of them. Self-discipline is benevolence and social commitment is creation, so he names his company "Rechsand."

Qin Shengyi regularly warns his employees that "Rechsand aims to meet the needs in certain particular parts effectively, so its profit is the economic reciprocation of that."

"Rechsand inscribed the motto which" embodies Rechsand's corporate culture. It not only is used to encourage employees to take the initiative to give their wisdoms and talents to achieve business goals, but also helps employees grasp their own values. This is Qin Shengyi's unique management thought, and the highest level of an administrator is to cultivate people.

(IX) "Poverty and misery lay the foundation of business" - be good at learning in adversity.

Famous philosopher Francis Bacon has said that "Miracles mostly appear in the bad luck." Famous musician Beethoven has said that "one advantage of remarkable person is that he is resolute in bad and tough conditions." Napoleon Hill has also said that "Every adversity, every failure, every heartache carries with it the seed on an equal or greater benefit. Sometimes, those things that seem to be adversity are, in fact, a good disguise." Qin Shengyi's miracle appears in up and downs as well. Thus, he is also a "remarkable person."

Qin Shengyi often says "Success comes from wisdom, but also from the endurance, which is the clockwork of innovation. My endurance is tempered out in poverty." Qin Shengyi was born in the old revolutionary base areas, Da Bie Shang. The land here develops him and scrutinizes his growth. The mountain remembers twenty years ago, when a farmer's son walks on the mountain road with a shoulder pole. One end of the pole is ten pounds of rice; the other is a jar of mother-made pickles. These are rations for the whole week of the child at high school. He has to get to school on foot over thirty li. This child who strives to study in difficulties is Qin Shengyi. At that time, his poor family cannot afford food of two cents in school. In 1979, he can only borrow two Yuan as the registration fee to take his first entrance examination for college.

His hometown is in Yuexi County, Da Bie Shan District, Anhui Province. He is surrounded by over a hundred miles of mountains. So his hometown is very remote. Because of poverty, he has never been to the county before he goes to Nanjing to school. He is the eldest at home, so he has to carry the burden of life at five or six years old by collecting firewood, and pasturing cattle. That is tantamount to an exercise of him. At that time, the national college entrance examination system has not recovered. In that case, his family considers it is useless to go to school since he has to return to farmland finally and his father orders his sister and him to weed a certain amount of grass. While he doesn't think so, he knows well the importance to study because knowledge can change his life. Therefore, he hides under the shade of a tree to read between work, hoping one day he could walk away from the mountains. Winter in the mountain is full of intense winds. Without cotton shoes to wear, he wraps sandals with brown hair, making "warm shoes." Perhaps that is his first invention. He takes his first college entrance examination in 1979 and falls short by two points of the admission standards. Later, he enters Nanjing School of Mechanical Engineering to study professional casting becoming the first ever secondary school student in his village, as well as the first one that leaves Anhui Province for studying.

Qin Shengyi graduates from secondary school in poverty, majoring in casting. Later he studies philosophy in college and studies law and business administration at the university while working and gets a master's degree. He has intensive Engels, "Dialectics of Nature," Marx's "Das Kapital," Mao Zedong's "On Practice," "Contradiction" and Hegel's "Great Logic" and "Small Logic," reads the classics in "Book of Changes," "The Analects of Confucius," "Moderate" and other treatises. He laments that "Poverty and misery lay the cornerstone of my initial success and form my values as well. In retrospect, that period of time is good for my life. It is my life's wealth, it makes me tough and smart, and it lays a solid foundation for my independent innovation, organizational innovation and sustained innovation."

Qin Shengyi says in a heroic way that "Innovation is a process to letting wisdom take hold and to sublimate theories. And it all comes from learning. It is reading that moistens the garden of innovation, and broadens the horizon of an innovator. Chinese traditional culture that lasts five thousand years opens my mind of wisdom. So my passion and dedication are all supported by knowledge. Keep learning and innovating is the motto of my life, which also needs knowledge to carry out. China is where I initiate and create my business, so my greatest wish is to make China's silica sand industry stronger and bigger. My greatest wish is to contribute more to build a resource-saving and environment-friendly society.

He admits "I have learned to cast, so I want to not only cast products, but also cast life, and cast a happy life for mankind. I always adhere to the innovative concept of 'I will create what you need.' and the mission to improve and beautify the living environment, to enhance the quality of life and contribute to society with my own wisdom, technology, products and services."

He vows that "My business journey is far from over; I will continue to create new telltale marks on it with wisdom my motherland gives me!"

Review

Qin Shengyi is not only a successful inventor, but also a successful entrepreneur. The reason why he can succeed can be summarized as he masters six subjects and integrates eight spirits.

The so-called "six subjects" refers to sinology, philosophy, economics, strategy, management and success. That is, he has both knowledge of extensive and profound ancient Chinese sinology theory, and is adept at theories of modern philosophy, economics, strategy, management and success. By saying "master," it also means he can use them flexibly to guide his thinking and behavior. While so-called "eight spirits" indicates spirits of enterprising, ethos, innovation, transcendence, practice, striving, dedication and winning. And "integrate" means he not only has these spirits, but also takes them as the spiritual motivator and acting pointer of his innovation and initiation. Experience of successful people at all times shows that, the people who can do that, whatever business they are engaging in, all will be successful, Qin Shengyi is an example.

Qin Shengyi often says "innovation of Rechsand is to meet needs, guide consumption and create the market. Rechsand is not trying to carve shares of the current market pie; instead, it identifies potential needs and turns them into products. That helps users solve the problem and creates a new market. ""Create a new market" here refers to getting out of the "red ocean" and exploring "blue oceans," or to abandon the "red ocean Strategy" and implement the "Blue Ocean Strategy." Because of this, Rechsand not only benefits at normal times, but also gains better efficiency during the uncommon international financial crisis.

Questions

1. What are red ocean strategy and blue ocean strategy?

2. What is the cornerstone of blue ocean strategy?
3. What are the differences between red ocean strategy and blue ocean strategy?
4. What are the six principles of formulating and executing blue ocean strategy?
5. What are the four action frameworks of blue ocean strategy?
6. What is the right strategic sequence?
7. What are the three characteristics of a good strategy?
8. How to create a blue ocean strategy?

Notes

(1) 〔Korea〕 W. Chan Kim, 〔U.S.〕 Renée Mauborgne, Blue Ocean Strategy, 1st edition, Commercial Press, 2005, p. vi-vii.

(2) 〔Korea〕 W. Chan Kim, 〔U.S.〕 Renée Mauborgne, Blue Ocean Strategy, 1st edition, Commercial Press, 2005, p. v-vi.

(3) Alternatives are broader than substitutes. Consider cinemas versus restaurants. Restaurants serve as alternatives of cinemas. Although restaurants are not direct competitors and not substitutes serving a distinct function, yet they can take away people who want to enjoy a night out, and these people are potential buyers of cinemas tickets. There are three tiers of noncustomers that can be transformed into customers. First Tier: "Soon-to-be" noncustomers who are on the edge of your market, waiting to jump ship. Second Tier: "Refusing" noncustomers who consciously choose against your market. Third Tier: "Unexplored" noncustomers who are in markets distant from yours.

(4) Zhang Xiuyu, How to be successful, 1st edition, Enterprise Management Press, January 2005, p.1.

(5) Zhang Xiuyu, How to be successful, 1st edition, Enterprise Management Press, January 2005, p.165.

(6) Zhang Xiuyu, How to be successful, 1st edition, Enterprise Management Press, January 2005, p.203.

(7) Zhang Xiuyu, How to be successful, 1st edition, Enterprise Management Press, January 2005, p.150.

(8) Zhang Xiuyu, How to be successful, 1st edition, Enterprise Management Press, January 2005, p.49.

(9) Zhang Xiuyu, How to be successful, 1st edition, Enterprise Management Press, January 2005, p.187.

(10) Zhang Xiuyu, How to be successful, 1st edition, Enterprise

Management Press, January 2005, p.76.

(11) Zhang Xiuyu, How to be successful, 1st edition, Enterprise Management Press, January 2005, p.151.

(12) Zhang Xiuyu, How to be successful, 1st edition, Enterprise Management Press, January 2005, p.289.

(13) Zhang Xiuyu, How to be successful, 1st edition, Enterprise Management Press, January 2005, p.109.

(14) Zhang Xiuyu, How to be successful, 1st edition, Enterprise Management Press, January 2005, p.289.

APPENDIX

Rechsand inscribed motto

Rechsand has self-discipline - benevolence (Ren in Chinese), and social commitment - creation (Chuang in Chinese). What is benevolence? The benevolent loves others. He will commit to satisfy the reasonable needs and help individuals tap their potential to fully realize their own values. Then what is innovation? Creation means innovation which means contradiction and solution. It breaks the routine and recombines elements in order to achieve greater, faster, better and more economical results. Innovation is not far from us; instead, it comes from our daily work, life and learning. Innovation is not esoteric; its key is just practice.

Rechsand purpose: charity, innovation, benefit and development.

Rechsand vision: a stronger Rechsand with billions and stands for hundreds of years.

Rechsand believes: No pain, no gain; challenge the limits, beyond you.

Rechsand values: to create value and realize it.

Rechsand concept of wealth: A gentleman makes money the right way. To create value is the only right path to wealth.

Rechsand behavior: be beneficial to all; do as you will do.

Rechsand work style: inseparability of knowledge and practice, speedy and strict enforcement; settlement of small issues within an hour and big ones within a day.

Rechsand work principle: start from the self, start from the events, start from now on.

Rechsand innovative concept: I will create what you need.

Rechsand innovation policy: analyze potential demand based on humanity; develop individual potential by strengthening self-cultivation; use and reuse the least quantity of natural resources to create wealth to meet social needs through technology innovation.

Rechsand business philosophy: to meet demand, guide consumption, and create markets.

Rechsand operating principle: individual production, full-service, to create value for customers and realize its own value.

Rechsand management philosophy: kindness oriented and advocating innovation

Be realistic and sensible in managing both personnel and subject matter.

Everyone does best for the company.

Be results-oriented with a positive mental attitude

Rechsand basic administration system: first, "three system approach," that is a system of assuming chief responsibility under the leadership of the board, a system of democratic centralism in decision-making and a system of reporting within 24 hours. Second an emphasis on interpersonal communications. Third, pay close attention to teamwork. Lastly, "two don't," which is don't leapfrog reporting work other than situations and don't leapfrog commands but understand the situation prior to taking action.

Rechsand production management system with three compatible principles:

To meet the needs depending on lean manufacturing

To work with honesty and integrity, abide by the laws, protect the environment, and be mindful of safety.

Be kindhearted, innovative, beneficial and growing.

Rechsand basic system of personnel management:

"One all," "two participate," "one change," and "three three combination."

One all - all member with labor contract.

Two participate - managers participate in work practice, while producers participate in management.

One change - change every unreasonable behaviors, habits, ideas, rules and regulations.

Three "Three" combines - combine seniors, middle-age and young; combine responsibilities, rights and interests; combine results, benefits and rates.

Rechsand basic working system:

Three-self principles - self-work, self-discipline and self-responsible.

Three-daily requirements - account daily, clear daily and revamp daily.

Three-all management system - all member quality, all members marketing and all members accounting.

One internalization - the internal marketization.

Rechsand mission: to improve and beautify the living environment, to enhance the quality of life and to contribute to society with one's own wisdom, technology, products and services.

BIBLIOGRAPHY

〔Korea〕 W. Chan Kim, 〔U.S.〕 Renée Mauborgne, *Blue Ocean Strategy*, 1st edition, Commercial Press, 2005.

〔U.S.〕 Napoleon Hill, *Everyone Can Be Successful*, 2nd edition, Hubei People's Publishing House in February 2001.

Zhang Xiuyu, *How to be successful*, 1st edition, Enterprise Management Press, January 2005.

〔U.S.〕 Michael Porter & Gary Hamel, *The Future of Strategy Management*, 1st Edition, Sichuan People's Publishing House, April 2000.

〔U.S.〕 Jack Trout, *Trout on Strategy*, 1st edition, China Financial and Economic Publishing House, October 2004, p. 157.

www.ingramcontent.com/pod-product-compliance
Lightning Source LLC
Chambersburg PA
CBHW052058230326
41599CB00054B/3022